New Pattern

English Language

for SBI/ IBPS Bank PO/ SO/ Clerk/ RRB Exams

- **Corporate Office :** 45, 2nd Floor, Maharishi Dayanand Marg, Corner Market, Malviya Nagar, New Delhi-110017

  Tel. : 011-49842349 / 49842350

Typeset by Disha DTP Team

Printed at Repro Knowledgecast Limited, Thane

For further information about the books from DISHA,

Log on to **www.dishapublication.com** or email to **info@dishapublication.com**

CONTENT

CHAPTER 1

Vocabulary

A set of all the words that exist in a particular language or subject is vocabulary. The word vocabulary can have at least three different meanings: 1) all of the words in a language; 2) the words used in a particular context and 3) the words an individual knows.

Learning vocabulary is a very important part of learning a language. The more words you know, the more you will be able to understand what you hear and read; and the better you will be able to say what you want to speak or write.

Every student at some time or the other faces the question "How do I increase my vocabulary?" This is because, people who might otherwise be very fluent in spoken English do not really take care to use new words for the purpose of communication; the current register of words is deemed enough.

An unfortunate fallout of this nonchalant complacency is that when these people actually face questions examining their vocabulary and its extent, they fall flat. An easy example will bear this out. Everyone knows that when we are asked to name the tip of a mountain or the highest point of something, we use the word 'peak'. But not everyone would know that words like zenith, apogee, crest and summit may be replacements for the same word. So the same meaning used in the form of another word might leave the student totally flummoxed. Therefore, it is important to start working on one's vocabulary as soon as possible for success in any competitive exam.

Given below are a few tips on the accepted methods and practices used to improve one's vocabulary:

(a) The practice of reading:

This is, sadly, lacking in most aspirants. With the advent of internet, reading has almost become passé. Reading is important not just because it increases general knowledge. That it definitely does; in addition what it does is help a student get into the habit of reading. It is also important to read a variety of subjects, because each subject has its own register of language and words are used with differing connotations in each register. So, for success in competitive exams, perusal of a few different sources of reading material is mandatory. The sources are:

(1) A general magazine e.g. India Today, Frontline, Outlook, Reader's Digest, Time, etc.
(2) A business magazine e.g. Business Today, Business India, Business World, etc.
(3) The daily newspaper e.g. The Times of India, The Hindu, The Indian Express, etc.

(b) Using a dictionary - the almost-extinct habit:

Even though the idea of using a dictionary does nothing to enthuse the common student, every one owns a dictionary but treats it like a sacred cow, not to be touched and defiled; of course, not that they are to be blamed too much for it; it is almost a habit now; but should be considered a necessary evil. A dictionary should be kept with the student while reading anything, so that an incomprehensible word can be looked up immediately. Procrastination invariably leads to the words remaining incomprehensible due to forgetfulness in looking up the word in the dictionary.

(c) Self-help books:

Quite a few self-help books claiming to improve Verbal Ability

are to be found in the open market, and one or two are actually helpful in this regard. Students are welcome to consult these books but are advised to do so after consulting discriminating people who have experience in this regard e.g. experienced English teachers or the English faculty, since they have better idea of the relative efficacy of these books.

(d) Thesaurus-the viable alternative:

If using a dictionary seems to be too boring to be considered for any length of time, using a thesaurus may be a more interesting alternative. In theory, it is the reverse of a dictionary, and basically gives the various synonyms and the types of usage of a word e.g. as a verb, adjective, noun etc. So it gives a lot of information about each word. If the student can remember even some of it, it will be a great advantage. The most commonly available thesaurus in the market is the Roget's Thesaurus, usually now used as a generic name by most publishers.

(e) The Word List:

The Word List is a comprehensive compendium of the words most commonly asked or used in the Management Examination question papers. Studying the Word List will also give the student a lot of information about the origin of various words, their roots etc. This is a particularly useful method of studying because knowledge of etymology helps the student gauge the meaning and usage of other words having the same roots, regardless of whether the student has come across the word earlier or not.

(f) Flip-Cards:

We strongly advocate this technique which is another tool to memorize words from the list. These are blank cards approximately double the size of your standard visiting card. After isolation of the exceptionally difficult words from the Word List, the student should write approximately five words on one side of the card and the corresponding meanings on the other. The advantages of using this type of tool are that (1) Cards are portable and the student can carry a card around with him/her anywhere and glance at it anytime. (2) The embarrassment factor which carrying a Word List around entails is absent here, and (3) At the time of the final run-up to the examination, the student, instead of revising the whole Word List, can just go through the set of Flip Cards that he or she has collected. The only problem is getting started and, to mix metaphors, once that initial hurdle is overcome the rest is smooth sailing!

(g) Gauging meanings:

This logically follows from the earlier method. It is advisable for the student to try and gauge the meaning of a word from the context of the sentence. This is an extremely effective method and very frequently, it is possible to find out the meaning of a newly seen word just by reading the whole sentence and getting the meaning of the sentence as a whole. e.g. in the sentence 'All of us tried our best to persuade him but he remained adamant'. Even if a student does not know the meaning of the word adamant per se, it is still possible to gauge the meaning from the context of the sentence i.e. unmoved, firm, intractable, etc.

It should be kept in mind by the students that none of the above methods are absolute in themselves. It is a combination of all these, or at least some of these, which will give one the best results.

ONE WORD - A SMALL COLLECTION

Abdicate	-	Renounce a throne or high office
Accelerate	-	Move faster
Accomplice	-	One associated with another especially in wrong-doing
Acoustics	-	Science of the production, transmission, reception and effects of sound
Actuary	-	One who calculates insurance and annuity premium etc.
Amnesty	-	General pardon
Abattoir	-	A building where animals are killed for meat (or slaughterhouse)
Aesthete	-	A person with a highly developed sense of beauty aesthetics
Agnostic	-	One who believes that nothing can be known about God
Agoraphobia	-	Fear of open spaces in public places
Alibi	-	It is Latin for elsewhere. It is actually a plea of having been elsewhere at the time of commission of an act. But it is now used in the sense of an excuse. Example: He offered no alibi for his absence from duty.
Alimony	-	Compensatory allowance given to wife after divorce
Altruist	-	One who is habitually kind to others
Ambivalent	-	A simultaneous attraction towards and repulsion from an object, person or action; Example: The attitude of educated Indians to love-marriages is ambivalent
Anachronism	-	That which appears to be old fashioned and does not belong to the present time
Anecdote	-	A short interesting or amusing story
Anthology	-	A collection of poems or writings
Aphorism	-	(or maxim) A wise saying in a few words
Aphrodisiac	-	A medicine drug causing sexual excitement
Apiary	-	A place where bees are kept
Apprentice	-	A person who works under someone to learn that person's skill
Arboreal	-	Those who live in trees
Armistice	-	(or cease-fire or truce) An agreement to stop fighting
Ascetic	-	One who avoids physical pleasures and comforts
Aviary	-	A place for keeping birds
Backwater	-	A part of a river out of the main stream, where the water does not move
Barbecue	-	A metal flame on which meat etc. is cooked over an open fire
Bibliography	-	A list of writings on a subject
Biennial	-	Happening once every two years
Blue Blood	-	The quality of being a noble person by birth
Bonsai	-	The art of growing a plant in a pot that is prevented from reaching its natural size
Bon Vivant	-	One who likes good wine and food and cheerful companions
Boulevard	-	A broad street having trees on each side
Bourgeois	-	Belonging to the middle class
Bric-a-brac	-	Small objects kept for decoration
Bullion	-	Bars of gold or silver
Cabal	-	A small group of people who make secret plans for political action
Cannibal	-	One who eats human flesh
Cardiac	-	Connected with the heart
Catch-22	-	A situation from which one is prevented from escaping by something that is part of the situation itself
Charlatan	-	One who deceives others by falsely claiming to have a skill
Celibacy	-	One who does not indulge in carnal pleasure
Cloak-and-Dagger	-	Stories that deal with adventure and exciting mystery
Clubfoot	-	A badly-shaped foot twisted out of position from birth
Coagulate	-	Change from a liquid into a solid by chemical action
Colonnade	-	A row of pillars supporting a roof or arches
Congenital	-	Existing at or from one's birth
Connotation	-	The feeling or ideas that are suggested by a word
Consortium	-	A combination of several companies, banks, etc. for a common purpose
Contretemps	-	An unlucky and unexpected event, socially uncomfortable position with someone
Corinthian	-	Typical of the most richly decorated style of ancient Greek buildings
Countervailing	-	Acting with equal force but opposite effect
Couture	-	The business of making and selling fashionable women's clothes
Crossroads	-	A point at which an important decision must be taken
Defeatism	-	The practice of thinking in a way that shows an expectation of being unsuccessful
Déja vu	-	The feeling of remembering something that in fact one is experiencing for the first time
Dragnet	-	A system of connected actions and methods for catching criminals
Dregs	-	Sediment in a liquid that sinks to the bottom and is thrown away
Drudgery	-	Hard uninteresting work
Eagle-eyed	-	Looking with very keen attention and noticing small details
Empirical	-	Based on practical experience of the world we see and feel
Enigmatic	-	That which is mysterious and very hard to understand

Entomology	-	The scientific study of insects
Epicurean	-	Lover of physical/material
Ergonomics	-	The study of the conditions in which people work most effectively with machines
Estuary	-	The wide lower part or mouth of a river
Expressionism	-	A style of painting which expresses feelings rather than describing objects and experiences
Farrier	-	One who makes and fits shoes for horses
Febrile	-	Of or caused by fever
Felony	-	A serious crime such as murder or armed robbery
Fluvial	-	Of, found in, or produced by rivers
Foible	-	A small rather strange and stupid personal habit
Foray	-	A sudden rush into enemy country
Fourth Estate	-	Newspapers and their writers, considered with regard to their political influence
Freckle	-	A small flat brown spot on the skin
Frontispiece	-	A picture or photograph at the beginning of a book
Fumigate	-	To clear of disease, bacteria etc. by means of chemical smoke
Gelatine	-	A clear substance used for making jellies
Geocentric	-	Having the Earth as the central point
Goatee	-	A little pointed beard on the bottom of the chin
Graffiti	-	Drawings or writing on a wall
Grange	-	A large country house with Farm buildings
Gubernatorial	-	Of a governor
Guinea pig	-	A person who is subject of some kind of test
Halitosis	-	A condition in which one has bad breath
Headstrong	-	Determined to do what one wants in spite of all advice
Heirloom	-	A valuable object passed on for generations
Hinterland	-	The inner part of a country
Histrionics	-	Behaviour resembling a theatrical performance
Hothead	-	One who does things too quickly, without thinking
Idolatry	-	The worship of idols
Implacable	-	Impossible to satisfy, change, or make less angry
Improvident	-	One who does not save for future
Incarnate	-	In physical form rather than in the form of a spirit or idea
Incorporeal	-	Without a body or form
Innate	-	Being talented through inherited qualities
Inseminate	-	To put male seed into a female
Intelligentsia	-	Those who are highly educated and often concern themselves with ideas and new developments
Intestate	-	Not having made a will
Invective	-	A forceful attacking speech used for blaming someone
Juxtapose	-	To place side by side or close together
Kimono	-	A long loose garment made of silk
Lackey	-	One who behaves like a servant by always obeying
Lead Time	-	The time taken in planning and producing a new product
Lecher	-	One who continually looks for sexual pleasure
Leonine	-	Of or like a lion
Levee	-	An embankment beside a river or stream or an arm of the sea, to prevent floods
Libertarian	-	One who believes that people should have freedom of expression
Lien	-	A legal claim or hold on employment or property, as security for a debt or charge.
Limerick	-	A humorous short poem with five lines
Linchpin/ Lynchpin	-	An important member which keeps the whole group together
Literati	-	People with great knowledge of literature
Logger	-	One whose job is to cut down trees
Lore	-	Old beliefs, not written down, about a particular subject
Lowbrow	-	One who has no interest in literature, art etc.
Machete	-	A knife with a broad heavy blade
Magnum Opus	-	A great work of art, theatre, film etc.
Malady	-	That which is wrong with a system
Malaise	-	A feeling of pain without any particular pain or appearance of disease
Malcontent	-	One who is dissatisfied with the existing state of affairs
Male Chauvinist	-	A man who believes that men are better than women
Megalomania	-	The belief that one is more important or powerful than one really is
Militia	-	Those trained as soldiers but not belonging to a regular army
Misnomer	-	A name wrongly or mistakenly applied
Moccasin	-	A simple shoe made of leather
Monomaniac	-	One who keeps thinking of one particular idea only
Moralistic	-	Having unchanging narrow ideas about right and wrong
Morbid	-	Having or expressing a strong interest in sad or unpleasant things
Mycology	-	The scientific study of fungi (plural of fungus)
Namesake	-	A person with the same name as yours is your namesake
Necromancy	-	The practice which claims to learn about the future by talking with the dead
Nemesis	-	Just and unavoidable punishment
Newfangled	-	New (idea, machine etc) but neither necessary nor better
Nihilism	-	The belief that nothing has meaning or value

Nosegay	-	A small bunch of flowers, to be carried or worn on a dress
No-win Situation	-	That which will end badly whichever choice one makes
Oar	-	A long pole used for rowing a boat
Obstetrics	-	The branch of medicine concerned with childbirth
Obtrude	-	To be pushed or to push oneself into undue prominence.
Obtrusive	-	Tending to be pushed or to push oneself into undue prominence
Obviate	-	To clear away or provide for, as an objection or difficulty
Odoriferous	-	Having a smell
Oligarchy	-	A collective government formed by a few persons
One-Upmanship	-	The art of getting an advantage over others without actually cheating
Ontology	-	The branch of philosophy concerned with the nature of existence
Opprobrium	-	The state of being scornfully reproached or censured
Ornithology	-	The scientific study of birds
Ostentation	-	A display dictated by vanity and intended to invite applause or flattery.
Ostracism	-	The state of not being included in a group
Palaeography	-	The study of ancient writing systems
Panacea	-	A remedy or medicine proposed for or professing to cure all diseases.
Panache	-	Being able to do things in a confident and elegant way.
Panegyric	-	A speeds or a piece of writing praising somebody or something
Pariah	-	One who is not accepted by society
Parricide	-	Act of murdering one's father, mother or other close relative
Parting Shot	-	A last remark made at the moment of leaving
Peeping Tom	-	One who secretly looks at others when they are undressing
Penance	-	Making oneself willingly suffer for one's wrongs
Perdition	-	Everlasting punishment after death
Perjury	-	A lie told on purpose in court
Persona non Grata	-	One who is not acceptable or welcome
Petrology	-	The scientific study of rocks
Phylum	-	A main division of animals or plants
Pithead	-	The entrance to a coalmine
Placate	-	To bring from a state of angry or hostile feeling to one of patience or friendliness.
Platitude	-	A written or spoken statement that has been made often before and is not interesting
Platonic	-	A friendly, not sexual, relationship between a man and a woman
Plebeian	-	Of the lower social classes
Poetaster	-	A writer of inferior quality poems
Poker Face	-	A face that shows nothing of what one is thinking or feeling
Porcine	-	Of or like a pig
Portend	-	To indicate as being about to happen, especially by previous signs
Post-Haste	-	In a great hurry
Pot-Boiler	-	A book of low quality produced quickly to make money
Powder Keg	-	Something dangerous that might explode
Précis	-	A shortened form of a piece of writing
Prescient	-	Able to imagine or guess what will probably happen
Prevaricate	-	To use ambiguous or evasive language for the purpose of deceiving or diverting attention.
Prima Donna	-	The main woman singer in an opera company
Prodigal	-	One who is wasteful or extravagant, especially in the use of money or property.
Propellant	-	An explosive for firing a bullet or a rocket
Proscribe	-	To reject, as a teaching or a practice, with condemnation or denunciation.
Prosody	-	The rules by which the patterns of sounds and rhythms are arranged in poetry
Pulmonary	-	Of or having an effect on the lungs
Punctilious	-	Strictly observant of the rules or forms prescribed by law or custom
Punter	-	One who makes a bet on horse race
Putsch	-	A sudden secretly planned attempt to remove a government by force
Quartet	-	Four singers or musicians performing together
Quixotic	-	Trying to do the impossible, often so as to help others, while getting oneself into danger
Raconteur	-	One who is good at telling stories in an interesting way
Raillery	-	Friendly joking at someone's weaknesses
Realpolitik	-	Politics based on practical facts rather than on moral or ideological aims
Recant	-	To withdraw formally one's belief (in something previously believed or maintained)
Recumbent	-	Lying down on the back or side
Reflation	-	A govt. policy of increasing the amount of money used to increase the demand for goods or services
Renaissance	-	A renewal of interest in some particular kind of art, literature, etc, a period of revival during 15th and 16th centuries in Europe
Rescind	-	To make void, as an act, by the enacting authority or by a superior authority.
Resonance	-	Sound produced in one object by sound waves from another
Retribution	-	A justly deserved penalty

Revisionism	-	The questioning of the main beliefs of an already existing political system
Riviera	-	A warm stretch of coast on the Mediterranean sea; popular with holiday makers
Rosary	-	A string of beads used for counting prayers
Saboteur	-	One who practices sabotage
Sapient	-	Wise and full of deep knowledge
Scaffolding	-	A structure built from poles and boards for workmen to stand on
Scuba	-	An instrument used for breathing while swimming underwater
Sexagenarian	-	One who is between 60 and 69 years old
Shaman	-	A priest believed to have magical powers and able to cure people
Shibboleth	-	A once-important custom which no longer has much meaning
Short-change	-	To give back less than what actually should be given back
Siamese twins	-	Those joined together from birth at some part of their bodies
Singsong	-	A repeated rising and falling of the voice in speaking
Smokestack	-	The tall chimney of a factory or a ship
Snippet	-	A short piece from something spoken or written
Somnambulism	-	The habit of walking about while asleep
Souvenir	-	An object kept as a reminder of something
Sprig	-	A small end of a stem or branch with leaves
Stallion	-	A fully-grown male horse kept for breeding
Standard-bearer	-	An important leader in a moral argument or movement
Stellar	-	Of the stars
Stoic	-	One who is indifferent to joys or sorrows
Stooge	-	One who habitually does what another person wants
Stratagem	-	A trick to deceive an enemy
Strobe Light	-	A light which goes on and off very quickly
Subcutaneous	-	Beneath the skin
Superannuated	-	Too old for work
Surreal	-	Having a strange dreamlike unreal quality
Sword of Damocles	-	Something bad that may happen at any time
Tactile	-	Of the sense of touch
Tarot	-	A set of 22 cards used for telling the future
Tautology	-	Needless repetition of meaning in other words; example: audible to the ear, return back, One after another in succession, etc.
Taxonomy	-	The system of putting plants and animals into various classes
Technocrat	-	A highly skilled specialist in charge of an organisation
Testamentary	-	Of or done according to a will
Thatch	-	Roof covering of straw, reeds, etc.
Thorax	-	The part between the neck and the abdomen
Thrombosis	-	Having a clot in a blood vessel or the heart
Topiary	-	The art of cutting trees and bushes into decorative shapes of animals and birds
Touchstone	-	Something used as a test or standard
Tract	-	A short piece dealing with a religious or moral subject
Transient	-	Lasting a very short time
Transmogrify	-	To change completely as if by magic
Treatise	-	A serious book or article that examines a particular subject
Troglodyte	-	One who lives in a cave
Trousseau	-	The personal outfit of a bride; clothes and accessories and linens
Tunnel Vision	-	A condition in which one can see only straight ahead
Turf	-	A surface made up of earth and a thick covering of grass
Tutelage	-	The act of training or the state of being under instruction
Tyro	-	One slightly skilled in or acquainted with any trade or profession
Underling	-	A person of low rank in relation to another
Unguent	-	A thick oily substance used on the skin to heal it
Unisex	-	Of one type used by both male and female
Valise	-	A small bag used while travelling
Vertebrate	-	A living creature which has a backbone
Vicissitude	-	A variation in circumstances or fortune at different times in your life or in the development of something
Vinous	-	Of or pertaining to wine
Waterloo	-	A severe defeat after a time of unusual success
Weakling	-	One who lacks physical strength or strength of character
Wean	-	To transfer (the young) from dependence on mother's milk to another form of nourishment
Wheeler-dealer	-	One who is skilled at making profitable or successful deals
Wretch	-	An unfortunate or unhappy person
Xenophobia	-	Fear of strange or foreign people, customs, etc.
Yeoman Service	-	Great and loyal service, help, or support
Yuppie	-	A young person in a professional job with a high income
Zeitgeist	-	The intellectual and moral tendencies that characterize any age or epoch

FOREIGN WORD AND PHRASES

Foreign words and phrases are generally not asked directly. But the knowledge of foreign words and phrases will help you in reading comprehension and other types of common questions. So, make yourself familiar with the common foreign words and phrases.

- **Ab initio** : from the beginning.
- **Addenda** : 'list of additions'. (addenda to a book)
- **Ad valorem** : according to value.
- **Ad infinitum** : to infinity.
- **A la carte** : according to the bill of fare. (a la carte dishes are available)
- **Alter ego** : the other self, intimate friend, (Kissinger was the alter ego of Nixon)
- **Amende honorable** : satisfactory apology, reparation.
- **Amour propre** : self love
- **Ancien regime** : a political or social system that has been displaced by another.
- **A posteriori** : empirical
- **A priori** : from cause to effect, presumptive. (every science cannot be taught a priori)
- **Apropos** : in respect of
- **An couran** : fully acquainted with matters.
- **Au fait** : completely familiar with
- **Au revoir** : until we meet again (to say au revoir at parting)
- **Avant propos** : preliminary matter, preface
- **Beau ideal** : the ideal of perfection.
- **Beaumonde** : the world of fashion.
- **Beaux esprits** : men of wit.
- **Bete noire** : a special aversion (Uncle Symond was my father's bête noire)
- **Bon voyage** : a good voyage or journey to you
- **Casus belli** : that which causes or justifies war.
- **Cause celebre** : a celebrated or notorious case in law
- **Charge d' affaires** : diplomat inferior in rank to an Ambassador but acting on his behalf in his absence.
- **Chef d' oeuvre** : masterpiece (Mona Lisa is Vinci's Chef-d' oeuvre)
- **Circa** : about ('circa 1930')
- **Contretemps** : an unexpected or untoward event; a hitch
- **Corrigenda** : a list of errors (in a book)
- **Coup d'etat** : violent change in government.
- **Coup de grace** : a finishing stroke. (The coup de grace of the Russian Revolution was the total annihilation of the Czar family)
- **Cul-de-sac** : a blind alley (The failure of the Policy of non-alignment in 1962 saw our foreign policy reach a cul-de-sac)
- **De facto** : actual or actually (de facto recognition to a state)

- **Dejure** : from the law, by law.
- **Denovo** : anew, again (trial of a case)
- **Denouement** : the end of a plot (in play)
- **De profundis** : out of the depths
- **Dernier resort** : last resort
- **Detente** : easing of strained relations especially between states / countries
- **Dramatis personae** : characters of a drama or play
- **Enfant terrible** : a terrible child; one who makes disconcerting remarks
- **En rapport** : in harmony
- **Entourage** : friends, group of people accompanying a dignitary.
- **Errata** : list of errors
- **Esprit de corps** : the animating spirit of a collective body, as a regiment.
- **Eureka** : a cry of joy or satisfaction when one finds or discovers something.
- **Ex-officio** : in virtue of his office.
- **Expose** : a statement
- **Expost facto** : acting retrospectively
- **Fait accompli** : a thing already done.
- **Faux pas** : a false step; slip in behaviour
- **Hoi polloi** : the rabble, ordinary people
- **Inextenso** : unextended small in extension
- **Ipso facto** : by that very fact.
- **Laissez faire** : non interference
- **Mal-a-propos** : ill-timed
- **Mutatis mutandis** : with the necessary changes (rules will come into force mutatis mutandis)
- **Noblesse oblige** : rank imposes obligation.
- **Nota bene** : note well
- **Par excellence** : pre-eminently.
- **Pari passu** : side by side.
- **Per se** : by itself.
- **Piece de resistance** : the main dish of a meal.
- **Poste restante** : to remain in the post office till called for. (said of letters)
- **Pro bone publico** : for the good of the public
- **Protégé** : one under the protection of another. (S. Vietnam is US's protege).
- **Quid pro quo** : an equivalent, something in return.
- **Raisond'etre** : the reason for a thing's existence.
- **Sanctum sanctorum** : holy of holies. (temple, church etc.)
- **Seiratim** : in a series
- **Sub rosa** : under the rose; confidentially
- **Sui gereris** : in a class by itself
- **Summon bonum** : the chief good.
- **Terra incognita** : an unknown country
- **Tour deforce** : a notable feat or strength of skill.
- **Ultra vires** : beyond one's authority
- **Vox populi, vox die** : The voice of the people is The voice of God.
- **Zeitgeist** : spirit of the age

WORD LIST

Given below is a list of words placed in alphabetical order. Each word is followed by a few of its synonyms. Note these words whenever you come across them. You should be familiar with most of the words for which synonyms are given if you have done all the exercises till this point thoroughly. So, this list will give you synonyms for the words which you know. Thus learning will be easier.

- **Abase** : Degrade, disgrace, humiliate
- **Abhor** : Hate, loathe, detest
- **Abridge** : Shorten, abbreviate
- **Adept** : Proficient, skilled, expert
- **Adherent** : Follower, stickler
- **Affliction** : Distress, sorrow, sadness
- **Alien** : Foreign, stranger, unknown
- **Alleviate** : Relieve, lighten, ease
- **Alms** : Gratuity, donation, grant
- **Apathy** : Indifference, neutrality
- **Apposite** : Apt, suitable, well chosen
- **Appraise** : Evaluate, estimate
- **Assent** : Agree, consent, acquiesce
- **Audacious** : Bold, courageous, daring
- **Aversion** : Dislike, detestation, hostility, hatred
- **Base** : Mean, low, ignoble
- **Brittle** : Frail, fragile
- **Callous** : Hard, indifferent, cold-blooded
- **Cause** : Make, originate, induce, generate, create
- **Censure** : Blame, condemn, reprove, reprimand
- **Character** : Letter, emblem, type, nature, disposition, quality
- **Charity** : Philanthropy, benevolence
- **Chaste** : Pure, immaculate, virgin, refined
- **Chatter** : Babble, ramble, talk, discourse
- **Colossal** : Huge, gigantic, enormous, big
- **Commensurate** : Equivalent, suitable, applicable, proportionate
- **Consequent** : Following, resultant, outcome
- **Cowardly** : Craven, dastardly, fearful, poltroon
- **Coy** : Modest, shy, reserved
- **Crafty** : Artful, adroit, dexterous, cunning, deceitful
- **Credence** : Belief, faith, trust, confidence
- **Criterion** : Test, touchstone, standard, yardstick
- **Cynical** : Captious, incredulous, sarcastic, morose
- **Dash** : Run, rush, fly
- **Deadly** : Fatal, lethal, destructive
- **Dearth** : Scarcity, lack, want
- **Debase** : Degrade, defame, disparage, humiliate
- **Decay** : Decompose, rot, decline in power, wealth, waste, wither, fade
- **Deceit** : Fraud, cheating, forgery
- **Decipher** : Translate, interpret, solve, explain
- **Decorum** : Decency, etiquette, propriety, gravity
- **Decree** : Law, edict, ordinance, mandate, judgement
- **Deformity** : Disfigurement, malformation, ugliness
- **Dejected** : Depressed, distressed, downhearted, downcast
- **Delectable** : Charming, delightful, pleasant
- **Delegate** : Commission, depute, authorise
- **Delicacy** : Softness, nicety, slenderness, refinement, purity
- **Delusion** : Illusion, fancy, error, false belief
- **Demeanour** : Behaviour, conduct, bearing
- **Demure** : Modest, coy, humane
- **Denomination** : Name, appellation, designation
- **Denounce** : Accuse, malign, criticise, defame, condemn
- **Deride** : Ridicule, mock, taunt
- **Descant** : Discourse, expatiate, enlarge
- **Desolate** : Lonely, deserted, solitary, devastated
- **Despise** : Condemn, dislike
- **Despondency** : Despair, dejection, hopelessness
- **Despotic** : Arbitrary, tyrannical, illegal
- **Destitute** : Needy, poor, miserable, indigent
- **Detest** : Despise, abhor, dislike
- **Dethrone** : Depose, remove (from office)
- **Devastate** : Ruin, demolition, ravage
- **Devoid** : Lacking, empty, vacant
- **Devout** : Religious, reverent
- **Dexterity** : Adroitness, cleverness, skill
- **Diabolical** : Fiendish, devilish, wicked
- **Diatribe** : Tirade, denunciation
- **Diffident** : Hesitating, doubtful, distrusting
- **Digression** : Excursion, deviation, misguidance
- **Diligence** : Care, industry, effort
- **Disavow** : Deny, refuse
- **Disconsolate** : Sad, cheerless, miserable
- **Discredit** : Disbelieve, doubt, disgrace
- **Disorder** : Disease, illness, untidiness, uncleanliness
- **Disparage** : Debase, decry, defame
- **Dispose** : Adjust, arrange, incline
- **Dissolute** : Corrupt, mean, lax, licentious
- **Distaste** : Abhorrence, dislike, detestation
- **Distorted** : Blurred, maligned, changed, disguised, deformed, misrepresented
- **Distress** : Affliction, depression, misery
- **Divine** : Heavenly, metaphysical, godlike
- **Divulge** : Reveal, uncover, disclose
- **Docile** : Amenable, tractable, submissive
- **Doctrine** : Precept, principle, teaching
- **Dogmatic** : Categorical, authoritative, firm, preachy
- **Dolt** : Blockhead, stupid, fool, idiot, dullard
- **Domicile** : Dwelling, home, residence
- **Dotage** : Senility, imbecility
- **Downright** : Simple, unquestionable, blunt, frank
- **Drench** : Soak, wet

- **Dubious** : Suspicious, doubtful, unreliable
- **Ductile** : Pliant, yielding, flexible
- **Dupe** : Cheat, befool, steal
- **Dwindle** : Shrink, diminish, decrease
- **Earnest** : Eager, ardent, intent, anxious, sincere
- **Eccentric** : Irregular, anomalous, abnormal, odd
- **Economise** : Save, retrench
- **Ecstasy** : Trance, enchantment, rapture
- **Efface** : Blot out, obliterate, destroy
- **Effeminate** : Womanly, weak, unmanly
- **Efficacy** : Energy, virtue, potence
- **Egotistic** : Self-centred, egoist, self-conceited
- **Egregious** : Conspicuously bad, sinful, monstrous, shocking
- **Elevated** : Elated, promoted, upgraded, risen
- **Eliminate** : Remove, replace, dismiss, discard
- **Eloquence** : Oratory, rhetoric, finery (of speech) fluency of expression
- **Emanate** : Originate, proceed, spring, issue
- **Emancipate** : Free, deliver, liberate
- **Embarrass** : Vex, confuse, entangle
- **Embezzle** : Steal, peculate, cheat
- **Embody** : Incorporate, include, comprise
- **Emulate** : Compete, rival, vie against, copy
- **Enchant** : Charm, bewitch, hypnotise
- **Encompass** : Surround, encircle
- **Endurance** : Patience, continuance, fortitude
- **Enfranchise** : Liberate, free, (also: give right to vote)
- **Enlighten** : Illuminate, edify, elaborate
- **Enrage** : Infuriate, madden, incense, irritate
- **Ensue** : Succeed, follow, result
- **Entangle** : Ravel, involve, perplex
- **Entice** : Allure, tempt, seduce, attract
- **Entreat** : Beseech, implore, beg
- **Entwine** : Encircle, surround, encompass
- **Enumerate** : Count, number one by one
- **Enunciate** : Declare, publish, propound, reveal
- **Epoch** : Era, time, age
- **Equivocal** : Doubtful, Ambiguous, uncertain
- **Erudite** : Learned, scholarly, lettered
- **Esteem** : Admire, appreciate, adore, respect
- **Eulogy** : Laudation, praise, extolling, felicitation
- **Evince** : Show, manifest, demonstrate
- **Exaggerate** : Amplify, overstate
- **Excerpt** : Extract, quotations
- **Exile** : Expulsion, banishment, expatriation
- **Exonerate** : Acquit, absolve, release
- **Exorbitant** : Excessive, too much, very high
- **Exuberant** : Abundant, plentiful
- **Exult** : Triumph, rejoice, delight
- **Fable** : Story, legend, myth, fiction
- **Facile** : Fluent, ready, glib (of writing), pliable, docile, tractable
- **Faction** : Clique, cabal, discord, section
- **Fallacy** : Deception, illusion, mistake
- **Falter** : Waver, hesitate, delay, flounder
- **Famine** : Hunger, starvation, scarcity of food
- **Fanatical** : Bigoted, enthusiastic
- **Farcical** : Droll, comic, extravagant
- **Fascinate** : Charm, bewitch, attract
- **Fastidious** : Particular, over-nice, squeamish
- **Felicitate** : Congratulate, compliment
- **Felicity** : Joy, happiness, good luck
- **Felon** : Criminal, sinner, guilty, bandit
- **Ferment** : Excite, agitate
- **Ferocity** : Fierceness, vehemence, fanaticism
- **Fervent** : Glowing, heated, impassioned
- **Fervour** : Warmth, glow, vehemence
- **Fetter** : Shackle, bind, imprison
- **Fickle** : Changeable, vacillating, varying
- **Fiendish** : Devilish, diabolical, malignant
- **Figurative** : Typical, imaginative, emblematic, metaphorical
- **Fissure** : Crevice, rift, narrow opening
- **Flaccid** : Soft, loose, weak
- **Flatter** : Adore, please, praise
- **Fleece** : Rob, despoil, cheat
- **Flounder** : Stumble, falter, wallow, struggle
- **Fluctuate** : Undulate, waver, vacillate
- **Flutter** : Flip, quiver, ruffle, agitate
- **Foray** : Incursion, inroad, venture
- **Forbearance** : Abstaining, refraining
- **Forebode** : Betoken, indicate, augur
- **Forlorn** : Disconsolate, cheerless, distressed, abandoned, lonely
- **Formidable** : Dreadful, difficult, hard to overcome
- **Frailty** : Weakness, delicacy, fragileness
- **Frisk** : Skip, dance, caper, frolic
- **Frivolous** : Vain, foolish, trivial
- **Frugal** : Economical, thrifty
- **Gainsay** : Contradict, dispute, controvert, deny
- **Gallantry** : Courage, bravery, heroism
- **Garrulous** : Prattling, chattering
- **Gawky** : Awkward, clumsy
- **Gay** : Happy, merry, joyous
- **Genteel** : Well-bred, well-cultured, polite, refined
- **Glimmer** : Shine, flash, gleam
- **Glisten** : Shine, beam, glow
- **Glutinous** : Sticky, viscous
- **Gluttonous** : Greedy, gorging, voracious
- **Gratification** : Satisfaction, enjoyment
- **Gravity** : Seriousness, importance, calmness
- **Grotesque** : Horrifying, contorted, bizzare, whimsical
- **Gullible** : Simple, easy, pliable, credulous
- **Hallucination** : Delusion, illusion, nightmare
- **Harangue** : a lengthy speech, oration
- **Haughty** : Arrogant, overbearing, imperious
- **Havoc** : Devastation, destruction, ruin
- **Heave** : Raise, lift
- **Hedge** : Fence, hem
- **Heed** : Advise, note, consider, mind
- **Herculean** : Colossal, laborious, excessive
- **Heterogeneous** : Dissimilar, unlike, different, diverse, varied
- **Hideous** : Terrific, horrible, filthy
- **Hilarious** : Exceedingly, funny, boisterously merry, amusing, joyous
- **Histrionic** : Theatrical, dramatic

- **Homage** : Deference, salute, worshipping
- **Hover** : remain in one place in the air, remain suspended, linger
- **Humane** : Compassionate, caring, benevolent
- **Idolise** : Adore, worship, admire
- **Immaculate** : Spotless, stainless, perfect
- **Imminent** : Impending, near, due, threatening
- **Impassioned** : Fervent, frenzied, fanatical
- **Impeachment** : Imputation, accusation
- **Implicit** : Implied, assumed, inferred
- **Impostor** : Cheat, conman, charlatan
- **Impunity** : Exemption (from punishment)
- **Inane** : Empty, silly, idiotic
- **Incense** : Infuriate, enrage, anger
- **Incessant** : Unceasing, continual
- **Incognito** : (Identity) Concealed, secretly, stealthily
- **Inculpate** : Blame, incriminate
- **Incumbent** : Compulsory, obligatory, binding
- **Incursion** : Inroad, foray, venture
- **Indefatigable** : Tireless, assiduous
- **Indict** : Accuse, charge
- **Indolence** : Apathy, inactivity, laziness, sluggishness, lethargy
- **Inexorable** : Relentless, indefatigable
- **Infallible** : Unfailing, unerring, certain
- **Infringe** : Break, violate, transgress, encroach
- **Inhibition** : Restraint, check
- **Iniquitous** : Unjust, wrong, unfair
- **Innocuous** : Harmless, mild, innocent
- **Insanity** : Madness, lunacy, mania
- **Insidious** : Deceitful, treacherous
- **Instantaneous** : Immediate, Sudden, quick
- **Integrity** : Oneness, entirety, completeness, honesty, wholeness, soundness
- **Intransigent** : Uncompromising, inflexible
- **Intrepid** : Brave, fearless
- **Intricate** : Complex, difficult, complicated
- **Intuition** : Insight, premonition, instinct
- **Inveterate** : Habitual, deep-rooted
- **Involuntary** : Compulsory, unwilled, reflex
- **Irresolute** : Wavering, confused, vacillating
- **Itinerant** : Travelling (on a circuit), wandering, nomadic
- **Jaded** : Tired, weary
- **Jargon** : cant, technical language, gibberish
- **Jocose** : Jocular, humorous
- **Jocular** : Inclined to joke
- **Jovial** : Merry
- **Judicious** : Prudent.
- **Juxtaposition** : Closeness, nearness
- **Lacerate** : Tear (tissue toughly), mangle
- **Lachrymose** : Given to shedding tears.
- **Lackadaisical** : Listless.
- **Laconic** : (Briskly) Short, concise, pithy
- **Languid** : Listless, spiritless
- **Lascivious** : Lustful.
- **Lassitude** : Weariness, tiredness
- **Latent** : Hidden, concealed
- **Legacy** : A bequest.
- **Levity** : Frivolity.
- **Libel** : Defamation.
- **Licentious** : Wanton.
- **Lithe** : Supple.
- **Loquacious** : Talkative.
- **Lustrous** : Shining.
- **Malaise** : A condition of uneasiness or ill-being.
- **Malevolence** : Ill-will.
- **Malleable** : Pliant.
- **Mawkish** : Sickening or insipid.
- **Mellifluous** : Sweetly or smoothly flowing.
- **Mendacious** : Untrue
- **Mesmerize** : To hypnotize.
- **Meticulous** : Over-cautious.
- **Mettle** : Courage.
- **Mien** : The external appearance or manner of a person.
- **Moderation** : Temperance.
- **Modicum** : A small or token amount.
- **Mordant** : Biting.
- **Moribund** : On the point of dying.
- **Morose** : Gloomy.
- **Multifarious** : Having great diversity or variety.
- **Mundane** : Worldly, as opposed to spiritual or celestial.
- **Munificent** : Extraordinarily generous.
- **Myriad** : A vast indefinite number.
- **Nadir** : The lowest point.
- **Nefarious** : Wicked in the extreme.
- **Neophyte** : Having the character of a beginner.
- **Noxious** : Hurtful.
- **Nugatory** : Having no power or force.
- **Obdurate** : Impassive to feelings of humanity or pity.
- **Obfuscate** : To darken; to obscure.
- **Oblique** : Slanting; said of lines.
- **Obstreperous** : Boisterous.
- **Odious** : Hateful.
- **Odium** : A feeling of extreme repugnance, or of dislike and disgust.
- **Ominous** : Portentous.
- **Onerous** : Burdensome or oppressive.
- **Onus** : A burden or responsibility.
- **Palate** : The roof of the mouth.
- **Palatial** : Magnificent.
- **Palliate** : To cause to appear less guilty.
- **Palpable** : Perceptible by feeling or touch.
- **Panoply** : A full set of armour.
- **Paragon** : A model of excellence.
- **Pariah** : A member of a degraded class; a social outcast.
- **Paroxysm** : A sudden outburst (of any kind of activity).
- **Paucity** : Fewness.
- **Pellucid** : Translucent.
- **Penchant** : A bias in favour of something.
- **Penurious** : Excessively sparing in the use of money.
- **Penury** : Indigence.

Peremptory	:	Precluding question or appeal.
Perfidy	:	Treachery.
Perfunctory	:	Half-hearted.
Peripatetic	:	Walking about.
Perjury	:	A solemn assertion of a falsity.
Permeate	:	To pervade.
Pernicious	:	Tending to kill or hurt.
Persiflage	:	Banter.
Perspicacity	:	Acuteness or discernment.
Perturbation	:	Mental excitement or confusion.
Petulant	:	Displaying impatience.
Phlegmatic	:	Not easily roused to feeling or action.
Pique	:	To excite a slight degree of anger in.
Plenary	:	Entire.
Plethora	:	Excess; superabundance.
Poignant	:	Severely painful or acute to the spirit.
Polyglot	:	Speaking several tongues.
Ponderous	:	Unusually weighty or forcible.
Portent	:	Anything that indicates what is to happen.
Pragmatic	:	Practical(values), empirical
Precarious	:	Critical, dangerous
Preclude	:	To prevent.
Precocious	:	Advanced (in development), over-forward, premature
Predilection	:	Preference, partiality, inclination
Predominate	:	To be chief in importance, quantity, or degree.
Preposterous	:	(Very) Absurd, ridiculous
Prerogative	:	(Special) Right, privilege
Presage	:	To foretell.
Prescience	:	Knowledge of events before they take place.
Preternatural	:	Extraordinary.
Prim	:	Stiffly proper.
Pristine	:	Primitive.
Probity	:	Virtue or integrity tested and confirmed.
Proclivity	:	A natural inclination.
Procrastination	:	Delay.
Prodigious	:	Large, immense
Profligate	:	Immoral, wanton, reckless, dissolute, licentious
Profuse	:	Produced or displayed in overabundance.
Prolix	:	Verbose.
Promiscuous	:	Indiscriminate, impure, casual
Propinquity	:	Nearness, proximity
Propitious	:	Kindly disposed.
Prosaic	:	Unimaginative.
Protagonist	:	Leading character), hero(ine)
Providential	:	Fortunate, lucky
Prudence	:	Caution.
Puerile	:	Childish.
Pugnacious	:	Quarrelsome
Puissant	:	Powerful, influential, mighty
Punctilious	:	Exact (in formalities), ceremonious, conscientious
Pungency	:	The quality of affecting the sense of smell.
Pusillanimous	:	Without spirit or bravery.
Putrefy	:	Decay, rot, decompose
Qualm	:	A fit of nausea.
Quandary	:	Doubt, dilemma, plight
Quibble	:	An utterly trivial distinction or objection.
Quiescence	:	Being quiet, still, or at rest; inactive
Quirk	:	Twist, quibble, deviation
Quixotic	:	(Foolishly) Chivalrous, unrealistic, whimsical
Rabble	:	Throng (of the vulgar), crowd, proletariat
Rabid	:	Furious, mad, fanatical
Raconteur	:	A person skilled in telling stories.
Raillery	:	Jesting (language), banter, ridicule
Ramify	:	To divide or subdivide into branches or subdivisions.
Rampant	:	Rife, widespread
Ramshackle	:	Dilapidated, tumbledown, rickety
Rapacious	:	Seize by force, avaricious
Raucous	:	Harsh.
Recalcitrant	:	Stubborn, refractory
Recluse	:	One who lives in retirement or seclusion.
Recondite	:	Incomprehensible to one of ordinary understanding.
Recuperate	:	To recover.
Redoubtable	:	Formidable.
Redundant	:	Wordy, repetitious, superfluous, needless
Refractory	:	Not amenable to control.
Regale	:	To give unusual pleasure.
Regicide	:	The killing of a king or sovereign.
Reiterate	:	To say or do again and again.
Relapse	:	To suffer a return of a disease after partial recovery.
Relegate	:	Assign a lower position, banish, demote
Repast	:	A meal; figuratively, any refreshment.
Repine	:	To indulge in fretfulness and faultfinding.
Reprisal	:	(Injury in) Return, retaliation, revenge
Reprobate	:	One abandoned to depravity and sin.
Repudiate	:	Disavow, disclaim
Resilience	:	The power of springing back to a former position
Resonance	:	Able to reinforce sound by sympathetic vibrations.
Revere	:	To regard with worshipful veneration.
Reverent	:	Humble.
Rotund	:	Round from fullness or plumpness.
Ruminate	:	To chew over again, as food previously swallowed and regurgitated.
Sagacious	:	Wise, shrewd, astute
Salacious	:	Obscene, foul, indecent, lecherous
Salubrious	:	Healthful; promoting health.
Salutary	:	(Morally) Healthy, salubrious, beneficial
Sanguine	:	Ardent, confident, optimistic
Sardonic	:	Ironical, scornful, derisive
Satiate	:	Gratify (fully), surfeit, saturate
Satyr	:	A very lascivious person.
Savour	:	To perceive by taste or smell.

- **Schism** : Disjunction, split
- **Scribble** : Hasty, careless writing.
- **Sedition** : Plotting (against government), incitement, insurgence
- **Sedulous** : Persevering in effort or endeavour.
- **Severance** : Separation.
- **Sinecure** : Any position (having emoluments with few or no duties).
- **Sinuous** : Curving in and out.
- **Sluggard** : A person habitually lazy or idle.
- **Solvent** : Having sufficient funds to pay all debts.
- **Somniferous** : Tending to produce sleep.
- **Somnolent** : Sleepy.
- **Soporific** : Causing sleep; also, something that causes sleep.
- **Specious** : Plausible.
- **Squalid** : Having a dirty, mean, poverty-stricken appearance.
- **Stanch** : To stop the flowing of; to check.
- **Stingy** : Cheap, unwilling to spend money.
- **Stolid** : Having or revealing little emotion or sensibility; not easily aroused or excited
- **Submerge** : To place or plunge under water.
- **Subterfuge** : Evasion.
- **Succinct** : Concise.
- **Sumptuous** : Rich and costly.
- **Supercilious** : Exhibiting haughty and careless contempt.
- **Supernumerary** : Superfluous.
- **Supersede** : To displace.
- **Supine** : Lying on the back.
- **Supplicate** : To beg.
- **Suppress** : To prevent from being disclosed or punished.
- **Surcharge** : An additional amount charged.
- **Surfeit** : To feed to fullness or to satiety.
- **Susceptibility** : A specific capability of feeling or emotion.
- **Taciturn** : Disinclined to conversation.
- **Taut** : Stretched tight.
- **Temerity** : Foolhardy disregard of danger; recklessness.
- **Terse** : Pithy.
- **Timorous** : Lacking courage.
- **Torpid** : Dull; sluggish; inactive.
- **Torrid** : Excessively hot.
- **Tortuous** : Abounding in irregular bends or turns.
- **Tractable** : Easily led or controlled.
- **Transgress** : To break a law.
- **Transitory** : Existing for a short time only.
- **Travail** : Hard or agonizing labour.
- **Travesty** : A grotesque imitation.
- **Trenchant** : Cutting deeply and quickly.
- **Trepidation** : Nervous uncertainty of feeling.
- **Trite** : Made commonplace by frequent repetition.
- **Truculence** : Ferocity.
- **Truculent** : Having the character or the spirit of a savage.
- **Turbid** : In a state of turmoil; muddled
- **Turgid** : Swollen.
- **Turpitude** : Depravity.
- **Ubiquitous** : Being present everywhere.
- **Umbrage** : A sense of injury.
- **Unctuous** : Oily.
- **Undulate** : To move like a wave or in waves.
- **Untoward** : Causing annoyance or hindrance.
- **Upbraid** : To reproach as deserving blame.
- **Vagary** : A sudden desire or action
- **Vainglory** : Excessive, pretentious, and demonstrative vanity.
- **Valorous** : Courageous.
- **Vapid** : Having lost sparkling quality and flavour.
- **Variegated** : Having marks or patches of different colours; also, varied.
- **Vehement** : Very eager or urgent.
- **Venal** : Mercenary, corrupt.
- **Veneer** : Outside show or elegance.
- **Venial** : That may be pardoned or forgiven, a forgivable sin.
- **Veracious** : Habitually disposed to speak the truth.
- **Veracity** : Truthfulness.
- **Verbiage** : Use of many words without necessity
- **Verbose** : Wordy
- **Verdant** : Green with vegetation.
- **Veritable** : Real, true, genuine
- **Vestige** : (A visible) trace, mark, or impression (of something absent, lost, or gone).
- **Virago** : Loud talkative women, strong statured women
- **Virtue** : Rare, curious, or beautiful quality.
- **Visage** : The face, countenance, or look of a person.
- **Vituperate** : To overwhelm with wordy abuse.
- **Vivify** : To endue with life.
- **Voluble** : Having great fluency in speaking.
- **Whimsical** : Capricious.
- **Winsome** : Attractive.

SYNONYMS AND ANTONYMS

This is the other very important area of the vocabulary section. This section tests widely and exhaustively one's knowledge of the language and word power, but goes beyond that to test your ability to remember words with similar meanings or opposite meanings. Or, alternately, to discover the similarity or proximity between the meaning of the given word with one of those in the options.

These exercises can get confusing sometimes because more than one option may appear as the right answer or none of them may look like the right answer. For such questions a student may consider the following strategies:

STRATEGY 1

If you do not know the meaning of the given word, think of a context in which you might have used it, that may help you to figure out the meaning, for example, in the question below find the word nearest in meaning to

MAGNIFY

(a) Forgive (b) diminish (c) swell (d) extract

Now if you do not know what magnify means think of a magnifying glass and what it does. It expands or makes a thing look bigger. So the right answer will be (c).

STRATEGY 2

If you cannot find a correct antonym in the given option think of the antonyms you know of and subsequently check if there is any word in the given options which is synonymous to the antonyms in your mind. For example

INDUSTRIOUS

(a) stupid (b) harsh (c) indolent (d) complex

If you don't know any of the words given as options think of antonyms you could think of, like lazy, idle. Now think of synonyms of lazy and you will know indolent is a synonym of lazy. So it will be the antonym to industrious. Formula → SYNONYM of ANTONYM is another ANTONYM.

STRATEGY 3

Look at the part of speech of the given word. A word may exist in various parts of speech. For example precipitate exists as a verb which means send rapidly into a certain state and also as a noun, precipitate, which means a substance deposited from a solution.

POLISH

(a) ruthlessness (b) honesty (c) indolence (d) gaucheness

Now is this the verb polish or noun polish? Since all options are nouns, this cannot be the verb polish related to shoes but noun polish which means culture and sophistication and the antonym to this would be gaucheness.

ANALOGIES

Analogy literally means a comparison or a comparable similarity. A student has to find a pair of words in the same relation or a similar relation as that of the given pair of words. Analogy is, in a sense, a test of vocabulary since you need to know the meaning of the words given, but in a broader sense it is a test of reasoning ability. To know the meaning of the words will not be enough if one is not able to understand clearly what the relation between the pairs of words is. Therefore, there are two things that are important to attempt a question on analogy:
(i)   meaning of all given words
(ii)   relationship between the given pairs of words

It is more convenient and time saving to first figure out the relation between the given pair and then compare it with the relations between the pairs in the options given for choice. Consider the following example
Pen : Write : : Book :
Now first determine the relation between the first two words, it is that of purpose, pen is used to write. Then determine the other word which will be in the same relation to the third word. Book is used to read, then
Pen : Write : : Book : read
There are different kinds of relationships that could be drawn from daily usage but some common relationships are given below:

1.   CAUSE : EFFECT
     Liquor : Intoxication → Liquor causes intoxication
     Wound : pain → wound causes pain.

In this relation the first word is the cause for the second and the second is the result of the first

2.   PURPOSE
     Bottle : Cork → a cork is used to close a bottle
     Dress : cloth → cloth is used to make a dress
     In this relation, one word is used for another, there is a purpose between the two

3.   OBJECT : ACTION
     Gun : Fire → you fire a gun
     Violin : play → you play a violin
     In this, one term is an object and the other one is action undertaken with the help of that object.

4.   ACTION : OBJECT
     foment : Riot → you foment a riot
     Wear : clothes → you wear clothes
     This is opposite to the previous relation, here the first word is the action and the second the object with which that action is done.

5.   PART : WHOLE
     Book : Literature → a book is a part of the larger body of literature
     Ship : fleet → ship is a part of the collection called fleet
     In this relation, the first word will in the same way be a constituent of a bigger body represented by the second word.

6.   **SYNONYMS**
     Abundant : ample → ample means the same as abundant
     Skilled : adroit → the two words are synonymous, i.e., they mean the same
     This relation is when both the words are synonyms.

7.   **ANTONYMS :**
     Abstinence : indulgence → indulgence means the opposite of Abstinence
     Legitimate : Unlawful → Legitimate means legal which is the opposite of unlawful.
     In this relation, the two words are opposite to each other in meaning.

8.   **SECONDARY SYNONYMS :**
     Callous : Indifference → The synonym of callous will be indifferent, since both words are adjectives but rather the noun form, indifference, has been given in the relation
     Brainwave: Inspired → The synonym of Brainwave is inspiration, but instead the second word in this relation is Inspired - the one who has inspiration.
     In this relation, the two words are not directly synonymous but a slight change of the part of speech has been made in the second word.

9.   **WORKER: ARTICLE CREATED**
     Carpenter : furniture → carpenter makes wooden furniture
     Compose : music → a composer composes or creates music
     In this relation, the first word is the doer and the second is the professional work done by the first.

10. **SYMBOL : QUALITY**
     Olive leaf : Peace → an olive leaf is a symbol of peace.
     Red : passion → the colour red symbolises passion.
     In this relation the first word is a symbol, and the second is the meaning represented by the symbol.

11. **CLASS : MEMBER**
     mammal : man → man belongs to the class of mammals.
     Doggerel : Poem → Doggerel is a class of poem which is bad in quality.
     In this relation the first word is a member belonging to the class denoted by the second word.

12. **ACTION : SIGNIFICANCE**
     Blush : embarrassment → if one blushes, that signifies that the person is embarrassed.
     Spasm : pain → a spasm indicates that the person is in pain.
     In this relation the first word is an action and the second is what that action signifies.

Although most of the questions asked in a competitive exam can be solved with the help of the given relationships, for subtle questions a student should apply reasoning to figure out the relation between the given words. Following are certain tips that would help a student to attempt analogy questions.

☛ **TIP 1**

The first and foremost step while attempting an analogy question should be to DEFINE THE RELATIONSHIP. To avoid any errors, first define the relationship on paper or in your mind before searching for options. Once you have defined the relationship analyse the given pairs in the light of the relationship.

(1) **ANXIOUS : REASSURANCE**
     → resentful : gratitude
     → perplexed : classification
     → insured : imagination
     → vociferous : suppression
     First, the relationship can be defined as 'need' i.e. an anxious person needs reassurance and then you can check the given pairs to find out that 'a perplexed person needs classification'. Thus this will be the right analogy.

(2) **SIMMER : BOIL**
     → Cook : Fry
     → Chill : Freeze
     → Roast : Stew
     → Slice : Cut
     Now, establish the relation between the two given words. It is that of degree. Simmer is the lower degree of boil. Just as chill is the lower degree of freeze.

☛ **TIP 2**

Always be careful about apparent and easy similarity. These are only to deceive the student as you would be attracted by these options. Always confirm all the options and be highly careful while considering an obvious answer.

e.g. **STUTTER : SPEECH**
     → Blare : hearing
     → Aroma : smelling
     → Astigmatism : sight
     → Novocaine : Touch
     Stutter is a defect of speech, so the relation between the two is that of defect. But Blare and hearing are closely related since blare means a harsh sound. This may attract the student, but this is not a relation of defect. This relation is in the third option, astigmatism is a defect of sight. So always avoid giving into the temptation of obviously correct answers.

☛ **TIP 3**

Sometimes a word has two meanings, while what may first come to your mind will be the more frequent use of that word, if you cannot find a logical relation between the two words. Go beyond the obvious meaning and link the word with the other meaning of the second word.

MAROON : SAILOR
     → Red : Ship
     → Crimson : flower
     → Stranded : Tourist
     → Colour : Dress
     Maroon also has two meanings the colour 'maroon' and the verb maroon which means being left alone or abandoned. Obviously the second meaning will make a logical relation with sailor, a sailor is marooned just as a tourist is stranded.

WORD USAGE

FILL IN THE BLANKS OR SENTENCE COMPLETION

Sentence completion questions test your ability to use your vocabulary and recognise logical consistency among the elements in a sentence. You need to know more than the dictionary definitions of the words involved. You need to know how the words fit together to make logical and stylistic sense.

Sentence completion questions actually measure one part of reading comprehension. If you can recognise how the different parts of a sentence affect one another, you should do well at choosing the answer that best completes the meaning of the sentence or provides a clear, logical statement of fact. The ability to recognise irony and humour will also stand you in good stead, as will the ability to recognise figurative language and to distinguish between formal and informal levels of speech.

Since the sentence completion questions contain many clues that help you to answer them correctly (far more clues than the antonyms provide, for example), and analysing them helps you warm up for the reading passages later on in the test, on the paper-and-pencil test, answer them first. Then go on to tackle the analogies, the antonyms, and, finally, the time-consuming reading comprehension section.

Sentence completion questions may come from any of a number of different fields - art, literature, history, philosophy, botany, astronomy, geology, and so on. You cannot predict what subject matter the sentences on your test will involve.

WHAT MAKES THE HARD QUESTIONS HARD?

1. **Vocabulary Level** :Sentences contain words like intransigence, nonplussed, harbingers. Answer choices include words like penchant, abeyance, and eclectic.

2. **Grammatical Complexity**: Sentences combine the entire range of grammatical possibilities : adverbial clauses, relative clauses, prepositional phrases, gerunds, infinitives, and so on in convoluted ways. The more complex the sentence, the more difficult it is for you to spot the key words that can unlock its meaning.

3. **Tone:** Sentences reflect the writer's attitude towards the subject matter. It is simple to comprehend material that is presented neutrally. It is far more difficult to comprehend material that is ironic, condescending, playful, sombre, or otherwise complex in tone.

4. **Style:** Ideas may be expressed in different manners ornately or sparely, poetically or prosaically, formally or informally, journalistically or academically, originally or imitatively. An author's style depends on such details as word choice, imagery, repetition, rhythm, sentence structure and length.

Work through the following fundas and learn techniques that will help you with vocabulary, grammatical complexity, tone, and style.

STRATEGY 1

BEFORE YOU LOOK AT THE CHOICES, READ THE SENTENCE AND THINK OF A WORD THAT MAKES SENSE

Your problem is to find the word that best completes the sentence in both thought and style. Before you look at the answer choices, see if you can come up with a word that makes logical sense in the context. Then look at all five choices. If the word you thought of is one of your five choices, select that as your answer. If the word you thought of is not one of your five choices, look for a synonym of that word. Select the synonym as your answer.

This technique is helpful because it enables you to get a sense of the sentence as a whole without being distracted by any misleading answers among the answer choices. You are free to concentrate on spotting key words or phrases in the body of the sentence and to call on your own "writer's intuition" in arriving at a stylistically apt choice of word.

See how the process works in a typical model question.

1. Because experience had convinced her that he was both self-seeking and avaricious, she rejected the likelihood that his donation had been................

    (A) redundant   (B) frivolous
    (C) inexpensive   (D) ephemeral
    (E) altruistic

This sentence presents a simple case of cause and effect. The key phrase here is self-seeking and avaricious. The woman has found the man to be selfish and greedy. Therefore, she refuses to believe he can do something.............. What words immediately come to mind? Selfless, generous, charitable? The missing word is, of course, altruistic. The woman expects selfishness (self-seeking) and greediness (avaricious), not altruism (magnanimity). The correct answer is Choice E.

Practice of Funda 1 extensively develops your intuitive sense of just the exactly right word. However, do not rely on Funda 1 alone. On the test, always follow up Funda 1 with Funda 2.

STRATEGY 2

LOOK AT ALL THE POSSIBLE ANSWERS BEFORE YOU MAKE YOUR FINAL CHOICE

Never decide on an answer before you have read all the choices. You are looking for the word that best fits the meaning of the sentence as a whole. In order to be sure you have not been hasty in making your decision, substitute all the answer choices for the missing word. Do not spend a lot of time doing so, but do try them all. That way you can satisfy yourself that you have come up with the best answer.

See how this Funda helps you deal with another question.

1. The evil of class and race hatred must be eliminated while it is still in an ....state; otherwise it may grow to dangerous proportions.

   (A) Amorphous   (B) overt

   (C) uncultivated   (D) embryonic

   (E) independent

On the basis of a loose sense of this sentence's meaning, you might be tempted to select Choice A. After all, this sentence basically tells you that you should wipe out hatred before it gets too dangerous. Clearly, if hatred is vague or amorphous, it is less formidable than if it is well defined. However, this reading of the sentence is inadequate: it fails to take into account the sentence's key phrase.

The key phrase here is 'grow to dangerous proportions'. The writer fears that class and race hatred may grow large enough to endanger society. He wants us to wipe out this hatred before it is fully-grown. Examine each answer choice, eliminating those answers that carry no suggestion that something lacks its full growth. Does overt suggest that something isn't fully-grown? No, it suggests that something is obvious or evident. Does uncultivated suggest that something isn't fully grown? No, it suggests that something is unrefined or growing without proper care or training. Does independent suggest that something isn't fully-grown? No, it suggests that something is free and unconstrained. Only one word suggests a lack of full growth: embryonic (at a rudimentary, early stage of development). The correct answer is Choice D.

STRATEGY 3

IN DOUBLE-BLANK SENTENCES, GO THROUGH THE ANSWERS, TESTING THE FIRST WORD IN EACH CHOICE (AND ELIMINATING THOSE THAT DON'T FIT)

In a sentence completion question with two blanks, read through the entire sentence to get a sense of it as a whole. Then insert the first word of each answer pair in the sentence's first blank. Ask yourself whether this particular word makes sense in this blank. If the initial word of an answer pair makes no sense in the sentence, you can eliminate that answer pair.

(Note: Occasionally this Funda will not work. In some questions, for example, the first words of all five answer pairs may be near-synonyms. However, the Funda frequently pays off, as it does in the following example.)

1. Critics of the movie version of The Colour Purple .... its saccharine, overoptimistic mood at odds with the novel's more ....tone.

   (A) applauded, sombre

   (B) condemned, hopeful

   (C) acclaimed, positive

   (D) denounced, sanguine

   (E) decried, acerbic

For a quick, general sense of the opening clause, break it up. What does it say? Critics..........the movie's sugary sweet mood.

How would critics react to something sugary sweet and over-hopeful? They would disapprove. Your first missing word must be a synonym for disapprove.

Now eliminate the misfits. Choices A and C fail to meet the test: applauded and acclaimed signify approval, not disapproval. Choice B, condemned, Choice D, denounced and Choice E, decried, however, all disapprobation; they require a second look.

To decide among Choices B, D, and E, consider the second blank. The movie's sugary, overly hopeful mood is at odds with the novel's tone: the two moods disagree. Therefore, the novel's tone is not hopeful or sugary sweet. It is instead on the bitter or sour side; in a word, acerbic, the correct answer is clearly Choice E.

Remember that, in double-blank sentences, the right answer must correctly fill both blanks. A wrong answer choice often includes one correct and one incorrect answer. ALWAYS test both words.

STRATEGY 4

WATCH FOR SIGNAL WORDS THAT LINK ONE PART OF THE SENTENCE TO ANOTHER

Writers use transitions to link their ideas logically. These transitions or signal words are clues that can help you figure out what the sentence actually means. Sentences often contain several signal words, combining them in complex ways.

1. Cause and Effect Signals

Look for words or phrases explicitly indicating that one thing causes another or logically determines another.

Cause and Effect Signal Words

Accordingly in order to	Because	
so...that	Consequently	Therefore
Given	thus	Hence when...then If...then

Look for words or phrases explicitly indicating that the omitted portion of the sentence supports or continues a thought developed elsewhere in the sentence. In such cases, a synonym or near-synonym for another word in the sentence may provide the correct answer.

Support	**Signal**	**Words**
Additionally	furthermore	Also
indeed	And	Likewise
as well	moreover	besides
too		

2. Contrast Signals (Explicit)

Look for functional words or phrases (conjunctions, adverbs, etc.) that explicitly indicate a contrast between one idea and another, setting up a reversal of a thought. In such cases, an antonym or near-antonym for another word in the sentence may provide the correct answer.

Explicit Contrast Signal Words

Albeit	nevertheless	Although
nonetheless	But	
Notwithstanding	despite	
on the contrary	even though	
on the other hand		however
rather than	in contrast	still
in spite of	while	instead of yet

3.   Contrast Signals (Implicit)

Look for content words whose meanings inherently indicate a contrast. These words can **turn a** situation **on its head**. They indicate that something unexpected, possibly even unwanted, has occurred.

Implicit Contrast Signal Words

anomaly	Anomalous	anomalously	illogically illogical
incongruity	incongruous	incongruously	
irony	ironic	ironically	
paradox	paradoxical	paradoxically	
surprise	surprising	surprisingly	
unexpected	unexpectedly		

Note the function of such a contrast signal word in the following question.

1.   Paradoxically, the more...........the details this artist chooses, the better able she is to depict her fantastic, otherworldly landscapes.

   (A) ethereal   (B) realistic

   (C) fanciful   (D) extravagant

   (E) sublime

The artist creates imaginary landscapes that do not seem to belong to this world. We normally would expect the details comprising these landscapes to be as fantastic and supernatural as the landscapes themselves. But the truth of the matter, however, is paradoxical: it contradicts what we expect. The details she chooses are realistic, and the more realistic they are, the more fantastic the paintings become. The correct answer is Choice B.

STRATEGY 5

USE YOUR KNOWLEDGE OF WORD PARTS AND PARTS OF SPEECH TO FIGURE OUT THE MEANINGS OF UNFAMILIAR WORDS

If a word used by the author is unfamiliar, or if an answer choice is unknown to you, two approaches are helpful.

1.   Break up the word into its component parts - prefixes, suffixes, and roots - to see whether they provide a clue to its meaning. For example, in the preceding list of Implicit Contrast Signal Words, the word incongruous contains three major word parts, in- here means not; con- means together; gru- means to move or conic. Incongruous behaviour, therefore, is behaviour that does not go together or agree with someone's usual behaviour; it is unexpected.

2.   Change the unfamiliar word from one part of speech to another. If the adjective embryonic is unfamiliar to you, cut off its adjective suffix -nic and recognise the familiar word embryo. If the noun precocity is unfamiliar to you cut off its noun suffix -ity and visualise it with different endings. You may think of the adjective precocious (maturing early). If the verb appropriate is unfamiliar to you, by adding a word part or two, you may come up with the common noun appropriation or the still more common noun misappropriation (as in the misappropriation of funds).

Note the application of this funda in the following typical example.

1.   This island is a colony; however, in most matters, it is .... and receives no orders from the mother country.

   (A) dichotomous   (B) methodical

   (C) heretical   (D) autonomous

   (E) disinterested

First, eliminate any answer choices that are obviously incorrect. If a colony receives no orders from its mother country, it is essentially self-governing. It is not necessarily methodical or systematic nor is it by definition heretical (unorthodox) or disinterested (impartial). Thus, you may rule out Choices B, C, and E.

The two answer choices remaining may be unfamiliar to you. Analyse them, using what you know of related words. Choice A, dichotomous, is related to the noun dichotomy, a division into two parts, as in the dichotomy between good and evil. Though the island colony may be separated from the mother country by distance that has nothing to do with how the colony governs itself. Choice D, autonomous, comes from the prefix auto-(self) and the root nom-(law). An autonomous nation is independent; it rules itself. Thus, the correct answer is autonomous, Choice D.

STRATEGY 6

BREAK UP COMPLEX SENTENCES INTO SIMPLER COMPONENTS

In analysing long, complex sentence completion items, you may find it useful to simplify the sentences by breaking them up. Rephrase dependent clauses and long participle phrases, turning them into simple sentences.

See how this funda helps you to analyse the following sentence.

1.   Museum director Hoving .... refers to the smuggled Greek urn as the "hot pot;" not because there are doubts about its authenticity or even great reservations as to its price, but because its .... of acquisition is open to question.

   (A) informally, costliness

   (B) characteristically, date

   (C) colloquially, manner

   (D) repeatedly, swiftness

   (E) cheerfully, mode

What do we know?

1.   The urn has been smuggled.

2.   Hoving calls it a "hot pot."

3.   It is genuine. (There are no doubts about its authenticity.)

4.   It did not cost too much. (There are no great reservations as to its price.)

In calling the smuggled urn a "hot pot", Hoving is not necessarily speaking characteristically or redundantly or cheerfully. He is speaking either informally or colloquially. (Hot here is a slang term meaning stolen or illegally obtained.) Its costliness is not being questioned. However, because the urn has been smuggled into the country, there clearly are unresolved questions about how it got here, in other words, about its manner of acquisition. The correct answer is Choice C.

Note that in sentence completion questions a choice may he complicated by an unusual word order, such as:

1.   placing the subject after the verb: To the complaints window strode the angry customer.

2. placing the subject after an auxiliary of the verb: Only by unending search could some few Havana cigars be found.

3. inverting the subject and verb to give the sense of "if": Were defeat to befall him today's dear friends would be tomorrow's acquaintances, and next week's strangers.

4 placing a negative word or phrase first, which usually requires at least part of the verb to follow: Never have I encountered so demanding a test!

In all these instances, rephrase the sentence to make it more straightforward. For example:

1. The angry customer strode to the complaints window.

2. Some few Havana cigars could be found only by unending search.

3. If defeat were to befall him, today's dear friends would be tomorrow's acquaintances, and next week's strangers.

4. I have never encountered so demanding a test!

IDIOMS AND PHRASES

- *Beat back* (to compel to retire) : The firemen were *beaten back* by angry flames and the building was reduced to ashes.

- *Boil down to* (to amount to) : His entire argument *boiled down* to this that he would not join the movement unless he saw some monetary gain in it.

- *Cast aside* (to reject, to throw aside) : Men will *cast aside* truth and honesty for immediate gains.

- *Cry down* (to deprecate) : Some of the Western powers did their best to *cry down* India's success in the war.

- *To cut off with a shilling* (to give someone a mere trifle in the will) : The father was so angry with the son over his marriage that *he cut him off with a shilling.*

- *Egg on* (to urge on) : Who *egged* you on to fight a professional boxer and get your nose knocked off?

- *Gloss over* (to ignore or avoid unpleasant fact) : Even if you are an important person your faults cannot be *glossed over.*

- *To laugh in one's sleeves* (to be secretly amused) : While I was solemnly reading my research paper to the audience, my friends were *laughing in their sleeves* for they knew what it was worth.

- *Play off* (to set one party against another for one's own advantage) : It best serves the interests of the super powers to *play off* one poor nation against another.

- *Pull one through* (to recover, to help one recover) : Armed with the latest medicines, the doctor *will pull him through.*

- *Cast a slur upon* (by word or act to cast a slight reproach on someone) : Many a man casts a *slur* on his own good name with some mean act.

- *To catch a Tartar* (to encounter a strong adversary) : When Hitler marched in to Russia he little knew that he would *catch a Tartar* in the tough people of that country.

- *To cut the Gordian knot* (to remove a difficulty by bold or unusual measures) : The Parliament threw out the Bill for Abolition of Privy Purses. The Government cut the Gordian knot by abolishing the privy purses through an ordinance.

- *To fall to one's lot* (to become one's fate): It fell to the lot of Sheikh Hasina and her colleagues to reconstruct the shattered economy of their nation.

- *To go on a fool's errand* (to go on an expedition which leads to a foolish end): Many people earlier believed that going to the moon was like *going on a fool's errand*

- *To go to the wall* (to get the worst in a competition): In the struggle of life, the weakest *goes to the wall.*

- *To go to rack and ruin, to go to the dogs* (to be ruined): If a big war comes, our economy will *go to the dogs.*

- *To have a bone to pick with one* (to have a difference with a person which has not yet been fully expressed). The extreme leftists *have a bone to pick* with the police and if ever they come to power there may be unpleasantness between the two.

- *To have the whip hand of* (to have mastery over): During the last decade, the right wing of the party has held the whip hand.

- *To have too many irons in the fire (to have so much work in* hand that some part of it is left undone or is done very badly): Let the Government not go in for privatization so fast. If they *have too many irons in the fire* they are bound to fare badly.

- *To have the tree or right ring* (To be genuine): Nixon's pronouncements on world peace do not *have the right ring.*

- *To keep the wolf from the door* (to keep away extreme poverty and hunger): Lakhs in India have to struggle everyday to *keep the wolf from the door.*

- *To make short work of (to* bring to sudden end): The locusts *made short work* of the ripe standing corn.

- *To make common cause with* (to unite, to co-operate with): During the last elections the princess *made a common cause with* the rightist parties. Both went down.

- *To make a virtue of necessity* (to do a very disagreeable thing as though from duty but really because you must do it): When a minister knows that he is going to be booted out of the cabinet he *makes a virtue of necessity* and resigns on health grounds.

- *To play second fiddle* (to take a subordinate part): With Mr. Phillip as the undisputed leader of the party, everyone else is content to *play second fiddle to him.*

- *To put one's shoulder to the wheel* (to make great efforts ourselves): No amount of foreign aid will pull us out of the economic morass; we have to *put our own shoulders to the wheel.*

- *To set store by* (to value highly): India, *surely sets much store by* the Indo Soviet Treaty of Friendship.

- *To take into one's head* (to occur to someone): The Manager *took it into his head* that by shutting off the electricity for a few hours daily he could save on refrigeration costs.
- *To throw cold water upon* (to discourage something): The doctor *threw cold water upon* my plans for a world tour by declaring that I could never stand the strain of it.
- *To throw up the sponge* (to give up a contest): Faced with stiff competition from big companies, many a small company will *throw up the sponge.*
- *To turn tail* (to retreat ignominiously): The enemy *turned tail* in the face of heavy onslaughts on its key positions.
- *To cook or doctor an account* (to tamper with or falsify the account): From the balance sheet presented to the shareholders, the company seemed to be flourishing, but it afterwards turned out that the Secretary had *cooked the accounts.*
- *To beard the lion in his den* (to oppose someone, in his stronghold): The Indian Army broke through strong Pakistani fortifications, and in the Kargil *bearded the lion in his own den.*
- *To bid fair to* (to give fair prospect of): His health is so good that he *bids fair to* live till he is sixty.
- *To blunt the edge of (to* make something less effective): Time *blunts the edge* of grief.
- *To burn the candle at both ends* (to use too much energy): Our resources are limited. Let us use them judiciously and not *burn the candle at both ends.*
- *To buy a pig in a poke* (to purchase a thing without previously examining it): Buying shares in a new Company started by unknown entrepreneurs is like buying a *pig in a poke.*
- *To cross or pass the Rubicon* (to take a decisive step forward): The Government will have to think of many things before nationalising the textile industry for once they *cross the Rubicon* there will be no going back.
- *To err on the safe side* (to choose a course which may in fact be inaccurate, but which will keep you safe from risk or harm): In going *in* for mixed economy rather than wholesale nationalisation the Government were *erring on the safe side.*
- *To feather one's nest* (to provide for oneself through dishonest means): Many tax collectors make a point of *feathering their* own *nests* well while they have opportunity.
- *To eat one's heart out* (to brood over one's sorrows or disappointments): Don't *eat your heart out* over failure in this competition.
- *To throw down the gauntlet, to take up the gauntlet* (to offer or give a challenge, to accept a challenge): It is not for a small country to throw down the gauntlet to the right and the left.
- *To run the gauntlet* (to undergo severe criticism or ill-treatment): Most trend-setting books have to *run the gauntlet* of the literary critics.
- *To force one's hands* (to compel one to do something unwillingly or earlier than he wished to do it): The Government wanted to do all that they could to meet the workers' demands. But the violence by the strikers *forced their hands* to declare a lockout.
- *To haul over the coals* (to scold a man, reprove him): If your bad habits become known, you will get *hauled over the coals* and richly deserve it.
- *To let the grass grow under your feet* (to be inert and passive to things around): The authorities should listen to students' grievances. By being indifferent they would only *let the grass grow* under *their feet* till it will be too late to turn these young people away from the path of violence.
- *To let loose the dogs of war* (to set in motion the destructive forces of war): Pakistan has *let loose the dogs of war* in Kashmir, through organized terrorism.
- *To muster in force* (to assemble in large numbers): The citizens *mustered in force* to welcome their beloved leader.
- *To rest on one's oars* (to suspend efforts after something has been attained): The agitators have been vigorously at work during the winter, but at present they seem to be *resting on their oars.*
- *To harp on the same string* (to keep repeating the same sentiment over and again): This gentleman *keeps harping on the same string:* he is from Oxford and deserves this and deserves that etc.
- *To rise like* a *phoenix from its ashes* (the phoenix was a fabulous Arabian bird. It had no mate but when about to die, made a funeral pile of wood and aromatic gums and on it burned itself to ashes. From the ashes a *young* phoenix was believed to rise): Germany was completely decimated in the Second World War. But it has *risen like* a *phoenix from its ashes.*
- *To* run *in the same groove* (to move forward on the same path, to advance in harmony): It is clear that the ideas of both reformers *run in the same groove.*
- *To scatter to the winds* (to waste, to scatter abroad): We have *scattered* to *the winds* what we had gained by our independence.
- *To see* some *thing through coloured glasses* (to regard something favourably because of one's prejudice): Pakistan has for long *looked at India through coloured glasses* and never trusted even the most genuine gestures for peace. (The world is a place of strife and one should not see it through coloured glasses.)
- *To show the white feather* (to show signs of cowardice): The agitators shouted and gesticulated but the moment the police appeared on the scene they seemed to *show the white feather.*
- *To sow broadcast* (to scatter widely or without stint): The emissaries of the banished king were *sowing sedition broadcast.*
- *To split hairs* (to make subtle and useless distinctions): Our rival company managed to steal a march on us by bringing out their software ahead of ours.
- *To stick at nothing* (the phrase implies readiness to stoop to baseness or deception to reach one's end): An ambitious politician will *stick* at *nothing* if he can only serve himself.
- *To strain every nerve* (to use one's utmost efforts): We have *to strain every nerve* to get over the poverty line.
- *To swallow the bait* (to catch others by guile, by offering them large promises): The candidate offered the people everything on earth and in the heavens if selected. The people *swallowed the bait* and elected him.
- To *talk shop* (to use the phrases peculiar to one's circumstances): Except for the undertakers, people of the same professions always *talk shop* at parties.

- To *tread on the heels* of (follow close behind): Famine *treads on the heels* of drought.
- *To win or gain* laurels *or to bear away palm* (to achieve success in a contest): The Indian Cricket Team *won* laurels on winning the World 20-20 Cup.
- *Argus-eyed* (jealously watchful): The husband of a pretty wife has got to be *Argus-eyed*.
- *Aegean stables: (to clean Aegean stables,* To correct a great abuse, from the stables of king Agues of Greece, whose stables had not been cleaned for thirty years): The law against prostitution has cleaned no Aegean stables; it has merely pushed it underground.
- *Backstairs influence* (influence exerted secretly and in a fashion not legitimate): The moneyed people do exercise *backstairs influence on* Parliament.
- *A cold comfort:* (something calculated to cause pain or irritation): The promise of a better future is only *cold comfort* to the frustrated youth of today.
- *A dog in the manger:* (said of a person who cannot himself use what another wants, and yet will not let that other have it): Stop being such a dog in the manger and let him ride your bike if you're not using it.
- *Elbow* room: (opportunity for freedom of action): Only give him *elbowroom* and he will succeed.
- *Lynch Law:* (the practice of punishing people where the punishment is inflicted by unauthorised persons and without judicial trial) Mob law denotes the same thing when carried out by a mob. In African countries they often resort to *lynch laws*.
- *A sheet anchor:* (the chief safety, the last refuge for safety): One's faith in God is one's *sheet anchor* in times of stress and strain.
- *The gift of the gab:* (fluency of speech): The *gift of the gab* combined with a slight cunning makes for a successful politician.
- *A mare's nest:* (a discovery that turns out to be false or worthless): There was much fanfare about the solar car. Later *it* turned out to be a mare's nest.
- *The milk of human kindness:* (kindly feelings a phrase used by Shakespeare.): With all their poverty, Indians do not lack *the milk of human kindness.*
- *Penelope's web* : (a work which seems to be going on and yet never comes to an end.): A housewife's chores are *a penelope's web.*
- *A snake in the grass:* (a secret foe.): How could I ever have trusted that snake in the grass?
- *All moonshine:* (foolish, idle, untrue statement.): The talk about welfare of the poor is all *moonshine.*
- *In a body:* (together) The striking workers went *in a body* to the Manager to present their demands.
- *Cheek by jowl:* (in the same position): There was a lawyer who never had a client *cheek by jowl* with a doctor who never had a patient.
- *Out at elbows:* (destitute): The rising prices and the new taxes may soon see most of us *out at elbows.*
- *Not worth his salt:* (good for nothing): A soldier who shivers at the boom of guns is not worth his salt.
- *With a pinch of salt:* (to take a statement with a grain of salt is to feel some doubt whether it is altogether true): Shaw's claim of having remained a celibate even after marriage has to be taken with a pinch of salt.
- *To be Greek or double Dutch to one:* (unintelligible): He spoke so fast that all he said was double Dutch to the audience.
- *To be within an ace of* (to be very nearly): He was within an ace of being shot.
- *To be at the beck and call:* (to be always ready to serve): You must not expect me to be at your beck and call, I have my own business to attend to.
- *To be at sea:* (confused, uncertain of mind): I am quite at sea in Mathematics.
- *To be in one's element: (to be in agreeable company or work):* Shaw is in his element when he is writing about the social ills of his time.
- *To be on wane: (to be on the decline):* (After the second World War, the British Empire was on the wane.)
- *To be on the carpet: (to be summoned to one's employer's room for reprimand):* (The unpunctual clerk was repeatedly on the carpet).
- *Chip of the old block (a son who is much like his father):* (The younger Nawab of Pataudi has proved to be a chip of the old block. He is as good a batsman as his father).
- *To pay one's way: (not get into debt):* (While at college, he paid his way by working as a newspaper vendor).
- *To weather the storm: (to come out of a crisis successfully):* (In a crisis it is unity which helps a nation to weather the storm).
- *To sail before the wind: (to go in the direction towards which the wind is blowing):* An opportunist is he who *sails before the wind (Its opposite is to sail close to the wind i.e. to break a law or principle)*
- *To sail under false colours:* (To pretend to be what one is not, to try to deceive): Phillips was sailing under false colours - he never told her he was a car mechanic.
- *To take the wind out of one's sails:* (Frustrating him by anticipating his arguments, take away his advantage suddenly): I was all ready to tell her that the relationship was over when she greeted me - that took the wind out of my sails.
- *Not fit to hold a candle to:* (One is inferior): For all his pious platitudes and political stunts, Mr. Nixon is not fit to hold a candle to Lincoln or Roosevelt.
- Hope springs eternal in the human breast: *one never loses hope.*
- *Fools rush in where angels fear to tread* : said of reckless persons.
- *He who pays the piper calls the tune*: One has to act according to the wishes of one's master
- *You cannot make a silk purse out of a sow's ear*: said of something impossible.
- *The last straw breaks the camel's back*: The smallest addition to an already heavy task makes it intolerable.
- *Distance lends enchantment to the old* : Things look nice and beautiful when they are not within reach.
- *Render unto Caesar what is Caesar's* : To be wise.
- *Nearer the Church, farther from heaven*: The more opportunity you have, the less you benefit from it.
- *Sweet are the uses of adversity*: Sufferings are to be welcomed

CONTEXTUAL MEANING

Contextual meaning or Contextual usage is another important word-based question. Contextual usage basically involves identifying the synonym/antonym of a word when it is used in a particular context so that the context provides you a clue to the meaning, even if the word is unfamiliar to you.

Example 1

MORIBUND : By the fourth century AD, the Roman Civilization was already moribund.

   (1)   extinct   (2)   forgotten
   (3)   flourishing   (4)   stagnant

In the context of the given sentence the meaning of the word will be stagnant, hence [4].

There may be sentences where most or even all of the options are synonymous to the highlighted word, but only one of them fits the particular context. This means that you have to be aware of the very subtle nuances of the words, making contextual usage more of a challenge to your command over words.

More Examples

GELID : It is hard to believe that any life could ever arise in the gelid environment of Titan.

   (1)   Frigid   (2)   Suffocation
   (3)   gelatinous   (4)   hostile

Gelid means icy cold or frozen. In the context also we can see that gelid can refer to a cold environment where no life can arise. The answer is [1].

Strategies for contextual usage :

The following steps and strategies will be useful while attempting contextual usage questions:

(1)   Read the highlighted word first; if it is familiar to you try to think of a synonym for it before going on to read the sentence or the option.

(2)   If it is not a familiar word, simply read the sentence and try to understand its meaning from the context. Think of a word that could suitably take its place.

(3)   Read the options if one of them is the word you thought of in step 1 or 2, or its close synonym, then choose that as an answer not before at least glancing at the other options and trying to see if one of them might be more suitable.

(4)   If none of the options is similar to the word you thought of in step 1 or 2, then read all the options and see if any of them suit the context of the sentence.

(5)   If you cannot understand the word from the context of the sentence or if you have trouble understanding the sentence itself, then look at the options. Sometimes the options can give you a clue, if you know where to look. For example, if all the options, except one, have a negative / positive connotation then the exception is likely to be the answer. Also sometimes the words in the options are much more familiar ones than the question word, so using them in the sentence instead of the question word should help you eliminate the wrong options.

HOMOPHONES

A **homophone** is a word which is pronounced the same as another word but differs in meaning, for example: carat, caret, and carrot. Homophones may be spelled differently, but the term also applies to different words that sound the same and are also spelled identically, such as "rose" (flower) and "rose" (past tense of "rise").

1	air, heir	26	foul, fowl
2	all, awl	27	gait, gate
3	allowed, aloud	28	hail, hale
4	ate, eight	29	genes, jeans
5	bail, bale	30	grate, great
6	bait, bate	31	hew, hue
7	band, banned	32	higher, hire
8	bard, barred	33	hoard, horde
9	berth, birth	34	idle, idol
10	bight, bite, byte	35	knew, new
11	billed, build	36	knight, night
12	board, bored	37	raise, rays, raze
13	brake, break	38	lessen, lesson
14	bridal, bridle	39	made, maid
15	ceiling, sealing	40	marshal, martial
16	censor, sensor	41	maize, maze
17	cereal, serial	42	medal, meddle
18	coarse, course	43	pail, pale
19	desert, dessert	44	pain, pane
20	dew, due	45	ode, owed
21	discreet, discrete	46	pause, paws
22	dual, duel	47	steal, steel
23	find, fined	48	peace, piece
24	flour, flower	49	praise, prays, preys
25	fore, four	50	lead, led

One Word with Different Meaninggs

Multiple meaning words are those which we use for different meanings in different contexts. The same word can be used as a noun, adjective or verb. English has adopted thousands of words from other languages like Spanish, French, Arabic and even Hindi. The same word but with different meaning can be found in its changed context.

In a similar way, words from different fields of professions e.g. medical, engineering, astronomy, law, business have become part of English Language to enrich it. Over the years, language has changed and more context based usage, (may be not having a direct linkage with the linguistic meaning of the word) has come in practice even by the connoisseurs of language.

Languages with such diversity use nuances of the words to convey the meaning. Sometimes due to this broader sense of words, language becomes ambiguous. But it is expected from the average learner like a Bank Officer that he should avoid this ambiguity related to these more often used words with wide scope of usage. Words that one would see in the Bank Officer's exam shall be from the daily use.

To score more in this particular section of exam -

One Key word - PRACTICE -can only help. Practice will increase your familiarity with the words.

- Read as much as you can particularly good weekly magazines and daily newspapers having columns from different fields like Engineering, Medicine, Law, Sports, and Politics etc.
- Note down the different meanings of the word from the dictionary or thesaurus.
- Make your own sentences using these words.
- Make a collection of these words and see them at least once in a day.

While attempting these questions, think at least one meaningful sentence you remember with that word or where you have seen that particular word and in which context.

In absence of familiarity a simple word can confuse and would lead to marking a wrong answer in the exam.

Let us take the example of the word **Hit-**

You can find this word on every page of a daily newspaper.

Sports - What a magnificent hit it was from the bat of Chris Gayle? (a stroke)

Business- Poor Monsoon to hit the growth rate of Agriculture Sector. (take a beating)

Politics- A US missile hit the Terrorist camp in Northern Pakistan. (an assault)

Entertainment - Jackie Chan has given another hit movie this year. (successful)

City- Power demand in Delhi hit a new high in this summer season. (reach)

Story- It suddenly hit his mind to not follow the monster blindly. (strike)

So in every example the same word is used in different contexts. Only practice can make one more familiar with the nuances of the usage of the same word.

In this section such words are selected which have a high probability of appearing in exam. Practising these will definitely enrich your understanding of the newly introduced section in the any exam.

EXERCISE

DIRECTIONS (Qs. 1-60): *Pick out the most effective pair of words from the given pair of words to make the sentence(s) meaningfully complete.*

1. Whether it be shallow or not, commitment is the .... , the bedrock of any .... loving relationship.
   - (a) expression, perfunctory
   - (b) foundation, genuinely
   - (c) manifestation, deep
   - (d) key, alarmingly
   - (e) basis, absorbing

2. Many people take spirituality very seriously and .... about those who don't, worrying about them and .... them to believe.
   - (a) think, criticizing
   - (b) pride, appraising
   - (c) rationalize, enabling
   - (d) wonder, pressing
   - (e) ponder, venturing

3. If you are .... you tend to respond to stressful situations in a calm, secure, steady and .... way.
   - (a) resilient, rational
   - (b) obdurate, manageable
   - (c) propitious, stable
   - (d) delectable, flexible
   - (e) supportive, positive.

4. Management can be defined as a process of.............. organizational goals by working with and through human and non-human resources to .... improve value added to the world.
   - (a) getting , deliberately
   - (b) managing, purposefully
   - (c) targeting, critically
   - (d) realizing, dialectically
   - (e) reaching, continuously

5. Although religion does not ....the acquisition of wealth, the tenor of its teaching is to..............an attitude of indifference to worldly things.
   - (a) proclaim, prohibit
   - (b) inhibit, induce
   - (c) manifest, proud
   - (d) delink, develop
   - (e) allow, criticise

6. Extreme poverty is as.............. to stagnation and impoverishment as ....wealth.
   - (a) dangerous, restrained
   - (b) provocative, permissible
   - (c) supportive, foul
   - (d) stupendous, corrupt
   - (e) liable, excessive

7. Part of the confusion in our societies.............. from our pursuit of efficiency and economic growth, in the .... that these are the necessary ingredients of progress.
   - (a) stems, conviction
   - (b) derives, evaluation
   - (c) emerges, consideration
   - (d) obtains, exploration
   - (e) extends, planning

8. The problem of housing shortage .... with the population explosion has also been .... by this policy.
   - (a) coped, highlighted
   - (b) dispensed, acknowledged
   - (c) compounded, addressed
   - (d) threatened, manifested
   - (e) projected, discussed

9. Complete and constant openness is a notion that can be.............. to absurdity. Am I.............. to stop everyone on the street and tell them my reaction to their appearance?
   - (a) consigned, communicated
   - (b) reduced, required
   - (c) attributed, requested
   - (d) projected, destined
   - (e) subjected, confined

10. When organizations............. creativity and risk-taking, the usual method of maintaining order and.............are indeed shaken.
    (a) encourage, decorum   (b) exhibit, durability
    (c) propose, humility   (d) enhance, supply
    (e) propagate, production

11. "Patriotism is the last refuge of the scoundrel," says Johnson. In the modern world where the cunning selfish people..............and the hardworking conscientious people ....the quotation holds good.
    (a) dominate, suppress   (b) thrive, suffer
    (c) enjoy, mutilate   (d) empower, subjected
    (e) harass, abdicate

12. In the role of a counsellor, you are an authority figure whose objective is to ....attentively and sensitively to employees who..............you with their feelings.
    (a) project, focus   (b) manage, direct
    (c) listen, trust   (d) concentrate, believe
    (e) consider, explain

13. If a junior executive neglects his professional development and ....education, he can easily and quickly become obsolete in a world changing at..............rates.
    (a) management, voluminous
    (b) higher, vulnerable
    (c) better, supreme
    (d) continuing, dizzying
    (e) value, profound

14. Man is .... He likes to know how things work. The search for understanding is ....in its own right.
    (a) evolving, prophetic
    (b) inquisitive, legitimate
    (d) appreciative, fundamental
    (d) curious, philosophical
    (e) social, judgmental

15. Our..............to understand the process of learning underlying beháviour change are..............by the fact that any given behaviour is determined jointly by many processes.
    (a) nature, determined   (b) scope, preceded
    (c) implications, followed (d) limitations, moderated
    (e) attempts, complicated

16. The Indian hospitality industry, which has been..............a prolonged slump, is now entering a new..............phase ready to enhance profitability.
    (a) witnessing, ambitious (b) observing, listless
    (c) demonstrating, efficient (d) recovering, debt
    (e) succumbing, lean

17. The society provides the individual security of life, ...of thought and sustenance for action. Every individual who..............from society is indebted to the society.
    (a) serenity, gains   (b) prosperity, benefits
    (c) objectivity, profits   (d) seriousness, derives
    (e) semblance, evolves

18. The..............of opinion which emerged at a recently concluded seminar was that the problem of dowry cannot be .... unless the law against it is made more stringent.
    (a) divergence, managed
    (b) sympathy, projected
    (c) consensus, tackled
    (d) similarity, curbed
    (e) convergence ..... appreciated

19. Despite ....of resources, the financially underprivileged students .... in their endeavour.
    (a) plenty, failed   (b) availability, gave
    (c) want, surrendered   (d) lack, succeeded
    (e) extremity, excelled

20. The work assigned to me is not..............though it is very..............
    (a) voluminous, careful   (b) challenging, easy
    (c) impossible, stupendous (d) exceptional, ordinary
    (e) meagre, difficult

21. Nothing is impossible in the world of politics. States which were ....foes and had their deadly missiles pointed at each other find themselves ....in military alliances.
    (a) implacable, partners   (b) intense, joining
    (c) deadly, approaching   (d) known, soliciting
    (e) enviable, grouping

22. ....of whether leaders are born or made, it is ....clear that leaders are not like other people.
    (a) Pursuant, manifestly
    (b) Sequel, amply
    (c) Regardless, unequivocally
    (d) Instead, purely
    (e) In spite, normally

23. There is a common talk today that women have made the.............. in many professions; that they have total freedom of opportunity. But the majority of women are still left .... at the unbreakable glass ceiling.
    (a) entry, inward   (b) grade, gazing
    (c) progress, trying   (d) mark, projecting
    (e) achievement, wondering

24. Inferring attitudes from expressed opinion has many .... People may .... their attitude and express socially acceptable opinions.
    (a) limitations, conceal   (b) advantages, show
    (c) drawbacks, support   (d) benefits, avoid
    (e) reasons, acknowledge

25. We should move towards a system where the banks can ....capital in the market with..............safeguards so that they continue to be public sector banks.
    (a) improve, proper   (b) strengthen, durable
    (c) raise, adequate   (d) stimulate, effective
    (e) provide, delicate

26. Human Resource Management is an..............of mind rather than a.............. of techniques.
    (a) organisation, quality (b) attempt, mix
    (c) evolution, measure   (d) attitude, set
    (e) expertise, collection

27. Statistics in an.............. tool for researchers that..............them to make inferences or generalisations about populations from their observations of the characteristics of samples.
    (a) outstanding, proposes (b) invaluable, proceeds
    (c) invaluable, enables   (d) important, proclaims
    (e) indispensable, enables

28. The Dalits have never had a............. of freedom in the suffocating society. They are a wounded people..............and broken.
    (a) glimpse, mitigated   (b) sigh, rejected
    (c) moment, criticised   (d) satisfaction, prohibited
    (e) breath, battered

29. His vision could be the............. that the policy-makers use to............. the banking sector.
    (a) roadmap, restructure   (b) manner, shape
    (c) blueprint, plan   (d) remedy, revise
    (e) approach, represent

30. A person's formal educational background may............. rich but complex information. To some degree education............. a person's knowledge and skill base.
    (a) reveal, advocates   (b) yield, indicates
    (c) exhibit, develops   (d) cover, evolves
    (e) surmount, shows

31. The RBI in consultation with Government of India has..............a working group to suggest measures for.............of weak public sector banks.
    (a) commissioned, appreciating
    (b) established, accommodation
    (c) reshaped, merger
    (d) constituted, revival
    (e) organised, development

32. The textile industry in India has.............rough weather in recent times. The textile mill is one of the few companies to have.............this storm.
    (a) overcome, empowered   (b) managed, absorbed
    (c) protested, fought   (d) withstood, survived
    (e) ventured, managed

33. With large classes, it is difficult for teachers to............. regular essay-type questions for homework because.............long answers would take too much time.
    (a) consider, writing   (b) revalue, concise
    (c) pursue, feeling   (d) handle, weighing
    (e) give, marking

34. Ours is a democracy and any.............or use of force is out of question. Methods of.............and education are best suited to a democratic regime.
    (a) attempt, coercion   (b) compulsion, persuasion
    (c) judgement, prayer   (d) inhuman, apprehension
    (e) implied, technology

35. The so-called civilised human race has_________ and ill-treated small and large animals in an attempt to prove his __________.
    (a) abused ...... supremacy
    (b) misuse ...... power
    (c) cruelty ...... altruism
    (d) advocated ...... worthlessness
    (e) beaten ...... generosity

36. He objected to the proposal because it was founded on a _________ principle and also was _________ at times.
    (a) faulty - desirable
    (b) imperative - reasonable
    (c) wrong - inconvenient
    (d) sound - acceptable
    (e) conforming - deplorable

37. The criterion for _________ a player should be based on his recent performance; but unfortunately, the journalists are _________ to be carried away by earlier successes.
    (a) condemning - satisfying
    (b) judging - prone
    (c) revealing - reluctant
    (d) eager - acclaiming
    (e) criticising - clean

38. For the last half century he _________ himself to public affairs _________ taking a holiday.
    (a) by - committed   (b) after - offered
    (c) devoted - without   (d) sacrificed - after
    (e) prepared - before

39. You will see signs of _________ everywhere, which speak well for the _________ of these people.
    (a) decoration - senses   (b) clear - debris
    (c) beauty - careful   (d) industry - prosperity
    (e) repairs - extravaganza

40. The recent _________ in oil prices has given an unexpected additional _________ to the cost-spiral.
    (a) slump, drawback   (b) cut, blow
    (c) rise, twist   (d) development, out
    (e) deterioration, impetus

41. _________ your colleagues for important decision-making activities ensures their _________ cooperation.
    (a) Counselling, whole-hearted
    (b) Helping, occasional
    (c) Guiding, meagre
    (d) Neglecting, enthusiastic
    (e) Dominating, unstinted

42. The only way to ensure best output from your vehicle is to provide it a _________ and _________ maintenance.
    (a) nurturing, expensive   (b) proper, timely
    (c) careful, costly   (d) trouble-free, everlasting
    (e) precious, healthy

43. The issues could be _________ amicably only because of his _________ handling of the situation.
    (a) dropped, haphazard   (b) raised, careful
    (c) discussed, enthusiastic (d) suppressed, emphatic
    (e) resolved, tactful

44. The ....with which he is able to wield the paintbrush is really..........
    (a) practice, good   (b) majesty, royal
    (c) sweep, fine   (d) energy, unnecessary
    (e) ease, remarkable

45. Nine members have .... about the decision, but the tenth one views it ....
    (a) solution, critically
    (b) consensus, similarly
    (c) disagreement, collectively
    (d) grievance, grudgingly
    (e) agreement, differently

46. Man needs food not .... for the body but for the soul also. The satisfaction of his physical wants does not imply his..............
    (a) merely, contentment   (b) properly, superiority
    (c) only, spirituality   (d) necessarily, commitment
    (e) certainly, entitlement

47. It is said that knowledge is power. The hunger for power is ....and therefore most difficult to ....
    (a) accumulative, subsume (b) enormous, apply
    (c) empowering, delegate   (d) insatiable, contain
    (e) evolutionary, rationalize

48. Nothing undermines the communication of a changed vision more than .... on the part of key............. that seems inconsistent with the vision.

(a) anything , issues   (b) behaviour, players
(c) advocacy, managers   (d) something, personnel
(e) philosophy, problems

49. Mountains and hills are a .... sight. I have always .... to see them.
(a) extraordinary, advocated
(b) stupendous, encouraged
(c) loving, prepared
(d) joyful, imagined
(e) fascinating, longed

50. Poetry is the language of the imagination and the ....
It relates to whatever gives .... pleasure or pain to the human mind.
(a) thinking, permanent   (b) analysis, temporary
(c) passions, immediate   (d) circumspection, sporadic
(e) visualization, constant

51. Success in business requires two things: a winning competitive .... and superb organizational ....
(a) advantage, satisfaction   (b) planning, advantage
(c) strategy, execution   (d) philosophy, motivation
(e) marketing, strategy

52. To .... in today's rapidly changing environment corporations need to .... their learning capability.
(a) develop, enlarge   (b) surpass, align
(c) project, assimilate   (d) service, mitigate
(e) compete, strengthen

53. People who have been through difficult, painful and not very .... change efforts often end up .... both pessimistic and angry conclusions.
(a) successful, drawing   (b) meaningful, projecting
(c) reliable, evolving   (d) strong, following
(e) challenging, lamenting

54. The human mind is never ....; it advances or it ....
(a) absolute, diminishes   (b) dynamic, stops
(c) perfect, disintegrates   (d) stationary, retrogrades
(e) happy, decomposes

55. If misery is the effect of ill fortune, it ought to be pitied, if of .... to be ....
(a) virtue, criticised   (b) calamity, reverenced
(c) virtue, protected   (d) vice, reverenced
(e) virtue, reverenced

56. It would be impossible for us to continue living in this world if each of us .... exactly what fate had in .... for him.
(a) follow, plan   (b) appreciate, strategy
(c) design, anticipation   (d) visualize, hidden
(e) knew, store

57. It is the .... of selfishness for men, who fully .... in their own case the great advantages of good education, to deny these advantages to women.
(a) parody, demand   (b) height, appreciate
(c) height, assimilate   (d) degree, appreciate
(e) level, advance

58. The learner should be .... to take a small first step one that will provide immediate success and .... the learning.
(a) encouraged, reinforce   (b) forced, organise
(c) directed, reorganise   (d) cautioned, reinforce
(e) encouraged, acknowledge

59. His death .... more tributes than have been paid at the .... of any other human being in history.
(a) brought, passing   (b) directed, helm
(c) delivered, description   (d) invited, living
(e) acknowledged, perpetuation

60. Only with executive .... can the organisation concentrate its energies on .... competitive advantage over time.
(a) position, embarking   (b) deployment, directing
(c) contingent, fabricating   (d) commitment, sustaining
(e) satisfaction, moulding

DIRECTIONS (Qs. 61-65): *In each of these questions, two sentences (I) and (II) are given. Each sentence has a blank in it. Five words (a), (b), (c), (d) and (e) are suggested. Out of these, only one fits at both the places in the context of each sentence. Number of that word is the answer*

61. I. He is _______ with whatever little he has.
II. They kept the _______ of the communication a secret.
(a) happy   (b) matter
(c) gist   (d) content
(e) sense

62. I. It is hard lo believe the _______ of operations involved in this activity.
II. The map is drawn to a _______ of 1 inch to 50 km.
(a) magnitude   (b) size
(c) scale   (d) proportion
(e) significance

63. I. Heavy snow did _______ the rescue efforts.
II. The food was kept in a _______ .
(a) delay   (b) bundle
(c) basket   (d) hamper
(e) holder

64. I. They left _______ after breakfast.
II. It is difficult to find a _______ person for this job.
(a) right   (b) immediately
(c) suitable   (d) best
(e) soon

65. I. He would always do _______ was told by his superiors.
II. He appeared on stage _______ a narrator of the drama.
(a) as   (b) what
(c) about   (d) whatever
(e) always

DIRECTIONS (Qs. 66-70): *In each of the following sentences there are two blank spaces. Below each sentence there are five pairs of words denoted by (a), (b), (c), (d) and (e). Find out which pair of words can be filled up in the blanks to make the sentence meaningfully complete.*

(SBI PO 2011)

66. _________ of illiteracy from a nation that is set to become the most populated in the world is by no _______ easy.
(a) Countering, task   (b) Driving, measure
(c) Curbing, way   (d) Eradication, means
(e) Removal, point

67. It is time to _______ ongoing programmes and _______ new horizons.

(a) value, choose   (b) speculate, experiment
(c) reject, consider   (d) scrutinise, impound
(e) assess, seek

68. This approach would ________ the enormous illiteracy problem to be ________ in a holistic manner.
(a) enable, tackled   (b) focus, viewed
(c) envision, dealt   (d) combine, judged
(e) review, countered

69. The ______ of criminalisation of politics needs to be ________ far more seriously.
(a) lacuna, dealt
(b) issue, addressed
(c) system, broken
(d) continuation, suppressed
(e) process, diverted

70. It would be proper for India to judge Pakistan by its ______ rather than ________ .
(a) credentials, potentials
(b) culture, politics
(c) actions, words
(d) promises, assurances
(e) nature, behaviour

DIRECTIONS (Qs. 71-75) : *The following questions consist of a single sentence with one blank only. You are given six words as answer choices and from the six choices you have to pick up two correct answers, either of which will make the sentence meaningfully complete.*

(IBPS PO/MT 2011)

71. The ability of a woman to do well does not .... on whether it is a man's world or not, because everyone has his/her own opportunities.
(1) trust   (2) depend
(3) reckon   (4) live
(5) rest   (6) believe
(a) (4) and (5)   (b) (2) and (3)
(c) (1) and (6)   (d) (2) and (5)
(e) (3) and (4)

72. Drugs worth ₹ 3 lakhs were .... from the apartment by the police.
(1) manufactured   (2) ruptured
(3) seized   (4) confiscated
(5) bought   (6) compared
(a) (1) and (4)   (b) (2) and (3)
(c) (3) and (5)   (d) (5) and (6)
(e) (3) and (4)

73. An organization .... to the mission of road safety has prepared an action plan for reducing accidents and related injuries and fatalities.
(1) specified   (2) inaugurated
(3) committed   (4) kicked off
(5) succumbed   (6) dedicated
(a) (3) and (6)   (b) (1) and (5)
(c) (3) and (5)   (d) (4) and (6)
(e) (1) and (3)

74. A man reportedly .... two passports with the same photograph, but under different names was arrested by the commissioner's Task Force.

(1) possessing   (2) examining
(3) surrendering   (4) mastering
(5) holding   (6) fixating
(a) (2) and (3)   (b) (3) and (6)
(c) (1) and (5)   (d) (1) and (4)
(e) (4) and (5)

75. The Hollywood star and the Bollywood heroine are being .... as the next big onscreen couple.
(1) labeled   (2) explained
(3) worshiped   (4) touted
(5) exclaimed   (6) shouted
(a) (2) and (4)   (b) (1) and (3)
(c) (2) and (6)   (d) (1) and (4)
(e) (3) and (4)

DIRECTIONS (Qs. 76-80) : *The following questions consist of a single sentence with one blank only. You are given six words denoted by A, B, C, D, E & F as answer choices and from the six choices you have to pick two correct answers, either of which will make the sentence meaningfully complete.*

(IBPS PO/MT 2012)

76. ____________ before the clock struck 8 on Saturday night, India Gate was swamped with people wearing black tee-shirts and holding candles.
(A) Minutes   (B) Time
(C) Later   (D) Quickly
(E) Since   (F) Seconds
(a) (B) and (E)   (b) (A) and (C)
(c) (A) and (F)   (d) (B) and (D)
(e) (C) and (E)

77. The state should take steps to __________ the process of teachers" appointments as the Centre has already sanctioned six lakh posts.
(A) fasten   (B) move
(C) hasten   (D) speed
(E) early   (F) quicken
(a) (D) and (F)   (b) (A) and (C)
(c) (C) and (F)   (d) (D) and (E)
(e) (B) and (D)

78. A senior citizen's son __________ threatened her every day and physically harmed her, forcing her to transfer her properly to him.
(A) superficially   (B) mistakenly
(C) allegedly   (D) miserably
(E) doubtfully   (F) purportedly
(a) (C) and (F)   (b) (A) and (E)
(c) (C) and (E)   (d) (D) and (F)
(e) (A) and (C)

79. Medical teachers said that the management had continued to remain to their cause leading to the stretching of their strike.
(A) unmoved   (B) lethargic
(C) unconcerned   (D) apathetic
(E) indifferent   (F) bored

(a)   (B) and (C)   (b)   (C) and (F)
(c)   (A) and (E)   (d)   (A) and (D)
(e)   (D) and (E)

80. The parents had approached the high court to the government order after their children, who passed UKG, were denied admission by a school.
(A) void   (B) quash
(C) annual   (D) stay
(E) lift   (F) post
(a)   (A) and (D)   (b)   (B) and (C)
(c)   (C) and (E)   (d)   (E) and (F)
(e)   (C) and (D)

DIRECTIONS (Qs. 81-85) : *Each question below has two blanks, each blank indicating that something has been omitted. Choose the set of words for each blank that best fits the meaning of the sentence as a whole.*

(IBPS PO/MT 2013)

81. In an effort to provide .... for higher education to all, most of the universities have been providing education without adequate infrastructure, thus churning out .... graduates every year.
(a)   chances, fresh
(b)   platform, capable
(c)   opportunities, unemployable
(d)   prospects, eligible
(e)   policy, incompetent

82. The move to allow dumping of mercury .... An outcry from residents of the area who ....that high levels of mercury will affect their health and destroy ecologically sensitive forest area.
(a)   resulted, insist   (b)   provoked, fear
(c)   incited, determined   (d)   activated, accept
(e)   angered, believe

83. Even as the ....elsewhere in the world are struggling to come out of recession, Indian consumers are splurging on consumer goods and to ....this growth, companies are investing heavily in various sectors.
(a)   economies, meet
(b)   countries, inhibit
(c)   governments, measure
(d)   nations, inflict
(e)   companies, counter

84. Drawing attention to the pitfalls of............... solely on Uranium as a fuel for nuclear reactors, Indian scientists warned that Uranium will not last for long and thus research on Thorium as its must be revived.
(a)   using, substitute
(b)   believing, replacement
(c)   depending, reserve
(d)   reckoning, option
(e)   relying, alternative

85. has been taken against some wholesale drug dealers for dealing in surgical items without a valid license and maintaining a stock of...............drugs.
(a)   Note, overwhelming
(b)   Step, impressive
(c)   Execution, outdated
(d)   Action, expired
(e)   Lawsuit, invalid

DIRECTIONS (Qs.86-90) : *Pick out the most effective pair of words from the given pair of words make the sentences meaningfully complete.*

(SBI PO 2014)

86. Weather officials have __ below-normal rains this year. If the predictions come true, farm output could __ as most of India's farmlands depend on rainwater for irrigation.
(a)   forecasted-shrank   (b)   forecast-shrank
(c)   forecast-shrink   (d)   predicted-expand
(e)   predictions-wan

87. It is the role of the state to ____ crime and protect people and property. If the state is unable to prevent a crime it falls upon the state to __ the victim.
(a)   prevent-support   (b)   preventing-encourage
(c)   prevent-supporting   (d)   forbid-discourage
(e)   forbid-discouraging

88. A person who is clean and tidy in how he dresses up commands better–from those around him than those "who have a–and unkempt appearance—
(a)   respectful - slovenly   (b)   respect - slovenly
(c)   respected - untidy   (d)   respect - tidy
(e)   respect - careful

89. Today we have achieved a milestone by completing 60 years of independence. It's now the time for everyone or every Indian to undergo–of the achievements we already made and also those that are to be still—
(a)   self-introspection, achiver
(b)   self-examination, achieve
(c)   introspection, achieved
(d)   search, found
(e)   cross-inspection, made

90. Education is an essential means of–women with the knowledge, skills and self-confidence necessary to fully— in the development process.
(a)   empower, include
(b)   empowering, participate
(c)   empowered, participating
(d)   empowerment, participate
(e)   strengthening, participate

DIRECTIONS (Qs. 91-95): *Five alternative a, b, c, d and e are given under each sentence, you are required to select the most suitable alternative to fill in the blank/blanks in the sentence to make it meaningful.*

(SBI PO Prelim 2015)

91. Intelligence is an ______ part of one's success.
(a)   inseparable   (b)   inimitable
(c)   indivisible   (d)   indispensable
(e)   None of these

92. Anjana impressed the interviewer with her concise, ____ answers.
(a)   allusive   (b)   revealing
(c)   pertinent   (d)   referential
(e)   None of these

93. The coach asked the players to ______ with his ideology or leave the team.
(a)   counter   (b)   align
(c)   favour   (d)   separate
(e)   None of these

94. The seminar helped _____ the students on the harmful effects of smoking and alcohol.
    (a) educate (b) learn
    (c) teach (d) insist
    (e) None of these
95. Rajeev was _____ legal aid to fight his extradition.
    (a) offered (b) granted
    (c) allowed (d) awarded
    (e) None of these

DIRECTIONS (Qs. 96-100) : *Each question given below has two blanks, each blank indicating that something has been omitted. Choose the set of words for each blank that best fits the meaning of the sentence as a whole.*

96. After having been friends for more than a decade, they had a _____ last year and have not _____ each other ever since.
    (a) fight, talked (b) argument, met
    (c) dispute, seen (d) quarrel, admired
    (e) difference, introduced
97. The workers, several of _____ had complained about their low wages earlier have now _____ to move to the court for the labour rights.
    (a) who, indicated (b) whom, decided
    (c) which, threatened (d) them, resolved
    (e) number, warmed
98. The hutment dwellers were jubilant when the government _____ an apartment to each of them at _____ rates.
    (a) demolished, fast (b) announced, less
    (c) provided, high (d) acquired, low
    (e) promised, subsidised
99. The organization was deeply _____ by difficulties a decade ago, but the new CEO brought many _____ changes in it and took it to a new high.
    (a) indebted, necessary (b) plagued, vital
    (c) coping, more (d) hurt, critical
    (e) shaken, inevitable
100. The Prime Minister who is _____ in his holiday home at the moment said that he was very _____ by the news of India winning the World Cup.
    (a) visiting, happy (b) residing, obliged
    (c) intruding, dejected (d) staying, pleased
    (e) resting, cheerful

DIRECTIONS (Qs. 101-105): *Select the correct alternatives.*

(SBI PO Main 2015)
101. The _____ you work, the _____ for your prosperity.
    (a) more, best (b) least, best
    (c) harder, better (d) decent, brightest
    (e) better, brighter
102. _____ you need a duplicate ration card, you must submit the _____ of your residence.
    (a) Should, proof (b) If, numbers
    (c) Had guarantee (d) Do, number
    (e) Would, document

103. It was my _____ that _____ to the serious problem.
    (a) desire, brought (b) negligence, led
    (c) fault, lauded (d) mistake, subjected
    (e) decision, put
104. Because he was _____ he left the party earlier and _____ home.
    (a) tired, brought (b) precarious, approached
    (c) preoccupied, sent (d) ill, contacted
    (e) unwell, returned
105. An impartial person _____ others without any _____ .
    (a) likes, reservation (b) judges, bias
    (c) blames, prudence (d) praises, point
    (e) wishes, malice

DIRECTIONS (Qs. 106-110) : *In each of the following sentence there are two blank spaces. Below each sentence there are five pair of words denoted by letters a, b, c, d, and e. Find out which pair of words can be filled up in the blanks in the sentence in the same sequence to make the sentence meaningfully complete.*

(SBI PO Prelim 2016)
106. He objected to the proposal because it was founded on a .... principle arid also was .... at time.
    (a) faulty ...... desirable
    (b) imperative .... reasonable
    (c) wrong ...... inconvenient
    (d) sound ..... acceptable
    (e) unconforming .... deplorable
107. The criterion for ..... a player should be his recent performance, but unfortunately, the journalists are ..... to be carried away by earlier successes.
    (a) condemning .... satisfying
    (b) judging ..... prone
    (c) revealing ..... reluctant
    (d) eager .... acclaiming
    (e) criticising .... clean
108. For the last half century, he ..... himself to public affairs .... taking a holiday.
    (a) by .... committed
    (b) after .... offered
    (c) devoted .... without
    (d) sacrified .... after
    (e) prepared .... before
109. You will see signs of ..... everywhere, which speak well for the .... of these people.
    (a) decoration .... senses
    (b) clear .... debris
    (c) beauty .... careful
    (d) industry .... prosperity
    (e) repairs .... extravaganza
110. The police arrested Ramesh on a .... of theft but for lack of evidence .... him.
    (a) crime .... imprisoned
    (b) punished .... complaint
    (c) left ...... condition
    (d) tip .... absconding
    (e) charge .... released

DIRECTIONS (Qs. 111 - 115) : *Each question below has two blanks, each blank indicating that something has been omitted. Choose the set of words for each blank that best fits the meaning of the sentence as a whole.*

(SBI PO Main 2016)

111. Drawing attention to the pitfalls of _____ solely on Uranium as a fuel for nuclear reactors, Indian scientists warned that Uranium will not last for long and thus research on Thorium as its ______ must be revived.
    (a) using, substitute   (b) believing, replacement
    (c) depending, reserve   (d) reckoning, option
    (e) relying, alternative

112. In an effort to provide ______ for higher education to all. most of the universities have been providing education without adequate infrastructure, thus churning out ______ graduates every year.
    (a) chances, fresh   (b) platform, capable
    (c) opportunities, unemployable (d) prospects, eligible
    (e) policy, incompetent

113. The move to allow dumping of mercury ______ an outcry from residents to the area who _______ that high levels of mercury will affect their health and destroy ecologically sensitive forest area
    (a) resulted, insist   (b) provoked, fear
    (c) incited, determined (d) activated, accept
    (e) angered believe

114. ______ has been taken against some wholesale drug dealers for dealing in surgical items without a valid license and maintaining a stock of ______ drugs.
    (a) Note, overwhelming   (b) Step, impressive
    (c) Execution, outdated (d) Action, expired
    (e) Lawsuit, invalid

115. Even as the ______ elsewhere in the world are struggling to come out of recession, Indian consumers are splurging on consumer goods and to ______ this growth, companies are investing heavily in various sectors.
    (a) economies, meet   (b) countries, inhibit
    (c) governments, measure (d) nations, inflict
    (e) companies, counter

DIRECTIONS (Qs. 116-120) : *In each of the following sentence there are three blank spaces. Below each sentence there are five options and each option consists of three words which can be filled up in the blanks in the sentence to make the sentence grammatically correct.*

116. Indian Cricket has seen many ______ captains. But Dhoni was certainly a/an ______ one in many ways. As skipper, he mainly focused on cultivating team spirit and creating ______ for young players.
    (a) exceptional, diminutive, chances.
    (b) sturdy, serendipitous, chances
    (c) stout, robust, opportunity
    (d) stalwart, extraordinary, opportunities.
    (e) common, exceptional, prospects.

117. Pakistani's Defense Minister Khwaja Muhammad Asif, for all practical purposes, recently __ Israel with a _______ nuclear attack, in response to a fake news report that the Israelis had said they would use nuclear____against Pakistan if it sent ground troops to Syria.
    (a) threatened, retaliatory, weapons
    (b) jeopardized, reciprocating, armor
    (c) admonished, riposte, weapon
    (d) rebuked, counter, armament
    (e) rebuffed, retorted, weapons

118. The line seems to be direct____to the establishment of a caliphate. But those who know the context of Faiz the poet, the man and his work correctly interpret it as a communist vision of life, with the ____________ of the ________ prevailing.
    (a) commendation, democracy, precariat
    (b) invocation, dictatorship, proletariat
    (c) intercession, autonomy, rabble
    (d) citation, anarchism, bourgeoisie
    (e) intervention, despot, common people

119. News and social media companies have a moral ___ to ensure that they do not, directly or otherwise, deliberately ___________ the facts to their audiences and pass them off for news. If it is a post-truth world we__, this becomes especially important.
    (a) obligation, distort, desire
    (b) commitment, tarnish, denounce
    (c) responsibility, misrepresent, inhabit
    (d) purport, besmirch, stigmatize
    (e) implication, enhance, reside

120. Activists in the country have long protested its __ society that essentially ___ women from travelling, marrying or attending college without permission from a male relative, who is called their__________ .
    (a) benevolent, forbid, steward
    (b) pre- adamite, prevent, custodian
    (c) pre-eminent, restrict, protector
    (d) venerable, condemns, manciple.
    (e) patriarchal, prohibits, guardian.

DIRECTIONS (Qs. 121 -160): *In each of the following questions four words are given of which two words are most nearly the same or opposite in meaning. Find the two words which are most nearly the same or opposite in meaning.*

121	(A) Prolixity	(B) Brevity
	(C) Agreement	(D) Proposition
	(a) A - B	(b) B - C
	(c) C - D	(d) A - C
	(e) A - D	

122.	(A) Suffuse	(B) Deplete
	(C) Fight	(D) Delay
	(a) B - C	(b) C - D
	(c) A - C	(d) A - D
	(e) A - B	

123.	(A) Forensic	(B) Delectable
	(C) Leaflike	(D) Charming
	(a) A - C	(b) B - D
	(c) A - D	(d) A - C
	(e) A - B	

124.	(A) Benevolent	(B) Alarming
	(C) Charitable	(D) Stupendous
	(a) A - B	(b) B - C
	(c) C - D	(d) A - C
	(e) B - D	

125	(A) Convenient	(B) Intolerant
	(C) Enduring	(D) Protestant
	(a) A-B	(b) A-C
	(c) B-C	(d) B-D
	(e) C-D	

126.	(A) Eject	(B) Spread
	(C) Mark	(D) Spout
	(a) B-D	(b) A-C
	(c) B-C	(d) A-B
	(e) A-D	

127	(A) Push	(B) Thrive
	(C) Flourish	(D) Arrange
	(a) A-C	(b) A-D
	(c) C-D	(d) B-C
	(e) B-D	

128.	(A) Refuse	(B) Discourage
	(C) Lurk	(D) Hide
	(a) A-C	(b) C-D
	(c) B-D	(d) B-C
	(e) B-D	

129.	(A) Delirious	(B) Confluent
	(C) Curt	(D) Gracious
	(a) A-B	(b) B-C
	(c) C-D	(d) B-D
	(e) A-D	

130.	(A) Punishment	(B) Divergence
	(C) Confluence	(D) Confidence
	(a) B-C	(B) B-D
	(c) C-D	(d) A-B
	(e) A-C	

131.	(A) Audacious	(B) Venturous
	(C) Abstruse	(D) Silent
	(a) A-C	(b) B-C
	(c) C-D	(d) A-B
	(e) B-D	

132.	(A) Encomium	(B) Extol
	(C) Eulogise	(D) Euphemise
	(a) A-B	(b) B-C
	(c) B-D	(d) A-D
	(e) C-D	

133.	(A) Recluse	(B) Pandemic
	(C) Transparent	(D) Opaque
	(a) A-B	(b) C-D
	(c) A-C	(d) A-D
	(e) B-D	

134.	(A) Diminutive	(B) Intelligent
	(C) Large	(D) Prolific
	(a) B-D	(b) C-D
	(c) A-C	(d) A-B
	(e) C-D	

135.	(A) Enormous	(B) Malign
	(C) Absorb	(D) Slander
	(a) A-C	(b) B-C
	(c) C-D	(d) B-D
	(e) A-D	

136.	(A) Withstand	(B) Climate
	(C) Hot	(D) Surrender
	(a) A-B	(b) B-C
	(c) A-D	(d) B-D
	(e) C-D	

137.	(A) Perky	(B) Lively
	(C) Honest	(D) Kind
	(a) A-B	(b) B-C
	(c) C-D	(d) B-D
	(e) A-C	

138.	(A) Reverie	(B) Stirring
	(C) Serene	(D) Fascination
	(a) A-D	(b) B-D
	(c) C-D	(d) A-B
	(e) B-C	

139.	(A) Pandemonium	(B) Scramble
	(C) Wriggle	(D) Order
	(a) A-B	(b) B-C
	(c) C-D	(d) A-D
	(e) A-C	

140.	(A) Stimulate	(B) Comprehend
	(C) Facilitate	(D) Understand
	(a) A-B	(b) B-C
	(c) A-C	(d) B-D
	(e) C-D	

141.	(A) Dense	(B) Graze
	(C) Pristine	(D) Fresh
	(a) B-C	(b) C-D
	(c) B-A	(d) A-C
	(e) B-D	

142.	(A) Enthralling	(B) Respecting
	(C) Projecting	(D) Alluring
	(a) A-B	(b) B-C
	(c) C-D	(d) A-D
	(e) B-D	

143.	(A) Swoop	(B) Perturb
	(C) Plunge	(D) Boil
	(a) A-D	(b) B-C
	(c) A-C	(d) B-D
	(e) C-D	

144.	(A) Concise	(B) Elegant
	(C) Indifferent	(D) Indecorous
	(a) B-C	(b) A-C
	(c) A-B	(d) C-D
	(e) B-D	

145.	(A) Acquit	(B) Defend
	(C) Forbid	(D) Condemn
	(a) B-C	(b) A-C
	(c) C-D	(d) B-D
	(e) A-D	

146.	(A) Fallacy	(B) Adage
	(C) Dictum	(D) Endorse
	(a) B-D	(b) C-D
	(c) B-C	(d) A-D
	(e) A-B	

147.	(A) Elevate	(B) Frugal
	(C) Exult	(D) Lament
	(a) C-D	(b) A-B
	(c) B-C	(d) B-D
	(e) A-D	

148.	(A) Surreptitious	(B) Taciturn
	(C) Exaggerate	(D) Covert
	(a) A-D	(b) A-B
	(c) A-C	(d) B-D
	(e) C-D	

149. (A) Handy   (B) Sparse
     (C) Redundant   (D) Exhausted
     (a) A-C   (b) B-C
     (c) B-D   (d) C-D
     (e) A-B

150. (A) Timid   (B) Conceited
     (C) Humane   (D) Modest
     (a) A-C   (b) B-D
     (c) B-C   (d) A-D
     (e) C-D

151. (A) Conversion   (B) Desistance
     (C) Substitution   (D) Cessation
     (a) A-B   (b) C-D
     (c) A-D   (d) B-D
     (e) A-C

152. (A) Concentration   (B) Dissociation
     (C) Distraction   (D) Deliberation
     (a) A-D   (b) B-C
     (c) A-C   (d) C-D
     (e) D-B

153. (A) Exaggeration   (B) Reiteration
     (C) Imagination   (D) Repetition
     (a) A-D   (b) B-D
     (c) C-D   (d) B-C
     (e) A-B

154. (A) Implies   (B) Leads
     (C) Confirms   (D) Connotes
     (a) C-B   (b) A-D
     (c) B-A   (d) D-C
     (e) D-B

155. (A) Surfaced   (B) Nurtured
     (C) Created   (D) Developed
     (a) B-A   (b) B-C
     (c) C-A   (d) C-D
     (e) B-D

156. (A) Expanded   (B) Proclaimed
     (C) Shrunk   (D) Facilitated
     (a) A-D   (b) B-D
     (c) C-D   (d) B-C
     (e) A-C

157. (A) Indelible   (B) Erasable
     (C) Insignificant   (D) Temporary
     (a) A-C   (b) C-B
     (c) A-B   (d) B-D
     (e) C-D

158. (A) Intangible   (B) Restless
     (C) Vast   (D) Meagre
     (a) C-A   (b) C-D
     (c) C-B   (d) B-A
     (e) B-D

159. (A) Cutting   (B) Establishing
     (C) Transferring   (D) Pruning
     (a) A-B   (b) C-D
     (c) B-C   (d) A-C
     (e) A-D

160. (A) Fixed   (B) Stiff
     (C) Indelible   (D) Soapy
     (a) A-B   (b) A-D
     (c) A-C   (d) B-C
     (e) C-D

DIRECTIONS (Qs. 161-164): *In each of the following sentence there are three blank spaces. Below each sentence there are five options and each option consists of three words which can be filled up in the blanks in the sentence to make the sentence meaningful and grammatically correct.*

161. As Prime Minister Narendra Modi travels through Sri Lanka for the UN Vesak Day celebrations, he will speak and hear much about the teachings of the world's greatest _____________, Gautama Buddha. He is also certain to be mindful of Sri Lanka's _____________with war, victory, militarism, the challenges of conflict resolution, and getting to peace and_____________.
    (a) peaceful, ignorance, settlement
    (b) antagonistic, undergo, agreement
    (c) nonviolent, encounter, estrangement
    (d) pacifist, experience, reconciliation
    (e) conciliatory, unfamiliarity, harmony

162. Most Tamil parents wanted their children to study and become civil servants, and even in the worst of times, _____________many difficulties to ensure that their sons and daughters attended school. ___________Tamil parents sat on dharna outside militant camps where their children had been_____________.
    (a) undergo, Ecstatic, recruited
    (b) underwent, wailing, conscripted
    (c) ignored, lamenting, levied
    (d) experienced, mourning, discharged
    (e) abided by, cheering, allocated

163. Rivers, it seems, have gone out of the lives of large numbers of people in India, in cities surely. They do become part of public_____________, but only as items of disputes between riparian states, or as beneficiaries - or victims - of large projects or when they go into _____________and cause havoc, sometimes even when they run dry. But the river as a part of people's day-to-day experiences is _______ _________ a matter of public conversation.
    (a) ignorance, deluge, hardly
    (b) speech, shortage, seldom
    (c) discourse, spate, rarely
    (d) sermon, paucity, scracely
    (e) talk, inundation, frequently

164. (1) Myanmar _____________ the recent terror attacks during the Amarnath Yatra in India as also various acts of terror _____________ by terrorists from across the borders.
    (2) He _____________ the scene between Gloucester and his sons as the act was _____________with an intention to harm the modesty of his family.
    (a) condemned, perpetrated
    (b) rebuked, persisted
    (c) reproached, achieved
    (d) reprimanded, enforced
    (e) clobbered, responded

DIRECTIONS(Qs. 165-175): *In each of the following sentences, there is a blank space, followed by some choices of words given in options. You have to determine which of these words fits well in all making them meaningful and grammatically correct. Word can be modified according to the tense of the sentence keeping the meaning of root word intact. If none of these words fit well, mark your answer as none of these.*

165. I.   The two currencies are approaching _______ for the first time in decades.
     II. Currently, there is rough _______ in the number of students entering and graduating from the school system.
     III. On one hand, the rising drinking among women is a sign of _______ .
     (a) incline   (b) dividend   (c) freedom
     (d) parity   (e) integration

166. I.   When the captain realised his efforts to steer his ship were __________, he commanded his officers to release the life boats.
     II. If appears that filling out job applications in this troubled economy is a __________ exercise.
     III. Unfortunately all resave attemts were _______ during the hurricane.
     (a) worthwhile   (b) useful   (c) vain
     (d) futile   (e) intense

167. I.   Homicide that occurs during the course of an attempted kidnapping is a _______ crime in some states.
     II. Like most homeowners, her house is her biggest _______ asset.
     III. The governor wasted his political _______ on an unpopular issue.
     (a) big   (b) intention
     (c) capital   (d) enhance
     (e) revival

168. I.   People are often _______ of their surroundings and upbringing.
     II. Together, the teams are working 24 hours a day for a _______ that promises much higher risk than it does profit.
     III. This book is the _______ of many years of hard work.
     (a) product   (b) determined
     (c) resource   (d) crucial
     (e) beginning

169. I.   She has an _______ dislike for/of her husband's friend.
     II. He was an _______ young man who was very determined to do well in school.
     III. After many years of _______ study, he received his medical degree.
     (a) brave   (b) intense
     (c) utter   (d) controlled
     (e) obvious

170. I.   There was a _______ on ethics within the agency.
     II. They detected high _______ of pollutants in the water.
     III. The _______ of PM2.5, the smallest particulate matter, is at 153 micrograms per cubic meter.
     (a) majority   (b) respect
     (c) concentration (d) polarity
     (e) outcome

171. I.   He made an _______ to swim across the lake.
     II. Do not _______ to repair the equipment without the proper tools.
     III. Police report that there has been an _______ on the actor's life.
     (a) futile   (b) way
     (c) think   (d) attempt
     (e) chance

172. I.   She opened the door and _______ cautiously into the room.
     II. Our understanding of this disease has _______ rapidly in recent years.
     III. He was _______ his own interests at the expense of his friend's.
     (a) develop   (b) clarify   (c) called
     (d) quick   (e) advanced

173. I.   They _______ moved away when they saw the oncoming car.
     II. we moved _______ to deal with our auditor's questions
     III. We made a _______ decision, but it turned out to be a good one.
     (a) seem   (b) clear
     (c) quick   (d) difficult
     (e) new

174. I.   He forgot his _______ and reached across the table for the salt.
     II. I objected to the _______ in which the decision was made.
     III. He had never been on a boat before, but he walked along the deck as if to the _______ born.
     (a) manner   (b) value
     (c) scope   (d) recognize
     (e) intense

175. I.   They are still considered refugees. Their _______ have not changed.
     II. They want to maintain the city's _______ as a major tourist attraction.
     III. He wants to improve his _______ in the community.
     (a) mind   (b) status
     (c) repots   (d) future
     (e) dignity

DIRECTIONS (Qs. 176-180): *There are two different sentences with a blank space in each question. Choose the word from the given options which fits into both the blanks appropriately without altering their meanings.*

176. (1) The only difficulty in this _______ is to secure debtors that will not die.
     (2) She was in a state of rare contentment, an _______ to the gaiety that was hers by nature.
     (a) accretion   (b) increase
     (c) enlargement   (d) accessory
     (e) None of the above

177. (1) He issued what was in reality an _______ proclamation, which President Lincoln was compelled to modify.
     (2) Friction increased between the races at the South after _______ .
     (a) abolition   (b) autarchy
     (c) exemption   (d) immune
     (e) emancipation

178. (1) It was feared that there could be a _______ unsettling of established governments and a new political order could come into being, oriented away from the traditional leadership of the region.
     (2) On the other hand, _______ emigration was not sufficient to remove the evil.
     (a) comprehensively (b) wholesale
     (c) voluminous   (d) extensive
     (e) haphazard

179. (1) The French President Emmanuel Macron's new centrist party is _____________ poised for a landslide victory in the parliamentary elections.
   (2) The opinion of parliament on two other questions during the session was, _____________, influenced by events in France.
   (a) evidently   (b) seemingly
   (c) ostensibly   (d) apparently
   (e) All of the above

180. (1) Parliament takes pride in asserting the supremacy of the institution, at times even ignoring what it perceives as judicial _____________ in its functioning.
   (2) It would have been enough to have cured the whole Roxburghe Club from _____________ with libraries and books for ever and ever.
   (a) concern   (b) examining
   (c) tracing   (d) meddling
   (e) quest

DIRECTIONS (Qs. 181-185) : *In each of the following questions four words are given of which two words are most nearly the same or opposite in meaning. Find the two words which are most nearly the same or opposite in meaning and find the number of the correct letter combination, that is your answer.*

(SBI PO 2010)

181. (A) consent   (B) nascent
    (C) emerging   (D) insecure
    (a) A - C   (b) B - D
    (c) B - C   (d) A - D
    (e) A - B

182. (A) elated   (B) eccentric
    (C) explicit   (D) abnormal
    (a) A - B   (b) B - D
    (c) A - C   (d) A - D
    (e) D - C

183. (A) abundance   (B) incomparable
    (C) projection   (D) plethora
    (a) A - C   (b) A - B
    (c) C - D   (d) B - D
    (e) A - D

184. (A) purposefully (B) inaccurately
    (C) inadvertently (D) unchangeably
    (a) A - C   (b) A - B
    (c) B - C   (d) B - D
    (e) A - D

185. (A) germane   (B) generate
    (C) reliable   (D) irrelevant
    (a) B - D   (b) B - C
    (c) A - B   (d) C - D
    (e) A - D

DIRECTIONS (Qs. 186-190) : *In each of the following questions four words are given, of which two are most nearly the same or opposite in meaning. Find the two words which are most nearly the same or opposite in meaning and mark the number of the correct letter combination as your answer.*

(SBI PO 2011)

186. (A) Discomfit   (B) Baffle
    (C) Epicure   (D) Enumerate
    (a) A-B   (b) A-C
    (c) A-D   (d) B-C
    (e) B-D

187. (A) Testimony   (B) Aura
    (C) Augment   (D) Decrease
    (a) A-B   (b) B-C
    (c) C-D   (d) A-D
    (e) B-D

188. (A) Unkempt   (B) Unremitting
    (C) Slackening   (D) Distasteful
    (a) A-B   (b) B-C
    (c) C-D   (d) A-D
    (e) B-D

189. (A) Gregarious   (B) Quixotic
    (C) Sociable   (D) Discernible
    (a) A-B   (b) B-C
    (c) C-D   (d) A-C
    (e) B-D

190. (A) Apathetic   (B) Wrath
    (C) Whirl   (D) Twirl
    (a) A-B   (b) A-C
    (c) A-D   (d) B-C
    (e) C-D

DIRECTIONS (Qs. 191-195) : *Below is given a single word with options to its meaning in different contexts. You have to select all those options which are synonyms of the word when the context is changed. Select the correct alterative from (a), (b), (c), (d) and (e) which represents all those synonyms.*

(IBPS PO/MT 2011)

191. **MASK**
    (1) Cover   (2) Hide
    (3) Conceal   (4) Disguise
    (a) Only (1)   (b) Both (2) and (4)
    (c) Only (2), (3) and (4)   (d) Only (1), (2) and (3)
    (e) All (1), (2), (3) and (4)

192. **REGULAR**
    (1) Present   (2) Common
    (3) Indiscriminate   (4) Uniform
    (a) Only (4)   (b) Both (2) and (4)
    (c) Both (1) and (3)   (d) Only (2), (3) and (4)
    (e) All (1), (2), (3) and (4)

193. **LABOUR**
    (1) Expedite   (2) To move faster
    (3) Controlled   (4) Toil
    (a) Only (4)   (b) Both (1) and (3)
    (c) Both (2), (3) and (4)   (d) Only (1), (3) and (4)
    (e) All (1), (2), (3) and (4)

194. **MEAN**
    (1) Imply   (2) Understand
    (3) Average   (4) Characterized by malice
    (a) Only (3)   (b) Both (1) and (4)
    (c) Only (1), (3) and (4)   (d) Only (1), (2) and (4)
    (e) All (1), (2), (3) and (4)

195. **ALONE**
    (1) Exclusively   (2) Morose
    (3) Solitary   (4) Human being
    (a) Only (1)   (b) Both (1) and (3)
    (c) Both (2) and (3)   (d) Only (1), (3) and (4)
    (e) All (1), (2), (3) and (4)

DIRECTIONS (Qs. 196-200): *In the following questions, a set of five words is given. Four of the words are related in some way, the remaining word is not related to the rest. You have to pick the word which does not fit in the relation.*

(SBI PO 2014)

196. (a) Disdain   (b) Disloyalty
     (c) Infidelity   (d) Unfaithfulness
     (e) Unreliability
197. (a) Astute   (b) Crafty
     (c) Wily   (d) Naive
     (e) Shrewd
198. (a) Discern   (b) Recognise
     (c) Discriminate   (d) Differentiate
     (e) Eviscerate
199. (a) Bewildered   (b) Perplexed
     (c) Confused   (d) Reserved
     (e) Flummoxed
200. (a) Pageant   (b) Pretense
     (c) Exhibition   (d) Lurid
     (e) Plush

DIRECTIONS (Qs. 201-205) : *In each of the following questions four words are given of which two words are most nearly the same or opposite in meaning. Find the number of correct letter combination.*

(SBI PO 2014)

201. (A) dominate   (B) radical
     (C) determined   (D) monopolise
     (a) A - B   (b) B - C
     (c) A - D   (d) B - D
     (e) C - D
202. (A) critical   (B) equitable
     (C) impartial   (D) unearth
     (a) A - B   (b) B - C
     (c) A - D   (d) B - D
     (e) C - D
203. (A) shining   (B) raise
     (C) flourish   (D) thrive
     (a) A - B   (b) B - C
     (c) C - D   (d) B - D
     (e) A - C
204. (A) Affable   (B) rude
     (C) pacify   (D) cajole
     (a) A - B   (b) B - C
     (c) C - D   (d) A - D
     (e) B - D
205. (A) energetic   (B) partial
     (C) diffuse   (D) dispassionate
     (a) A - B   (b) B - C
     (c) C - D   (d) A - D
     (e) B - D

DIRECTIONS (Qs. 206-212) : *In each of the following questions five options are given, of which one word is most nearly the same or opposite in meaning to the given word in the question. Find the correct option having either same or opposite meaning.*

(SBI PO Main 2016)

206. Snitch
     (a) Bode   (b) Stitch
     (c) Suffix   (d) Sneak
     (e) Parity
207. Porch
     (a) Peek   (b) Demur
     (c) Verandah   (d) Capitulate
     (e) Bigotry
208. Vituperate
     (a) Examine   (b) Variegate
     (c) Belittle   (d) Compliment
     (e) Baleful
209. Conundrum
     (a) Abjure   (b) Quash
     (c) Riddle   (d) Thrill
     (e) Vendetta
210. Praise
     (a) Portend   (b) Lash
     (c) Fidget   (d) Creak
     (e) Visage
211. Notional
     (a) Quixotic   (b) Unworldly
     (c) Ethereal   (d) Impalpable
     (e) Cosmic
212. Vacillate
     (a) Dally   (b) Hem
     (c) Dither   (d) Sway
     (e) Waffle

DIRECTIONS (Qs. 213-217) : *In each of the following questions five options are given, of which one word is most nearly the same or opposite in meaning to the given word in the question. Find the correct option having either same or opposite meaning.*

(IBPS PO Main 2016)

213. PRODIGY
     (a) Pauper   (b) Despondent
     (c) Demure   (d) Wanton
     (e) Epitome
214. NONDESCRIPT
     (a) Conducive   (b) Discern
     (c) Tantamount   (d) Defined
     (e) Emancipate
215. SAVANT
     (a) Glutton   (b) Postulant
     (c) Shrink   (d) Pluck
     (e) Itinerant
216. CORPULENT
     (a) Lean   (b) Gaunt
     (c) Emaciated   (d) Obese
     (e) Nobble
217. EMBEZZLE
     (a) Misappropriate   (b) Balance
     (c) Remunerate   (d) Clear
     (e) Perfection

DIRECTIONS (Qs. 218 to 249) : *The word given below has been used in sentences in four different ways. Choose the option corresponding to the sentence in which the usage of the word is incorrect or inappropriate.*

218. HAND
     (a) The board rejected the manager's plan out of hand.
     (b) When you have small children at home it is advisable to have a first aid kit at hand.

   (c)   He's an old hand at managing advertising campaigns.

   (d)   He is hand over glove with the new president of the company.

219. **PENCIL**

   (a)   I wanted to write a letter but couldn't put pencil to paper.

   (b)   The agent managed to pencil in a meeting at 4 pm.

   (c)   An active person would hate to become a pencil pusher.

   (d)   If you write well they will not blue-pencil the article.

220. **SHOW**

   (a)   The latest computers will be on show at the exhibition.

   (b)   She had shown herself unable to deal with money.

   (c)   It just goes to show what you can do when you really try.

   (d)   He showed me away by snoring during the concert.

221. **JOB**

   (a)   There was a job of work waiting for him that he was not looking forward to.

   (b)   That cup of tea was just the job.

   (c)   Sorting these papers out is going to be a tall job.

   (d)   He got six months for that last job he did.

222. **SORT**

   (a)   Let's sort these boys into four groups

   (b)   They serve tea of a sort on these trains.

   (c)   Farmers of all sort attended the rally.

   (d)   What sort of cheese do you use in pizza?

223. **HOST**

   (a)   A virus has infected the host computer

   (b)   Ranchi will play the host to the next national film festival

   (c)   Kerala's forests are host to a range of snakes

   (d)   If you host the party, who will foot the bil

224. **HIT**

   (a)   In his new book he hits off the American temperament with amazing insight.

   (b)   What will happen when the story hits the front page?

   (c)   This course will hit the high spots of ancient history.

   (d)   Critics hit off at the administration's new energy policy.

225. **NECK**

   (a)   The company that he founded in 1983 is now an albatross around his neck, making losses of several hundreds of thousands a year.

   (b)   Your little brother who cannot sit for still for five seconds is a pain in the neck.

   (c)   He stuck his neck out for the deal because he thought he could make some big money.

   (d)   The two companies are neck to neck in the competition to win over customers.

226. **EYES**

   (a)   She cried her eyes after her husband died in a gruesome car accident.

   (b)   We had a bird's eye view of the old town from the top of the city walls.

   (c)   Martha married an abusive younger man with a roving eye and a habit of spending his days at the country inn.

   (d)   She was a girl with stars in her eyes and dreams of becoming famous.

227. **NOTE**

   (a)   The author inciuded a note on the usage of the term.

   (b)   The chess player of note was invited to inaugurate the Sports Complex.

   (c)   Her photograph rings a note but I still can't remember who she is.

   (d)   There was a note of sorrow in her manner.

228. **PULL**

   (a)   Pill aside the curtains and let in some fresh air.

   (b)   I decided to pull away from the venture due to differences of opinion with my partners.

   (c)   Being a charismatic leader that he is, he can certainly pull the crowds.

   (d)   The municipal corporation has decided to pull down all illegal

229. **SHADE**

   (a)   Nina's bedroom was painted in a soft shade of pink

   (b)   Abdul is a dubious character who is suspected of being involved in several shady deals.

   (c)   The weary traveler rested for a while in the shade of a tree.

   (d)   The people in the strife torn region have been living in the shade of fear for several years.

230. **SORT**

   (a)   Let's sort these boys into four groups

   (b)   They serve tea of a sort on these trains.

   (c)   Farmers of all sort attended the rally.

   (d)   What sort of cheese do you use in pizza?

231. **HOST**

   (a)   A virus has infected the host computer

   (b)   Ranchi will play the host to the next national film festival

   (c)   Kerala's forests are host to a range of snakes

   (d)   If you host the party, who will foot the bill

232. **IMPLICATION**

   (a)   Death, by implication, is the only solution the poem offers the reader

   (b)   Several members of the audience misseed the implication of the minister's promise

   (c)   This letter will lead to the implication of several industrialists in the share market scam

   (d)   Everyone appreciated the headmaster's implication in raising flood relief in the village

233. **DISTINCT**

   (a)   Mars became distinct on the horizon in the month of August

   (b)   The distinct strains of Ravi's violin could be heard above the general din

   (c)   He is distinct about what is right and what is wrong

   (d)   Ghoshbabu's is a distinct case of water rising above its own level

234. **BUNDLE**

   (a)   He made a bundle in the share market

   (b)   It was sheer luck that brought a bundle of boy scouts to where I was lying wounded

   (c)   The newborn body was a bundle of joy for the family

   (d)   Mobile operators are offering a bundle of additional benefits

235. **HELP**

   (a)   This syrup will help your cold

   (b)   I can't help the color of of my skin

   (c)   Ranjit may help himself with the beer in the fridge

   (d)   Do you really expect me to help you out with cash?

236. **REASON**

   (a)   Your stand is beyond all reason

   (b)   Has she given you any reason for her resignation?

   (c)   There is little reason in your pompous advice

   (d)   How do you deal with a friend who doesn't listen to a reason?

237. **PAPER**

   (a)   Your suggestions look great on the paper, but are absolutely impractical

   (b)   Do you know how many trees are killed to make a truckload of paper?

   (c)   So far I have been able to paper over the disagreements among my brothers

   (d)   Dr. Malek will read a paper on criminalization of politics

238. **BUSINESS**

   (a)   I want to do an MBA before going into business

   (b)   My wife runs profitable business in this suburb

   (c)   If we advertise we will get twice as much business as we have now

   (d)   How you spend your money is as much my business as yours

239. **SERVICE**

   (a)   Customers have to service themselves at this canteen

   (b)   It's a service lift; don't get into it.

   (c)   I'm not making enough even to service the loan

   (d)   Jyoti's husband has been on active service for three months

240. **BOLT**

   (a)   The shopkeeper showed us a bolt of fine silk.

   (b)   As he could not move, he made a bolt for the gate.

   (c)   Could you please bolt the door?

   (d)   The thief was arrested before he could bolt from the scene of the crime.

241. **PASSING**

   (a)   She did not have passing marks in mathematics.

   (b)   The mad woman was cursing everybody passing her on the road.

   (c)   At the birthday party all the children enjoyed a game of passing the parcel.

   (d)   A passing taxi was stopped to rush the accident victim to the hospital.

242. **FALLOUT**

   (a)   Nagasaki suffered from the fallout of nuclear radiation.

   (b)   People believed that the political fallout of the scandal would be insignificant.

   (c)   Who can predict the environmental fallout of the WTO agreements?

   (d)   The headmaster could not understand the fallout of several of his good students at the public examination.

243. **FOR**

   (a)   He has a great eye for detail.

   (b)   We are waiting for the day.

   (c)   I can't bear for her to be angry.

   (d)   It couldn't be done for ever.

244. **HAND**

   (a)   I have my hand full, I cannot do it today.

   (b)   The minister visited the jail to see the breach at first hand.

   (c)   The situation is getting out of hand here!

   (d)   When the roof of my house was blown away, he was willing to lend me a hand.

245. **NEAR**

   (a)   I got there just after you left – a near miss!

   (b)   She and her near friend left early.

   (c)   The war led to a near doubling of oil prices.

   (d)   They came near to tear seeing the plight of the victims.

246. **RUN**

   (a)   I must run fast to catch up with him.

   (b)   Our team scored a goal against the run of play.

   (c)   You can't run over him like that.

   (d)   The newly released book is enjoying a popular run.

   (e)   This film is a run-of-the-mill production.

247. **ROUND**

   (a)   The police fired a round of tear gas shells.

   (b)   The shop is located round the corner.

   (c)   We took a ride on the merry-go-round.

   (d)   The doctor is on a hospital round.

   (e)   I shall proceed further only after you come round to admitting it.

248. **BUCKLE**

   (a)   After the long hike our knees were beginning to buckle.

   (b)   The horse suddenly broke into a buckle.

   (c)   The accused did not buckle under police interrogation.

   (d)   Sometimes, an earthquake can make a bridge buckle.

   (e)   People should learn to buckle up as soon as they get into a car.

249. **FILE**

   (a)   You will find the paper in the file under C.

   (b)   1 need to file an insurance claim.

   (c)   The cadets were marching in a single file.

   (d)   File your nails before you apply nail polish.

   (e)   When the parade was on, a soldier broke the file.

DIRECTIONS (Qs.250 – 256) : *In each question, there are five sentences. Each sentence has a pair of words that are italicized and highlighted. From the italicized and highlighted words, select the most appropriate words (A or B) to form correct sentences. The sentences are followed by options that indicate the words, which may be selected to correctly complete the set of sentences. From the options given, choose the most appropriate one.*

250. The cricket council that *was* [A] / *were* [B] elected last March **is** [A] / *are* [B] at sixes and sevens over new rules.

The critics *censored* [A] / *censured* [B] the new movie because of its social unacceptability.

Amit's explanation for missing the meeting was *credulous* [A] / *credible* [B]

She coughed *discreetly* [A] / *discretely* [B] to announce her presence.

  (a) BBAAA   (b) AAABA
  (c) BBBBA   (d) AABBA
  (e) BBBAA

251. The *further* [A] / *farther* [B] he pushed himself, the more disillusioned he grew.

For the crowds it was more of a *historical* [A] / *historic* [B] event; for their leader, it was just another day.

The old man has a healthy *distrust* [A] / *mistrust* [B] for all new technology. This film is based on a *real* [A] / *true* [B] story.

One suspects that the *compliment* [A] / *complement* [B] was backhanded.

  (a) BABAB   (b) ABBBA
  (c) BAABA   (d) BBAAB
  (e) ABABA

252. *Regrettably* [A] / *Regretfully* [B] I have to decline your invitation.

I am drawn to the poetic, *sensual* [A] / *sensuous* [B] quality of her paintings.

He was *besides* [A] / *beside* [B] himself with age when I told him what I had done.

After brushing against a *stationary* [A] / *stationery* [B] truck my car turned turtle.

As the water began to rise *over* [A] / *above* [B] the danger mark, the signs of an imminent flood were clear.

  (a) BAABA   (b) BBBAB
  (c) AAABA   (d) BBAAB
  (e) BABAB

253. Anita wore a beautiful *broach (A)/brooch(B)* on the lapel of her jacket.

If you want to complain about the amenities in your neighbourhood, please meet your *councillor (A)/counsellor (B)*.

I would like your *advice(A)/advise(B)* on which job I should choose.

The last scene provided a *climactic(A)/climatic(B)* ending to the film.

Jeans that *flair(A)/flare(B)* at the bottom are in fashion these days.   **(2008)**

  (a) BABAA   (b) BABAB
  (c) BAAAB   (d) ABABA
  (e) BAABA

254. The cake had lots of *currents(A)/currants(B)* and nuts in it.

If you engage in such *exceptional(A)/exceptionable(B)* behaviour, I will be forced to punish you.

He has the same capacity as an adult to *consent(A)/assent(B)* to surgical treatment.

The minister is *obliged(A)/compelled(B)* to report regularly to a parliamentary board.

His analysis of the situation is far too *sanguine (A)/ genuine(B)*.

  (a) BBABA   (b) BBAAA
  (c) BBBBA   (d) ABBAB
  (e) BABAB

255. She managed to bite back the *ironic(A)/caustic(B)* retort on the tip of her tongue.

He gave an impassioned and *valid(A)/cogent(B)* plea for judicial reform.

I am not *adverse(A)/averse(B)* to helping out.

The *coupé(A)/coup(B)* broke away as the train climbed the hill.

They heard the bells *peeling(A)/pealing(B)* far and wide.

  (a) BBABA   (b) BBBAB
  (c) BAABB   (d) ABBAA
  (e) BBBBA

256. We were not successful in *defusing(A)/diffusing(B)* the Guru's ideas.

The students *baited(A)/bated(B)* the instructor with irrelevant questions.

The *hoard(A)/horde(B)* rushed into the campus.

The prisoner's *interment(A)/internment(B)* came to an end with his early release.

The hockey team could not deal with his *unsociable (A)/ unsocial(B)* tendencies.

  (a) BABBA   (b) BBABB
  (c) BABAA   (d) ABBAB
  (e) AABBA

257. It would not be wrong to say that the politicians today are *leeches* (A) / *leaches* (B) feeding off the hard-working majority.

  II. He had been *gulled* (A) / *culled* (B) into believing that the documents were authentic

  III. The sole of the shoe should be designed in a manner such that it can take constant *abrasion* (A) / *aberration* (B).

  IV. He *attenuated* (A) / *accentuated* (B) the eccentricity of the already freakish costume by adopting theatrical attitudes and an air of satisfied negligence.

  V. She is the object of his unabashed *amorphous* (A) / *amorous* (B) intentions.

  (a) BAAAB   (b) BBBAB
  (c) AAABB   (d) ABAAA

258. I.   The animal approached us ***bellowing*** (A) / ***billowing*** (B) and pawing the ground with the strength of many earthly bulls.
    II.   I have seen this whole body of soldiers, upon a word of command, draw their swords at once, and ***brandish*** (A) / ***blandish*** (B) them in the air.
    III. I am surprised that plaintiffs' hyperbolic allegations and inflated damage claims are given any ***credence*** (A) / ***cadence*** (B).
    IV.   A number of the species are edible, while others have been recorded as ***deleterious*** (A) / ***delirious*** (B).
    V.   From the top of the hill I ***decried*** (A) / ***descried*** (B) a solitary rider.   **(2014)**
    (a) BABAB   (b) BBBAB
    (c) ABAAB   (d) AAAAB

259. I.   A survey of the history of Christianity tells a disturbing tale, one wherein ***diffident*** (A) / ***dissident*** (B) cries for reform resulted in dangerous accusation of heresy and witchcraft.
    II.   Certainly the Arabs have no interest in seeing another war ***conflagrate*** (A) / ***conflate*** (B) in the Gulf region.
    III. The government operates according to its own rules, bringing enormous benefits to the chosen few, and suffering and ***immiseration*** (A) / ***commiseration*** (B) to millions.
    IV.   If the minority in such case ***cedes*** (A) / ***secedes*** (B) rather than acquiesces, it will make a precedent which in turn will divide and ruin them.
    V.   The full moon beams like a ***beckon*** (A) / ***beacon*** (B) in the clear sky.   **(2014)**

    (a) BBAAB   (b) BAABB
    (c) ABBBA   (d) AAABB

260. (i)   The municipal ***councilor*** (A) / ***counselor*** (B) promised to improve civic amenities in the suburbs.
    (ii) Jean's ***adopted*** (A) / ***adoptive*** (B) patents dote on her and cater to her every whim.
    (iii) The ***venal*** (A) / ***venial*** (B) official was caught red – handed accepting bribe.
    (iv) We have now shifted our residence ***farther*** (A) / ***further*** (B) away from the main city.
    (v)   She claims to be of aristocratic ***dissent*** (A) / ***descent*** (B).
    (a) AAABB   (b) BBABB
    (c) ABBAB   (d) ABAAB

261. (i)   While evacuating people from the flood ravaged areas ***precedence*** (A) / ***precedent*** (B) was given to women and children.s
    (ii) The best was to reach the summit is by trekking up the hill, ***alternately*** (A) / ***alternatively*** (B) you can go on horse back
    (iii) His impeccable manners perfectly ***complimented*** (A) / ***complemented*** (B) his polished looks and fashionable attire.
    (iv) There has been a ***noticeable*** (A) / ***notable*** (B) improvement in Tarun's academic performance lately.
    (v)   You must be ***discreet*** (A) / ***discrete*** (B) about your plans
    (a) AABAB   (b) ABBBB
    (c) BABAA   (d) ABBAA

ANSWER KEY

No	Ans	No	Ans	No	Ans	No	Ans	No	Ans	No	Ans	No	Ans	No	Ans	No	Ans	No	Ans	No	Ans	No	Ans
1	(b)	23	(b)	45	(e)	67	(e)	89	(c)	111	(e)	133	(b)	155	(e)	177	(e)	199	(d)	221	(c)	243	(c)
2	(d)	24	(a)	46	(a)	68	(a)	90	(b)	112	(c)	134	(c)	156	(e)	178	(b)	200	(d)	222	(c)	244	(a)
3	(a)	25	(c)	47	(d)	69	(b)	91	(d)	113	(b)	135	(d)	157	(c)	179	(e)	201	(c)	223	(c)	245	(b)
4	(e)	26	(d)	48	(b)	70	(c)	92	(d)	114	(d)	136	(c)	158	(b)	180	(d)	202	(b)	224	(c)	246	(c)
5	(b)	27	(e)	49	(e)	71	(d)	93	(b)	115	(a)	137	(a)	159	(e)	181	(c)	203	(c)	225	(d)	247	(d)
6	(e)	28	(e)	50	(c)	72	(e)	94	(a)	116	(d)	138	(e)	160	(a)	182	(a)	204	(a)	226	(a)	248	(b)
7	(a)	29	(a)	51	(c)	73	(a)	95	(b)	117	(a)	139	(d)	161	(d)	183	(e)	205	(e)	227	(c)	249	(e)
8	(c)	30	(b)	52	(e)	74	(c)	96	(b)	118	(b)	140	(d)	162	(b)	184	(a)	206	(d)	228	(b)	250	(d)
9	(b)	31	(d)	53	(a)	75	(d)	97	(c)	119	(c)	141	(b)	163	(c)	185	(e)	207	(c)	229	(d)	251	(e)
10	(a)	32	(d)	54	(d)	76	(a)	98	(e)	120	(e)	142	(d)	164	(a)	186	(a)	208	(d)	230	(c)	252	(b)
11	(b)	33	(e)	55	(e)	77	(b)	99	(a)	121	(a)	143	(c)	165	(d)	187	(c)	209	(c)	231	(c)	253	(c)
12	(c)	34	(b)	56	(e)	78	(c)	100	(d)	122	(e)	144	(e)	166	(d)	188	(b)	210	(b)	232	(d)	254	(b)
13	(d)	35	(a)	57	(b)	79	(b)	101	(c)	123	(b)	145	(d)	167	(c)	189	(d)	211	(a)	233	(c)	255	(b)
14	(d)	36	(c)	58	(a)	80	(c)	102	(a)	124	(d)	146	(c)	168	(a)	190	(e)	212	(c)	234	(b)	256	(a)
15	(e)	37	(b)	59	(a)	81	(c)	103	(b)	125	(c)	147	(a)	169	(b)	191	(e)	213	(e)	235	(c)	257	(c)
16	(a)	38	(c)	60	(d)	82	(b)	104	(e)	126	(e)	148	(a)	170	(c)	192	(d)	214	(b)	236	(d)	258	(d)
17	(a)	39	(d)	61	(d)	83	(a)	105	(b)	127	(d)	149	(b)	171	(d)	193	(a)	215	(b)	237	(a)	259	(b)
18	(c)	40	(c)	62	(c)	84	(e)	106	(c)	128	(b)	150	(b)	172	(e)	194	(c)	216	(d)	238	(b)	260	(d)
19	(d)	41	(a)	63	(d)	85	(d)	107	(b)	129	(c)	151	(d)	173	(c)	195	(b)	217	(a)	239	(a)	261	(d)
20	(c)	42	(b)	64	(a)	86	(c)	108	(c)	130	(a)	152	(c)	174	(a)	196	(a)	218	(d)	240	(b)		
21	(a)	43	(e)	65	(a)	87	(a)	109	(d)	131	(d)	153	(b)	175	(b)	197	(d)	219	(a)	241	(a)		
22	(c)	44	(e)	66	(d)	88	(b)	110	(e)	132	(b)	154	(b)	176	(a)	198	(e)	220	(d)	242	(d)		

Hints & Explanations

71. (d) Option (d) is the answer and there are two reasons for it. First one is that from the context of situation independence of women from the man's world is indicated so some word to show dependency should be used. Depend and Rest both show dependence so these are the answers. Second one is that as blank space is followed by ON a word that connects grammatically so it should be used. Both 'depend on' and 'rest on' are the correct usage, so it confirms the selection on basis of the first reason. Other options are not logical.

72. (e) Confiscated – means to officially take something away from somebody, especially as a punishment.
Seized definitely fits in the blank therefore option E is correct.

73. (a) Organization and mission are two words which can be connected with committed or dedicated both the verbs - organizations committed/ dedicated to .....Objectives. Other words like kicked off/inaugurated/ succumbed do not match for objectives of organization.

74. (c) Holding and Possessing both gives the same meaning and sense to the sentence. Surrendering is inappropriate. Mastering can not be linked with passports. Fixating is also incorrect for the blank space as it gives no logical sense to the sentence. Examining can grammatically fit into the blank but not in the context of passage and would give a different direction to what is being said in the sentence.

75. (d) 'Next big thing' is always a projection or a decision based on current situation. It is neither worshipped nor shouted nor explained. Rather next big thing is touted or labeled on basis of projection.

91. (d) Indispensable means essential, and fits the blank.

92. (d) Pertinent means "relevant or applicable to the matter at hand". So it fits the blank.

93. (b) Align means to "adjust or support", and fits the blank.

94. (a) The correct answer here is educate. While the other words have similar meaning, they do not make the sentence grammatically correct.

95. (b) Legal aid is "granted". So, it fits the blank.

116. (d) "Stalwart, extra ordinary, opportunities" is the correct choice.
Stalwart means loyal, reliable, and hard-working.

117. (a) "threatened, retaliatory, weapons" is the correct choice.

"Retaliatory means the action of returning a military attack; counter-attack."

118. (b) Invocation means the action of invoking someone or something.
Proletariat means working-class people regarded collectively (often used with reference to Marxism).

119. (c) "responsibility, misrepresent, inhabit" fits the blanks most appropriately.

120. (e) Patriarchal means relating to or denoting a system of society or government controlled by men.
Prohibits means formally forbid (something) by law, rule, or other authority.

161. (d) Antagonistic means unsympathetic.
Estrangement means disaffection.
Conciliatory means pacific or peaceful.

162. (b) Conscripted means recruited.

163. (c) Spate means a sudden flood in a river.
Paucity means present in small amount.

164. (a) The word "condemned" means express complete disapproval of; censure. It fits into both the sentences perfectly as in the first case Myanmar deplored the recent terror attacks in India and in the second case a person criticizes an immoral act.
The other word "perpetrated" means carry out or commit (a harmful, illegal, or immoral action). Once again this word adds meaning to both the sentences. Other words given as options are irrelevant in defining the true meanings of the sentences. Hence "condemned, perpetrated" is the correct set of words.

165. (d) Correct choice is option D. Parity means the quality or state of being equal or equivalent

166. (c) Futile means incapable of producing any useful result, pointless.

167. (c) Correct choice is option C. Capital -of a crime : having death as a possible punishment or the money, property, etc., that a person or business owns

168. (a) Correct choice is option A. product means something that is made or grown to be sold or used, someone or something that is produced or influenced by a particular environment or experience .

169. (b) Correct choice is option B.
Intense means very great in degree, very strong, done with or showing great energy, enthusiasm, or effort, of a person or very serious

170. (c) Correct choice is option C.
Concentration means the ability to give your attention or thought to a single object or activity, the ability to concentrate.

171. (d) Correct choice is option D.
Attempt means to try to do (something) : to try to accomplish or complete (something) or an attempt on someone's life means an act of trying to kill someone or a usually unsuccessful effort to kill someone

172. (e) Correct choice is option E.
Advance means to move forward, to go forward or to make progress, to help the progress of (something). He was advancing his own interests at the expense of his friend's.

173. (c) Correct choice is option C.
quickly means at a fast speed; rapidly.
I. They quickly moved away when they saw the oncoming car.
II. we moved quickly to deal with our auditor's questions
III. We made a quick decision, but it turned out to be a good one.

174. (a) Correct choice is option A.
Manner means the way that something is done or happens, to the manner born means suited to a particular position, role, or status in a way that seems very natural

175. (b) Correct choice is option B.

176. (a) Accretion means a thing formed or added by gradual growth or increase.

177. (e) Emancipation means the fact or process of being set free from legal, social, or political restrictions; liberation.

178. (b) Wholesale means done on a large scale; extensive.

179. (e) All the given options fit into the blanks appropriately as all four words mean the same i.e. so as to give the impression of having a certain quality; apparently.

180. (d) Meddling means interfering in something that is not one's concern.

181. (c) The word **Nascent (Adjective)** means: beginning to exist; not yet fully developed.
The word **nascent** and **emerging** are synonymous.

182. (a) The word **Eccentric (Adjective)** means: considered by other people to be strange or unusual.
The word **eccentric** and **abnormal** are synonymous.

183. (e) The word **Plethora (Noun)** means: an amount that is greater than is needed; excess.
The word **Abundance (Noun)** means: a large quantity that is more than enough.

184. (a) The word **Inadvertently (Adverb)** means: unintentionally; without intending to; by accident.
The word **purposefully** and **inadvertently** are antonymous.

185. (e) The word **Germane (Adjective)** means: connected with something in an important or appropriate ways; relevant.
The word **germane** and **irrelevant** are antonymous.

191. (e) **Dictionary Meaning of MASK -**
1. A covering worn on the face to conceal one's identity,
2. A protective covering for the face or head.

194. (c) Dictionary Meaning of **MEAN -**
1. (a) To be used to convey; denote.
   (b) To act as a symbol of; signify or represent
2. To be mean – cheap, selfish or negativity attached to it.

195. (b) Dictionary Meaning of **ALONE -**
1. Being apart from others; solitary.
2. Being without anyone or anything else; only.
3. Considered separately from all others of the same class.

4. Being without equal; unique

    Synonyms: alone, lonely, lonesome, solitary

196. (a) Disdain means disrespect, to consider umworthy of one's consideration or respect. all the others are synonyms meaning unfaithfulness.

197. (d) Naïve means unsophisticatedly simple. All the others are synonyms meaning clever, shrewd.

198. (e) Eviscerate means deprive of essential contents. All the others are synonyms meaning infer.

199. (d) Reserved means to keep to oneself. All the others are synonyms meaning confused.

200. (d) Lurid means unpleasantly bright in color, shocking, sensational, horrifying. All the other words have positive connotations related to beauty pageant or contest.

201. (c) **Dominate (Verb)** = to control or have a lot of influence over somebody/something; to be the most important feature of something.

    Monopolise (Verb) = to have or take control of the larger part of something.

    Hence, synonymous relationship.

202. (b) **Equitable (Adjective)** = fair and reasonable; treating everyone in an equal way.

    Impartial (Adjective) = not supporting one person or group more than other; unbiased.

    Hence, synonymous relationship.

203. (c) **Flourish (Verb)** = to develop quickly and be successful; to grow well; thrive.

    Look at the sentence:

    Few businesses are flourishing in the present economic climate.

204. (a) **Affable (Adjective)** = pleasant, friendly and easy to talk to; genial.

    Rude (Adjective) = discourteous; impolite; showing lack of respect for other people.

    Hence, antonymous relationship.

205. (e) **Partial (Adjective)** = showing or feeling too much support for one person, idea etc. in a way that is unfair; biased.

    Dispassionate (Adjective) = not influenced by emotion; impartial.

    Hence, antonymous relationship.

206. (d) Snitch and Sneak both have same meaning. Snitch and Sneak both mean to inform on someone.

207. (c) A porch or verandah means a covered shelter projecting in front of the entrance of a building. Both have same meaning.

208. (d) Vituperate and compliment both are antonyms. Vituperate means to insult someone in violent language while, compliment means to praise someone politely.

209. (c) Conundrum or Riddle means a confusing and difficult problem.

210. (b) Praise means to express warm approval while lash means to beat with a stick.

211. (a) Notional or Quixotic means not existing in reality.

212. (c) Vacillate or Dither means to wave between different opinions or actions.

213. (e) Prodigy refers to a particular quality and its close meaning is the word 'epitome' that refers to, example of a particular quality or type.

214. (b) Nondescript refers to, lacking distinctive or interesting features or characteristics. Option (b) 'discern' has the nearest meaning that refers to, distinguish someone or something with difficulty by sight or with the others senses which means it lacks distinctive characteristics.

215. (b) Savant means a person who knows a lot about a particular subject. Option (b) postulant refers to a candidate, especially one seeking admission into a religious order that means he knows more about religion.

216. (d) Corpulent means fat or well-built and its same meaning is expressed in option (d) obese that means grossly fat or overweight.

217. (a) Embezzle means, steal or misappropriate money placed in one's trust or belonging to the organization for which one works. Its near word, option (a) 'misappropriate' means; dishonestly or unfairly take something, especially money, belonging to another for one's own use.

218. (d) The correct usage is 'hand in glove' which means 'in extremely close relationship or agreement'.

219. (a) The correct usage is 'put pen to paper' which means 'to start to write something'.

220. (d) 'show' is used to depict an occasion when a collection of things are brought together for people to look at. Show is also used to make it clear that you have a particular quality. Show can be used in 'goes to show' to say that something proves something. The correct usage in (d) should be "showed me up" which means to make somebody feel embarrassed by behaving badly.

221. (c) 'Job of work' means a work that you are paid to do or that must be done. 'just the job' means exactly what is needed in a particular situation. The correct expression in (c) should be 'a long job" which means a particular task or piece of work that you have to do. Job can also be used as sin statement (d) to describe a crime, especially stealing.

222. (c) In (c) sort has been used in incorrect manner, as it refers to sorts of farmers i.e. types. In (a), (b) and (d) the word sort has been used in the correct way.

223. (c) (c) is the correct choice, as over here host refers to home, which can't be taken in the sense. (a), (b) and (d) used the word host correctly.

224. (c) In option (a) use of the word 'hit' is correct. The phrase 'hits off' means to be friendly with each other immediately. Option (b) is also correct; 'hit the front page' means to be published in front page of a newspaper or magazine. Option (d) is correct; 'hit out' means to make a violent verbal attack. Option (c) is incorrect; it has wrong use of the idiom 'hit the high spots' which means visiting the most exciting places in a town. So option (c) is the correct answer.

225. (d) To stick one's neck out means to take a risk. If someone is described as a pain in the neck, it means he/she is an annoyance. If something is an albatross around your

neck, it's something that keeps causing you problems. The correct idiom in option (d) should be 'neck and neck' which is used if two persons are competing very closely. So option (d) is the correct answer.

226. (a) A bird's eye view means a view from a very high place which allows one to see a large area. Roving eye refers to people who are sexually attracted to persons other than their partner. The idiom 'stars in one's eyes' means to be dazzled or enraptured. Option (a) is incorrect as the correct phrase is 'to cry one's eyes out' not 'to cry one's eyes after'. So option (a) is the correct answer.

227. (c) In option (a) use of the word 'note' is correct. In the given context 'note' refers to explanation/s that the author has provided for reference of the readers. In option (b) the word 'note' has been used to refer a person who is distinguished or famous. In option (d) the word 'note' has been used correctly. The word 'note' is used in this context to refer to grief, condolence or similar emotional qualities. In option (c) there is incorrect use of the word 'note'. The word has been incorrectly used in the expression 'rings a note' in place of the idiom 'rings a bell'. The idiom 'rings a bell' is used to refer to something which evokes memory or recollection. So option (c) is the correct answer.

228. (b) In Statement 1, the word 'pull' implies to take something out of or away from a place, especially using physical effort.
    In Statement 3, the word 'pull' implies to attract a person or people.
    In Statement 4, the word 'pull' implies to remove or stop something because it is found to be offensive or not accurate.
    The correct answer is Statement 2, as the usage of word 'pull' here is inappropriate. Since 'pull away' implies to physically move away; however the statement implies metaphorical moving away.

229. (d) Statement 1 is correct, the word 'shade' here implies a colour, especially with regard to how light or dark it is or as distinguished from one nearly like it.
    Statement 2 is also correct; the word 'shady' here implies something/someone of doubtful honesty or legality.
    Statement 3 is also correct; the word 'shade' here implies the comparative darkness and coolness caused by shelter from direct sunlight.
    The correct answer is Statement 4 as the word 'shade' here is incorrect as 'fear' is an emotion/feeling, that does not have a shade.

230. (c) In (c) sort has been used in incorrect manner, as it refers to sorts of farmers i.e. types. In (a), (b) and (d) the word sort has been used in the correct way.

231. (c) Option (c) is the correct choice, as here 'host' refers to home which is not suitable here. (a), (b) and (d) used the word host correctly.

232. (d) Implication means a likely consequence, in this case (d) is eliminated as the word implication in this sentence does not make sense.

233. (c) The sentence (c) uses distinct in an incorrect manner, thus it is to be eliminated whereas (a), (b) and (d) use the word in the right sense.

234. (b) As a collective noun the phrase "bundle of boy scouts" is incorrect. Thus (b) has to be the answer.

235. (c) Sentence (c) is to be rejected as Ranjit may help himself "to" the beer in the fridge rather than help himself "with".

236. (d) is the incorrect sentence as "a" has been used with reason, which is inappropriate.

237. (a) "The paper" in sentence (a) has been incorrectly used as the word "the" refers to something in particular. Thus, (a) is the choice.

238. (b) is the incorrect sentence and has to be eliminated as it has to be "a" profitable business.

239. (a) The words 'serve themselves' should be used.

240. (b) The word has been correctly used in (a), (c) and (d) with meanings, a roll of fabric, fasten or lock and a sudden escape, respectively. In (b) the usage of 'bolt' would mean run, sprint etc, which is contradictory to the 1st part (As he could not move).

241. (a) In (a), the use of the word 'passing marks' is wrong, it should have been 'pass marks'. Other follow with the meaning of the word passing - transient, fleeting, brief, advance, etc.

242. (d) In options (a), (b) & (c), the use of the word 'fallout' is acceptable with its meaning but in (d) it does not make any sense - 'failure' would be a better word.

243. (c) This sentence is incorrect as 'Bear for her' do not make any sense. The correct sentence is : I can't bear her to be angry.

244. (a) The correct sentence is :
    I have my hands full, I cannot do it today

245. (b) 'near friend' is not appropriate and must be replaced with close friend.

246. (c) The sentence (c) has the wrong usage of 'run over'. Run over means (a) to overflow; as, a cup runs over, or the liquor runs over, (b) to go over, examine, or rehearse cursorily; as, We'll run over that song again, (c) to ride or drive over; as, to run over a child, (d) to go beyond; exceed; as, His speech ran over the time limit.

247. (d) The sentence (c) has the wrong usage of 'round'. The doctor is never on round, he is on rounds. Here rounds is a Noun. 'A round of tear gas shells' means a sequence of gun shots. 'Merry-go-round' and 'round the corner' are very common usages of 'round'. 'Come round' means (a) to recover consciousness; revive, (b) to change one's opinion, decision, etc., esp. to agree with another's, (c) to visit: Come around more often, (d) to cease being angry, hurt, etc.

248. (b) Sentence (e) is correct as 'buckle up' means to fasten one's belt, seat belt, or buckles: She won't start the car until we've all buckled up. Sentence (c) is correct as 'buckle' means to yield, surrender, or give way to another (often followed by under): She refused to take the medicine, but buckled under when the doctor told her

to. Sentence (a) is correct as 'buckle' also means to bend, warp, or cause to give way suddenly, as with heat or pressure. Similarly sentence (c) is correct. Thus sentence (b) is wrong as the correct sentence is 'The horse suddenly broke into a buckle'.

249. **(e)** Sentence (a) is correct as 'file' here refers to a folder, cabinet, or other container in which papers, letters, etc., are arranged in convenient order for storage or reference. Sentence (b) is correct as 'file' here refers to 'to make application', to file an insurance claim. Sentence (c) is correct as 'file' here refers to 'to march in a file or line, one after another, as soldiers'. Sentence (d) is correct as 'file' here refers to 'to reduce, smooth, or remove with or as if with a file'. Sentence (e) is wrong as 'A soldier broke the file' is the wrong usage and should be replaced by 'A soldier broke the rank'.

250. **(d)** 'Cricket Council' is a collective noun and will take the singular form of the verb i.e., was and is. The critics will censure or criticize the new movie not censor or edit. Explanation can be credible or believable not credulous or gallible. She coughed discreetly (which means careful or circumspect manner of doing things) not discretely (which means distinctly and separately). Hence, correct answer is option (d).

251. **(e)** 'Further' means degree or extent of something whereas 'further' is related to distance in space or time. So further is appropriate word in this sentence. An event can be historic or historical. 'Historic' means important, significant and 'historical' means ancient, past. But here historic is appropriate usage of word. 'Distrust' is a feeling of suspiscion and 'mistrust' is lack of trust but in this sentence distrust is correct.

The film is based on true story (connected with facts) not real (actually existing). One suspects that a compliment (a remark that expresses praise or admire) not complement (additional or supplement) was backhanded. So correct answer is option (e).

252. **(b)** Regretfully is a way of showing disappointment and Regrettably is someone is sorry about and wish had not happened. So one can decline invitation regretfully not regrettably. I am drawn to poetic, sensous (giving pleasure to senses) not sensual (physically passionate) quality of her paintings.

He was beside himself (means unable to control himself) not besides (in addition to or apart from) the rage.

Stationary is correct word because a truck can be stationary or not moving and not stationery or writing material.

Water rises above the danger mark not over. 'Above' denotes the higher place or position whereas over denotes the physical location. So correct answer is option (b).

253. **(c)** Sentence 1 - Brooch (A) is a clasp or ornament having a pin at the back for passing through the clothing and a catch for securing the point of the pin, whereas Broach (B) means to mention or suggest for the first time. In the context of the sentence, Brooch is the right choice.
Sentence 2 - Councillor (A) a member of a council, whereas a counsellor is a person who counsels; adviser.
In the context of the sentence, Councillor (B) is the right choice.
Sentence 3 - Advice (A) is the right choice as it is the Noun form, whereas Advise (B) is the verb form (used as, advise me). In the context of the sentence, Advice is the right choice.
Sentence 4 - Climactic (A) means pertaining to or coming to a climax and hence is the right choice.
Sentence 5 - Flair (A) means a natural talent, aptitude, or ability whereas, Flare (B) means to spread gradually outward, as the end of a trumpet, the bottom of a wide skirt, or the sides of a ship. In the context of the sentence, Flare is the right choice.
Thus the correct option is BAAAB

254. **(b)** Sentence 1 - Currants (B) are the fruits used for jams, jellies, desserts, or beverages, whereas Currents (A) means the movement of water in seas or rivers.
In the context of the sentence, Currants is the right choice.
Sentence 2 - Exceptional (A) is something good, whereas Exceptionable (B) is liable to exception or objection; objectionable. In the context of the sentence, Exceptionable (B) is the right choice.
Sentence 3 - Consent (A) is the right choice as it means to permit, approve, or agree; comply or yield, whereas Assent (B) means to agree or concur; subscribe to something.
Sentence 4 - Obliged (A) means, to require or constrain, as by law, command, conscience, or force of necessity, whereas Compelled (B) means to force or drive, esp. to a course of action. In the context of the sentence, Obliged (A) is the right choice.
Sentence 5 - Sanguine (A) is cheerfully optimistic, hopeful, or confident whereas, genuine (B) means exactly what something appears to be. In the context of the sentence, Sanguine (A) is the right choice.
Thus the correct option is BBAAA.

255. **(b)** Sentence 1 - Ironic (A) means poignantly contrary to what was expected or intended, whereas Caustic (B) means severely critical or sarcastic.
In the context of the sentence, Caustic (B) is the right choice.
Sentence 2 - Valid (A) is sound; just; well-founded, whereas Cogent (B) means to the point; relevant; pertinent.
In the context of the sentence, Cogent (B) is the right choice.
Sentence 3 - Adverse (A) means opposing one's interests or desire, whereas Averse (B) means having a feeling of opposition, distaste, or aversion; strongly disinclined. In the context of the sentence, Averse (B) is the right choice.
Sentence 4 - Coupé (A) means a short, four-wheeled, closed carriage, usually with a single seat for two passengers and an outside seat for the driver, whereas Coup (B) means A sudden appropriation of leadership or power; a takeover. In the context of the sentence, Coupé (A) is the right choice.
Sentence 5 - Peeling (A) is to strip or cut away the skin, rind, or bark from; pare, whereas, Pealing (B)

means a set of bells tuned to each other; a chime. In the context of the sentence, Pealing (B) is the right choice.

Thus the correct option is BBBAB.

256. (a) Sentence 1 - Defusing (A) means to make less dangerous, tense, or embarrassing, whereas Diffusing (B) means to spread or scatter widely or thinly; disseminate.

In the context of the sentence, Diffusing (B) is the right choice.

Sentence 2 - Baited (A) means 'to deliberately try to make somebody angry, whereas Bated (B) means to lessen by retrenching, deducting, or reducing.

In the context of the sentence, Baited (A) is the right choice.

Sentence 3 - Hoard (A) means to accumulate money, food, or the like, in a hidden or carefully guarded place for preservation, future use, etc, whereas Horde (B) means A large group or crowd. In the context of the sentence, Horde (B) is the right choice.

Sentence 4 - Interment (A) means the act or ceremony of interring; burial, whereas Internment (B) means confinement during wartime. In the context of the sentence, Internment (B) is the right choice.

Sentence 5 - Unsociable (A) means having, showing, or marked by a disinclination to friendly social relations; withdrawn, whereas, Unsocial (B) means outside the normal times of working. In the context of the sentence, Unsociable (A) is the right choice. Thus the correct option is BABBA.

257. (c) Leech refers to bloodsucking parasites that feed on others while leach means to drain away from soil, ash, or similar material. Gulled means fooled while culled means slaughtered. Abrasion means process of wearing down by friction and aberration means deviation or abnormality. To attenuate means to lessen the intensity of something and to accentuate means to intensify or emphasize. Amorphous means shapeless while amorous means passionate and lustful. The correct answer is AAABB. So option (c) is the correct answer.

258. (d) Bellow means to roar or shout while billow means to puff, swell or fill with something. Blandish means to coax someone with kind words and brandish means to exhibit something aggressively. Credence means belief in something and cadence means rhythm or beat. Delirious means to be in a disturbed state of mind while deleterious means harmful. To decry means to denounce or criticize someone while descry means to catch sight of something. The correct answer is AAAAB. So option (d) is the correct answer.

259. (b) Diffident means lacking self-confidence while dissident means a rebel or a non-conformist. Conflagrate means to inflame or incite and conflate means to mix different types of elements together. Immiseration means economic impoverishment and commiseration means pity or sympathy. Secede means to withdraw or disaffiliate from an organization while cede means to yield or surrender. Beacon means a shining example or a guiding light while beckon refers to a gesture to summon someone. The correct answer is BAABB. So option (b) is the correct answer.

260. (d) The word 'counselor' means a person who provides advice.

'Councilor' means a member of a council.

'Adopted' means legally take another's child and bring it up as one's own.

'Adoptive' means of a child or parent in that relationship by adoption.

'Venal' means showing or motivated by susceptibility to bribery; corrupt.

'Venial' means of a fault or offence slight and pardonable

'Further' is used for metaphorical or figurative distance.

'Farther' is used for physical distance.

So the correct answer is Option (d). ABAAB

261. (d) 'Precedence' means the condition of being considered more important than someone or something else; priority in importance.

'Precedent' means an earlier event or action that is regarded as an example or guide to be considered in subsequent similar consequences.

'Alternately' means set up or following by turns, one after the other.

'Alternatively' refers to or implies a choice between two things.

'Noticeable' is worthy of note; significant

'Notable' is useful or profitable.

"Discrete' means individually separate and distinct.

'Discreet' means careful and prudent in one's speech or actions.

So the right answer is Option (d). ABBAA

CHAPTER 2

Grammar

We can communicate well verbally but when it comes to answering grammar-based questions, we commit mistakes. Grammar is not a set of rules but in reality a mere description of the language used by all of us. Grammar forms an important part in the English section of any competitive examination. The typical kind of questions can be categorized as follows: (a) Fill in the blanks (b) Identifying errors in sentences and (c) Correcting the sentences. The questions can be handled easily and you can score well if your basics are clear.

HOW THIS CHAPTER WILL HELP YOU

This chapter will help you to understand how language and components of language work. It is oriented towards making you more confident user of English by giving you an insight into correct usage. The material provided is user-friendly with adequate examples and 'practice exercises'.

If you make a concentrated effort, it will not only prepare you for the forthcoming competitive exams but also fine-tune your communication skills.

READING: To supplement your efforts, you should build up reading habits. This can be of any kind - magazines, newspapers or novels. But, one should consciously look at the usage. Good reading habits will definitely build up your understanding of grammatical usage and help you in being successful in competitive exams.

NOUNS

A Noun is a word used as a name of a person, place or thing.
There are five kinds of Noun –
(a) Proper Noun   (b) Common Noun
(c) Collective Noun   (d) Abstract Noun
(e) Material Noun.

FOLLOWING ARE CERTAIN RULES OF GRAMMAR REGARDING NOUNS THAT WOULD BE USEFUL IN A COMPETITIVE EXAM:

1. Proper nouns are sometimes used as common nouns.
   For example :
   (a) Amitabh is **Gandhiji** of our class. (Incorrect)
   (b) Amitabh is the **Gandhiji** of our class, (Correct)
   Here Gandhiji does not mean Mahatma Gandhi. The word here stands for the possessor of the qualities that Gandhiji is most known for - truth and non-violence. Thus Gandhiji is being used as a metaphorical common noun.

FOLLOWING ARE RULES REGARDING THE NUMBER OF THE NOUN :

2. Some nouns have the same form both in singular as well as in plural.
   For example :
   (a) A deer **was** caught.
   (b) Deer **were** caught.
   Here, the singular and plural form of the noun Deer is the same. Like Deer there are other nouns that have the same form **in singular as well as plural form**. *For example*: sheep, apparatus, species, series, hundred, dozen, hair etc. Preceding adjectives and articles decide whether the word is used in the singular form or plural form.

For example :
(a) He paid eight **hundred** rupees for this pair of shoes.
(b) India again won the **series**.

3. Nouns denoting large numbers are used both in singular and plural form
   For example :
   (a) Three **hundred** people attended the function.
   (b) **Hundreds** of people attended the party.
   In sentence (a), 'hundred' is preceded by number 'three'. So 'hundred' will take no plural form. Word 'three hundred' indicates plurality. But in sentence (b), 'hundred' is not preceded by any number. So to indicate plurality, we will write 'hundreds'. **So, rule is that when words like hundred, dozen, thousand, pair, score are not preceded by any word denoting number then they take the plural form, otherwise not.**
   Consider some more *examples* :
   (a) Coca-Cola paid **lakhs** of rupees to Aamir Khan for promoting their product.
   (b) I brought two **dozen** bananas.

4. Tell which sentence is correct:
   (a) Since long no news **has** been heard.
   (b) Since long no news **have** been heard.
   Sentence a is correct. The reason is that **some nouns are always used as singular though they look like plural nouns.** That's why we should never use the plural verb with these words. Other similar words are politics, mathematics, physics, gallows, means, billiards, ethics, summons, innings.
   For example :
   (a) **Politics** is not my cup of tea.
   (b) I received **summons**.
   (c) Sachin once again played a superb **innings**

5. Tell which sentence is correct:
    (a) The spectacles that you are wearing **are** really nice.
    (b) The spectacles that you are wearing **is** really nice.
    Sentence a) is correct. The reason being that **some noun words are always used in the plural form**.
    For example : trousers, arms, drawers, assets, scales, alms, thanks, cards; ashes, riches, premises, scissors, credentials, proceeds.

6. Tell which sentence is correct:
    (a) The cattle **was** grazing in the field.
    (b) The cattle **were** grazing in the field.
    Sentence (b) is correct. The reason being that **some nouns are always used as plurals though they look like singular**. Other nouns like this are public, people, folk, mankind, poultry, sheep, police, gentry, peasantry, bulk, majority, etc.
    For example:
    (a) The majority **are** with the leader.
    (b) Police, though late, **have** come.
    (c) Public wants results.

7. Tell which sentence is correct.
    (a) This project will lead to lots of **expenditures**
    (b) This project will lead to lots of **expenditure**.
    Sentence (b) is correct. The reason is that **some nouns are always used as singular. Preceding adjectives or the verb form indicates the singularity or plurality**. Other nouns are expenditure, furniture, information, machinery, issue, offspring, alphabet, scenery, poetry.
    For example :
    (a) All the **furniture** was bought last year.
    (b) All the **Information** was given to him.

8. Meaning of some nouns in plural form is very **different** from the meaning of nouns in singular form. Hence, that form should be used which will convey the right meaning.
    For example:
    (a) I opened the letter and read its **contents**.
    (b) Her mouth was fixed in a smile of pure **content**.
    (c) The conflict between **good** and evil is age-old.
    (d) We must produce **goods** at competitive prices.
    (e) Delhiites breathe the most polluted **air** in the world.
    (f) She was just putting on **airs** when she came to visit me.
    (g) We should renounce the use of **force** to settle our dispute.
    (h) Families of people who died as a result of services in the **forces** should not be ignored.
    (i) I was very excited on my **return** to my home village.
    (j) Early **returns** in the ballot indicate majority for opposition.
    Other nouns having different meanings in the singular and plural form are:

Singular with meaning	Plural with meaning
Advice - counsel	Advises - information
Respect - regard	Respects - compliments
Compass - extent or range	Compasses - instrument
Custom - habit	Customs - duties levied on
Ground - Earth	Grounds - reasons
Iron - metal	Irons - fetters made of iron
Mean - average	Means - way or method
Respect - regard	Respects - polite greetings
Colour - hue	Colours - appearance
Physic - medicine	Physics - natural science

9. Please go through the following singulars and plurals as plural forms are commonly known but their **singular forms are** not commonly known.

Singular Form	Plural form
Agendum	Agenda
Alumnus	Alumni
Index	Indices
Phenomenon	Phenomena
Criterion	Criteria
Radius	Radii
Formula	Formulae
Memorandum	Memoranda

10. Some noun words have **two plurals with different meanings**. So, that plural form should be selected which will convey the right meaning.
    For example :
    (a) I have one **brother** and one sister (meaning- children of the same parents).
    (b) Why should only select **brethren** be allowed to attend the meeting? (meaning - members of the same society, organisation)
    (c) I took off my shoes and **clothes** (meaning- things that people wear).
    (d) Cotton, Nylon, Silk are different kinds of **cloths** (meaning- kinds or pieces of cloth).
    Other nouns having two plurals with different meanings are:

Singular	Plural with different meaning
Die	Dies - stamps
	Dice - small cubes used in games
Genius	Geniuses-persons of great talent
	Genie - spirit
Quarter	Quarter - fourth part
	Quarter(s) - lodging
Manner	Manner - Method
	Manners - Correct behaviour
Pain	Pain - Suffering
	Pains - Careful efforts
Spectacle	Spectacle - sight
	Spectacles - eye-glasses
Penny	Pence - indicate amount of money
	Pennies - number of coins

FOLLOWING ARE RULES REGARDING GENDER OF THE NOUN :

11. Collective nouns, even when they denote living beings, are considered to be of the **neuter gender**.
    For example :
    (a) Mr. Smith had a herd of cows. He kept a herdsman to look after **her**.
    (b) Mr. Smith had a herd of cows. He kept a herdsman to look after **it**.

Sentence b) is correct. Though herd consists of cows (females), herd is not a feminine noun as it a collective noun.

12. Young children and the lower animals are also referred to as of the **neuter gender**.

For example :

(a) The baby loves **his** toys. (Incorrect)

(b) The baby loves **its** toys. (correct)

(c) The mouse lost **his** tail when the cat pounced on him. (Incorrect)

(d) The mouse lost its tail when the cat pounced on it. (correct)

We are often uncertain regarding the gender of the animals. The mouse here may be a male or a female. So, English language prefers the easy way out: treat it as of the neuter gender.

13. When objects without life are personified they are considered of

(i) The masculine gender if the object is remarkable for strength and violence. Ex. Sun, Summer, Winter, Time, Death etc.

(ii) The feminine gender if the object is remarkable for beauty, gentleness and gracefulness. Ex: Earth, Moon, Spring, Nature, Mercy etc.

For example:

(a) The Sun came from behind the clouds and with **her** brilliance tore the veil of darkness. (Incorrect)

(b) The Sun came from behind the clouds and with **his** brilliance tore the veil of darkness. (Correct)

Convention does not see brilliance as a womanly quality, but a manly one.

(a) Nature offers **his** lap to him that **seeks** it. (Incorrect)

(b) Nature offers **her** lap to him that **seeks** it. (Correct)

The offering of a lap is usually the mother's role. Hence, Nature here should be treated as a feminine noun.

Tell which sentence is correct.

(a) The earth goes round the sun in 365 days. Can **you calculate her speed**?

(b) The earth goes round the sun in 365 days. Can **you calculate its speed**?

Sentence b is correct. The error being made here is that personification is being brought where it does not exist. In the above statement the earth is being treated as a body (a thing), not a person. The scientist here is not concerned with the womanly qualities of the planet. So, neuter gender should be applied.

FOLLOWING ARE RULES REGARDING APOSTROPHE:

14. Rules regarding apostrophe S ('s):

(a) Singular noun: 's is added after the word.

(b) Singular noun: Only an apostrophe is added when there are too many hissing sounds. *For example*: Moses' laws, for goodness' sake, For justice' sake.

(c) Plural nouns ending in s like boys, cows: only (') is added after the word

(d) Plural nouns not ending in s like men, children: ('s) is added after the word.

(e) 'S is added primarily after the living things and personified objects. *For example*: Governor's bodyguard, horse's head, Nature's law, Fortune's favourite.

(f) 'S is not used with inanimate or non-living things. *For example*: leg of the table, cover of the book.

(g) But in nouns that denote time, distance or weight, ('s) is used. *For example*: a stone's throw, in a year's time, the earth's surface.

(h) Some other common phrases where ('s) is used are to his heart's content, at his wit's end, out of harm's way.

(i) When a noun consists of several words, the possessive sign is attached only to the last word.

For example:

(a) The Queen's **of England** reaction is important in the Diana episode. (Incorrect)

(b) The Queen **of England's** reaction is important in the Diana episode. (Correct)

Do not be mistaken that since it is the Queen's reaction, the ('s) should come after queen. You might think that putting it after England would make the reaction England's and not the Queen's. This is short-sightedness. Do not see Queen and England in isolation, Queen of England is one whole unit and the apostrophe should come at its end.

(j) When two nouns are in apposition, the possessive sign is put to the latter only.

For example :

(a) I am going to Stephen **Hawking's the scientist's country**. (Incorrect)

(b) I am going to Stephen **Hawking the scientist's country**. (Correct)

(k) When two or more nouns show joint possession, the possessive sign is put to the latter only.

For example:

(a) Amitabh and Ajitabh are Bachchanji's sons. So Bachchanji **is Amitabh's and Ajitabh's father**. (Incoreect)

(b) Amitabh and Ajitabh are Bachchanji's sons. So Bachchanji **is Amitabh and Ajitabh's father**. (Correct)

(l) When two or more nouns show separate possession, the possessive sign is put with both.

For example.

(a) The audience listened to Javed and Vajpayee's poems. (Incorrect)

(b) The audience listened to Javed's and Vajpayee's poems. (Correct)

PRONOUNS

A pronoun is a word used instead of a noun.

Now consider the following cases :

1. Since a pronoun is used **instead of a Noun**, it must be of the same number, gender and person as the noun for which it stands. *For example*: Those **beggars** are idle. **They** refuse to work for their living.

2. Consider the following two sentences.
   (a) After a few hearings the jury gave its verdict. (Pronoun 'its is used in place of noun 'jury').
   (b) The **jury** were divided in **their** opinions. (Pronoun 'their' is used in place of noun 'jury'

   You must be wondering why different pronoun 'its' and 'their' is used in place of the same noun 'jury' The reason is when a pronoun stands for a **collective noun** it must be in the singular number and neutral gender. (Sentence a). But when collective noun conveys the idea of separate individuals comprising the whole, the pronoun standing for it must be of the plural number. In sentence b, it is clear that members of the jury are not behaving as whole.

   For example :
   (a) The **committee** is reconsidering its decision.
   (b) The **committee** decided the matter without leaving their seats.

PRONOUNS IN SENTENCES FOUND BY CONJUNCTION :

3. When two or more singular nouns are joined by '**and**', the pronoun used for them must be **plural**.

   For example : Rama and Hari work hard. **Their** teachers praise **them**.

   But when two Singular nouns joined by '**and**' refer to the same person or thing, the pronoun should be singular.

   For example : The Secretary and Treasurer is negligent of **his** duty.

   Here the same person is acting as Secretary and Treasurer. That's why singular pronoun is used.

4. When two singular nouns joined by '**and**' are preceded by 'each' or 'every', then the pronoun must be singular

   For example : Every soldier and every sailor was in **his** place.

5. When two or more singular nouns are joined by '**or**', '**either...or**', '**neither...nor**', the pronoun is generally singular.

   For example :
   (a) Neither Abdul nor Rehman has done his lessons.
   (b) Either Rama or Hari must help **his** friend.

6. When a plural and a singular noun are joined by '**or**' or '**nor**', the pronoun must be in the plural

   For example : Either the manager or his assistants failed in **their** duty.

7. When two things which have been **already mentioned** are referred to, 'this' refers to the thing last mentioned and 'that to the thing first mentioned.

   For example : Alcohol and Tobacco are both injurious: **this** perhaps less than **that**.

RULES REGARDING PERSONAL PRONOUNS :

8. Tell which sentence is correct-
   (a) The presents are for you and **me**.
   (b) The presents are for you and **I**.

   Sentence a is correct. Pronoun has to agree with the case. Here it is the **objective case**. So, 'me' should be used instead of 'I'. *For example* : My uncle asked my brother and me to dinner.

9. Tell which sentence is correct
   (a) He loves you more than **I**.
   (b) He loves you more than **me**.

   Sentence a is correct 'Than' is a conjunction joining clauses. And the case of the pronoun to be used may be found by writing the clauses in full. So, in sentence a.) two clauses joined by 'than' are 'He loves you more' and 'I love you'. Being a subjective case, 'I' should be used.

   For example:
   (a) He is taller than **I** (am).
   (b) He loves you more than (he loves) **me**.

10. When a pronoun refers to more than one noun or pronouns of different persons, it must be of the first person plural in preference to the second and of the second person plural in preference to the third.

    For example :
    (a) You and I, husband and wife, have to look after **your** home. (Incorrect)
    (b) You and I, husband and wife, have to look after **our** home. (Correct)

    Now, common sense tells us that if we are a couple, wife and husband, the feeling of togetherness is expressed by our home, not your home. And so does grammar.

    Rule: 123. I stands for first person, 2 for second person and 3 for third person. The order of precedence is: 1 before 2 and 2 before 3. In the given example, we have 2 and 1. So I will apply; that is, first person. The number, of course, will be plural.

    Let us take another *example*.
    (a) You and Hari have done **their duty**. (Incorrect)
    (b) You and Hari have done **your** duty. (Correct)

    Applying 123 rule. You = 2 and Hari = 3. So, 2. Second person plural gives 'your'.

    Similarly ,when all the three persons are taken into account, it has to be I; that is, first person plural.
    (a) You, he and I have not forgotten your roots. (Incorrect)
    (b) You, he and I have not forgotten **our roots**. (Correct)

11. **Each, either and neither** are always singular and are followed by the verb in the singular.

    For example :
    (a) Neither of the accusations **is** true.
    (b) Each boy took **his** turn.
    (c) Each of the ladies performs **her** duty well.

12. (A) Please consider the following sentences.
    (a) This is the boy. **He** works hard. (**He** subjective case)

   (b) This is the boy. **His** exercise is done well. (**His** is possessive case)

   (c) This is the boy. All praise **him**. (**Him** is objective case)

13. An apostrophe is never used in 'its', 'yours' and 'theirs'.

14. The complement of the verb **be**, when it is expressed by a pronoun, should be in the nominative form.

For example.

   (a) It was **he** (not **him**),

   (b) It is **I** (not **me**) that gave the prizes away.

   (c) It might have been **he** (not **him**).

15. The case of a pronoun following **than** or **as** is determined by mentally supplying the verb.

For example :

   (a) He is taller than **I** (**am**).

   (b) I like you better than **he** (**likes you**).

   (c) They gave him as much as (**they gave**) **me**.

16. A pronoun must agree with its Antecedent in **person, number and gender.**

For example:

   (a) All passengers must show **their** (**not his**) tickets.

   (b) I am not one of those who believe everything **they** (**not I**) hear

RULES REGARDING DEMONSTRATIVE PRONOUNS :

17. **That** is used-

   A. **After adjectives in the superlative degree.**

     For example-

     (a) This is the best **that** we can do.

     (b) He is the best speaker **that** we ever heard.

   B. After the words **all, same, any, none, nothing, only.**

     For example:

     (a) Man is the only animal **that** can talk.

     (b) He is the same man **that** he has been.

   C. After **two antecedents**, one denoting a person and the other denoting an animal or a thing.

     For example : The man and his pet **that** met with an accident yesterday died today.

18. **What** and **That** refer to persons as well as things.

RULES REGARDING RELATIVE PRONOUNS :

19. On combining each of the above pairs into one sentence

     (a) This is the boy **who** works hard (Who in place of He)

     (b) This is the boy **whose** exercise is done well. (**whose** in place of His)

     (c) This is the boy **whom** all praise. (**Whom** in place of Him)

The above sentences show when to use who, whose and whom. Who is the subjective case, Whose the possessive case and Whom the objective case.

20. Who is used for persons only. It may refer to a singular or plural noun.

For example :

   (a) He **who** hesitates is lost.

   (b) Blessed is he **who** has found his work.

21. Whose can be used for persons as well as things without life also.

For example :

   (a) This is the hotel **whose** owner is a criminal.

   (b) This is the person **whose** will power is extraordinary.

22. Which is used for inanimate things and animals. 'Which' is used for both singular and plural nouns.

For example :

   (a) I have found the book **which** I had lost last week.

   (b) The horse, **which** won the race yesterday, is my favourite.

23. When 'which' is used for selection, it may refer to a person as well as things.

For example :

   (a) Which of the packets is yours?

   (b) Which of the boys has not done his homework?

24. **Who, Which, Whom, That, Whose** should be placed as near to the antecedent as possible.

For example :

   (a) I with my family reside in Delhi, which consists of my wife and parents.

     This sentence is wrong as **which** relates to 'my' family'. So 'which' should be placed as near to family' as possible. So, the correct sentence is

   (b) I with my family which, consists of my wife and parents, reside in Delhi.

25. **Who** is used In the **nominative** cases and **whom** in the **objective** cases.

For example :

   (a) There is Mr. Dutt, **who** (not **whom**) they say is the best painter in the town.

   (b) The Student, whom (not who) you thought so highly of, has failed to win the first prize.

26. When the **subject** of a verb is a **relative pronoun**, the verb should agree in number and person with the antecedent of the **relative.**

For example :

   (a) This is **one** of the most interesting **novels that have** (not **has**) appeared this year. (Here, antecedent of **relative pronoun that** is **novels** and not **one**)

   (b) This is the only **one** of his **poems that is** (not **are**) worth reading. (Here the antecedent of **that** is **one** and not **poems**. Kindly note the difference between sentence **a and b**)

OTHER USEFUL RULES :

27. None is used in the singular or plural as the sense may require.

For example:

   (a) Each boy was accompanied by an adult but there were none, with the orphan (Incorrect)

   (b) Each boy was accompanied by an adult but there **was** none with the orphan. (Correct)

   (c) I am used to many guests everyday but there **was** none today. (Incorrect)

   (d) I am used to many guests everyday but there **were** none today. (Correct)

28. When 'one' is used as **pronoun**, its possessive form 'one's' should follow instead of his, her etc.

For example : One must put **one's best** efforts if one wishes to succeed.

29. With **let** objective case of the pronoun is used.

For example : let **you** and **me** do it.

30. If a pronoun has two antecedents, it should agree with the **nearer one**.

    For example :
    (a) I hold in high esteem everything and **everybody who** reminds me of my failures.
    (b) I hold in high esteem everybody and **everything, which** reminds me of my failures.

31. In referring to **anybody, everybody, anyone, each** etc., the pronoun of the masculine or the feminine gender is used according to the context.

    For example.
    (a) I shall be glad to help **everyone** of my **boys** in **his** studies.
    (b) I shall be glad to help **everyone** of my **girls** in **her** studies.

    (c) I shall be glad to help everyone of my **students** in **his** studies.

    But when gender is not determined, the pronoun of the **masculine gender** is used as in sentence c.

32. (A) The pronoun **one** should be used throughout, if used at all.

    For example:
    (a) **One** must use **one's** best efforts if one wishes to succeed.
    (b) **One** should be careful about what one says.

    (B) **Plural** is commonly used with **none**.

    For example.
    (a) **None** of his poems are well known.
    (b) **None** of these words are now current.

33. **Anyone** should be used when **more than two** persons or things are spoken of.

    For example : She was taller than **anyone** of her five sisters.

TENSES

1. Tense is the form taken by a verb to indicate time and **continuance** or **completeness** of action. The continuance or completeness of action is denoted by four subcategories.

   (a) Simple Tense : It is used for habitual or routine actions in the Present Tense, action which is over in the Past Tense & action to happen in the Future Tense.

   (b) Continuous Tense : The action is incomplete or continuous or going on.

   (c) Perfect Tense : The action is complete, finished or perfect with respect to a certain point of time.

   (d) Perfect Continuous Tense : The action is going on continuously over a long period of time and is yet to be finished.

2. The different tenses and the verb forms used in each tense are given below :

Singular with meaning	Plural with meaning
Name of Tenses	**Verb form used in Tenses**
Present simple / indefinite	Verb / verb + s/es
Present continuous/Progressive	Is/am/are + verb + ing
Present perfect	Has / have + third form of verb
Present perfect continuous	Has/have + been + verb + ing
Past simple / indefinite	Second form of verb only
Past continuous / Progressive	Was/were + verb + ing
Past perfect	Had + third form of verb
Past perfect continuous	Had been + verb + ing
Future simple / indefinite	Shall / will + verb
Future continuous / Progressive	Shall / will + be + verb + ing
Future perfect	Shall/will + Have + past participle
Future perfect continuous	Shall/will + have been + verb + ing

3. The **simple Present tense** is used
   A. To express a **habitual action**.
      For example : I **get** up every day at five o'clock.
   B. To express **general truths**.

   For example : Fortune **favours** the brave.
   C. In **vivid narrative**, as substitute for the simple past.
      For example : Immediately the Sultan **hurries** to his capital.
   D. To indicate a **future event that is part of a fixed programme or time table**.
      For example : The train **leaves** at 5:20 am.
      Note: We can also use **will leave** in place of **leaves**.
   E. It is used to introduce **quotations**.
      For example : Keats **says,** 'A thing of beauty is a joy forever'.
   F. In exclamatory' sentences beginning with **here** and **there** to express what is actually taking place in the present.
      For example : Here comes the bus!
   G. When two actions of the **future** are being talked about, one dependent on the other, the former action is represented by present simple and the latter by future simple.
      For example : We shall go when the child comes back home.

4. **The present continuous tense** is used
   (I) For an action **going on at the time of speaking**.
       For example : The boys are **playing** cricket in the ground.
   (II) For a temporary action that may not be actually happening at the time of speaking but was happening in the recent past and is still happening in recent future.
        For example : I **am reading** Sidney Sheldon now a days.
   (III) To express **changing or developing situations**.
         For example : India is **progressing** day by day.
   (IV) For an action that is planned or arranged to take place in the **near future**.
        For example : I am **going** to cinema tonight.
        Note: But it is not good to use the present continuous for slightly distant future. So, don't say
   (a) I am **going** to cinema next week.
       Rather, use the future simple. So, it is better if you say
   (b) I **will go** to cinema next week.

(V) When the reference is to a particularly obstinate habit, the present continuous is used instead of present simple. An adverb like always, continually, constantly is also used.

For example : It is no use scolding him; he always **does** what is forbidden. (Incorrect)

Note: that his doing what is forbidden has become a die-hard habit. The habit persists in spite of advice or warning. So, we should use the present continuous.

For example : It is no use scolding him; he **is always doing** what is forbidden. (Correct)

5. The **present perfect tense** is used

(I) To indicate the completed activities in the **immediate past**.

For example : He has just gone out.

(II) Action completed in the immediate past or an action of the past whose effect lingers in the present.

For example : **I wrote** three books. (Incorrect)

The given sentence appears to be incomplete. The reader of the sentence immediately queries. 'When did you write three books?" It would be a different case if you said

For example : **I wrote books**.

Then the reader would infer that you wrote books in the past as a profession or hobby. But when you are being so specific as to say "three books", we immediately feel the need of a time frame. Since no time frame is mentioned, we assume it to be 'by now'. So, we have something to the effect.

For example : I have **written** three books by now.

This 'by now' is implied and need not be written. So,

For example : I have **written** three books. (Correct)

(III) The present perfect is never used with adverbs of the past time. In such cases the past simple should be used.

For example : India **has** won the match last week (Incorrect)

"Last week" is not immediate past. You may therefore be tempted to use the present perfect. But remember that the immediate past here does not go unindicated. Last week is being used as an adverb of past time. So,

For example : India **won** the match last week. (Correct)

(IV) To express past actions whose time is not given and not definite - actions with their effect continuing in the present.

For example :

a) I **have** never **known** him to be angry.

b) **Have** you **read** 'Gulliver's Travels'?

(V) To describe the past events when we think more of their effect in the present than of the action itself.

For example : I **have** cut my finger.

(VI) For long actions and situations which started in the near past and went on until very recently.

For example : I **have read** three chapters since this morning.

6. The **present perfect continuous** tense is used for an action, which began at some time in the past and is still continuing. With the present perfect continuous tense an adverb or phrase that expresses time is used.

For example :

(a) I **have been reading** this book since morning.

(b) They **have been building** the bridge for several months.

7. The **simple past tense** is used

(I) To indicate an action **completed in the past**. Generally, adverbs or adverb phrases of past time are used in the past simple tense.

For example:

(a) The steamer **sailed** yesterday.

(b) He **went** home some time back.

(II) To express imaginary present situations or imaginary future events that may not happen.

For example :

(a) If I **had** longer holidays, I would be very happy.

(b) If I **got** rich, I would travel all over the world.

(III) When this tense is used without an adverb of time, then time may be either implied or indicated by the context.

For example : I **didn't** sleep well. (i.e., last night)

(IV) For past habits 'used to' is added to the verb.

For example : She used to **carry** an umbrella.

8. The **past continuous** tense is used

(I) To denote an action going on at some time in the past. The time of the action may or may not be indicated.

For example :

(a) It **was getting** darker.

(b) We **were listening** to the radio all evening.

(II) When a new action happened in the middle of a longer action. In this case Past simple and Past continuous are used together. Past simple is used for the new action.

For example : The Light **went** out while **I was reading**.

(III) For persistent habits in the past.

For example : She **was always chewing** gum.

9. The **past perfect tense** is used when **two actions happened in the past**. In this case it is necessary to show which action happened earlier than the other. Here **past perfect is used for the action, which happened earlier**.

For example :

(a) When I reached the station the train **had started**.

(b) **I had done** my exercise when Hari **came** to see me.

10. **Past perfect continuous tense** is used when an action that began before a certain point of time in the past & was continuing at the given point of time in the sentence. A time expression like **since last year, for the last few days** is generally put after perfect continuous tense.

For example : At that time he **had been writing** a novel for **two months**.

Here, **At that time** is the given point of time and **for two months** is the point of time in the past.

11. The **simple future** is used for an action that has **still to take place**.

For example :

(a) I **shall** see him tomorrow.

(b) Tomorrow **will** be Sunday.

12. The **future continuous** tense

(I) Represents an action as going on at **sometime in the future**.

For example : I **shall be reading** the paper then.

(II) Represents the future events that are planned.

For example : He **will be meeting** us next week.

13. The **future perfect tense** is used to indicate the **completion of an event by a certain future time**.

For example : I **shall have written** my exercise by that time.

14. The **future perfect continuous tense** indicates an action represented as being in progress over a period of time that will end in the future. Generally time period is mentioned along with it.

For example : By next July we shall have been living here for four years.

15. Other rules to be followed : Events occurring at the same time must be given in the same tense.

For example : When he fainted his brother was with him.

16. Will or Shall cannot be used twice in the same sentence even if both the actions refer to the future tense.

For example :

(a) I shall come if he will call me. (Wrong)

(b) I shall come if he calls me. (Right)

17. With the phrases as if and as though the past tense and plural form of the verb should be used.

For example :

(a) He behaves as if he is a king. (Wrong)

(b) He behaves as if he were a king. (Right)

18. With the word 'wish' four verbs are used namely were, had, could, would. 'Were' is used when the wish seems to be unrealisable.

For example : I wish I were a king.

'Had' is used when our wish is a lament over the past happening. *For example* : I wish I had accepted that job. 'Would' is used when we refer to the future. *For example* : I wish I would get a ticket.

'Could' is used when we wish that something that has happened already should have happened otherwise.

For example : He did not go because he was busy yesterday. I wish he could go with you.

19. 'For' is used for a period of time. *For example* : He has been working for two hours.

'Since' is used with a point of time. *For example* : He has been working since morning.

20. In case of conditional sentences 'had' and 'would have' are used.

For example : If I had met him I would have invited him.

ARTICLES

1. **A** or **an** does not refer to a particular person or thing. It leaves indefinite the person or thing spoken of.

For example : I saw a doctor. (means I saw any doctor)

2. **An** is used before a word beginning with vowel sound (please note a word beginning with vowel sound and not necessarily a vowel itself).

For example : an ass, an enemy, an inkstand, an orange, an umbrella, an hour.

3. **An** is placed before an abbreviation if the first letter of an abbreviation is F, H. L, M, N, R, S or X.

For example :

(a) An MBA was required for the post.

(b) An SAO is an officer of high rank

4. A is used before a word beginning with a consonant sound.

For example : a boy, a woman a horse, a one-rupee note, a university, a European (both university and European begin with a consonant sound of 'yu')

5. **A** and **an** are used with words 'few' and 'little' if they refer to a small number or a small amount. Words 'few' and 'little' without the articles means almost none.

For example:

(a) We have little time to spare. (means almost no time)

(b) We have a little time to spare. (means some time)

(c) Few persons were present at the meeting. (means almost no one was present)

(d) A few persons were present at the meeting. (means some were present)

6. A is used in the following senses :

A) In its original numerical sense of one.

For example:

(a) Not a word was said.

(b) A word to the wise is sufficient.

(B) In the vague sense of a **certain time.**

(C) In the sense of any, to single out an individual as the representative of a class.

For example : A pupil should obey his teacher.

(D) To make a common noun of a proper noun.

For example : A Daniel came to judgement. (A Daniel = A very wise man)

7. **The** points out a particular person or thing or someone or something already referred to.

For example :

(a) I saw the doctor. (means I saw some particular doctor)

(b) The book you want is out of print.

8. **The** is used with names of gulfs, rivers, seas, oceans, groups of islands and mountain ranges.

For example :

The Persian Gulf, The Red Sea, The Indian Ocean, The British Isles, The Alps.

9. **The** is used before the name of certain books.

For example : The Vedas, The Puranas, The Ramayana.

But we never say 'The Valmiki's Ramayana'. The is not used when the name of a book is mentioned along with the author's name. So, 'Valmiki's Ramayana' is correct.

10. **The** is used before the names of things unique of their kind.

For example : the sun, the sky, the ocean, the sea.

11. **The** is used before a plural common noun if it refers to a particular group among the class and not the whole class.

For example : Drive away the cows from the field.

12. **The** is used before a proper noun only when it is qualified by an adjective.

For example : The great Rani of Jhansi, the immortal Kalidas.

13. **The** is used before superlatives.
For example :
(a)   Sachin was the best batsman in the world.
(b)   The best person should win.

14. **The** noun if emphasis is laid on the use of such a noun. Here, noun can be proper or abstract noun
(a)   the time for doing it.
(b)   occasion to help the distressed.

15. **The** is used with ordinals.
For example :
(a)   He was the first student to finish his homework.
(b)   The second chapter of the book is very interesting.

16. **The** is used before an adjective when the noun is understood.
For example :
(a)   The poor are always with us. (Here poor means poor people which is understood.)
(b)   The weak and the strong. (Here weak means weak people and strong means strong people.)

17. No article is used before a common noun when it refers to all the members of the class.
For example :
(a)   Man is mortal.
(b)   Fish has high protein content.
(c)   What kind of flower is it?

18. The is used before a common noun to give it the meaning of an abstract noun.
For example : The devil in him begins its misdeeds now and then.

19. No article is used before the names of materials such as gold, stone, wine, iron, wheat, wood, cloth.
For example :
(a)   Gold is a precious metal.
(b)   Wheat grows in Uttar Pardesh, Haryana and Madhya Pardesh.
(c)   Iron is a useful metal.
Note: But it is correct to say
For example : An iron is a useful gadget.
Because here we are not taking about material iron, but the object which is used to make clothes smooth.

20. No article is used before proper nouns.
For example :
(a)   Delhi is the capital of India.
(b)   Newton was a great philosopher.
But consider the following examples where an article is used before a proper noun.
(a)   This man is a second Newton.
(b)   Bombay is the Manchester of India.
Here Newton and Manchester are not used as proper nouns but as common nouns. The first sentence means that this man is as great as Newton and the second sentence means that Bombay is a great manufacturing city like Manchester.

21. No articles are used before a common noun used in its widest sense.
For example :
(a)   The science has developed much in the past hundred years. (Incorrect)
(b)   Science has developed much in the past hundred years. (Correct).

22. No article is used before the noun following 'Kind of':
For example :
(a)   What kind of a hobby is this? (Incorrect)
(b)   What kind of hobby is this? (Correct)

23. No article is used before abstract nouns.
For example :
(a)   Wisdom is the gift of heaven.
(b)   Honesty is the best policy.
But consider the following examples where an article is used before an abstract noun.
(a)   The wisdom of Solomon is famous.
(b)   I cannot forget the kindness with which he treated me.
Here the article is used before the abstract noun as the abstract noun has been qualified by an adjective or adjectival clause.

24. No article is used before languages, subject of arts and science.
For example :
(a)   We are studying English.
(b)   Geometry is the toughest subject I have ever studied.

25. No article is used before words such as school, college, church, bed, table, hospital, market, prison.
For example :
(a)   I went to school till last year.
(b)   I have never been to hospital.
But an article is used before these words when reference is made to a definite place.

26. No article is used before the name of relations like father, mother, aunt, uncle.
For example : Mother would like to see you.
But if someone else's mother is being talked about then **the** should be used.
For example : The mother would like to see you.

27. Article should not be used before positions that are held at one time by one person only.
For example :
(a)   S D Sharma was elected the president of the country. (Incorrect)
(b)   S D Sharma was elected president of the country. (Correct)

28. Please consider this sentence
(a)   I have a black and white cat.
Here I mean that I have one cat that is partly black and partly white.
Now, consider this sentence
For example : I have a black and a white cat.
Here I mean that I have two cats one is black and the other white. Hence the rule is that when two or more adjectives qualify the same noun, the article is used before the first adjective only. But when they qualify different nouns, the article is used before each adjective separately.
Consider one more *example.*
(a)   The President and Chairman is absent.
(b)   The President and the Chairman are present.
Sentence a means that only one person is acting as president as well as chairman. Sentence b means that two different persons are acting as the President and the Chairman and both the persons are present.

ADJECTIVES

Adjectives are the words that describe the qualities of a noun or pronoun in a given sentence.

CONSIDER THE FOLLOWING :
1. Tell which sentence is correct
    (a) Flowers are plucked freshly.
    (b) Flowers are plucked fresh.
    Sentence b is correct as, adjective is correctly used with a verb when some quality of the subject rather than verb is to be expressed. Here, fresh describes the word Flowers (a noun) and not plucked (a verb).

RULES REGARDING DEMONSTRATIVE ADJECTIVE :
2. **This** and **that** are used with the singular nouns and these and those are used with plural nouns
    For example :
    (a) This mango is sour.
    (b) These mangoes are sour.
    (c) That boy is industrious
    (d) Those boys are industrious.
3. **This** and **these** indicate something near to the speaker while that and those indicate something distant to the speaker.
    For example :
    (a) This girl sings.
    (b) These girls sing.
    (c) That girl sings.
    (d) Those girls sing.

RULES REGARDING DISTRIBUTIVE ADJECTIVES:
4. **Each** is used when reference is made to the individuals forming any group. Each is also used when the number of the group is limited and definite.
    For example :
    (a) I was in Shimla for five days and it rained each day.
    Every is used when reference is made to total group or when the number is indefinite.
    For example :
    (a) Every seat was taken.
    (b) I go for a movie every week.
    (c) Leap year falls in every fourth year.
5. Each, either, neither and every are always followed by the singular noun.
    For example :
    (a) Each boy must take his turn.
    (b) Every word of it is false.
    (c) Neither accusation is true.

RULES REGARDING ADJECTIVES OF QUANTITY:
6. **Some** is used in affirmative sentences to express quantity or degree.
    For example : I shall buy some bananas.
    Any is used in the negative or interrogative sentences to express quantity or degree.
    For example :

(a) I shall not buy any bananas.
(b) Have you bought any bananas?
But some is an exception to the above rule. Some is used in interrogative sentences, which are commands or requests.
For example : Will you please lend me some money?
7. **Few** is used for countable objects and *little* is used for non-countable objects.
8. Little means not much. So use of the word little has a negative meaning.
    For example :
    (a) There is little hope of his recovery.
    (b) He has little appreciation of hard work.
        A little means some though not much. So, use of a little has a positive meaning.
    For example :
    (a) There is a little hope of his recovery.
    (b) He has a little appreciation of hard work.
    The little means not much but all there is.
    For example :
    (a) The little information he had was quite reliable.
    (b) The little knowledge of management he possessed was not sufficient to stand him in good stead.
9. Few means not many. So use of the word few has a negative meaning.
    For example : Few men are free from faults.
    A few means some. So use of 'a few' has a positive meaning.
    For example : A few men are free from faults.
    The few means not many, but all there are.
    For example : The few remarks that he made were very good.
10. Only uncountable nouns follow much, little, some, enough, sufficient and whole.
    For example :
    (a) I ate some rice.
    (b) There are not enough spoons.

RULES REGARDING INTERROGATIVE ADJECTIVES :
11. **What** is used in the general sense and **which** is used in a selective sense.
    For example :
    (a) Which of you haven't brought your book?
    (b) What sort of man is he?

RULES REGARDING DEGREES OF COMPARISON OF ADJECTIVES :
12. The comparative form ending in 'er' is used when we are comparing one quality in two persons.
    For example : Anjali is wiser than Rahul.
    But if we wish to compare two qualities in the same person then the comparative form ending in 'er' is not used.
    For example : Anjali is wise than brave.
13. When two objects are compared with each other, the latter term of comparison must exclude the former.

For example :

(a) Delhi is bigger than any other city in India.

If we say

(b) Delhi is bigger than any city in India.

Then we are saying Delhi is bigger than Delhi, as any city in India includes Delhi also. And this is obviously wrong.

14. In a comparison by means of a superlative the latter term should include the former.

For example :

(a) Delhi is the biggest of all cities in India.

(b) Of all men he is the strongest.

Kindly note the difference in this and the previous rule.

15. **Later** and **latest** refer to time.

For example :

(a) He came later than I expected.

(b) This is the latest news.

Latter and **last** refer to position.

For example :

(a) The last player could not bat as he was injured.

(b) The latter chapters are very interesting.

Latter is used when there are two only, last when there are more than two.

For example :

(a) Of Manohar, Syam and Joshi, the latter is a driver. (Incorrect)

(b) Of Manohor, Syam and Joshi, the last is a driver. (Correct)

16. **Elder** and **eldest** are used only of persons (usually members of the same family).

For example :

(a) My elder sister is doing MBA from IIM, Ahemdabad.

(b) My eldest brother is getting married today.

Older and **oldest** are used of both persons and things.

For example :

(a) This is the oldest building in the city.

(b) Anthony is the oldest boy in the class.

17. Further means more distant or advanced whereas farther is a variation of further and means at a distance – both the words can be used to indicate physical distance.

For example :

(a) No one discussed the topic further.

(b) Calcutta is farther from the equator than Colombo.

18. The comparative degree is generally followed by 'than', but comparative adjectives ending in 'is' or 'are' are followed by the preposition 'to'.

For example :

(a) Raj is inferior to Aman in intelligence.

(b) Aman is superior to Raj in intelligence.

(c) He is junior to me.

(d) Who was captain prior to Dhoni?

19. Adjectives such as square, round, perfect, eternal, universal, unique do not admit of different degrees. So they cannot be compared. Thus strictly speaking we cannot say that a thing is more square more round or more perfect. But sometimes we do make exceptions to this rule.

For example : This is the most perfect specimen I have seen.

20. When the comparative form is used to express selection from two of the same kind or class, it is followed by 'of' and preceded by 'the'.

For example :

(a) Raj is stronger of the two boys.

21. When 'than' or 'as' is followed by the third person pronoun, the verb is to be repeated.

For example : Raj is not as clever as his brother is.

22. When 'than' or 'as' is followed by first or second person pronoun, the verb can be omitted.

For example : He is more intelligent than you.

23. In comparing two things or classes of things the comparative should be used.

For example :

(a) Of two evils choose the lesser (not least).

(b) Which is the better (not best) of the two?

24. A very common form of error is exemplified in the following sentence.

(a) The population of London is greater than any town in India.

(b) The population of London is greater than that of any town in India.

Sentence b is correct as the comparison is between the population of London and the population of any town in India.

25. Double comparatives and superlatives should be avoided.

For example :

(a) Seldom had the little town seen a more costlier funeral. (Wrong)

(b) Seldom had the little town seen a costlier funeral. (Right)

(c) Seldom had the little town seen a more costly funeral. (Right)

26. Preferable has the force of comparative and is followed by to. Phrase 'more preferable' should not be used.

For example :

(a) Coffee is more preferable to tea. (Wrong)

(b) Coffee is preferable to tea. (Right)

27. Less refers to quantity whereas fewer refers to number.

For example :

(a) No fewer than fifty miners were killed in the explosion.

(b) We do not sell less than ten kg of tea.

28. Certain adjectives do not really admit of comparison because their meaning is already superlative. Such words are unique, ideal, perfect, complete, universal, entire, extreme, chief, full, square, round. Therefore phrases like most unique, more round, fullest etc. are wrong.

29. If there is a gradual increase it is generally expressed with two comparatives and not with positives.

For example :

(a) It grew hot and hot. (Incorrect)

(b) It grew hotter and hotter. (Correct)

OTHER COMMON RULES :

30. 'Verbal' means 'of or pertaining to words' whereas 'oral' means 'delivered by word of mouth or not written'. Hence the opposite of written is oral, not verbal.

For example :

(a) His written statement differs in several important respects from his oral (not verbal) statement.

(b) The boy was sent with a verbal message to the doctor.

31. 'Common' means shared by all concerned. If a fact is a common Knowledge, it means the knowledge of the fact is shared by all. Everyone knows about it. 'Mutual' means in relation to each other. If you and I are mutual admirers, it means I admire you and you admire me. We might also have a common admirer who admires both of us.

    (a) We stopped smoking on the advice of a mutual friend. (Incorrect)

    (b) We stopped smoking on the advice of a common friend (Correct)

    It is apparent that there are two or more than two of us. Apart from us, there is a person (friend). Since he is a friend to all of us, this friend is being shared by all of us. So, he is a common friend. Now, look at this sentence.

For example : We stopped smoking on mutual advice. It means I advised you not to smoke and you advised me not to smoke.

OTHER COMMON ERRORS :

32. Other common errors.

    (a) These kind of questions is often asked in the examinations. (Incorrect)

    (b) This kind of question is often asked in the examinations. (Correct)

    (c) He is as good if not better than his brother. (Incorrect)

    (d) He is as good as if not better than his brother. (Correct)

    (e) The future do not hold much for you. (Incorrect)

    (f) The future does not hold much for you. (Correct)

VERBS

1. Two or more singular subjects connected by 'and' usually take a verb in the plural.

   For example : Hari and Rama are there.

2. If two singular nouns refer to the same person or thing, the verb must be singular.

   For example : My friend and benefactor has come.

3. If two subjects together express one idea, the verb may be in the singular.

   For example : The horse and carriage is at the door.

4. Two or more singular subjects connected by 'or', 'nor', either... or, neither...nor take a verb in the singular.

   For example : Neither he nor I was there.

   But when subjects joined by 'or', 'nor' are of different numbers, the verb must be plural, and the plural subject must be placed next to the verb.

   For example : Rama and his brothers have done this.

   When the subjects joined by 'or', 'nor' are of different persons, the verb agrees in person with the nearest one.

   For example :

   (a) Either he or I am mistaken.

   (b) Neither you nor he is to blame.

5. When words are joined to a singular subject by 'with', 'together with', 'in addition to', 'as well as', then also number of the verb remains singular.

   For example : The Chief with all his men, was massacred.

6. Following examples exemplify the common mistakes committed:

   (a) His diet was abstemious, his prayers long and fervent. (Wrong as subjects are not in the same number.)

   (b) His diet was abstemious, his prayers were long and fervent. (Right)

   (c) He never has and never will take such strong measures. (Wrong)

   (d) He never has taken, and never will take such strong measures. (Right)

   (e) Ten new members have been enrolled and seven resigned (Wrong)

   (f) Ten new members have been enrolled and seven have resigned. (Right)

   (g) Being a very hot day, I remained in my tent. (Wrong as participle being is referring to none)

   (h) It being a very hot day, I remained in my tent. (Right)

   (i) Sitting on the gate, a scorpion stung him. (Wrong as participle sitting is not referring to any word)

   (j) While he was sitting on the gate, a scorpion stung him (Right)

7. The verb lay (lay, laid, laid) is transitive and is always followed by an object. The verb lie (lie, lay, lain) is intransitive and cannot have an object.

   For example :

   (a) Lay the child to sleep.

   (b) Let me lie here.

   (c) I laid the book on the table.

AGREEMENT OF THE SUBJECT WITH THE VERB:

1. A verb must agree with its subject in number and person. Often due to "Error of Proximity" the verb is made to agree in number with a noun near it instead of with its proper subject.

   For example :

   (a) The quality of the mangoes were not good. (Wrong since subject is quality, a singular and not mangoes.)

   (b) The quality of the mangoes was not good (Right).

   (c) His knowledge of Indian vernaculars are far beyond the common. (Wrong)

   (d) His knowledge of Indian vernaculars is far beyond the common. (Right)

2. Verb should be singular even when some words are joined to a singular subject by 'with', 'as well as' etc,

   For example :

   (a) The chairman, with the directors, is to be present.

   (b) Silver, as well as cotton, has fallen in prices.

3. Two or more singular subjects connected by 'or', 'nor' require singular verb.

   For example :

   (a) No nook or corner was left unexplored.

   (b) Our happiness or our sorrow is largely due to our own actions.

4. If two singular nouns express one idea, the verb is in the singular.

   For example :

   (a) Bread and Butter are essential for one's life. (Incorrect)

   (b) Bread and Butter is essential for one's life. (Correct)

5. **Either, neither, each, everyone, many a** must be followed by a singular verb.

   For example :

   (a) Neither of the two men was very strong.

   (b) Every one of the prisons is full.

   (c) Many a man has done so.

   (d) He asked whether either of the applicants was suitable.

6. When the subjects joined by 'or', 'nor' are of different numbers, the verb *must* be plural, and the plural must be placed next to the verb.

   For example :

   (a) Neither Rekha nor her friends was present at the party. (Incorrect)

   (b) Neither Rekha nor her friends were present at the party. (Correct)

7. When a plural noun denotes some specific quantity or amount considered as a whole, the verb is generally singular.

   For example :

   (a) Five hours are too short a time to judge one's character. (Incorrect)

   (b) Five hours is too short a time to judge one's character. (Correct)

   This is so because five hours is considered as one chunk.

8. **Two nouns** qualified by each or every, even though connected by 'and' require a singular verb.

   For example : **Every boy and every girl was given a packet of sweets.**

9. 'None' though singular commonly takes a plural verb.

   For example : None are so deaf as those who will not hear.

10. Tell which sentence is correct.

    (a) Put in to bat first, a huge total was expected from India.

    (b) Put in to bat first, India was expected to pile up a huge total.

    Now: who has been put in to bat first? A huge total of India? Common sense tells us it must be India. But the sentence a, as it stands, appears otherwise. So, sentence b is correct.

    (a) Being a rainy day, I decided to take my umbrella.

    (b) It being a rainy day, I decided to take my umbrella.

    The sentence a, as it stands, gives us the impression that being a rainy day qualifies I. This is simply not true. I am not a rainy day. So sentence b is correct.

11. **When** a plural noun denotes some specific quantity or amount considered as a whole, the verb is generally singular.

    For example :

    (a) One hundred paise is equal to one rupee.

    (b) Six miles is a long distance.

    (c) Fifty thousand rupees is a large sum.

ADVERBS

A word that modifies the meaning of a verb is called an Adverb.

SOME IMPORTANT RULES :

1. Adverbs of manner such is well, fast, quickly, carefully, calmly etc. are placed after the verb if there is no object and after the object if there is one.

   For example :

   (a) It is raining heavily.

   (b) She speaks English well.

2. Adverbs of time such as always, often, sometimes, never, generally, ever, merely, seldom etc. are placed before the verb they qualify.

   For example :

   (a) I seldom meet him. (Right)

   (b) I meet him seldom. (Wrong)

   Adverbs of degree refer to words which show "how much", "in what degree" or "to what extent" does the action takes place.

   CONSIDER THE FOLLOWING:

3. Meaning of too is more than enough. Too denotes some kind of excess.

   For example :

   (a) He is too weak to walk.

   (b) It is never too late.

   Hence, use of very in place of too is wrong.

   For example : Instead of saying that

   (a) Cow's milk is too nutritious

   We should say that

   (b) Cow's milk is very nutritious.

4. Enough is placed after the word it qualifies.

   For example : Everyone should be strong enough to support one's family.

   It will be wrong if we write 'Everyone should be enough strong to support one's family'.

5. Much is used with past participles.

   For example :

   (a) He was much disgusted with his life.

   (b) The news was much surprising.

   Very is used with present participles.

   For example :

   (a) He is very disgusted with his life.

   (b) The news is very surprising.

6. Very and much are also used to emphasise superlative form of adjectives/adverbs-

   For example :

   (a) Rishi is the very best boy in his class.

   (b) Rishi is much the best boy in his class.

   Adverbs of Affirmation or Negation refer to words that assert the action emphatically.

Consider these *examples* :
(a) He certainly was a winner among them.
(b) Luckily he survived the crash.

CONSIDER THE FOLLOWING :

7. No sooner should always be followed by than.
    For example :
    (a) No sooner I saw him I trembled with fear. (Wrong)
    (b) No sooner did I see him than I trembled with fear. (Right)
8. 'Not' should not be used with the words which have negative meaning if we want the sentence to be negative.
    For example :
    (a) I received no letter neither from him nor from her. (Wrong)
    (b) I received letter neither from him nor from her. (Right)
9. 'Of course' is used to denote a natural consequence. It should not be used in place of certainly, undoubtedly.
    For example :
    (a) Of course he is the best player. (Wrong)
    (b) He is certainly the best player. (Right)

FOLLOWING ARE COMMON RULES OF ADVERBS IN GENERAL:

10. Only is used before the word it qualifies.
     For example :
     (a) Only I spoke to him.
     (b) I only spoke to him.
     (c) I spoke to him only.
11. Else is followed by but and not by than.
     For example : It is nothing else but hypocrisy.
12. 'As' is often used in a sentence though there is no need for it. *For example* :
     (a) He is elected as the President. (Wrong)
     (b) He is elected President. (Right)
13. 'Perhaps' means possibly whereas 'probably' means most likely. *For example* :
     (a) Where is Govinda? Perhaps he is not here. (Wrong)
     (b) Where is Govinda? Probably he is not here. (Right)

PREPOSITIONS

1. **In** is used with the names of countries and large towns; **at** is used when speaking of small towns and villages.
    For example :
    (a) I live in Delhi.
    (b) I live at Rohini in Delhi.
2. **In** and **at** are used in speaking of things at rest; **to** and **into** are used in speaking of things in motion.
    For example :
    (a) He is in bed.
    (b) He is at the top of the class.
    (c) He ran to school
    (d) He jumped into the river.
    (e) The snake crawled into its hole.
3. **On** is often used in speaking of things at rest; and **upon** for the things in motion. *For example*:
    (a) He sat on a chair.
    (b) The cat sprang upon the table.
4. **Till** is used for time and **to** is used for place.
    For example :
    (a) He slept till eight o'clock.
    (b) He walked to the end of the street.
5. **With** often denotes the instrument and **by** the agent.
    For example :
    (a) He killed two birds with one shot.
    (b) He was stabbed by a lunatic with a dagger.
6. **Since** is used before a noun or phrase denoting some point of time and is preceded by a verb in the perfect tense.
    For example :
    (a) I have eaten nothing since yesterday.
    (b) He has been ill since Monday last.
    From is also used before a noun or phrase denoting some point of time but is used with non-perfect tense.
    For example :
    (a) I commenced work from 1st January.
    (b) He will join school from tomorrow.

For is used with a period of time.
For example :
(a) He has been ill for five days.
(b) He lived in Bombay for five years.
7. Use of **in** before a period of time means at the end of period, but use of **within** before a period of time means before the end of the period.
    For example :
    (a) I shall return in an hour. (means I shall return at the end of an hour).
    (b) I shall return within an hour. (means I shall return before the end of an hour).
8. **Scarcely** should be followed by **when** and not by **but**.
    For example : Scarcely had he gone, when **(not** than) a policeman knocked at the door.
9. The phrase 'seldom or ever' is wrong 'Seldom or never' is right.
    For example : Such goods are made for export, and are **seldom or never** used in this country.
10. Examine the following sentence
     (a) This is as good, if not better than that. (Wrong)
     (b) This is as good as, if not better than, that. (Right)
     (c) This is as good as that, if not better. (Right)
11. **Beside** means at the side of while **besides** means in addition to. *For example* :
     (a) Beside the ungathered rice he lay.
     (b) Besides being fined, he was sentenced to a term of imprisonment.
12. **Above** and **Below** merely denote position While **over** and **under** also carry a sense of covering or movement.
     (a) The bird flew above the lake. (Wrong)
     (b) The bird flew over the lake. (Correct)
     Here over is used to denote upward position and movement also.

13. **During** is used when reference is made to the time within which something happens. **For** is used when we are talking about how long something lasts.

(a) There are few incidents of irregularity **for** the emergency years. (Wrong)

(b) There are few incidents of irregularity during the emergency years. (Correct)

14. **Compare** is followed by **to** when it shows that two things are alike. It is followed by **with** when we look at the ways in which two things are like and unlike each other. *For example* :

(a) Sanath Jayasuria's batting may be compared to the sales of a useful book, they score right from the beginning. (Right)

(b) Sanath Jayasuria's batting may be compared with the sales of a useful book; they score right from the beginning. (Wrong)

(c) If we compare Delhi University with the regional ones, we find the former to be much more efficient. (Right)

(d) If we compare Delhi University to the regional ones, we find the former to be much more efficient. (Wrong)

CONJUNCTIONS

1. **Since** as conjunction means
   (A) From and after the time when.
      For example :
      (a) Many things have happened since I left the school.
      (b) I have never seen him since that unfortunate event happened.
   (B) Seeing that,
      For example :
      (a) Since you wish it, it shall be done.
      (b) Since that is the case, I shall excuse you.

2. **Or** is used
   (A) To introduce an alternative.
      For example :
      (a) You must work or starve.
      (b) You may take this book or that one.
      (c) He may study law **or** medicine **or** engineering **or** he may enter into trade.
   (B) To introduce an alternative name or synonym.
      For example : The violin **or** fiddle has become the leading instrument of the modern orchestra.
   (C) To mean otherwise.
      For example : We must hasten or night will overtake us.

3. If is used to mean
   (A) On the condition or supposition that.
      For example :
      (a) If he is here, I shall see him.
      (b) If that is so, I am content.
   (B) Admitting that.
      For example : If I am blunt, I am at least honest.
   (C) Whether
      For example : I asked him if he would help me.
   (D) Whenever.
      For example : If I feel any doubt I enquire.

4. **That** is used
   (A) To express a reason or cause.
      For example :
      (a) Not that I loved Caesar less but that I loved Rome more.
      (b) He was annoyed that he was contradicted.
   (B) To express a purpose and is equivalent to in order that.
      For example : He kept quiet that the dispute might cease.
   (C) To express a consequence, result or effect.
      For example : He bled so profusely that he died.

5. **Lest** is used to express a negative purpose and is equivalent to 'in order that... not', 'for fear that'.
   For example :
   (a) He lied lest he should be killed.
   (b) I was alarmed lest we should be wrecked.

6. **While** is used to mean
   (A) During that time, as long as.
      For example : while there is life there is hope.
   (B) At the same time that.
      For example : While he found fault, he also praised.

7. **Only** means except that, but, were it not that.
   For example :
   (a) A very pretty woman, only she squints a little.
   (b) The day is pleasant, only rather cold.

8. The conjunctions **after, before, as soon as, until** are not followed by clause in the future tense. Present simple or present perfect tense is used to express a future event.
   For example :
   (a) I will phone you after I arrive here.
   (b) I will phone you after I have arrived here.

9. **As if** used in the sense of as it would be is generally followed by a subject + were + complement.
   For example :
   (a) He loves you as if you were his own child.
   (b) Sometimes she weeps and sometimes she laughs as if she were mad.

10. The clause that begins with **as if** should be put into the simple past tense, if the preceding clause expresses a past action. But if it expresses a past action it should be followed by the past perfect tense.
    For example :
    (a) He behaves as if he were a lord.
    (b) He behaved as if he had been a lord

11. While **as long as** is used to express time in sense of how long, **Until** is used to express time in sense of before.

    For example :

    (a) Until you work hard you will improve. (Wrong)

    (b) As long as you work hard you will improve. (Right)

    (c) He learnt little as long as he was 15 years old. (Wrong)

    (d) He learnt little until he was 15 years old. (Right)

12. **No sooner** should be followed by verb + subject and than should begin another clause.

    For example :

    (a) No sooner had I reached the station than the train left.

    (b) No sooner did the bell ring than all the students rushed in.

13. When **as well as** is used, finite verb should agree in number and person with the first subject.

    For example : He as well as us is innocent.

14. **As well as** should never be used in place of **and** if the first subject is preceded by the word 'both'.

    For example :

    (a) Both Rani as well as Kajol came. (Wrong)

    (b) Both Rani and Kajol came. (Right)

15. **Because** is generally used when the reason is the most important part of a sentence.

    For example : Some people like him because he is honest and hard working.

    Since is used when the reason is already known or is less important than the chief statement.

    For example : Since you refuse to cooperate, I shall have to take legal steps.

    For is used when reason is given is an afterthought.

    For example : The servant must have opened the box, for no one else had the key. For never comes at the beginning of the sentence and for is always preceded by a comma.

16. **Scarcely** should be followed by when and not by than.

    (a) Scarcely had he arrived than he had to leave again. (Wrong)

    (b) Scarcely had he arrived when he had to leave again. (Right)

17. Conjunctions such as either..or, neither.. nor, not only..but also, both..and, whether, or etc. always join two words or phrases belonging to the same parts of speech.

    For example :

    (a) Either he will ask me or you. (Wrong)

    (b) He will ask either me or you. (Right)

    (c) Neither he reads nor write English (Wrong)

    (d) He neither reads nor writes English. (Right)

    (e) Either you shall have to go home or stay here. (Wrong)

    (f) You shall have either to go home or stay here. (Right)

18. Conjunctions like neither...nor, either..or, should be followed by the same part of speech.

    For example :

    (a) He neither agreed to my proposal nor to his. (Wrong)

    (b) He agreed neither to my proposal nor to his. (Right)

19. Conjunction is not used before an interrogative adverb or interrogative pronoun in the indirect narration.

    For example :

    (a) He asked me that where I stayed. (Wrong)

    (b) He asked me where I stayed. (right)

20. **Although** goes with yet or a comma in the other clause.

    For example :

    (a) Although Manohar is hardworking but he does not get a job. (Wrong)

    (b) Although Manohar is hard working, yet he does not get a job. (Right)

21. **Nothing else** should be followed by 'but' not by 'than',

    For example :

    (a) Mr. Bureaucrat! This is nothing else than red-tapism. (Wrong)

    (b) Mr. Bureaucrat! This is nothing else but red-tapism. (Right)

22. The correlative conjunctions **indeed... but** are used to emphasise the contrast between the first and the second parts of the statement.

    For example :

    (a) I am indeed happy with my school but it produces famous men. (Wrong)

    (b) I am indeed happy with my school but it does not produce famous men. (Right)

    (c) I am indeed happy with my school that it produces famous men. (Right)

23. In a **"not only ... but also..."** sentence, the verb should agree with the noun or pronoun mentioned second, that is; the one after 'but also', because this is the part being emphasised.

    For example :

    (a) Not only the students but also the teacher were responsible for what happened in the class. (Wrong)

    (b) Not only the students but also the teacher was responsible for what happened in the class. (Right)

24. **Such ... as** is used to denote a category whereas **such ...that** emphasises the degree of something by mentioning its consequence.

    For example :

    (a) Each member of the alliance agrees to take such action that it deems necessary. (Wrong)

    (b) Each member of the alliance agrees to take such action as it deems necessary. (Right)

    Here "it seems necessary" is not a consequence of "such action". The sentence wants to imply that the action belongs to the category "as it deems necessary" In other words, what kind of action? Such action as it deems necessary.

    (a) She looked at him in such distress as he had to look away. (Wrong)

    (b) She looked at him in such distress that he had to look away. (Right)

    Here, "he had to look away" is a consequence of "she looked at him in such distress." In other words, the degree of the distress of looking at him was such that (not as) he had to look away.

PHRASAL VERBS

Phrasal Verbs are a particular kind of expression, wherein the verb is made of two or more components. Mostly the combining components are verbs and prepositions. When divided these components will have a meaning of their own but would not suggest anything about the meaning of the phrasal verb. Consider the following sentences.

(a) This sword has been **handed down** from father to son in the family for many generations.

(b) I have been **looking forward** to meeting you since long now.

(c) The patient **came out** of the delirium only when given tranquilizers.

(d) We had almost decided to **give up** on the search when we made the discovery.

Phrasal verbs are idiomatic expressions and have a particular meaning different from that of the combining verbs and prepositions. Following are some phrasal verbs with their meanings.

(a) sit in – to attend or take part as a visitor

(b) sit out – to stay till the end of

(c) come round – to accept circumstances and adjust yourself to them

(d) get on – to manage one's life

(e) turn out – to have a particular result

(f) turn up – to arrive unexpectedly

(g) show off – to brag or boast

(h) sort out – to successfully deal with a problem

(i) hand in – to give something to someone in authority

(j) sit down – to take a seat

(k) sit up – to rise from a supine position

(l) give in – to yield to some pressure

(m) come forth – to find something

(o) switch on – to start something

(p) turn down – to refuse or reject an offer

(q) turn in – to expose

(r) look into – probe, or investigate a matter

(s) look after – take care of

(t) take off – to remove something

(u) put out – to extinguish

(v) try on – to wear some clothes for first time

(w) turn down – lower the volume

(x) turn on – to start a machine

(y) put in – to invest something (matter or abstract)

(z) look out – be careful of some danger

Following are some sentences using Phrasal Verbs

- Don't **throw away** your opportunity to enter this University.

- Many people **believe in** astrology and tarot cards now-a-days.

- Quickly **get in** the car, we're getting late.

- You can **put forward** your point in today's meeting.

- To **sit through** his speech was very difficult.

- I don't understand why you **put up** with his insolent behaviour.

- I could **see through** his intentions the first time I met, but kept quiet to give him a chance to reform.

- Please, **fill in** all the necessary information in this form.

- I am sure you will not **let** me **down**; I've full faith in your capacities.

- Why are you **taking it out** on me? I'm not the one responsible for the mishap.

QUESTION TAGS

Consider the following examples

(1) You wanted that, didn't you?

(2) He is coming tonight, isn't he?

(3) You wouldn't report me, would you?

Now, look at the last part of all the above sentences preceded by the comma. These are very small questions added to the sentence and are called question Tags. Remember only the question tag is a question and not the entire sentence. So, one can say that a Question Tag is an added brief question to a statement. Usually a question tag consists of two words- an auxiliary verb in the positive or negative form and a pronoun.

How to form question tags?

Three things are to be kept in mind while making a question tag :

(a) The right auxiliary Verb to be used in the question.

(b) The right pronouns to be used in the tag.

Both (a) and (b) should be in agreement with the verb and noun in the main statement.

(c) Whether the verb in the question tag should be positive or negative.

Rules to form Question Tags

I. If the main statement is positive, the auxiliary verb will be negative and vice versa e.g.

- He saw that, didn't he?

- But he isn't going to England, is he?

II. If there is a single subject/noun/pronoun in the main sentence, the corresponding pronoun/the same pronoun will be used in the question tag. e.g.,

- **You** are coming with us, aren't **you?**
- **Reena** is leaving tonight, isn't **she?**

III. If there is more than one noun/pronoun in the main sentence then the corresponding pronoun to the active subject will be used in the Question tag. e.g.

- After all this time **you'd** think he'd have forgotten, wouldn't **you?**
- **You** wouldn't refuse me, would **you?**

IV If the verb in the main sentence is an active verb without any auxiliary verb, then the verb used in the Question tag will be the form of verb 'do' that corresponds with the tense in the main sentence.

- He knows it's true, **doesn't** he?

- You wanted to come with me, **didn't** you?
- I told you so, didn't I?
- She never informed us, did she?
- If the main sentence has an auxiliary then it is used in the question tag, but with opposite affirmation, i.e., a positive auxiliary in the main sentence transforms to a negative auxiliary in the question tag and vice versa e.g.
- He **will** be coming, **won't** he?
- You **were** there at the party, **weren't** you?
- You would appear for this exam, **wouldn't** you?
- He **didn't** call us, **did** he?
- She **doesn't** live here anymore, **does** she?

MODALS

The verbs like can, could, may, might, would, shall, should and ought are called modal verbs or modals. They are used with ordinary verbs to express meanings such as possibility, permission, certainly, etc.

(1) **Can** usually expresses ability or capacity
I can swim across the river.
Can you lift this table?

(2) **Can** is also used to express permission
You can go now.

(3) **May** is a more formal modal used to express permission
You may come in.
May I leave the room now?

(4) **May** is also used to suggest possibility in an affirmative sentence.
He may be at home
It may rain tomorrow.

(5) **Can** is used to suggest possibility in negative/interrogative sentence.
Can this be true?
It cannot be so.

(6) **May** when used in a negative sentence suggests an improbability whereas can suggests impossibility.
He may not come today.
She cannot sing.

(7) **Could** and **might** are used as past tense forms of can and 'may'.
I could swim across the river when I was young.
I thought he might be at home.

(8) **Might** suggests less possibility or probability than may.
I might go to Bangalore next week suggests the probability of going is less than a sentence with 'may' will suggest.

(9) **Could** is used as a polite form of seeking permission or making a request.
Could you pass me the plate?
Could I please talk to Mr. Grover?

(10) **Shall** is used with first person and will in all the persons to denote future action.
I shall need the money tomorrow.
When will you come next?

(11) **Shall** is used with the second and third person to express command, promise or threat.
You shall never come near my child.
You shall be punished for this.
We shall go for a picnic this Sunday.

(12) Will You? indicates an invitation or request.
Will you dine with us tonight?
Will you lend me your car for a week?

(13) **Should** and **would** are used as past forms of shall and will.
I expected that I would get a first class.
She would sit for hours listening to the radio.

(14) **Should** is used to express duty or obligation.
We should obey the laws.
You should keep your promise.

(15) **Should** is used to express a supposition
If it should rain, they will not come.

(16) **Should** can also be used to express probability.
He should be in the library.

(17) **Must** is used to express necessity.
You must improve your spelling.

(18) **Must** is also need to express obligation, and is a stronger word than should.
We must follow the law.

(19) **Must** is also used to express logical certainty.
Living alone in such a big city must be difficult.

(20) **Ought** is used to express moral obligation and is stronger than both should and must.
We ought to love our parents.

(21) **Ought** is also used to express probability sometimes when the probability is very strong.
The book ought to be very useful.

POINTS TO REMEMBER

1. **Abstract Noun :** Abstract noun refers to quality, action or state of a thing that can only be felt by us.
For example : Laughter, greatness, faith, poverty, courage, kindness, fear, bravery, childhood etc. Abstract noun is always uncountable and has no plural form.

2. **Accusative Case :** See Objective case.

3. **Active Voice :** A verb is in the active voice when its form shows that the person or thing denoted by the subject does something or, in other words, is doer of the action.

4. **Adjectives :** Adjective is a word used with a noun to add something to its meaning. Adjective is used with the noun to describe or point out the person, animal, place or thing the noun names, or to tell the number or quantity.

5. **Adverbs :** Adverb is a word that modifies the meaning of a verb, an adjective or another adverb.
For example :
(a)   P T Usha runs fast.
(b)   Govinda reads quite clearly.

6. **Antecedent :** Antecedent is a noun or noun-equivalent to which a relative pronoun refers.
For example : 'Cloud' is antecedent in the sentence. The cloud that thunders does not rain.

7. **Apposition :** When one noun follows another to describe it, the noun which follows is said to be in apposition to the noun which comes before it. Both the nouns are in the same case.
For example : In the sentence, Stephen Hawking, the scientist, has written A Brief History of Time. The noun scientist is in apposition to the noun Stephen Hawking.

8. **Case :** The use of different forms of a noun or pronoun to show its relation to the remaining sentence is called case. Three different types of cases are Nominative case, Objective or Accusative case and Possessive or Genitive case.

9. **Collective Noun :** Collective noun refers to a group of similar persons or things. Though collective noun refers to more than one thing, it is always singular in form.
For example : Army, Family, Herd, and Committee.

10. **Common Noun :** Common noun is a name that can be applied to all the members of a class. In other words it refers to all the persons and things of the same kind. Like proper noun it does not refer to a particular person or thing.
For example : man, woman, elephant, village, crowd, army, family, nation.

11. **Complement :** Complement of the verb is the word or words which are used to make the sense of, the sentence complete.
For example :
(a)   They made him.
(b)   They made him king.
Sentence a carries no complete sense or meaning. But when the word king is added to it, the sentence carries full sense. So, here king is the complement.

12. **Concrete Noun :** Concrete noun is the opposite of abstract noun. Concrete noun refers to a thing that can be identified or sensed by our senses.
For example : House, Brick, Telephone, Rose.

13. **Countable Noun :** As the name suggests, a countable noun is one that can be counted,
For example : ten Girls, 25 rupees. Depending upon how the plural form of a countable noun is obtained, countable noun can be categorised as Regular countable noun and Irregular countable noun.

14. **First Person:** First person denotes the person or persons speaking.

First Person *(Masculine or Feminine)*

Case	Singular	Plural
Nominative	I	We
Possessive	My, mine	Our, ours
Objective	Me	Us

15. **Intransitive Verb :** When a verb is so used in a sentence that its effect is limited to its subject or the doer of the action only, it is called intransitive.
For example : Compare these two sentences.
a)   This boy is eating.
b)   This boy is eating mango.
In sentence a), effect of eating mango is limited to subject, (boy) only. But in sentence b), the effect of eating mango passes from subject (boy) to an object (mango). It is intransitive verb if we get answer to; who eats it?' Hence, sentence a uses intransitive verb but sentence b is not using intransitive verb. It is called transitive verb.

16. **Irregular Countable Noun :** Plural form of these countable nouns is not obtained by adding 's ', 'es' or 'ies' after the word.
For example : plural of person is people, tooth is teeth.

17. **Nominative Case :** Here noun or pronoun is used as the subject of a verb. To find the nominative put "who or what" before the verb.

18. **Noun :** A noun is a word used as the name of a person, place, thing or idea. A noun can be a Common noun or a Proper noun, an Abstract noun or a concrete noun, a countable noun or non-countable noun and a collective noun.

19. **Object:** Also called Predicate. The part which tells something about the subject is called object.

20. **Objective Case:** Also called Accusative Case. Here noun or pronoun is used as the object of the verb. To find the objective case put 'whom' or 'what' before the verb and its subject

21. **Passive Voice :** A verb is in the passive form when its form shows that something is done to the person or thing denoted by the subject.

22. **Personal Pronoun :** Personal pronoun refers to an individual or Individuals. Personal pronouns are of three different types - First person, Second person and Third person.

23. **Possessive Case :** In this form of the noun, ownership or possession is shown. Possessive case is also used to denote authorship, origin, kind etc. The possessive case answers the question 'whose.'

24. **Predicate :** Please see Object.

25. **Preposition :** A preposition is a word placed before a noun or pronoun to show in what relation the person or thing denoted by it stands in regard to something else.

26. **Pronoun :** A pronoun is a word used instead of a noun. Pronouns are classified as personal, relative, reflexive, demonstrative, indefinite, interrogative, reciprocal pronoun.

27. **Proper Noun :** Unlike common noun, proper noun refers to a particular member of a class. Proper noun is the name of some particular person or thing. Proper nouns are always written with a capital letter at the beginning. *For example* : names of all people, places.

28. **Regular Countable Noun :** Plural form of these words is obtained by adding 's', 'es' or converting 'y' to 'ies' after the word. *For example* : plural form of Book is books, city is cities.

29. **Relative Pronoun :** Relative pronoun refers or relates two clauses. Relative pronoun refers to some noun which is called its antecedent.

For example : I met Hari who has just returned.

30. **Second Person :** Second person denotes the person or persons spoken to.

Second Person *(Masculine or Feminine)*

Case	Singular	Plural
Nominative	You	You
Possessive	Your, yours	Your, yours
Objective	You	You

31. **Sentence :** Sentence is a group of words which makes completes sense. In a sentence we name some person or thing and say something about that person or thing.

32. **Subject :** The part which names the person or thing we are speaking about is called subject of the sentence.

33. **Third Person :** Third person denotes the person or persons spoken of,

Third Person			
Singular/ Plural			
Case	Masculine	Feminine	Neuter	All Genders
Nominative	He	She	It	They
Possessive	His	Her, hers	Its	They, their
Objective	Him	Her	It	Them

34. **Transitive Verb :** When an action/word or verb is so used in a sentence that its effect is not limited to its subject only but passes to another person or thing, it is called Transitive verb.

For example : A boy is eating a mango. For details kindly see definition of Intransitive Verb.

35. **Uncountable Noun :** Unlike countable nouns it cannot be counted. *For example* : Water, Milk, Sand, News, information. But if an uncountable thing is placed in a thing that can be counted, then the uncountable noun can be counted.

For example : one bottle of milk. Uncountable nouns can never be plural, though some uncountable nouns may appear to be plurals. *For example* : News.

36. **Voice :** Voice is that form of a verb which shows whether what is denoted by the subject does something or has something done to it. *For example* :

(a)   Rama helps Hari.

(b)   Hari is helped by Rama.

In sentence a, the form of the verb denotes that the person denoted by the subject, Rama, does something. In sentence b, the form of the verb shows that something is done to the person denoted by the subject, Hari.

EXERCISE

DIRECTIONS (Qs. 1-60): *Read each sentence to find out whether there is any error in it. The error, if any, will be in one part of the sentence. The letter of that part is the answer. If there is no error, the answer is (e). (Ignore errors of punctuation, if any).*

1. (a) The driver of that car /(b) is sounding horn for /(c) the last ten minutes /(d) but nobody tells him to stop. /(e) No error

2. (a) If you go on letting /(b) your dog chase cars /(c) he will end by being /(d) run down one day. /(e) No error

3. (a) He heard the guard /(b) blowing the whistle and knew /(c) it is time for him /(d) to enter the train. /(e) No error

4. (a) He telephoned from a public call-box /(b) so that the call /(c) would not be traced /(d) to his own address. /(e) No error

5. (a) It has been better /(b) to put your money in a bank /(c) than to keep it under /(d) your bed in a suitcase. /(e) No error

6. (a) If you would have read /(b) the instructions carefully /(c) you would not have /(d) answered the questions wrongly. /(e) No error

7. (a) I can see through /(b) her sudden friendliness; /(c) she wants me to look over /(d) her dog while she is away. /(e) No error

8. You may not know it (a)/ but this engine is (b)/ claimed to have twice (c)/ as powerful as the previous one. (d)/ No error (e)

9. Nothing ever becomes real (a)/ till it is experienced. (b)/ Even a proverb is no proverb to you (c)/ till your life has illustrated with it. (d)/ No error (e).

10. I remember my childhood days (a)/ when I was used to go (b) to the farm with my father (c) and help him in his work. (d)/ No error (e).

11. I missed the last train (a)/ which I usually catch (b)/ and have to stay at the station (c)/ on my way back home yesterday. (d)/ No error (e).

12. Sureshbabu, who is living (a)/ in this town since 1955, (b)/ is a well-known scholar of history (c)/ and a distinguished musician. (d)/ No error (e).

13. If you had read (a)/ the relevant literature carefully (b)/You would have answered (c)/ most of the questions correctly. (d) No error (e).

14. The house where the dead man was found (a)/ is being guarded by police (b)/ to prevent it from being entered (c)/ and the evidence interfered with (d)/No error (e).

15. We were happy that (a)/ the audience responded well (b)/ and gave all the speakers (c)/ a patiently listening. (d)/ No error (e).

16. He received timely support (a)/ from his elder brother (b)/ who is working abroad (c)/ for the last six years. (d)/ No error (e).

17. The notorious gang opened (a)/ the door quietly and (b)/ escaped in the dark with (c)/ whatever they would collect. (d)/ No error (e).

18. One of the security men (a)/rushed forward and asked (b)/ me whether (c)/ had anything objectionable. (d)/ No error (e).

19. We could not (a)/ believe that one (b)/ of us was (c)/ responsible with the act. (d)/ No error (e).

20. We are now (a)/ reliably learnt that (b)/ he was involved (c)/ in the bank robbery. (d) No error (e).

21. I do not know (a)/ what most people feel (b)/ depressed and dejected (c)/ even with the slightest provocation. (d)/ No error (e).

22. She had such pretty (a)/ that she thinks (b)/ she can afford to be (c)/ careless about her clothes. (d)/ No error (e).

23. After carefully examining (a)/ all the medicine bottles (b)/ he submitted a detailed report (c) to the higher authorities. (d)/ No error (e).

24. All of you have the liberty (a)/ to come home (b)/ as per the convenient (c)/ and discuss the problems. (d)/ No error (e).

25. He was persuaded (a)/ by his friends (b)/ to end his fast (c)/ because of his condition deteriorated. (d) No error (e).

26. I know who (a)/ this job should be (b)/ entrusted to (c)/ for smooth handling. (d)/ No error (e).

27. They have the nasty habit of (a)/ looking down upon people (b)/ and criticised them (c)/ for no reason. (d)/ No error (e).

28. Nowadays, the cost of living (a)/ is so high that (b)/ people find it difficult (c)/ to make both ends meeting. (d)/ No error (e).

29. Karnavati is (a)/ one of the leading (b)/ business centres (c)/ in our state. (d)/ No error (e).

30. As I reached the hospital (a)/ I had found, a great rush of visitors (b)/ whose relatives had been admitted there (c)/ for one or the other ailment. (d)/ No error (e)

31. One should study the history (a)/ of his country because it alone can satisfy (b)/ one's natural curiosity to know (c)/ what happened in the past. (d)/ No error (e)

32. It is interesting to note (a)/ that the greatest lines in poetry are simple (b)/ and yet there is with them some quality (c)/ which makes them outstandingly great. (d)/ No error (e)

33. In order to make human life happy, (a)/ man should live (b)/ as far as possible (c)/ in perfect harmony with nature. (d)/ No error (e)

34. You have heard (a)/ of Socrates, I suppose. (b)/ Undoubtedly he was one (c)/ of the greatest man of the world. (d)/ No error (e)

35. My daughter never (a)/would write to me (b)/so I never know (c)/what she is doing. (d)/No error (e).

36. Whenever we have a puncture (a)/she just sits in the car (b)/and reads a book (c)/while I changed the wheel. (d)/ No error (e).

37. He walked to the market (a)/with both his servants (b)/on either side of his (c)/to help him buy things. (d)/No error (e).

38. Ganesh, who has been (a) driving all day (b)/was extremely tired (c)/and wanted to stop. (d)/No error (e).

39. Everyone was reading quietly (a)/when suddenly the door (b)/burst open and a (c)/complete stranger rushed in. (d)/No error (e).

40. My secretary is so (a)/careful of her work that (b)/none has so far found (c)/any error in her work. (d)/ No error (e)

41. Our conclusion is that (a)/ between Vinayak and (b)/ Lobo, Vinayak is (c)/ the most honest. (d)/ No error (e)

42. The new project group (a)/ would first look into the tender conditions (b)/ of both basic and value-added (c)/ services before submit its bid. (d)/ No error (e)

43. I would have committed (a)/the same mistake of signing (b)/ the sale deed if my agent (c)/ would not have forewarned me. (d)/ No error (e)

44. The team leaders encourages (a)/ the participants who have (b)/ difficulty in performing (c)/ the assigned task. (d)/ No error (e)

45. We are happy that (a)/ our prime minister (b)/ with the members (c)/ of his cabinet are to be present at the function. (d)/No error (e)

46. Neither the size nor the colour (a)/ of clothes which (b)/ I purchased for him (c)/ yesterday were right. (d)/ No error (e)

47. I heard to my surprise (a)/ that the present (b)/ I send him was not (c)/ to his taste. (d)/ No error (e)

48. Let us refer (a)/ this matter to the principal. (b)/ We shall abide (c)/ with his decision. (d)/ No error (e)

49. If I would have come (a)/ a little earlier, I would have (b)/got a glimpse (c)/ of my beloved leader. (d)I No error (e)

50. Whey you buy something (a)/ on the instalment system (b)/ you are not required to pay (c)/ the whole price at once. (d)/No error (e)

51. I am waiting for you (a)/ for the last two hours (b)/ but you did not bother (c)/ to turn up in time (d)/ No error (e)

52. He is certainly a man (a) / whom I know very well (b) / is trustworthy beyond doubt (c) / and meticulous in his habits. (d) / No error (e) /

53. No sooner did (a) / we reach the station (b) / than the train had (c) / started moving out of the station. (d) / No error (e)/.

54. I am sure about it, (a)/ nobody has lived (b) / in that house (c) / for a hundred years. (d) / No error (e) /

55. There were no less (a) / than forty boys (b) / in the class (c) / when this happened. (d) / No error (e) /

56. I am glad to hear (a) / that you narrowly escaped (b) / being run over by (c) / a speeding car yesterday. (d) / No error (e) /

57. This laboratory of physics is (a)/ not only equipped with (b)/ all state-of-the-art instruments (c)/ but also with outstanding physicists. (d)/ No error (e)

58. No method of making (a)/ other people agree to (b)/ your view-point is (c)/ as effective as this method. (d)/ No error (e)

59. I was pretty sure that (a)/ he would support my views (b)/ for changing the age-old (c)/ and static structure of our organisation. (d)/ No error (e)

60. I did not like his (a)/ comments on my paper (b)/ but I had no alternative (c)/ as I had agreed to keep quiet. (d)/No error (e)

DIRECTIONS (Qs. 61-70) : *Read each sentence to find out whether there is any grammatical error or idiomatic error in it. The error, if any, will be in one part of the sentence. The letter of that part is the answer. If there is 'No error', the answer is '(e)'. (ignore errors of punctuation, if any).*

(IBPS PO/MT 2012)

61. The Government has asked individuals (a)/ with income of over 110 lakhs to (b)/ electronic file tax returns for the year 2011-12 (c)/ something which was optional till last year (d)/ No error (e).

62. The power tariff had already (a)/been increased twice in (b)/ the last 15 months and the Electricity Board had also (c)/ levied additional monthly charges to consumers (d)/ No error (e)

63. Despite of curfew (a)/in some areas, minor (b)/ communal incidents were reported (c)/ from different areas of the walled city (d)/ No error (e)

64. This comes (a)/at a time (b)/ when fund allocation (c)/ is been doubled. (d)/ No error (e)

65. As the prison will get (a)/an official telephone facility soon, the prisoners (b)/ wont have to make calls in discreet manner (c)/ through smuggled mobile phones. (d)/ No error (e)

66. The area was plunged into (a)/darkness mid a wave of (b)/ cheering and shouting (c)/ slogans like 'Save The Earth'. (d)/ No error (e)

67. The poll contestants approached (a)/the commission complanining that the hoardings (b)/ violated the code of conduct (c)/ and influenced public perception (d)/ No error (e)

68. The country has (a)/adequate laws but problems (b)/ arise when these are not (c)/ implemented in letter and spirit (d)/ No error (e)

69. The Management feels that (a)/the employees of the organisation are (b)/ non-productive, and do not want (c)/ to work hard. (d)/ No error (e)

70. As far the issue of land encroachment (a)/in villages is concerned, people will (b)/ have to make a start from their villages by (c)/ sensitising and educating the villagers about this issue. (d)/ No error (e)

DIRECTIONS (Qs.71-75): *Read each sentence to find out whether there is any grammatical mistake/error in it. The error if any, will be in any part of the sentence. Mark the number of that part with error as your answer. If there is 'No error', mark (e).*

(SBI PO 2013)

71. There cannot be any situation where/(a) somebody makes money in an asset/ (b) located in India and does not pay tax/ (c) either to India or to the country of his origin./ (d) No error (e).

72. India has entered a downward spiral / (a) where the organised, productive/ (b) and law abide sectors are subjec to / (c) sevage amounts of multiple taxes./ (d) No error (e).

73. The bank may have followed/ (a) an aggressive monetary tightening policy/ (b) but its stated aim of / (c) curbin inflation have not been achieved/ (d) No error (e).

74. Equal opportunities for advancement/ (a) across the length and breadth / (b) of an organisation will/ (c) keep many problems away. /(d) No error (e).

75. A customised data science degree/ (a) is yet to become/(b) a standard programme/ (c) to India's premier educational institutes./ (d) No error (e).

DIRECTIONS (Qs. 76-80) : *Read each sentence to find out whether there is any error in it. The error, if any, will be in one part of the sentence. The number of that part is the answer. If there is no error, the answer is (e). (Ignore errors of punctuation, if any.)*

(IBPS PO/MT 2014)

76. The ongoing merger among /the two companies will/ (a) (b) have an adverse/impact on consumers. No error (c) (d) (e)

77. It is evident that/the banking sector has underwent/ (a) (b) tremendous changes during/the past two decades. No error (e)

78. According to the consultant/a more detail analysis of/ (a) (b) customer needs / and product pricing is required. No error (c) (d) (e)

79. Over the next five years / the government needs to invest/ (a) (b) at less 350 billion dollars/in rural infrastructure. No error (c) (d) (e)

80. The lack of no funds / has resulted in several / delays in (a) (b) launching our / new product in India. No error (c) (d) (e)

DIRECTIONS (Qs.81-85) : *Read each sentence to find out whether there is any grammatical error in it. The error if any, will be in one part of the sentence, the number of that part is the answer. If there is no error, mark (e). (Ignore errors of punctuation. if any)*

(SBI PO 2014)

81. In the first two months of this fiscal, tractor sales has seen (a)/a drop of about five percent (b)/ however, the industry is waiting for the monsoon (c)/ to really arrive at a firm conclusion about growth prospects for the current year. (d)/No error (e)

82. Dolphins are truly out of the ordinary because of their intelligence (a) / and. among the many creatures that share the earth form (b)/they come closest to humankind in terms of (c)/familial traits, emotions and learining. (d)/ No error (e)

83. Corruption indulged in by the high and mighty adversely impacts (a)/ our nation and in the coming months (b) / we may see revival of efforts (c)/ to tackle such large scale corruption. (d)/ No error (e)

84. It is notable and welcome that the ministry of (a)/ environmental and forests is to issue approvals online (b)/ in a time bound manner, with clear timelines (c)/in place for the various sub-steps along the way. (d)/No error (e)

85. To portray (a)/ what a fairness cream does without (b)/ any sort of comparison or visual (c)/ references are very difficult. (d)/ No error (e).

DIRECTIONS (Qs. 86-90) : *Read each sentence to find out whether there is any grammatical error in it or a wrong word has been used. The error, if any, will be in one part of the sentence which has been printed in bold and has been numbered (a), (b), (c) or (d). The number of that part is the answer. If there is no error, the answer is (e) i.e. 'No error'. (Ignore the errors of punctuation, if any.)*

(IBPS PO Prelim 2015)

86. The **convergence of** (a)/Indian accounting standards with International Financial Reporting Standards (IFRS) **beginning** (b)/in April is **expecting to** (c)/ see power companies **struggling with** (d)/ significant first-time adoption impact. No error (e)

87. **Researchers at** (a)/ the Indian Institute of Science (IISc), Bangalore, are **mapping** (b)/ India's solar hot spots-where **round-the-year** (c)/ sunlight makes it **viable of** (d)/ companies to set up solar power plants. No error (e).

88. Though their qualifications span **a diverse** (a)/ range, there is **an equal** (b)/ number of graduates and those who have just completed School, **each set** (c)/ **making up** (d)/ close to 30% of these households. No error (e)

89. **As if** (a)/ the most dangerous moment for any dictatorship **is when** (b)/ it **starts to** (c)/ reform, North Korea looks ready to turn that truism **on its head.** (d)/ No error (e)

90. **It so happens** (a)/ that this happy campy ritual is their **way of life** (b)/ and **one into which** (c)/ they don't **particularly welcome** (d)/ voyeuristic intrusions. No error (e)

DIRECTIONS (Qs. 91-95): *Read each sentence given below and find out whether there is an error in it. The error if any will be one of the sentence which are marked as A, B, C and D. If there is no error, the answer will be (E) i.e. No error. (Ignore the errors of punctuation, if any)*

(IBPS PO Main 2015)

91. The low learnings levels is due to the fact (a)/ that the state spends 87% of its budget (b)/ on salaries of its teachers (c)/ and not on infrastructure development for students (e)/ No error (e).

92. Recent incidents of tigers straying have brought to focus (a)/ the lack of proper regulatory mechanism and powers with the forest department (b)/ to take action against the resorts (c)/ mushroom in forest fringes (d)/ No error (e).

93. The beauty of the palace comes alive (a)/ When over a lakh bulbs (b)/ is switched on between 7pm and 7.45pm (c)/ on specific days (d)/ No error (e)

94. In view of the rising complaints (a)/ of unscrupulous financial institutes duping people with luring them (b)/ with handsome returns on their investment, the police have appealed (c)/ to the citizens to stay away from such companies (d)/ No error (e)

95. More and more cab drivers are approaching the regional transport office (RTO) (a)/ to obtain identity cards (b)/ after the transport office intensified action against errant drivers (c)/ in the last couple of months (d)/ No error (e).

DIRECTIONS (Qs. 96 to 100): *Read each sentence to find out whether there is any grammatical error in it. The error, if any will be in one part of the sentence. The letter of that part is the answer. If there is no error, the answer is 'D'. (Ignore the errors of punctuation, if any)*

(SBI PO Prelim 2015)

96. "The Patient is comparatively better (a)/ today and I hope (b)/ that he will recover soon" (c)/ said the doctor (d)/ No error (e)

97. All the members (a)/ of the committee are (b)/ kindly requested to appear (c)/ in the next morning (d)/ No error (e).

98. This is the new (a)/ book "One Night @ the call centre" authored by Chetan Bhagat which my father (b)/ bought it (c)/ for you (d)/ No error (e)

99. The passing marks (a)/ in Economics is thirty three (b)/ but he has secured (c)/ just twenty-nine (d)/ No error

100. As my neighbourers (a)/ are very co-operative (b)/ I do not (c)/ feel any difficultly in living in this locality (d)/ No error (e).

DIRECTIONS (Qs. 101-105): *Read each sentence to find out whether there is any error in it. The error, if any, will be in one part of the sentence, the name of the part is the answer. If there is no error, the answer is (e).*

(SBI PO Main 2015)

101. She asked me (a)/ Where I was going to (b)/ and what I had done (c)/ the previous day. (d)/ No error (e)

102. Yesterday in the night (a)/ he came (b)/ by bus (c)/ and was disturbed. (d)/ No error (e)

103. Within two hours (a)/ we will approach (b)/ near Agra (c)/ by car. (d)/ No error (e)

104. Throughout the whole year (a)/ there was (b)/ not a single day (c)/ without any incidence of violence. (d)/ No error (e)

105. The P.M. said (a)/ that it was his decision (b)/ and that nobody (c)/ could get it changed. (d)/ No error (e)

DIRECTIONS (Qs. 106-110) : *Read each sentence to find out whether there is any grammatical mistak error in it. The error if any, will be in one part of the sentence. Mark the number of the part with error as your answer. If there is no error, mark (E).*

(SBI PO Prelim 2016)

106. To run a company effectively (A)/ it is very important (B)/ in knowing the strengths and weaknesses (C)/ of the employees. (D)/ No error (E)
    (a) A   (b) B
    (c) C   (d) D
    (e) E

107. The land records (A)/ of this district (B)/ will computerise (C)/ by next year. (D)/ No error (E)
    (a) A   (b) B
    (c) C   (d) D
    (e) E

108. The Head Office has (A)/ issued instructions that (B)/ the performance of all Zonal Managers (C)/ have to assess by a committee. (D)/ No error (E)
    (a) A   (b) B
    (c) C   (d) D
    (e) E

109. She has promised to (A)/ donate the funds to (B)/ establish a library in many (C)/ villages in India. (D)/ No error (E)
    (a) A   (b) B
    (c) C   (d) D
    (e) E

110. We have already (A)/ submitted our application (B)/ and expect to receive (C)/ our licence in thirty days.(D)/ No error (E)
    (a) A   (b) B
    (c) C   (d) D
    (e) E

DIRECTIONS (Qs. 111-120): *Identify the error in the sentences given below, if there is no error, click option (e).*

(IBPS PO Prelim 2016)

111. (a) The need to set up
    (b) a good library in the locality
    (c) has been in the minds of people
    (d) for some time now
    (e) No error

112. (a) Most people would have
    (b) attended the union meeting
    (c) if they had
    (d) had longer notice of it.
    (e) No error

113. (a) He took to
    (b) reading Times
    (c) for better knowledge
    (d) of the facts.
    (e) No error

114. (a) When children have difficulty understanding
    (b) a certain mathematical process, it is often because
    (c) their teachers do not understand it conceptually
    (d) themselves and do not present it in a way that children can understand.
    (e) No error.

115. (a) Studies show that the lives of millions of mothers
    (b) and their children could be saved if countries would
    (c) invest in programs that ensures a healthy pregnancy,
    (d) and safe childbirth.
    (e) No error.

116. (a) Film viewers claim that
    (b) the number of scenes depicting alcohol consumption
    (c) have increased dramatically over
    (d) the last decade.
    (e) no error

117. (a) Forty percent of the people alive today have
    (b) never made a phone call, but
    (c) thirty percent still have no electricity connections
    (d) to their homes.
    (e) no error

118. (a) Workers with less
    (b) personal problems are
    (c) likely to be
    (d) more productive in their work.
    (e) no error.

119. (a) Everyone who visits Singapore
     (b) is impressed by its cleanliness,
     (c) which is mainly a result of rigorous implementation
     (d) of their strict laws.
     (e) No error
120. (a) The bridal dress was
     (b) most unique: the prince
     (c) designed it and his
     (d) mother provided the lace fabric.
     (e) No error

DIRECTIONS (Qs.121-160): *Which of the phrases (a), (b), (c) or (d) given below should replace the phrase given in bold in the following sentence to make the sentence meaningful and grammatically correct? If the sentence is correct as it is and no correction is required mark (e) as the answer.*

121. He admitted admiringly that he had never come across a painting which **did not please him more.**
     (a) pleased him more
     (b) would have pleased him
     (c) had not pleased him more
     (d) had been pleased him any more
     (e) No correction required
122. It **has always been** better to use preventive measures than to cure illness
     (a) had always been
     (b) is always
     (c) was always
     (d) would have always been
     (e) No correction required
123. He had deliberately kept the matter pending so that people **should be bribed** him.
     (a) could be bribed
     (b) should bribe
     (c) could be bribing
     (d) should have bribed
     (e) No correction required
124. Because of a shortage the government had appealed to the people **to be extravagant** with water.
     (a) for being extravagant
     (b) to be saving
     (c) to be economical
     (d) to be economic
     (e) No correction required
125. He **was found absorbing** in his studies when I reached there.
     (a) was to find absorbed
     (b) was found absorbed
     (c) had been found absorbing
     (d) had to be found absorbing
     (e) No correction required
126. The guide warned us that we **had better be prepared** for a long, hard day.
     (a) had been better prepared
     (b) should better be prepared
     (c) should be prepared with
     (d) had been better preparing
     (e) No correction required
127. Income tax rates are usually **associated to one's** annual income.
     (a) related to one's
     (b) dependent to one's
     (c) depended on one's
     (d) associated with one's
     (e) No correction required
128. All that I have described **have been taken** place in the last four decades.
     (a) have taken
     (b) has been taken
     (c) has taken
     (d) was taken
     (e) No correction required
129. The fees charged by the architect for the plans of the new building **were unreasonable high.**
     (a) were unreasonably high
     (b) were unreasonably higher
     (c) had been unreasonably higher
     (d) had been unreasonable high
     (e) No correction required
130. There are many **new emerging** fields in information technology and electronics.
     (a) newly emerging
     (b) new emergent
     (c) new emergency
     (d) newly emergent
     (e) No correction required
131. People in underdeveloped countries **are distressing because of** the antagonistic attitude of developed countries.
     (a) have been distressing with
     (b) are distressed because
     (c) are distressed at
     (d) were distressing by
     (e) No correction required
132. He **had been behaved** impolitely and suffered owing to that.
     (a) was behaved
     (b) had behaved
     (c) have been behaved
     (d) would have behaved
     (e) No correction required
133. It has become a **commonly practise to talk about** women's liberation.
     (a) commonly practised talk about
     (b) common practice to talk about
     (c) common practice of talking with
     (d) commonly practising to talk about
     (e) No correction required
134. He is so brisk himself that he cannot **tolerate any efficiency.**
     (a) tolerate hardly any inefficiency
     (b) hardly tolerates lethargy
     (c) tolerate any haste
     (d) tolerate any delay
     (e) No correction required
135. No person with a **reasonably self-esteem** would ever like to succumb to any pressure.
     (a) reasonable self-esteem
     (b) reasonable self-esteemed
     (c) reasonably self-esteemed
     (d) reasonably a self-esteem
     (e) No correction required

136. It is the temple where religious rites are celebrated **as they were for** centuries.
    (a) as they have been for
    (b) so were they for
    (c) as they are for
    (d) as they were before
    (e) No correction required

137. By the time he had won his commission, the senior officer **had to start seeking** employment elsewhere.
    (a) had started seeking
    (b) were started seeking
    (c) had been started to seek
    (d) were to have started seeking
    (e) No correction required

138. The congestion on the streets must **be seen to believe.**
    (a) have been to believe
    (b) have been seen for believing
    (c) have seen for belief
    (d) be seen to be believed
    (e) No correction required

139. He had begun to develop the qualities that he **was going to need** in later years.
    (a) was going to be needed
    (b) had gone to need
    (c) was later to need
    (d) had been gone to need
    (e) No correction required

140. All **round is emptiness and silence,** the silence, it seems, of a land that man has not yet set foot upon.
    (a) around is emptiness and silence
    (b) round is empty and silent
    (c) round are emptiness and silence
    (d) around are empty and silence
    (e) No correction required

141. He was quite sure that none of them **were aware of** the truth.
    (a) were aware from
    (b) was aware of
    (c) were beware of
    (d) had aware of
    (e) No correction required

142. I was **too overwhelmed to** make any decision.
    (a) too much overwhelm to
    (b) so overwhelmed to
    (c) extremely overwhelmed about
    (d) quite overwhelming to
    (e) No correction required

143. **Shocked of finding** an unknown person, the army officer briskly caught hold of him.
    (a) Shockingly found
    (b) Shocked at finding
    (c) Shocked by finding
    (d) Finding as a shock
    (e) No correction required

144. No sooner did he reach the station than the train **had started moving.**
    (a) had started movement
    (b) had been moving
    (c) had been started movement
    (d) started moving
    (e) No correction required

145. He **has even venturing into** areas which he had shunned.
    (a) had even venturing into
    (b) even is being venture into
    (c) has even been venturing into
    (d) has even been ventured in
    (e) No correction required

146. **When the boy regain** consciousness he wanted to eat something.
    (a) If the boy regain
    (b) When the boy regained
    (c) Despite the boy regain
    (d) On the boy regaining
    (e) No correction required

147. The social worker wanted **to bring about** little changes in the lives of the people of that village.
    (a) to bring back
    (b) to bring up
    (c) to bring forth
    (d) bringing about
    (e) No correction required

148. Raghunath proposes to **lay claim for** the insurance company as soon as he recovers from the accident.
    (a) lay claim to
    (b) lay claim on
    (c) laying claim towards
    (d) lay claim against
    (e) No correction required

149. The new concession announced by the Government will have only a **marginalised effect on** the lives of the people.
    (a) marginal effect off
    (b) margin of effect on
    (c) marginal effect on
    (d) marginalising effect in
    (e) No correction required

150. The Charitable Hospital works **under the auspices from** the Welfare Trust of an Industry.
    (a) under the auspices by
    (b) by the auspices from
    (c) through the auspices from
    (d) under the auspices of
    (e) No correction required

151. Government **should not stop to spending** money on arms and ammunition in the wake of the present strained relations.
    (a) should not stop spending
    (b) shall not be stopped to spend
    (c) will not stop to spend
    (d) should not be stopping to spend
    (e) No Correction Required

152. The one-act play was so humorous that it **was hardly impossible** to keep a straight face.
    (a) is hardly impossible
    (b) was almost impossible
    (c) is hardly possible
    (d) was barely impossible
    (e) No Correction Required

153. One of the politicians **have open admittance** that he had resorted to corrupt practices.

(a)   have opened admittance
(b)   has opened admittance
(c)   has openly admitted
(d)   have been open admittances
(e)   No Correction required

154. The **unkind comments passed by** her superiors made her resign.
(a)   unkindly comments passing by
(b)   unkind comments passing on
(c)   unkind comments posed by
(d)   unkindly comments passed on
(e)   No correction Required

155. The ban on public meetings **have been lifted temporarily** in view of the auspicious occasion.
(a)   have been temporarily lifted
(b)   have been lifting temporarily
(c)   had been lifting temporary
(d)   has been lifted temporarily
(e)   No Correction Required

156. **Finishing his breakfast,** he started working on the problem that had been awaiting disposal for a long time.
(a)   His breakfast finished
(b)   His breakfast having finished
(c)   Having finished his breakfast
(d)   Finished his breakfast
(e)   No correction required

157. **One of the function of** a teacher is to spot cases of maladjustment.
(a)   One of the functions of
(b)   Most of the functions of
(c)   Some of the functions
(d)   One of the functions by
(e)   No correction required

158. In our friends' circle it is customary for each of the members **to buy their own tickets.**
(a)   buying their own tickets
(b)   are buying their own tickets
(c)   buying his own tickets
(d)   to buy his own ticket
(e)   No correction required

159. Where the distance is not too much I prefer walking on foot **than waiting for a bus.**
(a)   than wait for the
(b)   than no waiting for
(c)   to waiting for a
(d)   rather than waiting for a
(e)   No correction required

160. **Being a pleasant morning,** he went out for a walk along the seashore.
(a)   With a pleasant morning
(b)   It being a pleasant morning
(c)   Being a pleasing morning
(d)   As a pleasant morning
(e)   No correction required

DIRECTIONS (Qs. 161-165) : *Which of the phrases (a), (b), (c) and (d) given below each sentence should replace the word/ phrase printed in bold in the sentence to make it grammatically correct ? If the sentence is correct as it is given and no correction is required, mark (e) as the answer.*

(IBPS PO/MT 2012)

161. US secretary of state made it clear that time **running out** for diplomacy over Iran's nuclear programme and said that talks aimed at preventing Tehran from acquiring a nuclear weapon would resume in April.
(a)   runs out   (b)   was running out
(c)   ran out   (d)   run
(e)   No correction required

162. While the war of the generals **rage on,** somewhere in small town India, wonderful things are happening, quietly and minus fanfare.
(a)   rage   (b)   raging
(c)   rages on   (d)   raged on
(e)   No correction required

163. According to WWF, the small island nation of Samoa was **the first in switch off** its lights for Earth Hour.
(a)   first to switch of   (b)   the first to switch off
(c)   the first of switch off   (d)   first in switch of
(e)   No correction required

164. The campaign is significant **because not just** the youths are directly appealing to the world but because their efforts challenge the chimera of normalcy in the area.
(a)   not just because   (b)   just not because
(c)   not just   (d)   because just
(e)   No correction required

165. The doctor's association has threatened to go on indefinite strike **support of** their teachers.
(a)   on supporting to   (b)   to supporting
(c)   for support   (d)   in support of
(e)   No correction required

DIRECTIONS (Qs. 166-170) : *Which of the phrases (a), (b), (c) and (d) given below should replace the phrase given in bold in the following sentence to make the sentence grammatically correct. If the sentence is correct as it is and 'No correction is required', mark (e) as the answer.*

(SBI PO 2014)

166. British Airspace has been **focusing on build** European links.
(a)   focusing on built
(b)   focusing on forged
(c)   focusing on forging
(d)   concentrating to build
(e)   No correction required

167. The appetite of banks for funds was lost under the onslaught of the slowdown, corporates refused to borrow even as **bank deposits flourished.**
(a)   bank deposits flourishing
(b)   bank deposits swelled
(c)   bank deposits were enhanced
(d)   bank deposits flummoxed
(e)   No correction required

168. The 8th century revival of Byzantine learning is **an exemplary phenomenon** and its economic and military precursors have yet to be discovered.
(a)   phenomenon yet to be discovered.
(b)   a phenomenon incompletely explained
(c)   an inexplicable phenomenon
(d)   an unidentifiable phenomenon
(e)   No correction required

169. NASA is all set to start building the world's first spacecraft **that collected samples** from an asteroid in 2018.
  - (a) that will collect samples
  - (b) that has collected samples
  - (c) that will have collected samples
  - (d) who will collect samples
  - (e) No correction required
170. A sculpture by a veteran artist **that stands** in the lawns of National Art Gallery was found damaged.
  - (a) that stood
  - (b) that had stood
  - (c) that was standing
  - (d) that has stood
  - (e) No correction required

DIRECTIONS (Qs. 171-175) : *Which of the phrases (a), (b), (c) and (d) given below should replace the phrase given in bold in the following sentence to make the sentence grammatically correct ? If the sentence is correct as it is and no correction is required, mark (e) as the answer.*

(IBPS PO/MT 2014)

171. They didn't pay any heed to their superior's instructions : **I did neither.**
  - (a) I either did
  - (b) Either 1 did not
  - (c) Neither didn't I
  - (d) Nor did I
  - (e) No correction required
172. Every poet **gives voice to** his anger and his compassion through his poems.
  - (a) voiced to give
  - (b) gives voice for
  - (c) gave voice against
  - (d) voiced at giving
  - (e) No correction required
173. The police nabbed a notorious criminal who **had been terrorising builders and extorted** money from them for the past two years.
  - (a) was terrorising builders and extorted
  - (b) had not been terrorised builders and extorted
  - (c) had been terrorising builders and extorting
  - (d) had terrorised builders and extorted
  - (e) No correction required
174. Managers frequently encounter situations where they need **to help others solved** problems.
  - (a) to helping others solved
  - (b) help others solved
  - (c) to help others solve
  - (d) help others solving
  - (e) No correction required
175. From among various alternatives we should choose the one which **is viable and consumes less** time and energy.
  - (a) is viable and consuming lesser
  - (b) is viability and consumes less
  - (c) being viable and consumes less
  - (d) has viable and consuming less
  - (e) No correction required

DIRECTIONS (Qs. 176-180): *Which of the phrases (a), (b), (c) and (d) given below each sentence should replace the phrase printed in bold in the sentence to make it grametically correct ? If the sentence is correct as it is given and no correction is required mark (e) as the answer.*

(SBI PO Main 2015)

176. The Governor has a good collection of **paintings adoring the walls** of the Raj Bhavan.
  - (a) painting adoring the wall
  - (b) painting adoring the walls
  - (c) painting sticking the walls
  - (d) painting adorning the walls
  - (e) No correction required
177. The principals and teachers **at the selected English Medium** School were contacted.
  - (a) of the selected English Medium
  - (b) at the select English Medium
  - (c) upon the selected English Medium
  - (d) of the section English Medium
  - (e) No correction required
178. Besides these norms, **the data was also analyzed** to form the sub groups.
  - (a) the data had analyzed also
  - (b) the data were also concluded
  - (c) the data were also analyzed
  - (d) an data were analyzed also
  - (e) No correction required
179. He does not know the Mount Everest **is the Most highest mountain** peak.
  - (a) is a more highest mountain
  - (b) is the most high mountain
  - (c) is the higher mountain
  - (d) is the highest mountain
  - (e) No correction required
180. Walking in the morning in open air **is being observed to be better** for the health of the people who live in congestion.
  - (a) was observer the best
  - (b) hand been proved far better
  - (c) has been observed good
  - (d) was proved far better
  - (e) No correction required

DIRECTIONS (Qs. 181-185) : *Which of the pair of phrases (a), (b), (c) and (d) given below should replace the phrase given in bold in the following sentence to make the sentence grammatically meaningful and correct? If the sentence is correct as it is and no correction is required, mark (e) as the answer.*

(IBPS PO Main 2016)

181. According to author Dishantgautam, a novel is difficult to write when compared to a play is like **going for** an election where one has to appeal to a thousand people at a time whereas in a book one appeals to one only person.
  - (a) simpler, running in
  - (b) faster, voting through
  - (c) easier, running for
  - (d) fool proof, voting on
  - (e) No correction required
182. We have in America a **collection** speech that is neither American, Oxford English, nor colloquial English, but **a mixture** of all three.
  - (a) motley, an enhancement
  - (b) hybrid, a combination

    (c)   nasal, a blend

    (d)   mangled, a medley.

    (e)   No correction required

183. Alice Walker's The Temple of My Familiar, far from being a tight, **focused** Narrative, is instead **a cheaper** novel that roams freely and imaginatively over a halfmillion

    (a)   traditional , a chronological

    (b)   provocative , an insensitive

    (c)   forceful , a concise

    (d)   focused , an expansive

    (e)   circuitous , a discursive

184. Jayashree was habitually so docile and **erratic** that her friends could not understand her sudden **hostile** her employers.

    (a)   accommodating, outburst against

    (b)   erratic, envy of

    (c)   truculent, virulence toward

    (d)   hasty, annoyance toward

    (e)   apologetic, hostile

185. The village headman was unlettered, but he was no fool, he could see through the **mystery** of the businessman's proposition and promptly **moved** him down.

    (a)   deception, forced   (b)   naivete, turned

    (c)   potential, forced   (d)   sophistry, turned

    (e)   No correction required

DIRECTIONS (Qs. 186 -196): *In each of the following questions two/three sentences are given. These sentences are combined into a single sentence and given as four alternatives below each question. You have to select one sentence which is grammatically correct and conveys the same meaning as conveyed by the two/three sentences and mark the letter of that sentence as your answer. If none of the four sentences given as alternatives below each question is correct, mark 'e', None of the above sentences is correct, as the answer.*

186. Her father was listening keenly. Rupa noticed this.

    (a)   Rupa noticed that her father had listened keenly.

    (b)   Rupa had noticed that her father was listening keenly.

    (c)   Rupa noticed that her father is listening keenly.

    (d)   Rupa noticed that her father was listening keenly.

    (e)   None of the above sentences is correct.

187. The sun is very important to men. Men have long known this.

    (a)   Men have long known how important the sun is to them.

    (b)   The sun is very important to them is known to men.

    (c)   The sun has been very important for men is known to them.

    (d)   The men know the sun is very important to them.

    (e)   None of the above sentences is correct.

188. He got up. He wound the cloth around his head.

    (a)   Having got up, he had wound the cloth around his head.

    (b)   Getting up he did wound the cloth around his head.

    (c)   Getting up, he wound the cloth around his head.

    (d)   Having getting up, he wound the cloth around his head.

    (e)   None of the above sentences is correct.

189. They watched. They wondered. They were unable to find the reason.

    (a)   They watched and wondered till they were unable to find the reason.

    (b)   They watched and wondered but were unable to find the reason.

    (c)   They had watched and wondered but were unable to find the reason.

    (d)   They watched and wondered despite being unable to find the reason.

    (e)   None of the above sentences is correct.

190. I was very much overwhelmed. I did not make any decision.

    (a)   I was so overwhelmed to make any decision.

    (b)   I could not make any decision as I was very much overwhelmed.

    (c)   I was too overwhelmed to make any decision.

    (d)   Being very much overwhelmed, I did not make any decision.

    (e)   None of the above sentences is correct.

191. He is sure to receive his pay. It is due to him. Why then does he worry?

    (a)   Why does he worry, till he is sure to receive his pay due to him?

    (b)   Why should he worry as the pay due to him is sure to be received?

    (c)   Why does he worry as he should be sure to receive the pay due to him?

    (d)   Why does he worry, since the pay due to him is sure to be received?

    (e)   None of the above sentences is correct.

192. Should you need a duplicate licence you must submit an application along with a copy of your ration card.

    (a)   Unless you submit an application along with a copy of your ration card you will not get a duplicate licence.

    (b)   You should require a duplicate license if you submit an application along with a copy of your ration card.

    (c)   If you submit your application along with your ration card you do not need duplicate license.

    (d)   If you submit an application along with your ration card you will get only a license.

    (e)   None of these

193. Although the strike of transporters continues, I shall come.

    (a)   I shall come if the strike of transporters continues.

    (b)   I shall not be able to come if the strike of transporters continues.

    (c)   Even though I come, the strike of transporters is going to continue.

    (d)   Whether or not the transporters strike continues I shall come.

    (e)   None of these

194. The Manager would like you to help him locate the default.

    (a)   If you help him locate the default, the Manager would like you.

    (b)   The Manager desires that you should provide him the necessary assistance to locate the default.

    (c)   The Manager feels that if you do not help him the fault will not be located.

    (d)   The Manager expects that the default should be located only with your help.

    (e)   None of these

195. The judge remarked that not all the accused were really guilty.
    (a) The judge remarked that some of the accused were guilty while others were not.
    (b) The judge remarked that all the accused were not innocent.
    (c) The judge remarked that all those accused cannot be necessarily guilty.
    (d) The judge remarked that all those who are accused may contain some who are really guilty.
    (e) None of these
196. Unlike the tribals who are very hardworking, the urban communities cannot withstand physical strain.
    (a) The tribals do not like to withstand physical strain as the urban communities do.
    (b) The urban communities are hardworking but they do not like to undertake physical strain.
    (c) The tribals can withstand physical strain whereas urban communities cannot.
    (d) Because the tribals are hardworking they can tolerate physical strain.
    (e) None of these

DIRECTIONS (Qs. 197-201): *In each of the following questions there is a sentence with a phrase/idiom printed in bold, followed by five options. Find out the option which expresses the meaning of the phrase/idiom correctly.*

197. To speak of one language for the world as leading to one purpose is to **put the cart before the horse.**
    (a) reverse the proper order of events
    (b) invite dictatorship
    (c) accelerate a backward movement
    (d) indulge an unrealistic proposition
    (e) None of these
198. He was somewhat **taken aback** by the news that the police intended to prosecute him.
    (a) strike   (b) terror-stricken
    (c) surprised and upset   (d) fainted
    (e) enchanted
199. I have got enough money in my pocket to last me the rest of my life provided I **drop dead** this afternoon.
    (a) save   (b) rescue
    (c) commit suicide   (d) die suddenly
    (e) None of these
200. Not one of his insulting remarks **caused a ripple on the surface of her composure.**
    (a) caused anger   (b) had noticeable effect
    (c) caused injury   (d) evoked attention
    (e) None of these
201. Suresh knows that the good times are over, but he says, "we still feel **footloose and fancy-free.**"
    (a) a comeback   (b) easy
    (c) original condition   (d) the presence
    (e) boundless

DIRECTIONS (Qs. 202-211): *In each question below, an incomplete sentence is given which is followed by three possible fillers denoted by (A), (B) and (C). Find out which one, two or three of these fillers can make the sentence meaningfully complete and grammatically correct.*

202. ____ when the audience started throwing rotten eggs towards him.

A   No sooner did he stand up to address
B   No much before he stood up
C   He had hardly stood up
    (a) Only C   (b) Only B
    (c) Only A or B   (d) Only B or C
    (e) Any one of the three
203. ____ sacrifice their own self for the welfare of the common man.
A   Not all men devoted to social service
B   Only dedicated men
C   In exceptional cases certain anti-social elements
    (a) Only C   (b) Only A or C
    (c) Only B or C   (d) Only A or B
    (e) Any one of the three
204. Natural calamities such as floods, earthquakes, etc occur so suddenly and unexpectedly that ____
A   people get hardly any time to save themselves
B   man realises his limitations and supremacy of nature
C   devastation cannot be prevented
    (a) Only A   (b) Only B
    (c) Only A or B   (d) Only A or C
    (e) Any one of the three
205. ____ the poor students had managed to come out successfully with flying colours.
A   Despite lack of resources
B   Owing to adverse circumstances
C   It was a mere coincidence that
    (a) Only A   (b) Only A or C
    (c) Only B or C   (d) Only A or B
    (e) Any one of the three
206. They appreciated my act of bravado because the life I saved was ____.
A   insignificant for them
B   extremely precious
C   reverent to them
    (a) Only B   (b) Only C
    (c) Only A or B   (d) Only B or C
    (e) Any one of the three
207. He always delays in taking any action. It makes others suffer a lot.
A.   His taking action on time makes...
B.   Others suffer a lot because of ...
C.   On account of his procrastination ...
    (a) A, B and C   (b) A and B only
    (c) B and C only   (d) A and C only
    (e) None of these
208. Don't add so much chilli powder to the soup. Consumers are only small children.
A.   Because small children do not allow chilli powder ...
B.   Since, small children do not consume more soup...
C.   Adding more chilli powder to soup makes the small children like ...
    (a) None   (b) A only
    (c) B only   (d) C only
    (e) A and C only
209. The quality of the fabric was not impressive. We changed our plan of purchasing.
A.   The quality of the fabric being ...
B.   We changed our ...
C.   In spite of the unimpressive ...

(a) Only A (b) Only B
(c) Only C (d) A and B only
(e) All the three A, B and C

210. Madhuri has been consistent in her studies. Her performance in the examination was nothing else but excellent.
A. Despite being consistent in her studies ...
B. Madhuri's performance in the examination was not excellent because...
C. Because Madhuri was only consistent and not intelligent, her performance...
(a) Only A (b) Only B and C
(c) Only A and C (d) All the three A, B and C
(e) None of these

211. It is very cold here. You must bring warm clothes with you.
A. Since, you must ...
B. As it is very ...
C. If it is very ...
(a) Only A (b) Only B
(c) Only C (d) A and C only
(e) B and C only

DIRECTIONS (Qs. 212-216): *Please select the most appropriate option, out of the five options given for each of the following sentences, which, in your view, should be grammatically and structurally correct. Please note that the meaning & context of the sentence must not change.*

(IBPS PO Main 2016)

212. (a) Although I already knew the answer and he invited me to visit him often, since I just have seen her in the square, I was never determined to yield this point.
(b) Although I have already known the answer and he invited me to visit him often but since I just have seen her in the square, I was not determined to yield this point.
(c) Although I knew the answer already, and he has often invited me to visit him, since I just have seen her in the square, I am never determined to yield this point.
(d) Although I already know the answer and he often invited me to visit him , since I have just seen her in the square, I am determined never to yield this point.
(e) None is true.

213. (a) If I have enough money I would have backpack around Europe. But unfortunately I was broken.
(b) If I have had enough money, I would have done backpack around Europe. But, unfortunately I am broke.
(c) If I had enough money I would backpack around Europe. But, unfortunately I am broke.
(d) If I have enough money I would backpack around all over the Europe. But unfortunately I am broke.
(e) None is true.

214. (a) The judges finally distributed the awards among the most active children talking at length among themselves.
(b) The judges finally distributed the awards talking at length among themselves.
(c) The judges, talking at length among themselves finally distributed the awards among the most active children.
(d) The judges distributed finally talking at length among themselves the awards among the most active children.
(e) None is true.

215. (a) I have been ill for fortnight and the Management and the school sports committee as well prefer to elect me the Captain of school team. Initially I thought that it is only in a fun but I was wrong.
(b) I had been ill for the fortnight and the Management and the school sports committee preferred to elect me the Captain of school team. Initially I thought that it was only in a fun but I was wrong.
(c) I have been ill for a fortnight and the Management as well as the school sports committee prefers to elect me Captain of school team. Initially I thought that it was only in fun but I was wrong.
(d) I was ill for fortnight thus the Management as well as the school sports committee preferred to elect me the Captain of school team. Initially I thought that it was only in a fun but I was wrong.
(e) All are true

216. (a) If you try to understand the concept in the class you will not only remember it but also will not be able to put to use while solving even the difficult exercises.
(b) If you tried to understand the concept of the whole class, you will not only remember it, but also can put to use while solving even the difficult exercises.
(c) If you tried to understand the concept in the class, you would not only remember it but also can put it to use while solving even the difficult exercises.
(d) If you tried to understand the concept in the class, you would not only remember it but also could put it to use while solving even the difficult exercises.
(e) None is true.

DIRECTIONS (Qs. 217-220) : *Given below are five sentences that form a paragraph. Identify the sentence(s) or part(s) of sentence(s) that is/are correct in terms of grammar and usage (including spelling, punctuation and logical consistency). Then, choose the most appropriate option.*

---

217. A. A tarot is one of the most wonderful of human inventions.
B. Despite all the outcry of philosophers, this pack of pictures,
C. in whom destiny is reflected as in a mirror with multiple facets,
D. remains so vital and exercises so irresistible an attraction on
E. imaginative minds that it is hardly possible that it could ever be abolished.
(a) A only (b) A and B
(c) D and E (d) D only
(e) None of these

218. 1. In every democratic and more-or-less secular countries,
2. similar questions arise about precise extent to which religious sub-cultures
3. should be allowed to live on their own rules and laws.
4. One set of questions emerge when believers demand, and often get,
5. an opt-out from the law of the land.
(a) 3 & 5 (b) 3 only
(c) 5 only (d) 2, 3 & 5
(e) None of these

219. A. Since the breakdown of political formality, pictures have stood for a different message, for which the umbrella term is "down to earth".
B. This down-to-earthness has myriad elements, most of it contradictory or impossible.
C. For instance, to be down-to-earth you have to like sport; to like sport you have to choose a team; but if you go and see your team, you are no longer down-to-earth because you can afford a ticket.
D. If you pretend that you can't afford a ticket, you're disingenuous; if you shrug and say, "I can get a free ticket to anything, I'm prime minister", you're reasonable but you have squandered the advantage you gained in liking sport in the first place.
E. Realistically, all one can do is pretend you're too busy to watch sport, which works OK for the harassed, sleep-deprived, Thatcher-model premier, but couldn't possibly wash for David "Fruit Ninja" Cameron.
(a) A, C and E   (b) B, D and E
(c) B, C and D   (d) A, B and E
(e) None of these

220. A. The central question to answering in judging the proportionality of this sentence is whether the desire to punish a whistleblower driven by moral outrage stems from the alleged harm he did US military and diplomatic interests, or whether it derives more from sheer embarrassment.
B. The judge presiding, Col Denise Lind, had already thrown out the gravest of charge, that of "aiding the enemy".
C. Col Lind had also limited the admissibility of evidence regarding the "chilling effects" that Mr Manning's actions had on US diplomacy by releasing 250,000 state department cables.
D. A military witness conceded there was no evidence that anyone had been killed after being named in the releases.
E. Mr Manning's recent apology for his actions does not, and should not, detract from the initial defence he gave for it, when he spoke of his shock at the "delightful bloodlust" displayed by that helicopter crew, or his belief that stimulating a debate about the wars was the right thing to do.
(a) A, B and E   (b) B, C and D
(c) A, C and D   (d) A, C and E
(e) None of these

DIRECTIONS (221-235): *Following questions consist of two sentences. Read each sentence to find out whether there is any grammatical error in it and mark your answer accordingly from the given options.*

221. I. There is no objection to his joining the dance classes if he is willing to learn classical dance.
II. Being the only people there, their presence was considered to be the most important.
(a) if there is an error only in the first sentence;
(b) if there is an error only in the second sentence;
(c) if there are errors in both sentences; and
(d) if there is no error in either of the sentences.
(e) if there are more than two errors in either of the sentence.

222. I. It is surprising to note that a man who has lived in this town since birth, he doesn't know where the post office is.
II. I was surprised at not having seen him at the rally even though he was addressing it.
(a) if there is an error only in the first sentence;
(b) if there is an error only in the second sentence;
(c) if there are errors in both sentences; and
(d) if there is no error in either of the sentences.
(e) if there are more than two errors in either of the sentence.

223. I. It is time you mend your ways.
II. Hardly had the train left the station than the ticket checker entered the compartment.
(a) if there is an error only in the first sentence;
(b) if there is an error only in the second sentence;
(c) if there are errors in both sentences; and
(d) if there is no error in either of the sentences.
(e) if there are more than two errors in either of the sentence.

224. I. On a windy day like this I prefer playing indoors than going out.
II. Had she asked me for my umbrella, I may have lent her to save her from rain.
(a) if there is an error only in the first sentence;
(b) if there is an error only in the second sentence;
(c) if there are errors in both sentences; and
(d) if there is no error in either of the sentences.
(e) if there are more than two errors in either of the sentence.

225. I. She does not seem to be aware of her mother's illness.
II. As I noticed, he appeared to be unreasonably anxious about pleasing his boss.
(a) if there is an error only in the first sentence;
(b) if there is an error only in the second sentence;
(c) if there are errors in both sentences; and
(d) if there is no error in either of the sentences.
(e) if there are more than two errors in either of the sentence.

226. I. This kind of questions does not appear in competitive examinations.
II. It was you who suggested that she give these entry passes to each participant on his arrival.
(a) if there is an error only in the first sentence;
(b) if there is an error only in the second sentence;
(c) if there are errors in both sentences; and
(d) if there is no error in either of the sentences.
(e) If there are more than two errors in either of the sentence.

227. I. One should seek an audience with the minister, if he wants to air his grievances.
II. The cinema hall is full; there is no place for anyone else.
(a) if there is an error only in the first sentence;
(b) if there is an error only in the second sentence;
(c) if there are errors in both sentences; and
(d) if there is no error in either of the sentences.
(e) if there are more than two errors in either of the sentence.

228.
- I. Whom do you mean to insult by your taunts except Peter and I.
- II. He tried all the compartments in the train but could not find his suitcase in anyone of them.
- (a) if there is an error only in the first sentence;
- (b) if there is an error only in the second sentence;
- (c) if there are errors in both sentences; and
- (d) if there is no error in either of the sentences.
- (e) if there are more than two errors in either of the sentence.

229.
- I. Privatisation offers the most ideal situation for consumers because private sector focuses on quality.
- II. Little precaution would have prevented you from that accident.
- (a) if there is an error only in the first sentence;
- (b) if there is an error only in the second sentence;
- (c) if there are errors in both sentences; and
- (d) if there is no error in either of the sentences.
- (e) if there are more than two errors in either of the sentence.

230.
- I. It was noted that the speeches of prime minister were better than those of the opposition leaders.
- II. Peter and I will conduct function tomorrow.
- (a) if there is an error only in the first sentence;
- (b) if there is an error only in the second sentence;
- (c) if there are errors in both sentences; and
- (d) if there is no error in either of the sentences.
- (e) if there are more than two errors in either of the sentence.

231.
- I. Last winter he went to his hometown and enjoyed very much.
- II. The ruling party stood for Surrogacy bill and was ready to stake its political existence.
- (a) if there is an error only in the first sentence;
- (b) if there is an error only in the second sentence;
- (c) if there are errors in both sentences; and
- (d) if there is no error in either of the sentences.
- (e) if there are more than two errors in either of the sentence.

232.
- I. Troy was taken by Greeks; this formed the basis of a story which has become famous.
- II. The majority of legislators recommends that effective measures should be taken against bank frauds.
- (a) if there is an error only in the first sentence;
- (b) if there is an error only in the second sentence;
- (c) if there are errors in both sentences; and
- (d) if there is no error in either of the sentences.
- (e) if there are more than two errors in either of the sentence.

233.
- I. According to the Bible, it is the meek and the humble who shall inherit the heaven.
- II. He was passing by the famous monument when the accident occurred.
- (a) if there is an error only in the first sentence;
- (b) if there is an error only in the second sentence;
- (c) if there are errors in both sentences; and
- (d) if there is no error in either of the sentences.
- (e) if there are more than two errors in either of the sentence.

234.
- I. He fixed a metal ladder on the wall so as to be able to water the flowerpots on it.
- II. It was surprising that neither the house nor its content was destroyed in the fire.
- (a) if there is an error only in the first sentence;
- (b) if there is an error only in the second sentence;
- (c) if there are errors in both sentences; and
- (d) if there is no error in either of the sentences.
- (e) if there are more than two errors in either of the sentence.

235.
- I. He will not be able to attend the function as he is already late by an hour, will he?
- II. The foremost criterion of selection the panel adopted was the grades an aspirant had got under the supervision of a particular teacher.
- (a) if there is an error only in the first sentence;
- (b) if there is an error only in the second sentence;
- (c) if there are errors in both sentences; and
- (d) if there is no error in either of the sentences.
- (e) if there are more than two errors in either of the sentence.

DIRECTIONS (Qs 236-240): *Following question consists of three sentences. Read each sentence to find out whether there is any grammatical error in it and mark your answer accordingly from the given options.*

236.
- I. Of all the employees, James was less worried when the list of retrenchment was announced for the year.
- II. Whole India was shocked over the incident of hijacking of Air India Boeing Jet by militants from Pakistan.
- III. Neither does he call nor does he send a message.
- (a) if there is an error only in the Ist sentence;
- (b) if there is an error only in the Ind sentence;
- (c) if there is an error in IIIrd sentence;
- (d) if there are errors in Ist & IInd sentence;
- (e) if there are errors in IInd & IIIrd sentence;

237.
- I. The landscape of Ooty is by far more enchanting of all.
- II. He told me as blunt as he could the reasons why he was opposed to my candidature.
- III. Her house looks at the lake.
- (a) if there is an error only in the Ist sentence;
- (b) if there is an error only in the IInd sentence;
- (c) if there is an error in the IIIrd sentence;
- (d) if there are errors in Ist & IInd sentence;
- (e) if there are errors in all the sentences.

238.
- I. It was barely midnight when I arrived home and found him sitting at the doorstep waiting for me.
- II. I don't know why you have been unreasonably anxious to know her name.
- III. His job is commensurate with his qualifications, leadership and interpersonal skills.
- (a) if there is an error only in the Ist sentence;
- (b) if there is an error only in the IInd sentence;
- (c) if there is an error in the IIIrd sentence;
- (d) if there are errors in Ist & IInd sentence;
- (e) if there is no error in any sentence;

239.
- I. After toiling very hardly over a long period of time, he began to realize that people recognised him as a superstar.

II.   The woman who is certain of her judgement is surely a match for a man who knows his own mind.
III. Sushie does not play piano, and neither does Rishi.
(a)   if there is an error only in the Ist sentence;
(b)   if there is an error only in the IInd sentence;
(c)   if there is an error in the IIIrd sentence;
(d)   if there are errors in Ist & IInd sentence;
(e)   if there is no error in any sentence;

240. I.   Travelling by car is as quick as or perhaps quicker than by train.
II.   She has been trying to search for the lost keys for the last two hours.
III. Smoking is injurious to health as well as making you smell bad
(a)   if there is an error only in the Ist sentence;
(b)   if there is an error only in the IInd sentence;
(c)   if there is an error in the IIIrd sentence;
(d)   if there are errors in Ist & IInd sentence;
(e)   if there is no error in any sentence;

DIRECTIONS (Qs 241-245) : *Which of the phrases (a), (b), (c) or (d) given below each sentence to make it grammatically correct? If the sentence is correct as it is given and 'No correction is required', mark (e) as the answer.*

241. There is no other way to end war **except** disarmament.
(a)   apart from   (b)   rather than
(c)   excluding   (d)   than
(e)   No correction required

242. The jail is in the news again **with the finding** of a pistol and some bullets.
(a)   to finding   (b)   with find
(c)   finding   (d)   one found
(e)   No correction required

243. The space-crunched city throws up several stories of struggle that schools **have had put up with** to win playground for their students.
(a)   have had to put up to
(b)   had put up on
(c)   have had to put up with
(d)   had to put up to
(e)   No correction required

244. **Emotions rang high** as both families were taken to the police station last night.
(a)   Emotions went higher
(b)   Emotion become high
(c)   Emotionally high
(d)   Emotions ran high
(e)   No correction required

245. Work at all the court complexes was paralysed as lawyers went **on a day-long strike** as a mark of protest.
(a)   for a one day strike
(b)   for a strike
(c)   on a day's long strike
(d)   on a day-long striking
(e)   No correction required

DIRECTIONS (246-250): *Each question below has two blanks, each blank indicating that something has been omitted. Choose the set of words for each blank which best fits the meaning of the sentence as a whole.*

246. Forest department officials said that when the elephants were made to_______from their trucks they went straight to the spot where they had been _______during the camp.
(a)   jump, killed   (b)   alight, tied
(c)   enter, hurt   (d)   step, played
(e)   exit, enjoyed

247. Excise official seized pouches of whisky_______a bus travelling_______Maharashtra.
(a)   from, to   (b)   in, for
(c)   for, towards   (d)   inside, on
(e)   through, till

248. Organisations_______for the victims_______the inhuman and unjust attitude of the government.
(a)   fighting, applauded
(b)   lobbying, supported
(c)   working, condemned
(d)   stand, opposed
(e)   trying, spoke

249. A collision between two buses_______six people dead, _______the driver of one of the buses.
(a)   made, also   (b)   left, including
(c)   caused, combined   (d)   resulted, except
(e)   got, surpassing

250. The court_______revenue authorities and PCB officials to _______teams and visit pharma units.
(a)   directed, form   (b)   announced, arrange
(c)   commanded display   (d)   ruled, make
(e)   told, carve

DIRECTION (251-255) : *In each of the following sentences, there is a blank space, followed by some choices of words given in options. You have to determine which of these words fits well in all making them meaningful and grammatically correct. Word can be modified according to the tense of the sentence keeping the meaning of root word intact. If none of these words fit well, mark your answer as none of these.*

251. A. Sanjna prepared a/an _______ breakfast in the morning.
B. The minister did not_______as to what it meant by this.
C. The French grand opera was full of hugely_______stage effects.
(a)   special   (b)   detail
(c)   elaborate   (d)   ornamented
(e)   inclined

252. A. He'd known love and trust only in the earliest _______ of his life, when he had a family before he entered the dark age of his people.
B. Jackson helped set up the presentation on the _______, and then took a seat at the back of the lecture hall as the students meandered in.
C. Fisher_______a surprising victory in the primary against Jim Mattox.
(a)   time   (b)   level
(c)   phase   (d)   point
(e)   stage

253. A. There were many skirmishes between them, but a common danger soon forced them to _______ their hostilities.
B. He can_______for a month a municipal council, mayor or deputy-mayor; certain decisions of the municipal councils require his approval.
C. Within two miles of the falls is a wonderful_______bridge.

(a) suspend   (b) freeze
(c) alter   (d) defer
(e) rusticate

254. A. The poets - especially the authors of the New Comedy strongly _________ humanity, and insist on the fundamental equality of the slave.
B. Schools in the city had done much to _________ on their pupils the doctrines of Theodore of Mopsuestia.
C. The _________ of such knowledge is an education for peace.
     (a) support   (b) inculcate
     (c) condemn   (d) burden
     (e) oppose

255. A. Sophia stared at him, struggling to _________ on his face when all she wanted to do was study every inch of his perfect body.
B. When nations are young and when they are poor, they usually _________ on two things: the military and civil order.
C. Causes of the heating problem could now be coming into _________ .
     (a) conclude   (b) study
     (c) concentrate   (d) focus
     (e) stress

DIRECTION (Qs 256-260): *Read each sentence to find out whether there is any grammatical mistake/error in it. Choose the sentence /option which is CORRECT without any errors in it.*

256. (a) While walking on the sidewalk, Hina found a sparkly girl's bracelet.
(b) After finally setting off on the trail, the morning felt more exciting.
(c) She tried to sneak out of the house her mother saw her leaving.
(d) He ran through the field as fast as he could. All the while rain was soaking him to the bone.
(e) According to newspaper reports there are more Internet users in small towns than metros.

257. (a) The officer yielded for the temptation and demanded extra amount.
(b) He is either foolish or coward, if not both.
(c) The attorney-general repeated the verdict word by word.
(d) Found guilty on theft, the accused was sentenced two years in jail.
(e) I complimented him on his inclusion in the national team.

258. (a) You toil not, neither do you spin, yet God takes care of you and your little ones.
(b) The prospect of reform were not much more favourable in Prussia.
(c) Dolly sure loves her mother but the relationship between mother and daughter is reversed.
(d) They had no abstract ideas; in their minds all were concrete, visible and tangible.
(e) The problem is, you did not either ask or listen.

259. (a) I'm sure neither Shiela nor Sarah are surprised at Peter not paying for the bill.
(b) We're still working with Rahul. He's on denial about everything. I almost pity the man.
(c) I was about to deny, but she kept a finger on my lips.
(d) She started to put the pillow down and caught the movement in the mirror out of the corner of her eye.
(e) Trying to write is very much like trying to put a Chinese puzzle together.

260. (a) It would only cause him more trouble, both to the trip and wagging tongues.
(b) We all know the stories of people who win the lottery and let's face it, for too often no good comes of it.
(c) The cause of the destruction of the French army in 1812 is clear to us now.
(d) Sanjna looked in the mirrors and could not distinguish her reflection than the others.
(e) The real important thing to remember is that language learning requires a lot of practice.

ANSWER KEY

1	(b)	24	(c)	47	(c)	70	(b)	93	(c)	116	(c)	139	(e)	162	(c)	185	(a)	208	(a)	231	(a)	254	(b)
2	(c)	25	(d)	48	(d)	71	(d)	94	(b)	117	(b)	140	(a)	163	(b)	186	(d)	209	(d)	232	(c)	255	(d)
3	(c)	26	(a)	49	(a)	72	(c)	95	(e)	118	(a)	141	(b)	164	(a)	187	(a)	210	(e)	233	(c)	256	(d)
4	(c)	27	(c)	50	(d)	73	(d)	96	(a)	119	(d)	142	(e)	165	(d)	188	(c)	211	(b)	234	(c)	257	(e)
5	(a)	28	(d)	51	(a)	74	(e)	97	(c)	120	(b)	143	(b)	166	(c)	189	(b)	212	(e)	235	(d)	258	(a)
6	(a)	29	(d)	52	(a)	75	(d)	98	(c)	121	(a)	144	(d)	167	(b)	190	(d)	213	(c)	236	(d)	259	(e)
7	(c)	30	(b)	53	(c)	76	(a)	99	(a)	122	(b)	145	(c)	168	(c)	191	(e)	214	(c)	237	(e)	260	(c)
8	(c)	31	(b)	54	(b)	77	(b)	100	(a)	123	(b)	146	(b)	169	(a)	192	(a)	215	(c)	238	(e)		
9	(d)	32	(c)	55	(a)	78	(b)	101	(b)	124	(c)	147	(e)	170	(e)	193	(d)	216	(b)	239	(a)		
10	(b)	33	(e)	56	(e)	79	(c)	102	(a)	125	(b)	148	(d)	171	(d)	194	(b)	217	(c)	240	(e)		
11	(c)	34	(d)	57	(b)	80	(a)	103	(c)	126	(b)	149	(c)	172	(e)	195	(a)	218	(c)	241	(d)		
12	(a)	35	(b)	58	(a)	81	(a)	104	(a)	127	(a)	150	(d)	173	(a)	196	(c)	219	(b)	242	(e)		
13	(e)	36	(d)	59	(c)	82	(b)	105	(c)	128	(c)	151	(a)	174	(c)	197	(a)	220	(a)	243	(c)		
14	(d)	37	(c)	60	(c)	83	(c)	106	(c)	129	(a)	152	(b)	175	(e)	198	(c)	221	(b)	244	(d)		
15	(d)	38	(a)	61	(e)	84	(b)	107	(e)	130	(e)	153	(c)	176	(d)	199	(d)	222	(a)	245	(e)		
16	(c)	39	(d)	62	(d)	85	(d)	108	(d)	131	(c)	154	(e)	177	(b)	200	(b)	223	(c)	246	(b)		
17	(d)	40	(b)	63	(a)	86	(a)	109	(c)	132	(b)	155	(d)	178	(c)	201	(e)	224	(c)	247	(a)		
18	(d)	41	(d)	64	(d)	87	(d)	110	(d)	133	(b)	156	(c)	179	(d)	202	(a)	225	(d)	248	(c)		
19	(d)	42	(d)	65	(a)	88	(d)	111	(c)	134	(d)	157	(a)	180	(e)	203	(e)	226	(d)	249	(b)		
20	(a)	43	(d)	66	(b)	89	(d)	112	(d)	135	(a)	158	(d)	181	(c)	204	(d)	227	(c)	250	(a)		
21	(b)	44	(a)	67	(c)	90	(c)	113	(b)	136	(a)	159	(c)	182	(b)	205	(a)	228	(a)	251	(c)		
22	(a)	45	(d)	68	(c)	91	(e)	114	(a)	137	(a)	160	(b)	183	(d)	206	(a)	229	(c)	252	(e)		
23	(e)	46	(d)	69	(e)	92	(d)	115	(c)	138	(d)	161	(a)	184	(c)	207	(c)	230	(d)	253	(a)		

Hints & Explanations

1. (b) It should be 'has been sounding horn'.
2. (c) Replace 'by' with 'up'.
3. (c) It should be 'was' in place of 'is'.
4. (c) Change 'would not be traced' to 'could not be traced'.
5. (a) Change the first part as ———— It is/would be better ...
6. (a) The sentence should start as ———— If you had read ...
7. (c) The right phrase will be 'to look after' in place of 'to look over'.
35. (b) Replace *would write* by *writes*.
36. (d) Replace *changed* by *change*
37. (c) Replace *his* by *him*.
38. (a) Replace *has* by *had*.
40. (b) Replace 'of' with 'in'.
41. (d) Here there is a comparison between two persons, so it should be 'more honest' in place of 'most honest'.
42. (d) 'Submit' should be 'submitting'.
43. (d) Replace 'would not have' with 'had not'.
44. (a) 'team leaders encourages' should be replaced by 'team leaders encourage' or 'team leader encourages'.
45. (d) Replace 'are' with 'is' because the subject (prime minister) is singular here.
46. (d) Replace 'were' with 'was'.

47. (c) It should be 'the present I sent for him'.
48. (d) It should be *by* his decision.
49. (a) The sentence should begin as, 'if 1 had come ...'
50. (d) Replace 'at once' with 'at the beginning'
51. (a) The sentence should start as, I had been waiting for you.......'
52. (c) It should be " *and who is* ..." In the given form, the subject 'of is' is missing.
53. (c) Delete had. In a "No sooner...than..."structure, than is followed by a subject followed by past simple tense.
54. (b) *For a hundred years* indicates that the verb should be in the perfect continuous tense. Hence replace 'has lived' by 'has been living'.
55. (a) *Boys* is countable. Hence replace 'less' by 'fewer'.
57. (b) It should be "equipped not only with" instead of "not only equipped with".
58. (a) Here, as we are comparing two methods for a single purpose, the sentence should start as – 'No other method'.
59. (c) Views should always be followed by 'on' instead of 'for'.
60. (c) Delete 'I'.

62. (d) Here, levied additional monthly charges on consumers is used.

63. (a) Here, Despite curfew is used.

64. (d) Here, Has been doubled is used.

65. (a)   66. (b)   67. (c)

68. (c) Here, arise when they are not is used.

69. (e) No error

71. (d) If should be 'either in India or in the country of his origin

72. (c) and law abiding ....

73. (d) .... has not been achieved instead of have

74. (e) the sentence is correct (no error)

75. (d) in India's ..... in place of to India's ...

76. (a) Substitute between for among

77. (b) Substitute undergone

78. (b) Substitute detailed

79. (c) Substitute at least

80. (a) Delete no.

81. (a) Here subject (tractor sales) is plural. Hence, ... tractor sales have seen .... should be used.

82. (b) It is preposition related error. Hence, ... that share the earth with us should be used.

83. (c)

84. (b) Here, Noun i.e., environment and forests is .... should be used.

85. (d) Here, Infinitive i.e., To portray is subject. Hence, singular verb i.e. references is very difficult should be used.

92. (d) 'Mushrooming' should be used-which would serve as an adjective.

93. (c) 'Are' should replace 'is'- verb should agree with 'bulbs'

94. (b) 'By' should replace 'with' - which means 'by the way of'

96. (a) Either you have to remove "comparatively" or convert "better" to "good" in the sentence. The meaning of "comparatively" is - to evaluate anything using comparison estimate by comparison, etc. hence you should use either "better" or "comparatively good" in order to make the sentence correct.

97. (c) "Kindly" will not be used here; because "kindly" and "requested" are never used simultaneously "kindly" and "please" are used in Active Voice to denote "request"; while denote "kindly" and "please" in Passive Voice, "Requested" is generally used.

98. (c) The use of "it" is superfluous here, as the usage of the Object of "bought"- the book: is correct in the sentence.

99. (a) Instead of "passing marks" you should use "pass marks", because "passing marks" is not correct

100. (a) You should use "neighbours" instead of "neighbourers" because, there is no word in English like "neighbourers". The meaning of "neighbours" is people who live or are situated nearby.

101. (b) Delete 'to'. It is superfluous.

102. (a) Replace 'Yesterday in the night' by last night.

103. (c) Replace 'will approach' with 'will be approaching'.

104. (a) Use of whole is superfluous.

105. (c) Use of that is superfluous.

111. (c) 'The need to set up a good library in the locality has been in the minds of the people' is correct. Therefore option (c) requires an article-the, otherwise the expression is not correct.

112. (d) Most people would have attended the union meeting if they had had a longer notice of it. Therefore option (d) is wrong and article 'a' should be used before longer.

113. (b) He took to reading the Times for better knowledge of the facts, is the correct sentence. Therefore in option (b) article 'the' will be used before the name of a newspaper, Time.

114. (a) When children have difficulty in understanding a certain mathematical process, it is often because their teachers do not understand it conceptually themselves and do not present it in a way that children can understand. Therefore option (a) difficulty will take the preposition 'in' to be correctly expressed.

115. (c) Invest in programs that ensure a healthy pregnancy, is the correct use.

116. (c) The number of scenes depicting alcohol consumption has increased dramatically over--- is the right use. Therefore the number as the subject will take a singular verb 'has', in option (c).

117. (b) The provided information is based on a single theme therefore the two parts of the sentence should be connected by conjunction 'and' not by 'but'. The conjunction 'But' is used when the flow of information is in opposite direction.

118. (a) Less is used when you're referring to something that can't be counted or doesn't have a plural, fewer is used for 'countable' and less for 'uncountable'. In the given sentence, since 'problems' are countable, 'fewer' should be used.

119. (d) Here the singular subject Singapore will take pronoun its in option (d).

120. (b) Most unique is the wrong comparative. In option (b) So, it should be 'the gown was unique'.

161. (a) runs out.

162. (c) rages on.

163. (b) the first to switch off.

164. (a) not just because.

165. (d) in support of.

168. (c) For the candidate.

181. (c) Difficult will replace easier and going for an election will be running for election.

182. (b) We have in America a hybrid speech....... But a combination of all three is the correct improvement.

183. (d) Far from being a tight focused Narrative.......instead an expansive novel

184. (c) So docile and truculent that.......sudden virulence toward

185. (a) See through the deception......and promptly forced him down.

207. (c) B. Others suffer a lot because of his procrastination in taking any action.
C. On account of his procrastination others suffer a lot.

209. (d) A. The quality of the fabric being unimpressive, we changed our plan of purchasing.
B. We changed our plan of purchasing on finding the quality of the fabric unimpressive.

211. (b) B. As it is very cold you must bring warm clothes with you.

212. (e) None of the above sentence is structurally and grammatically correct.

213. (c) If I had enough money I would backpack around Europe. But, unfortunately I am broke.

214. (c) The judges, talking at length among themselves finally distributed the awards among the most active children.

215. (c) I have been ill for a fortnight and the Management as well as the school sports committee prefers to elect me Captain of school team.

216. (b) If you tried to understand the concept of the whole class, you will not only remember it, but also can put to use while solving even the difficult exercises.

217. (c) In sentence A there is incorrect use of article 'a' before 'tarot'; it should be 'the tarot'. Sentence B has an incorrect phrase 'all the outcry'; it should be 'all the outcries'. Sentence C has incorrect use of pronoun 'whom' in place of 'which'. Sentences D and E do not contain any error, so option (c) is the correct answer.

218. (c) Sentence 1 is incorrect because there is incorrect use of the word 'countries' in place of 'country'. Sentence 2 is also incorrect; article 'the' is required before 'precise extent to which ....'. In sentence 3 there is incorrect use of preposition 'on' after 'to live...'. It should be 'live by....'. There is subject-verb disagreement in sentence in sentence 4, so it is also incorrect. Only sentence 5 is correct grammatically, so option (c) is the correct answer.

219. (b) Sentences A and C are correct grammatically. In sentence B, there is incorrect use of the singular pronoun 'it' to refer to plural noun 'elements'. The correct sentence should be - "...elements, most of them...". There is incorrect use of phrase 'gained in' in sentence D in place of 'gained by'. The phrase 'gained in' means an increase or growth in something. Sentence E is also incorrect because the different pronouns have been used in the sentence. 'One' should be replaced by 'you' to make the sentence correct. So option (b) is the correct answer.

220. (a) Sentences C and D are correct grammatically. Sentence A is incorrect as there is wrong use of 'ing' after the word 'answer'. An 'infinitive' should not be followed by the '-ing'. Sentence B is wrong because there is wrong use of degree of comparison in 'gravest of charge', it should be 'gravest of charges' instead. Sentence E has the error of subject-verb disagreement. The plural pronoun 'them' should be used to refer to plural word 'actions' instead of 'it'. So option (a) is the correct answer.

221. (b) First sentence is grammatically correct. In the second sentence, add 'they' before 'being' which is the subject of the sentence; this is a dangling modifier because we do not know who the only people are there.

222. (a) In sentence (I), 'he' is superfluous. Sentence (II) is correct.

223. (c) 'It's time' is followed by the past tense verb which isn't actually a past tense, but the subjunctive is in past. In second sentence, 'than' should be replaced by 'when'.

224. (c) With 'prefer' use 'to' and not 'than'. Ex- I prefer tea to coffee. In second sentence, conditional sentence form: if + Past Perfect, Conditional II (= would/might+ have + Past Participle). Ex- If I had found her number, I would have called her.

225. (d) Both sentences are grammatically correct.

226. (d) Both sentences are grammatically correct.

227. (c) One is only used to talk about people in general, and is not used to refer to an individual. Hence, its possessive is one's and not 'his/her'. In the second sentence, 'place' should be replaced by 'there are no seats'.

228. (a) With 'except' use objective case 'me' instead of subjective 'I'. Second sentence is correct.

229. (c) 'the most' is redundant in the first sentence. In the second sentence, 'a little' should replace 'little'.

230. (d) Both sentences are correct.

231. (a) 'Enjoyed' should be followed by 'himself'. Second sentence is correct.

232. (c) Say 'The Greeks' instead of 'Greeks'. In the second sentence, 'the majority of legislators' should take a plural verb.

233. (c) Both sentences are correct.

234. (c) You put up a ladder against the wall. In the second sentence, 'content' should be in plural meaning everything that is included in a collection and that is held or included in something.

235. (d) Both sentences are correct.

236. (d) Say 'least' worried. In the second sentence, use 'the' before 'whole'. Sentence (III) is correct.

237. (e) Instead of 'more enchanting', use 'the most enchanting'. In the sentence (II), replace 'blunt' with 'bluntly.' 'Looks out on something' is correct usage.

238. (e) All three sentences are correct.

239. (a) Use 'toiling very hard' instead of 'hardly'. Sentence (II) & (III) are correct.

240. (e) All three sentences correct.

241. (d) 'None other than', 'no other way...than' will take comparative 'than'.

242. (e) The sentence is grammatically correct and no correction is required.

243. (c) 'To put up with' means to bear or suffer patiently; tolerate. Here schools have gone through the struggle and have put up with the struggle to win playground for their students.

244. (d) If emotions are running high, people are angry or emotional about something.

245. (e) To go on a day-long strike means to go on a strike that lasts a whole day. Hence, sentence requires no improvement.

246. (b) 'alight' means to get out of a vehicle, especially a train or bus. 'Tied' means fastened or attached with string or similar cord.

247. (a) 'From' indicates the point in space at which a journey, motion, or action starts. 'To' is here used to express motion in the direction of (a particular location).

248. (c) 'Working' here means engaging in physical or mental activity in order to achieve a result; 'Condemn' means to express complete disapproval of; censure.

249. (b) 'Left' here means to cause (someone or something) to be in a particular state or position.
' Including' means 'containing as part of the whole being considered.'

250. (a) 'Direct' here means give (someone) an official order or authoritative instruction. 'Form' means 'bring together parts or combine to create (something)'.

251. (c) Elaborate breakfast means fancy or showy, if you elaborate you add details to something, elaborate stage effects means fancy or showy effects that would mesmerise.

252. (e) Stage denotes any distinct time period in a sequence of events; a large platform on which people can stand and can be seen by an audience; plan, organize, and carry out (an event).

253. (a) The verb 'suspend' means 'stop a process, activity or a habit'; make inoperative or stop; suspension bridge means a bridge in which the weight of the deck is supported by vertical cables suspended from further cables that run between towers and are anchored in abutments at each end.

254. (b) The verb 'inculcate' means teach and impress by frequent repetitions or admonitions; Noun 'inculcation' means the act of inculcating, or teaching or influencing persistently and repeatedly so as to implant or instil an idea, theory, attitude, etc.

255. (d) The verb 'focus' here means direct one's attention on something; noun 'focus' means the concentration of attention or energy on something.

256. (d) Sentence is grammatically correct.

257. (e) Sentence is grammatically correct.

258. (a) Sentence is grammatically correct.

259. (e) Sentence is grammatically correct.

260. (c) Sentence has no error.

◈ ◈ ◈

CHAPTER 3

Reading Comprehension

INTRODUCTION

If one wants to find a success mantra in today's highly competitive world with ever expanding boundaries of knowledge, then it has to be – "know the right thing at the right time, make right use of it in just the right words" – we all have our own bank of knowledge, some have more than others, but what is the point of knowing if you don't know how to use your knowledge well. It is just like owning a guitar without knowing how to play it. But the good thing is you can easily learn to play it if you are committed and have the right guidance.

It is also true about reading comprehension which is all about knowing the right thing, making the right use of it, in the right words. It is the magical guitar on which you can play your success tune. But to learn to play this guitar you need constant effort and a right direction. So, why not begin now ?

Why do you think reading comprehension questions are asked from the primary level in school examinations to a level as high as competitive examinations for management or administrative work? Very simply put, in the present era which has a plethora of information, facts, knowledge, it is important for any officer, most of all, for a manager to be able to extract out relevant information from the given draft in minimum possible time and use it for the execution of the assigned project in the best possible way. Remember, as a Manager, you will be required to know details of your company, your staff, your client, your projects, your rivals. But it does not stop here for this you can find out and store on your desktop easily, the real managerial task is to use the available information cleverly to achieve maximum profit target. And this is what reading comprehension exercises give you a practice in. Therefore, a student must approach this section not only as a preparation exercise but as skill that he/she will use for the rest of his/her life. Having said how important Reading comprehension is, I would like the students to know that the reading comprehension section checks not your IQ rather your ability to analyse data and produce conclusions most useful and tangible for positive results. Every student should therefore, keep in mind that this section demands Aptitude more than Intelligence. So, with right direction and determined practice even an average student can excel in this area. Remember you can play guitar if you want to, hard enough.

Let's proceed with understanding reading comprehension.

WHAT IS READING COMPREHENSION?

Interestingly, Reading Comprehension is an activity your brain is constantly engaged in. Whatever you do is reading Comprehension for brain. e.g. Reading newspaper, watching billboards on roadside, watching TV, talking with a person, listening to music etc. Reading a newspaper is obviously reading comprehension you would have understood. We read the news printed on the paper, we understand what it means, we analyse the news for ourselves, by which I mean, sometimes we agree or disagree with the opinion expressed in the newspaper article. If it is a report we select the useful portion of news and store it in our memory to be used later. We like or dislike the subject chosen by the writer, sometimes we are made to think or question our beliefs or mindset by some articles, this is data analysis, then we remember what seems important or useful to us in the newspaper and forget much of the news in the paper everyday.

The same procedure happens even when you are watching hoarding on the roadside. The advertisements are the data for your brain. It is raw information that your brain understands and processes. Remember how many times you say after watching an Ad, "Oh, this is not real", "Oh! Does it happen this way, I didn't know that", "This is a good Ad". All of the above reactions when studied closely are a judgment, fact-collection, opinion formation.

You don't remember everything about every Ad, only the part appealing to you finds a place in your memory. This is Data Selection. Same for watching TV and listening to music, your mind reads information, comprehends it, processes it, selects the useful section and stores it for future, rejects the useless part. So, to make Reading Comprehension easy we can draw a flow chart of the entire process.

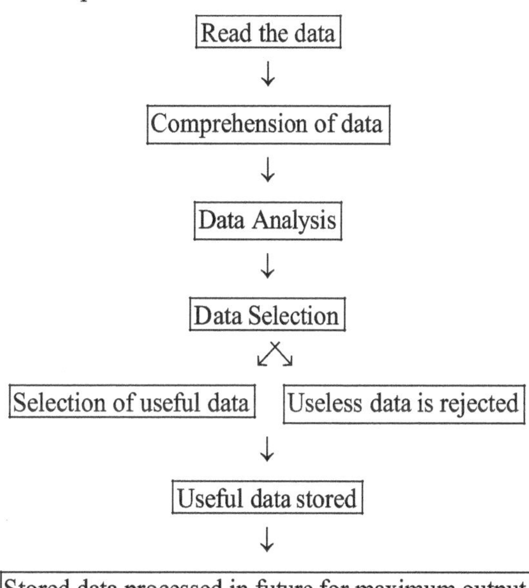

The entire process of Reading Comprehension could be divided into 7 simple steps. But here is a need for a reckenor. Though reading comprehension is what our brain practices all the time, yet we do not always perform very well when attempting a reading comprehension question, why?

Because what the brain does is at an ordinary simplistic level and we are unaware of even that. But what is required of an aspiring student is a conscious, skilful, determined effort to master the art of reading comprehension.

Let's illustrate all the seven steps involved in Reading Compression describing what we ordinarily do and what are the special concepts a students should keep in mind while attempting the Reading Comprehension section with some useful tips.

STEP 1 : Reading is the obvious important pre-requisite of the RC section. How well you read, in what manner do you read a given passage, would determine the level of your comprehension and consequently the analysis of information. Reading in the right way is very important.

WHAT is the RIGHT way of READING ?

As I have mentioned before that we are constantly engaged in the process of reading information from our surroundings. Only we do not do it skilfully in the right direction. This is what a student has to practice doing to read everything rightly. **HOW**? Even an apparently simple process of reading involves many factors that affect the output of reading. How intelligently can you mould these factors will, in turn, improve the quality of reading. These factors are :

- Subject of data
- Interest areas of the reader
- Concentration span of the reader
- Reading speed
- Retaining capacity
- Reading Aptitude

I.   SUBJECT OF DATA

It is proven by research that our brains or brains of different people do not respond to different kinds of data in a similar manner or to a similar extent. Just like we all have our area of expertise, I might know a lot about space science while your knowledge of Automobile may be vast. On the other hand, my idea of latest cars, engines and their power may be meagre and you may find yourself fumbling if questioned about planetary movements, composition of stars etc. This is a reflection of reading habits. Ordinarily, we do selective reading, e.g; while reading a newspaper many students are used to skipping the Business news and jumping straight to sports page while many others simply refuse to look at the editorial page and drool all over the page 3 or entertainment section. Whereas reading has many advantages, it is neither feasible nor advisable for a student to read everything available on all topics under the sun. But it is important, nevertheless, for you to have some basic knowledge about most subjects. This will

(1) improve your general awareness,

(2) boost your confidence,

(3) sharpen your analytical skills because you would be able to use information from different sections and even do a comparative study, if needed, it will also.

(4) improve your thinking skills because as the quantity of facts will increase, you will be pushed to think about all of them. In this manner you will improve many of your skills, not just one. Also, one should not forget that as a manager one needs to know about not just one field but many. Marketing requires more than just the knowledge of specific sector.

So, to begin with a student should open oneself to reading about varied subjects and not just a selected few. Then it becomes important to decide how much to read and from where to read. The best and age-old golden option is Newspaper. A good student MUST develop a habit of reading a newspaper properly everyday. You would say that you do already. In that case, answer the following questions and check yourself?

*   What is the most influential political news of the last week ?

*   What important discovery or research has been made in the field of science, technology or medicine in the gone month?

*   Which book was released by an Indian or American author in the gone week ?

*   Who is the Chief Minister of Gujarat ?

*   When did Einstein die ?

*   What is article 377 of the Indian constitution?

*   What was Rowlatt Act ? Which year was it passed?

*   Who is rated the best Badminton player in the world ?

*   Who is playing Danial Pearl's wife in the Hollywood film being made on the Journalist's life and murder by terrorists ?

*   Which film received the National Award this year?

Check your calibre as a reader now on the basis of the following result card.

Correct Answers	Result
0 – 3	Poor Reader
4 – 7	Average Reader
8 – 10	Good Reader

Now, you know yourself and what are your weaknesses. You would have noticed for yourself while answering the questions.

That despite reading the newspaper everyday you are not updated about the goings-on in every field. This is the first step towards becoming a good reader. You should choose wisely what newspaper or magazines you read. Most advisable would be The Hindu, Indian Express, The Times of India. You can choose from the following magazines India Today, Frontline, Outlook, The Economist. You should also read some books on History, Philosophy and literature as and when you have the time. Though reading must be done selectively so as not to waste time, don't read all articles and reports in the newspaper but intelligently choose after having read all headlines.

☛ **TIP**

Use this reading habit to improve your vocabulary. Each day list the new words you come across. Classify them under subjects, e.g. Science, Sports, Politics, Literature. Learn their meanings and use them frequently. This will help you understand the jargon of different fields.

Now, let us quickly recall all that we have stated and discussed in this section and list the

MUST DOs FOR A GOOD READER

* Read about different fields, don't restrict yourself to one.
* Do intelligent reading, don't waste time reading junk information.
* Read only from good newspapers and magazines
* Utilise maximum time, read while travelling, waiting etc.
* Try to indulge in a discussion everyday about what you read that day
* Improve your vocabulary alongside reading

II. INTEREST OF READER

This factor is closely connected to the first factor. In fact, it is this factor that chiefly decides the subjects we choose to read about. Just like all fingers in a hand are not of the same size, our interest in every field cannot be of the same level. This is why we choose certain fields and eliminate others. e.g. while walking on the road, if there is a large poster of a bike newly launched in market, it is more likely that a teenage or a young boy would stop by to read the details about the bike rather than a girl who would probably stop by to read information on Jewellery or garments ranges. This is just difference of interests. This is the difference that decides the store of one's knowledge. Ordinarily, it is alright for a person to seek information about one feels drawn to the area of his/her interest. But a student should develop a habit of arousing an interest in different kind of fields equally.

Why is this important ?

Let us suppose that you have interest in fields A, B, D and F but you do not find fields C and E appealing at all. In that case, if you get a passage for Reading Comprehension from areas A, C and E, then you would attempt the first comprehension well because it is an area of your interest, therefore, you will be eager to know more about it, you will, therefore, read it with more concentration and finish reading in less time. Since you have some previous knowledge about the subject, the matter will not be completely new to you and therefore, you will be able to deal with it better. But for

the other two passages, because of lack of interest in the topic, your engagement with the data will be half hearted. Owing to this, the comprehension process will slow down and the analysis will not be of the same quality as the first. It is, therefore, clear that the interest of the student in given passage greatly affects his/her performance in attempting the exercise. This is why it becomes important for an aspiring student to develop some interest at least in various fields whether it be science, politics, history, medicine, space, diplomacy, technology, literature, business, economy or world affairs etc.

This is where the first factor also comes into play. If a student reads from different topics, expands his/her reading to various field, he/she will automatically develop some interest in all the fields and also attain some knowledge about each sector. Combining the two, the efficiency of a student in attempting the RC section will be greatly improved.

☛ **TIP**

For maximum utility of time, you can depend on News Channels. You can select certain talk shows aired on some good English news channels like NDTV, CNN IBN or TIMES NOW and watch them regularly. This will improve your general awareness, give you an analytical perspective, keep you updated with news from different sectors, and also improve your English.

An Inquisitive mind is a gift for student. Always maintain a desire to know more, keep yourself curious about every subject. Do not hesitate in discussing your opinions, asking questions, expressing your views with friends, teachers or experts. This kind of interaction and communication will greatly increase your interest and knowledge and you will be drawn towards reading automatically. Always keep in mind that developing these habits will help you reap long term benefits.

III. CONCENTRATION SPAN OF READER

Not only in reading but any task to be executed requires concentration. But reading requires it more. So, most students from primary to senior level are heard complaining about lack of concentration as the reason for their poor performance. It has become a popular belief that concentration is naturally endowed on people and so some students have great concentration while others remain restless and cannot concentrate properly. Contrary to the popular belief, the truth is that even concentration can be achieved through effort.

Scientifically a human brain is not tuned to keep itself associated with a particular object for long time and that is why many of us face concentration problems. But these problems are easy to handle also. From usual experience you would know that while reading data of your interest, your mind exhibits more concentration. Why can you sit through a movie with complete concentration but not your maths book or even a newspaper for that matter? Because, things that you find entertaining stimulate your brain in a manner which is positive and, hence, you achieve higher level of concentration. Here again we see the first two factors affecting the third. If you develop interest in many subjects, your concentration will automatically increase. But there is a hitch, you can improve concentration by increasing interest and you can increase interest by reading more. But if you have poor concentration then you cannot read more. It is, therefore, a vicious circle.

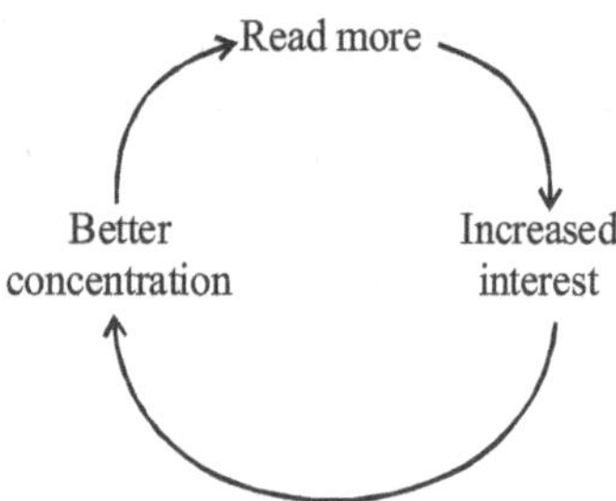

It, therefore, becomes important to improve your concentration first, to be able to then work on other factors. There are certain tricks that a student may follow to improve his/her concentration.

☛ **TIP 1**

Always start with shorter, simpler pieces with subject of your interest and gradually move to heavier, more difficult passage. Through this you will first strengthen your confidence, build up your momentum and will be more prepared to deal with longer passages.

☛ **TIP 2**

Always supervise your reading. Mark every time you get distraction or lose concentration. In this manner you will find out how many times you lost concentration in an hour, with every passing hour make a stronger effort to be more concentrated. You will find out that with each hour number of the marks will decrease.

IV. READING SPEED

From a competitive point of view, 'Time is money,' the faster you read, the more time you will have for comprehension and analysis. If you have followed the first three factors carefully then you will realise that your reading speed will improve greatly itself. But you must keep in mind certain points while trying to read fast. Often what students do is, in their attempt to read fast, they increase the speed of reading words without trying to either understand or retain the information. Remember-

Reading Comprehension = Reading + Comprehension. You must read at a fast speed but not at the cost of comprehension because in that case you'll have to read the

passage again and, therefore, the time you saved by reading fast will be consumed in re-reading.

☛ **TIP 1**

Your Reading speed is the number of words you can read and understand per minute. Remember if you don't understand because you're reading very fast, it is of no use.

☛ **TIP 2**

Calculate your reading speed. In this manner you will be able to supervise your improvement.

V. RETAINING CAPACITY

This is the most important part of Reading. If a student is able to read well, read with concentration, read fast and if not able to retain useful information of the data then all is lost. A good reader need not come back to the passage again and again to look for answers. The first reading of this passage should, therefore, be done with much care and attention so that the reader retains most of the matter.

You can follow some simple steps to improve your retaining capability. Every time you read a passage, make a mental note of the following :

(a)　title of the passage
(b)　basic theme of the passage
(c)　the positions that the passage takes or the points that the passage makes
(d)　conclusion of the passage.

VI. READING APTITUDE

Reading Aptitude is different from reading skills. The points and factors discussed up till now, constitute reading skill and are regarding the manner you read. Reading Aptitude is what gives an upper edge to a student in the RC section or even otherwise if developed properly.

What is Reading Aptitude?

By reading aptitude, we mean the approach that you take while reading a passage or reading anything. The mindset with which you read it and what is your motive or expectation from the passage. Simply put, Reading aptitude is what you want from reading. If your approach is a reading piece only for the purpose of reading to collect facts to add to your existing store of knowledge or only as a practice to improve your reading speed or merely as an examination exercise you would not receive the same results as you will if you read the passage with a different attitude.

Consider every piece of written information as a prospective useful draft.

Begin with the rule of WIIFM - what's in it for me. Once you have used your wisdom to decide if the passage is worth reading. Approach the passage as a mystery novel. There are hidden clues you must look for. From the beginning stay a careful, clever reader. Remember the first reading itself should give you all you may need to have from a passage.

If there are facts in the passage, quickly decide, as you read, which of these are important enough to be memorized and memorize them.

If there is an argument in the passage, keep trail of how the argument proceeds and what are the different evidences offered.

In such a passage, as you read, involve your mind with the passage and form an opinion about the argument.

If a passage is about philosophy offering a philosophical perspective as you read, form a short summary of the philosophical theory in simple words.

If the essay describes a process or an event, then as you read on, form a chain of events in your mind.

Keeping these points in mind, will improve your reading and retaining efficiency greatly. What we have to target and achieve is not GOOD READING rather what we must try and attain is EFFECTIVE READING. A good reader may or may not be just as good at comprehension and analysis but an Effective Reader would definitely perform in comprehension and Analysis of data just as well. So, try and be an EFFECTIVE READER.

STEP 2 : Comprehension follows reading and simply put means understanding the passage. But there are different categories of compositions and the time of comprehension for each would principally vary. Nevertheless, there are some basic principles one must keep in mind while attempting to comprehend a passage.

* To make comprehension easy, follow the paragraph division of the passage.

* As you read each paragraph, mark the important points stated in the paragraph.

* When you have read the passage once, decide onto the basic theme of the passage.

* Quickly re-read the marked section of each paragraph and form a basic argument skeleton of the passage in your mind.

* Do not make reading a one way process rather treat it as a dialogue.

* Keep your brain actively involved in reading. Treat the passage as if its writer is talking to you. Make it move like a discussion, respond to what is being said in the passage. In this manner your comprehension level will increase greatly.

* If you do not understand a word, do not panic, you can make out the meaning of the word by fitting it into the larger sense of the sentence, similarly, if you don't understand a phrase, try to fit it into the argument of the paragraph to ascertain its meaning.

* In case the subject of the paragraph is completely new to you, you must proceed with more care and cleverness. Approach the passage with confidence and an open mind. Do not get taken aback by field-specific jargon, these big and difficult sounding words would not affect your understanding of the composition much.

The different types of compositions that one can come across while attempting RC exercise are :

(1) Narrative.

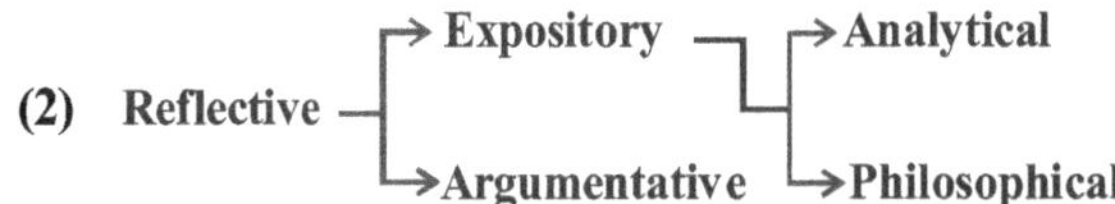

(2) Reflective

(3) Imaginative.

Let us now consider each type of passage and how should one deal with it.

1. **Narrative Passage :** A narrative passage usually tells a story which means a sequence of events. Thus, a narrative passage gives an orderly account of a series of related events or the successive particulars of an event. A narrative passage could be of various kinds. (1) biographics (2) History (3) Fiction (4) Execution of a process. The following is a paragraph from a narrative passage.

Recently I spent several hours sitting under a tree in my garden with the social anthropologist William Ury, a Harvard University professor who specializes in the art of negotiation and wrote the bestselling book, *Getting to Yes*. He captivated me with his theory that tribalism protects people from their fear of rapid change. He explained that the pillars of tribalism that humans rely on for security would always counter any significant cultural or social change. In this way, he said, change is never allowed to happen too fast. Technology, for example, is a pillar of society. Ury believes that every time technology moves in a new or radical direction, another pillar such as religion or nationalism will grow stronger - in effect, the traditional and familiar will assume greater importance to compensate for the new and untested. In this manner, human tribes avoid rapid change that leaves people insecure and frightened.

In a narrative passage, the questions asked are chiefly about the main ideas discussed in the narrative, some opinions of the narrator or about the general factual information provided through the passage and student must, therefore, concentrate on the main points of the narrative and select them as important. You can follow this simple procedure for attempting the comprehension of a Narrative passage.

If it is a biography, choose the important events of the life of the person, his/her most important works, Principles and ideas that govern the person's life.

If it is a historical narrative, keep in mind the important stages of the event, the cause and the consequences, important people involved in the happenings of the event and their views. Also, it is always important to give weightage to the opinion of the author if expressed in the narrative.

If it is a narrative about a process or an incident then find out the following :-

* theme of narration
* basic exposition, i.e. the chief idea being narrated
* statements that the narrator supports
* idea or statements author does not agree with
* certain factual descriptions in the passage
* train of thought as the narrative moves

2. Reflective Passage :

(a) **Expository Passage :** An expository passage is the most rigid and restricted form of composition. It is also the most common kind of writing. Exposition means to set forth a subject. So, an exposition composition would mean an orderly setting forth of facts and ideas. Its purpose is to explain its language is clear and direct. Its appeal is to the intellect. What you would mostly come across in an exposition essay will be definition, comparisons and contradictions. Exposition is defined in the dictionary as Explanation. Thus a student can expect a straight statement like tone in the passage. These are easier to deal with and can be mastered with practice and relatively less effort.

The following is a paragraph from an expository passage. The painter is now free to paint anything he chooses. There are scarcely any forbidden subjects, and today everybody is prepared to admit that a painting of some fruit can be as important as a painting of a hero dying. The impressionists did as much as anybody to win this previously unheard-of freedom for the artist. Yet, by the next generation, painters began to abandon the subject altogether, and began to paint abstract pictures. Today the majority pictures painted are abstract.

Thus, for a painting to succeed it is essential that the painter and his public agree about what is significant. The subject may have a personal meaning for the painter or individual spectator; but there must also be the possibility of their agreement on its general meaning. It is at this point that the culture of the society and period in question proceeds the artist and his art. Renaissance art would have meant nothing to the Aztecs–and vice versa. If, to some extent, a few intellectuals can appreciate them both today it is because their culture is an historical one: its inspirations is history and therefore it can include within itself, in principle if not in every particular, all known developments to date.

As you can read yourself an expository essay in itself gives you a serial line of thought. What you have to do, in this case, is understand critically the exposition being made. Pay attention to the following when attempting an exposition essay.

* main subject of the exposition
* illustrations made about its different aspects
* analysis done by the writer on the various definitions & statements
* Agreements or disagreements made by the writer with some views.

Let's take the following questions as an example-
Which of the following is not necessarily among the attributes needed for a painter to succeed?
(1) The painter and his public agree on what is significant
(2) The painter is able to communicate and justify the significance of its subject selection.
(3) The subject has a personal meaning for the painter
(4) The painting of subject is inspired by historical developments.

The first option is clearly stated as a reason for the success of a painter and, thus, can be eliminated. The second option, if one thinks intelligently, is linked to the first. If only the painter is able to communicate or justify the significance of its subject selection, can there be any agreement between the painter and the public? This too, thus, gets eliminated. The third and the fourth options offer an ambiguity because both appear in the passage. A close study of the language of the statement and the question is required here. The question asks for a reason which is not necessarily required for the success of a painting, which means it may cause the success of a painting but not necessarily. The third option appears with a 'may' in the passage and can, therefore, be a possible answer. The fourth option is not the answer because the passage states that a painting can earn the appreciation of intellectuals if its inspiration is history and there is no 'may' or chance involved here. Thus, the fourth option can also be eliminated and we have our correct answer as option (3).

(b) **Argumentative Passage :** An argumentative passage includes an argument and an argument is possible only about a subject that invites argument, conflicting opinions. Such an essay admits difference of opinions and, therefore, the purpose of an argumentative essay is to persuade the readers to adopt a certain idea, attitude or course of action and if possible to resolve the conflict implicit in the subject. The following is an example of a argumentative passage : The detective story, the adult analogue of juvenile adventure tale has at times been described as a glorification of intellectualized conflict. However, a great deal of the interest in the plots of these stories is sustained by withholding the unravelling of a solution to a problem. The effort of solving the problem is in itself not a conflict if the adversary (the unknown criminal) remains passive, like Nature whose secrets the scientist supposedly unravels by deduction. If the adversary actively puts obstacles in the detectives' path towards the solution, there is genuine conflict. But the conflict is psychologically interesting only to the extent that it contains irrational components such as a tactical error on the criminal's part or the detectives' insight into some psychological quirk of the criminal or something of the Art. Conflict conducted in a perfectly rational manner is psychologically no more interesting than western standard e.g. Tie-tac-toe, played perfectly by both players, is completely devoid of psychological interest. Chess may be psychologically interesting but only to the extent that it is played not quite rationally. Played completely rationally, chess would be no different from tic-tac-toe.

Internal conflicts are always psychologically interesting. What we vaguely call "interesting" psychology is in very great measure the psychology of inner conflict. Inner conflict is also held to be an important component of serious literature as distinguished from less serious genres. The classical tragedy, as well as the serious novel, reveals the inner conflict of central figures. The superficial adventure story, on the other hand, depicts only external conflict; that is, the threats to the person with whom the reader (or viewer) identifies stem in these stories exclusively from external obstacles and from the adversaries who create them. On the most primitive level this sort of external conflict is psychologically empty. In the fisticuffs between the protagonists of good and evil, no psychological problems are involved or, at any rate, none are depicted in juvenile representations of conflict. While dealing with an argumentative passage the reader should follow the following method to deal any question-

Narrow down the argument to its basis

> Track the history of the question/conflict in the passage
>
> Take a stand yourself or be clear as to what is author's stand
>
> Analyse the necessary idea expressed in the passage
>
> Keep track of the evidence or examples offered by the author in support of his/her argument
>
> Make note of the counter argument

Following this method the students should find out the right answer to the above mentioned question from the following option:

(a) Internal conflicts, rather than external conflicts, form an important component of serious literature as distinguished from less serious genres.

(b) Only juveniles or very few adults actually experience external conflict while internal conflict is more widely prevalent in society

(c) In situations of internal conflict, individuals experience a dilemma in solving their own preferences for different outcomes

(d) There are no threats to the reader in case of external conflicts

Examples of **Analytical** and **Philosophical passages** are given below. A student should follow the same method as for the expository passage and keep similar factors in mind. Spare a moment to take stock of what's been happening in the past *few* months. Let's start with the oil price, which has rocketed to more than \$65 a barrel, more than double its level 18 months ago. The accepted wisdom is that we shouldn't worry our little heads about that, because the incentives are there *for* business to build new production

and refining capacity, which will effortlessly bring demand and supply back into balance and bring crude prices back to \$25 a barrel. As Tommy Cooper used to say, 'just like that'.

Then there is the result of the French referendum on the European Constitution, seen as thick-headed luddites railing vainly against the modem world. What the French needed to realise, the argument went, was that there was no alternative to the reforms that would make the country more flexible, more competitive, more dynamic. Just the sort of reforms that allowed Gate Gourmet to sack hundreds of its staff at Heathrow after the sort of ultimatum that used to be handed out by Victorian mill owners. An alternative way of looking at the French "non" is that our neighbours translate "flexibility" as "you're fired."

Finally, take a squint at the United States. Just like Britain a century ago, a period of unquestioned superiority is drawing to a close. China is still a long way from matching America's wealth, but it is growing at a stupendous rate and economic strength brings geo-political clout. Already, there is evidence of a new scramble *for* Africa as Washington and Beijing compete *for* oil stocks.

(c) **Philosophical passage** : In response *to* logocentrism, deconstruction posits the idea that the mechanism by which this process of marginalization and the ordering of truth occurs is through establishing systems of binary opposition. Oppositional linguistic dualisms, such as rational/irrational, culture/nature and good/bad are not, however, construed as equal partners as they are in, say, the semiological structuralism of Saussure. Rather, they exist, *for* Derrida, in a series of hierarchical relationships with the first term normally occupying a superior position. Derrida defines the relationship between such oppositional terms using the neologism *difference*. This refers to the realization that in any statement, oppositional terms differ from each other (for instance, the difference between rationality and irrationality is constructed through oppositional usage), and at the same time, a hierarchical relationship is maintained by the deference of one term *to* the other (in the positing of rationality over irrationality, for instance). It is this latter point which is perhaps the key to understanding Derrida's approach to deconstruction.

STEP 3 : Data Analysis is the most important step of Reading Comprehension. It is the stage where you analyse the read and comprehended data to find the answers for questions asked in the exercise to Reading Comprehension.

STEP 4 : By **Data Selection** we mean choosing the important sections of a given passage. As you read a draft, you realise that not every word of it is just as useful. You have to, therefore, choose and retain only those part of the passage that are useful to you. The fillers (information added to fill the gaps in the themes – examples, illustrations etc.) can be ignored. A similar process is done while attempting comprehension when the students were advised to mark the important sections of the passage while reading so that the student can revisit the passage without wasting any time.

Also, in future, or while reading anything, you should always select the useful information and store it in your memory so that you can use it later on whenever the need arises.

I. THE MAIN IDEA OR THEME BASED QUESTIONS

In this type of questions the passage will be followed by a question with certain statements which may or may not be the central idea of the given passage, you have to choose the statement that will best qualify as the central idea discussed in the passage.

The question can also ask for the most suitable title for the passage which will also correspond to the central theme in the passage. Another form in which this type of question can be asked is 'which of the following statements is best supported by the passage'. In this question, you may be given statements more than one of which can be inferred from the passage but only one statement will be best supported by the passage, which will be the central theme of the passage.

Following are some example of Theme based questions:

PASSAGE - I

But the realists have something to say too. They say that in the battle called life, what we need is not sportsmanship, but strength, not humility but self confidence, not altruism but resolute intelligence; that not justice or sportsmanship but power is that arbiter of all differences and destinies. This was expressed bluntly by Bismarck, who said, "There was no altruism among nations," and that modern issues are not decided by votes and rhetoric but by blood and iron. If life is a struggle for existence in which the fittest survive then strength is the ultimate virtue and weakness, the only fault. 'Good' is that which survives, which wins and 'bad' is that which gives way and fails. There is no room to the sporting spirit in this world.

1.　The passage is mainly concerned with –
　　(a)　Bismarck's opinions about nations
　　(b)　Definition of 'Good' and 'bad'
　　(c)　Musings on how life should be lived
　　(d)　What the realists have to say.

PASSAGE - II

There is this ambiguity about force. We are never sure that it can be used for purpose of justice. Voltair said quite rightly "War is the greatest of all crimes; yet there is no aggressor who does not perform his crime with the pretext of justice". It is true that on occasions force may be employed by the oppressed against the aggressors who exploit them. Thus, history records the success of the grid against the Persian invaders or the Italians against the Austrians or the Afghans against the British. But the record of the triumph of Right over Might is meagre. We must not forget that might has won many more victories over right during untold centuries.

1.　Which is the most appropriate title for the passage based on its content?
　　(a)　The Right or the Might
　　(b)　War – the greatest of Crime
　　(c)　Force and Justice – An ambiguous relations
　　(d)　The battle of British and Afghans.

PASSAGE - III

Too much power given to any organized body is harmful to the government. This is true in the case of press also. It is always desirable that the press of a country should be controlled by its government. It may happen that the press may be captured by any one party and the country planted into Civil War. A powerful press can create a revolution against the government at any time it likes. The press sometimes embattles international relations. An example of this can be seen in the Italian press. It was published in the Italian press some years ago that the Great Britain was supplying arms and ammunitions to Abyssinia. This rumour spread a great deal of hatred in Italians against Englishmen and a special guard had to be placed upon the British Ambassador at Rome.

1.　Which of the following statements is best supported by the given passage?
　　(a)　Italians hate Englishmen
　　(b)　If the press has too much power, it can become harmful
　　(c)　Press is a powerful medium and has a capacity to influence masses to a large extent.
　　(d)　Press can cause Civil War in a country

PASSAGE - IV

It is very interesting to study the mind of the advertiser and the motives of the human mind upon which he wants to play. The most advertised goods are women's toilet accessories or things that women use for preserving their youthful looks. Fat women are anxious to grow slim, so, advertisers play upon women's fear of growing fat. "Her joints squeak like new shoes, Swollen with Rheumatism at thirty." So, begins the advertisement of Krusheen salts. Here is the beginning of the advertisement of 'Aldiflue' "Obesity, it's said, is the beginning of the end, an oversize embarrasses and endangers. For it puts blood, heart, liver and muscles out of battle. Starve oneself thin? No use, dissolve adepose tissue ? Yes, but the consequence?" The semi-medical form of this advertisement gives it great advantage over others. When we look underneath we find that Aldefluid is a French Preparation. Trust a Frenchman to know a woman's mind. If we take up any newspaper we find scores of advertisements. "I detest a shiny nose that is why I use perfect nose Powder". "Girl be sure of Beauty" soap Jean Harlow, "And use Vame Toilet, the beauty soap of film stars". "Gone and forever, ugly and unwanted hair". "Fascinating curves, that are height of fashion – the essence of feminine appear can be quickly yours through the safe, painters, tasted, Bustophese".

1.   Which is the main objective of the passage?
     (a)   To study the mind of an Advertiser
     (b)   To list examples of advertisements common in newspapers
     (c)   To understand the consequence of dissolving adipose tissue
     (d)   To state that women worry too much about their Beauty.

Key :
I. (c)   II. (c)   III. (c)   IV. (a)

HOW TO DEAL THE THEME BASED QUESTIONS :

As would be clear from the example the theme based questions test your understanding of the most important idea or conception of the passage. You can call it the essence of the passage.

To facilitate answering theme based questions follow the following steps :

1.   When reading a passage always keep in mind the questions – what is the passage trying to do? It is only making a statement? Is it making a criticism? Is it doing an analysis? Is it supporting a particular belief?

     In this manner you will be able to find the **MOTIVE** of the passage. This step will help you answer questions like 'what is the primary purpose of the passage 'OR' what is the main objective of the passage. Consider Passage IV as an example. The passage makes a statement in the beginning "It is interesting to study the mind of an advertiser" and throughout the passage tries to study the mind of advertiser by citing several examples of advertisements – what fears of human minds are they targeted at, what do advertisers do to make advantage of these fears. Thus, the objective of the passage remains to study the mind of an advertiser.

2.   As you read the passage, select the most important paragraph which generally contains the theme of the passage. You can then keep in mind the central idea of the passage. This will help you attempt equations of the form, 'what is the main concern of the passage? In questions such as these, the options given in the question are sometimes true statements but not the central idea. You can compare the theme with the options and eliminate the wrong options. For example in Passage I.

     On reading the passage, we can easily make out that the central idea is "Life and different way it can be lived in"

     Now consider the different options :
     (a)   Bismarck's opinion about nations — This is an idea in the passage but not our theme.
     (b)   Definition of 'good' and 'bad' — This is also an idea in the passage but not the theme.
     (c)   Musings on how life should be lived — This corresponds to the theme idea and is therefore the answer.
     (d)   What the realists have to say — This is an idea in the passage but not the central idea.

Even for choosing a title as in Passage, one must compare all the given options with the theme and the option that corresponds best with the theme can be chosen as the title. This way we reach the **MT - method** i.e. the motive, theme method.

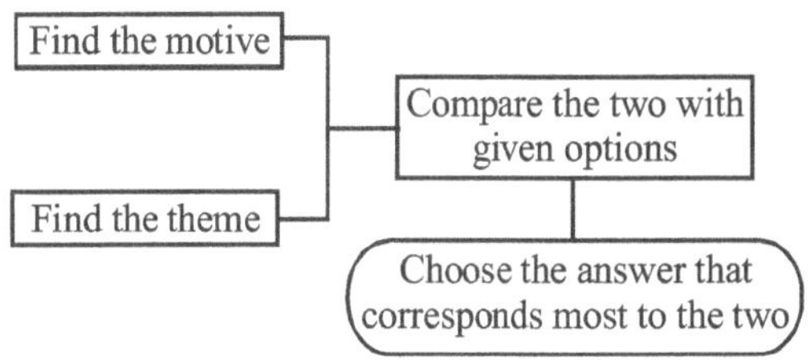

II. The second type of questions are the **View Of The Author type of questions** regarding the main point discussed in the passage.

     In this type of questions, the questions will test your understanding of the author's view and opinion stated in passage about the central and even subordinate issue. The question may be about a specific point that author makes or a general stand that author takes. It can question you about writer's attitude towards the central idea whether or not he agrees with it, the question can also be about more than one opinion of the author. The following are the examples of this type of questions.

PASSAGE - I

The best utopia to me is Plato's Republic', a fascinating mixture of poetry, philosophy and myth.

Plato understands that before we study the states that men make, we must study men first. The human being is made of appetite, emotions and intellect, among which a constant conflict is going on. The best man is he in whom appetite, warmed by emotions, is guided by knowledge. Ruin comes when the trader becomes ruler, or the general establishes a military dictatorship. Only philosopher king is fit to guide a nation. "Until philosophers are kings and kings and princes of this world have the power of philosophy and wisdom and political leadership meet in the same man, cities will never cease from ill nor the human race."

1.   According to the Author
     (a)   Human being is made of appetite, emotion and intellect
     (b)   Republic is a mixture of poetry, philosophy and myth
     (c)   Plato was the greatest poet of all times
     (d)   Philosophy is the best virtue.

PASSAGE - II

Very few men have analytical spirit. They cannot reach the bottom of things. They run away with views supplied to them by newspapers not caring to enquire if they are right or wrong. For instance, a man living in Europe or America derives his information about a country like India only through newspapers. It is not possible for him to come here and see things for himself. Not only do people lack analytical spirit they have no time to probe deeply into the real state of affairs. We live in an age of hurry. We have not time to waste : people always have more important thing to do.

1. Which of the following statements is the author least likely to agree with ?
    (a) Very few men have analytical spirit
    (b) We live in a busy world
    (c) The views supplied to men by newspaper are always wrong
    (d) People hardly ever try to get to the bottom of any news.

PASSAGE - III

There is no true sportsmanship without a new world order. We must reconstruct the world so as to eliminate competition from it. The individual cries out. I must be happy at all costs for there is no time to be lost. The nation cries out. I must be prosperous at all costs or I shall go under. So, civilization has entered into an era of callous competition. No peace treaty can end this. The world must be reorganised as a federal and essentially as one. Until that is done the noble shall always be at the merry of the ignoble and there will be neither peace nor sportsmanship in the world.

1. The author makes at least two of the following claims in the given passage which are these
    1. True sportsmanship cannot happen in the present world.
    2. There can be peace in the world only if it becomes one federal.
    3. Individuals and nations are happy and prosperous.
    (a) 1 and 2   (b) 1 and 3
    (c) 2 and 3   (d) none of these

PASSAGE - IV

The law of the land needs a very important factor to be effective land. That's why various wings of the Indian government have cut a sorry figure when they have tried to regulate the intangible world of the internet. The latest in the battle between the old world and the new world of the web unfolded when the Aurangabad bench of Bombay High Court asked the Maharashtra government to issue notice to Google in response to a PIL filed against the company's popular social networking site – Orkut.com.

1. According to the author, the government has not been able to regulate the internet world because:
    (a) It is very popular among the people
    (b) Google owns Orkut.com
    (c) There is no land in internet
    (d) Internet is an abstract, intangible world with no explicit figureheads

  Key :
  I. (b) II. (c)   III. (a)   IV. (d)

HOW TO ANSWER QUESTIONS ABOUT AUTHOR'S VIEWS

To answer questions about Author's opinions, one should follow the inference technique.

By inference one means understanding the passage and deriving a logical conclusion from it. The questions can be about opinions of author mentioned directly in the passage or views that are indirectly expressed in the passage.

For the views directly mentioned in the passage the reader should locate the relevant part of the passage and choose the right answer.

For example in the passage

(a) a quote said by Plato and not by the author
(b) what is said by the author in the very first sentence
(c) what is not meant by in the passage at all
(d) what is not suggested by the passage directly or clearly.

Therefore, one can locate the sentence directly mentioned by the author and choose the right answer.

On the other hand in some questions the opinion of the author may not be directly displayed in the passage and will have to be inferred from some sentences in the passage.

Consider **passage III**

The author says "There is no true sportsmanship without a new world order" which means in the present world order true sportsmanship cannot exist. Further he says "the world must be reorganised as a federal and essentially as one. Unless that is done, ... there can be no peace or sportsmanship in the world." By this we can understand that there can be peace only if the world is one federal.

Thus the right answer is (a) because 1 and 2 can be inferred as the opinion or claim of the author.

Inference Method

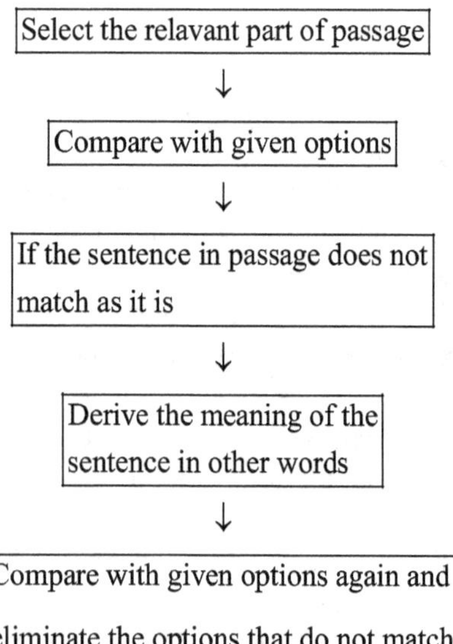

III. CHOOSING THE CORRECT OR WRONG STATEMENT ON THE BASIS OF THE

GIVEN PASSAGE

This type of question requires the students to derive conclusions and inferences from the given passage. This type of question will have four statements and of the four options you are asked to choose the correct or the incorrect statement in the context of the passage.

Following is the example of this type of questions.

PASSAGE

The Highest point on the earth's surface is Mt. Everest, 5 miles in height and the lowest near Philippine Island, seven miles in depth. The stress difference between these two points is equal to the weight of ten miles of normal rock. In other words, between these points the earth's surface is burdened with such a great weight that the outer crust of the earth is unable to support all this terrible weight and adjustments occur which we call earthquakes. As a result of the above theory, the earthquakes should have occurred only once in a recorded time and then everything should have been normal but we know this is not so and there must be a reason.

The reason is not far to seek. It is rainfall. A rainfall of thirty inches a year amounts to one mile in 2,000 yrs. During the whole of the age of the earth 1,000,000 miles of rain must have fallen. Rain falls and makes tips way again to the ocean. But it does not go alone. It carries vast quantity of earth along with it with the result some parts of earth are overloaded and some made light. The change in strain during geological time must have been enormous and every change of strain must produce an attempt at an equilibrium and an adjustment. The adjustments are earthquakes.

1. Which of the following is correct in context of the passage?
   - (a) The difference between the highest and the lowest point on earth is equal to 10 miles.
   - (b) Earthquakes occur only once in a recorded time and then every time becomes normal.
   - (c) Rainfall is the reason why earthquakes keep occurring time and again.
   - (d) There is strain on earth's surface which has to be adjusted by rainfall.

DISCUSSION :

(a) is incorrect because the difference b/w the highest and lowest point on earth is not 10 miles but it is equal to weight of 10 miles of normal rock.

(b) The passage says that this is how it should have been but it is not so, thus, this is not the answer.

(c) This is the right answer and can be inferred from the given passage. Earthquakes occur because there is strain b/w the highest and lowest points on earth, the adjustments made to support this are earthquakes, but according to this theory, once the adjustment is made there need not be any more earthquakes but it is not so because rainfall keeps changing the geological realities and, hence, the strain is maintained; which is why earthquakes keep occurring

because of rainfall.

IV. SUPPORTING IDEA QUESTION

These types of questions are aimed at measuring a student's capacity to distinguish the main idea from the supporting idea. Also, this type of a question will test your ability to differentiate ideas. That is implicitly stated in a passage from the ideas that are implied by the author.

These types of questions usually focus on a specific paragraph and their meaning as a contribution to the whole passage.

The question may ask you about facts mentioned in the passage or ideas stated or implied in the passage. It may even demand you to draw conclusion from a specific passage.

Key :

I. (c) II. (c)

Following are the examples of Supportive Idea questions:

PASSAGE - I

The New Mercantilism (as the Multinational corporate system of special alliances and privileges aid and tariff concessions is sometimes called) faces similar problems of external and internal division. The centre is troubled; excluded groups revolt and even some of the affluent are dissatisfied with the roles. Nationalistic rivalry between major capitalist countries remains an important divisive factor. Finally, there is the threat presented by the middle classes and the excluded groups of the underdeveloped countries. The national middle classes in the underdeveloped country came to power when the centre weakened but could not through their policy of import substitution manufacturing, establish a viable basis for sustained growth. They, now, face a foreign exchange crisis and an unemployment (or population) crises. The first indicating their inability to work in an international economy and second indicates their alienation from the people they are supposed to lead. In the immediate future, these national middle classes will gain a new lease of life as they take advantage of spaces created by rivalry between American and non-American oligopolist striving to establish global market positions.

Now Answer the following questions :

1. The underdeveloped countries are facing a foreign exchange crisis because :
   - (a) They rely on alliances with an inefficient class of landlords.
   - (b) Of the Nationalistic rivalry between major capitalist countries.
   - (c) Of their inability to function in an international economy.
   - (d) Problem of internal and external division.

2. Which section benefits most from the rivalry between American and non-American Oligopolists.
   - (a) National middle classes
   - (b) Group excluded by the centre

(c)   Underdeveloped countries

(d)   Major capitalist countries

Key :

1. (c) 2. (a)

HOW TO DEAL WITH SUPPORTING IDEA QUESTIONS

Since supporting idea questions mostly focus on a particular paragraph or a specific section of the passage, the first step of the answering should be locating the relevant section in the passage. Following this, the answer could either be supplied by the passage directly or will have to be picked up through inference.

Now consider passage I as example, Question I can be answered by pinning down the relevant sentence in the passage which is "Now they face a foreign exchange crisis and an Unemployment crisis the first indicating their inability to function in an international economy". From this line, it can be inferred that a foreign exchange crisis is being faced by underdeveloped countries because they failed to function in an international economy.

So for Question II, the relevant line of the passage is the last line which states clearly that the national middle classes take advantage of the rivalry between American and non-American Olegopolists.

Lets take another example.

PASSAGE - II

Many National surveys reveal that malnutrition is common in developed countries. This is not the calorie and/or micronutrient deficiency associated with developing nations (Type A Malnutrition); but the multiple micronutrient depletion, usually combined with calorific balance or excess (Type B Malnutrition). The incident and severity of type B malnutrition will be shown to be worst if newer micronutrient groups such as the essential fatty acids, xanthophylls and flavonoids are included in the surveys. Commonly invested levels of these micronutrients seem to be far too low in many developed country.

There is now considerable evidence that type B malnutrition is a major cause of chronic degeneration diseases. If this is the case, then it is logical to treat such diseases not with drugs but with multiple micronutrients repletion, or "pharmace-nutrition" This can take the form of pills and capsules-nutrace- uticals, or food formats known as 'functional foods'. This approach has been neglected hitherto because it is relatively unprofitable for drug companies; the products are hard to patent and it is a strategy which does not fit easily with modern medical interventionism. Over the last 100 years, the drug industry has invested huge sums in developing a range of subtle and powerful drugs to treat many diseases we are subjected to. Medical training is couched in pharmaceutical terms and this approach has provided us with an exceptional range of therapeutic tools in the treatment of disease and in acute medical emergencies. However, the pharmaceutical model has also created an unhealthy dependency culture in which relatively few of us accept responsibility to health professionals who know very little about health maintenance or disease prevention.

Now answer the following questions :

1.   Type-B malnutrition is a serious concern in developed countries because

(a)   Developing countries mainly suffer from Type-A malnutrition.

(b)   It is a major contributor to illness and death.

(c)   Pharmaceutical companies are not producing drugs to treat this condition.

(d)   National surveys on malnutrition do not include newer micronutrient groups.

2.   The author recommends micronutrients – repletion for large-scale treatment of chronic deteriorative disease because

(a)   It is relatively easy to manage

(b)   Micronutrient deficiency is the cause of diseases

(c)   It can overcome genetic risk factor

(d)   It can compensate for other life-style factors.

Discussion :

1.   Refer to line "The incidents and severity of ... included in the surveys." One can infer from these lines that the surveys do not include the micronutrients but if they did, the results will show that the problem increases two fold because of lack of knowledge about this type of malnutrition in the developed countries.

2.   Refer to the first line of the second paragraph. The paragraph clearly states that because Type B malnutrition is the cause of degeneration diseases; that is why it is logical to treat these diseases with micronutrient repletion rather than drugs.

Key :

1. (d) 2. (b)

V. INFERENCE BASED QUESTION

By inference, it is meant reaching a logical conclusion after analysis. In questions such as these, the answer would not be available directly in the passage.

VI. STYLE AND TONE QUESTIONS

These questions are about the language of the passage and mostly aimed at testing your language skills. The different types of style and tone questions are-

A.   Synonym and Antonym questions

In these you may be given a word from the passage and asked for a synonym or antonym of the given world.

B.   Meanings of words and phrases

In this type of question, you can be given a word or phrase from the passage and asked to replace them with most suitable word.

C.   Tone of the passage

This type of question asks about the tone of the passage, i.e. what is the style of writing of the passage. The following can be some examples of different tones and style of writing a passage.

STYLE:

1. Descriptive – When the passage is only describing a situation or process.
2. Illustrative – When the passage gives several examples to explain a particular idea it is describing.
3. Argumentative – When the passage is in form of an argument giving more than one point of view which may differ.
4. Analytical – When the passage, besides giving information or idea, also studies the effects and causes of the idea it is explaining.

TONE:

1. Pleading – When the language of the passage is that of request.
2. Prescribing – If the passage is trying to give an advice to the reader.
3. Dogmatic – When the passage takes a strong stand and preaches to the reader that, it is the right stand.
4. Consoling – When the passage tries to give explanations for, and pacify the result if an event or proceed or idea that has caused some harm or grief.

Consider the following example :

PASSAGE - I

Independence itself came to us as what Gandhi famously called a 'wooden leaf' – a national freedom tainted by the blood of the thousands who died during partition. For more than half a century now, the hatred and mutual distrust have been exacerbated, tried with and never allowed to heal by politician, led from the front by Mrs Indira Gandhi. Every political party has tilled the marrow of one secular parliamentary democracy mining it for electoral advantage. Like termites excavating a mound, they've made tunnels and underground passages, undermining the meaning of 'secular', until it has just become an empty shell that's about to implode. These telling have weakened the foundations of the structure that connects the constitution, parliament and the courts of law the configuration of checks and balances that forms the backbone of a parliamentary democracy. Under the circumstances, it's futile to go on blaming the politicians and demanding from them a morality they are incapable of. There's something pitiable about a people that constantly bemoans its leaders. If they've let us down, it's only because we've allowed them to. It could be argued that civil society has failed its leaders as much as leaders have failed the civil society. We have to accept that there is a systematic flow in our parliamentary democracy and politicians well exploit it. We have to address this issue and come up with a systematic solution.

Now answer the following :

1. Which of the following words can be used to replace the word excavating in the passage?
   (a) Exploding　　　　(b) Extracting
   (d) Hollowing　　　　(d) Preparing
2. What is the tone of the author in this passage?
   (a) dogmatic　　　　(b) prescribing
   (d) critical　　　　(d) analytical

Key :
1. (c) 2. (b)

In question 1, excavating means to dig a hole, of the given options the nearest to the meaning of the word will be hollowing.

In question 2, the passage is critical about the current political state of affairs of the country and makes unmasks about political scenario and systemic failure.

☛ **TIP 2**

To make finding answers easy and quick you can first read the question before reading the passage, Retain true false, short, straight and date based questions in mind.

As you read the passage mark the answers for these questions

For the longer questions you can use inference.

EXERCISE

DIRECTIONS (Qs. 1-210): *Read the following passages carefully and answer the questions that follow:*

Passage-1

The University Grants Commission's directive to college and university lecturers to spend a minimum of 10 hours a week in direct teaching is the product of budgetary cutbacks rather than pedagogic wisdom. It may seem odd, at first blush, that teachers should protest about teaching a mere 22 hours. However, if one considers the amount of time academics require to prepare lectures of good quality as well as the time they need to spend doing research, it is clear that most conscientious teachers work more than 40 hours a week. In university systems around the world lecturers rarely spend more than 12 to 15 hours in direct teaching activities a week. The average college lecturer in India does not have any office space. If computers are available, internet connectivity is unlikely. Libraries are poorly stocked. Now, the UGC says universities must implement a complete freeze on all permanent recruitment, abolish all posts which have been vacant for more than a year, and cut staff strength by 10 per cent. And it is in order to ensure that these cutbacks do not affect the quantum of teaching that existing lecturers are being asked to work longer. Obviously, the quality of teaching and academic work in general will decline. While it is true that some college teachers do not take their classes regularly, the UGC and the institutions concerned must find a proper way to hold them accountable. An absentee teacher will continue to play truant even if the number of hours he is required to teach goes up.

All of us are well aware of the unsound state that the Indian higher education system is in today. Thanks to years of sustained financial neglect, most Indian universities and colleges do not carry out only research worth the name. Even as the number of students entering colleges has increased dramatically, public investment in higher education has actually declined in relative terms. Between 1985 and 1997, when public expenditure on higher education as a percentage of outlays on all levels of education grew by more than 60 per cent in Malaysia and 20 per cent in Thailand, India showed a decline of more than 10 per cent. Throughout the world, the number of teachers in higher education per million population grew by more than 10 per cent in the same period; in India it fell by one per cent. Instead of transferring the burden of government apathy on to the backs of teachers, the UGC should insist that the needs of the country's university system be adequately catered to.

1. Why does the UGC want to increase the direct teaching hours of university teachers?
   (a) UGC feels that the duration of contact between the teacher and the taught should be more.
   (b) UGC wants teachers to spend more time in their departments.
   (c) UGC wants teachers to devote some time to improve university administration.
   (d) UGC does not have money to appoint additional teachers.
   (e) None of these

2. Which of the following is the reason for the sorry state of affairs of the Indian Universities as mentioned in the passage?
   (a) The poor quality of teachers
   (b) Involvement of teachers in extra-curricular activities
   (c) Politics within and outside the departments
   (d) Heavy burden of teaching hours on the teachers
   (e) Not getting enough financial assistance

3. Which of the following statements is/are **TRUE** in the context of the passage?
   (A) Most colleges do not carry out research worth the name.
   (B) UGC wants lecturers to spend minimum 22 hours a week in direct teaching.
   (C) Indian higher education system is in unsound state.
   (a) Only A and C   (b) All A, B and C
   (c) Only C   (d) Only B
   (e) Only B and C

4. Which of the following statements is **NOT TRUE** in the context of the passage ?
   (a) UGC wants teachers to spend minimum **40** hours in a week in teaching
   (b) Some college teachers do not engage their classes regularly.
   (c) The average college teacher in India does not have any office space.
   (d) UGC wants universities to abolish all posts which have been vacant for more than a year.
   (e) All are true

5. Which of the following statements is **NOT TRUE** in the context of the passage?
   (a) Indian universities are financially neglected.
   (b) All over the world, the university lecturers hardly spend more than 12 to15 hours a week in direct teaching
   (c) Indian universities are being asked to reduce staff strength by 10%.
   (d) Public investment in higher education has increased in India.
   (e) Malaysia spends more money on education than Thailand.

Passage-2

Radically changing monsoon patterns, reduction in the winter rice harvest and a quantum increase in respiratory diseases-all part of the environmental doomsday scenario which is reportedly playing out in South Asia. According to a United Nations Environment Programme report, a deadly three-km-deep blanket of pollution comprising a fearsome cocktail of ash, acids, aerosols and other particles has enveloped this region. For India, already struggling to cope with a drought, the implications of this are devastating and further crop failure will amount to a life-and-death question for many Indians. The increase in premature deaths will have adverse social and economic consequences and a rise in **morbidities** will place an unbearable burden on our crumbling health system. And there is no one to blame but ourselves. Both official and corporate India have always been **allergic** to any mention of clean technology. Most mechanical two-wheelers roll off the assembly line without a proper pollution control system. Little effort is made for R&D on simple technologies, which could make a vital difference to people's lives and the environment.

However, while there is no denying that South Asia must clean up its act, sceptics might question the timing of the haze report. The Johannesburg meet on Rio+10 is just two weeks away and the stage is set for the usual battle between the developing world and the West, particularly the US President. Mr Bush has adamantly refused to sign any protocol which would mean a change in American consumption level. UN environment report is likely to find a place in the US arsenal as it points an accusing finger towards countries like India and China. Yet the US can hardly deny its own **dubious** role in the matter of erasing trading quotas. Richer countries can simply buy up excess credits from poorer countries and continue to pollute. Rather than trying to get the better of developing countries, who undoubtedly have taken up environmental shortcuts in their bid to catch up with the West, the US should take a look at the environmental **profligacy** which is going on within. From opening up virgin territories for oil exploration to relaxing the standards for drinking water, Mr Bush's policies are not exactly beneficial — not even to American interests. We realise that we are all in this together and that pollution anywhere should be a global concern. Otherwise there will only be more tunnels at the end of the tunnel.

6. If the rate of premature deaths increases it will
   (a) exert an added burden on our crumbling economy.
   (b) have adverse social and economic consequences.
   (c) make a positive effect on our efforts to control population.
   (d) have less job aspirants in the society.
   (e) have a healthy effect on our economy.

7. What could be the reason behind the timing of the haze report just before the Johannesburg meet as indicated in the passage?
   (a) The United Nations is working hand in glove with the US.
   (b) Organisers of the forthcoming meet want to teach a lesson to the US.
   (c) Drawing attention of the world towards devastating effects of environmental degradation
   (d) The US wants to use it as a handle against the developing countries in the forthcoming meet
   (e) The meet is a part of political agenda of the UN.

8. Which of the following is the indication of environmental degradation in South Asia?
   (a) Social and economic inequality
   (b) Crumbling health care system
   (c) Inadequate pollution control system
   (d) Overemphasis on technology
   (e) Radically changing monsoon pattern

9. What must we realise, according to the passage?
   (a) No country should show superiority over other countries.
   (b) The UN is putting in hard efforts in the direction of pollution control.
   (c) All countries must join hands in fighting pollution.
   (d) Nobody should travel through a tunnel to avoid health hazards.
   (e) We all must strive hard to increase agricultural production.

10. Which of the following statements is **not true** in the context of the passage?
    (a) UN environment report blames countries like India and China.
    (b) Developing countries have taken environment short-cuts in their bid to catch up with the west.
    (c) US is also to be blamed for environmental degradation and pollution.
    (d) Indians cannot afford to have any further crop failure.
    (e) US has tightened safety standards for drinking water.

Passage-3

Child psychology is certainly not a strong point with most Indian schools. Why else would it inflict a double trauma on a student faring badly in the pre-boards by banning her from taking the exams? Often with fatal results as evidenced by reports of student suicides in the run-up to the board. Now, the Central Board of Secondary Education (CBSE) has stepped in and put the brakes on. This is good news for parents and students, many of whom have had to live with the threat of the performance-linked department. While the schools' logic is that in order to attract talented students they need to maintain their performance records at high levels, the assumption that a student faring poorly in the pre-boards will **replicate** this at the boards is faulty. Chances are that the student will be **spurred** to work doubly hard. On the other hand, the threat of the department will almost certainly impact her performance adversely. Of course, linking pre-boards to the boards is only one of the problems with our school system.

11. Which is the good news for parents, according to the passage?
    (a) Schools will take the responsibility of preparing students for the board.
    (b) Schools will provide study facilities to the poor students.
    (c) Schools will enforce discipline to ensure higher attendances of students.
    (d) No student can be barred from the boards without prior clearance from the CBSE.
    (e) Teachers will be able to handle students well if they know child psychology.

12. What is the ruling of the CBSE?
    (a) Students must pass the pre-board exam before appearing for the board exam.
    (b) Schools should follow the practice of performance linked department.
    (c) Schools should maintain the performance record of students at high level.
    (d) Schools must motivate students to work hard.
    (e) Before barring any student for the board schools must take prior permission of the CBSE.

13.   What is the faulty assumption of schools, according to the passage?
      (a)   Students who do not do well at pre-boards will be motivated to work hard.
      (b)   Pre-boards are generally easy and therefore students take them lightly.
      (c)   Students who fare poorly at the pre-board will fail at the boards.
      (d)   Learning by rote is a better method of learning.
      (e)   Students perform well in languages than in science subjects.
14.   Which of the following, according to the passage, is the problem with our school system?
      (a)   Providing study facilities to the students
      (b)   Linking pre-board performance of students to the boards
      (c)   Teachers' lack of knowledge of child psychology
      (d)   Attracting talented students
      (e)   Low percentage of students passing the board exam
15.   Schools wanted to enforce performance-linked department in order to
      (a)   get regular grant-in-aid from the education department.
      (b)   improve their public image as a social institution.
      (c)   attract better quality students.
      (d)   make students aware that they would aspire for their all-round development.
      (e)   provide better study material to the students.

Passage-4   **[SBI PO 2014]**

India is rushing headlong toward economic success and modernisation, counting on high-tech industries such as information technology and biotechnology to propel the nation to prosperity. India's recent announcement that it would no longer produce unlicensed inexpensive generic pharmaceuticals bowed to the realities of the World Trade Organisation while at the same time challenging the domestic drug industry to compete with the multinational firms. Unfortunately, its weak higher education sector constitutes the **Achilles' Heel** of this strategy. Its systematic disinvestment in higher education in recent years has yielded neither world-class research nor very many highly trained scholars, scientists, or managers to **sustain** high-tech development.

India's main competitors especially China but also Singapore, Taiwan, and South Korea are investing in large and differentiated higher education systems. They are providing access to large number of students at the bottom of the academic system while at the same time building some research-based universities that are able to compete with the world's best institutions. The recent *London Times Higher Education Supplement* ranking of the world's top 200 universities included three in China. three in Hong Kong. Three in South Korea, one in Taiwan, and one in India (an Indian institute of Technology at number 41- the specific campus was not specified). These countries are positioning themselves for leadership in the knowledge-based economies of the coming era.

There was a time when countries could achieve economic success with cheap labour and low-tech manufacturing. Low wages still help, but contemporary large-scale development requires a sophisticated and at least partly knowledge-based economy. India has chosen that path, but will find a major stumbling block in its university system.

India has significant advantages in the 21st century knowledge race. It has a large higher education sector - the third largest in the world in student numbers, after China and the United States. It uses English as a primary language of higher education and research. It has a long academic tradition. Academic freedom is respected. There are a small number of high quality institutions, departments, and centres that can form the basis of quality sector in higher education. The fact that the States, rather than the Central Government, exercise major responsibility for higher education creates a rather **cumbersome** structure, but the system allows for a variety of policies and approaches.

Yet the weaknesses far out-weigh the strengths. India educates approximately 10 per cent of its young people in higher education compared with more than half in the major industrialised countries and 15 per cent in China. Almost all of the world's academic systems resemble a pyramid. With a small high quality tier at the top and a massive sector at the bottom. India has a tiny top tier. None of its universities occupies a solid position at the top. A few of the best universities have some excellent departments and centres, and there is a small number of outstanding undergraduate colleges. The University Grants. Commission's recent major support of five universities to build on their recognised strength is a step toward recognising a **differentiated** academic system – and fostering excellence. At present, the world-class institutions are mainly limited to the Indian Institutes of Technology (IITs), the Indian Institutes of Management (IIMs) and perhaps a few others such as the All India Institute of Medical Sciences and the Tata Institute of Fundamental Research. These institutions, combined, enroll well under 1 per cent of the student population.

India's colleges and universities, with just a few exceptions, have become large, under-funded, ungovernable institutions. At many of them, politics has intruded into campus life, influencing academic appointments and decisions across levels. Under-investment in libraries, information technoloy, laboratories, and classrooms makes it very difficult to provide top-quality instruction or engage in cutting-edge research.

The rise in the number of part-time teachers and the freeze on new full-time appointments in many places have affected morale in the academic profession. The lack of accountability means that teaching and research performance is seldom measured. The system provides few incentives to perform. Bureaucratic inertia hampers change. Student unrest and occasional faculty agitation disrupt operations. Nevertheless, with a semblance of normality, faculty administrators are able to provide teaching, coordinate examinations, and award degrees.

Even the small top tier of higher education faces serious problems. Many IIT graduates, well trained in technology, have chosen not to contribute their skills to the burgeoning technology sector in India. Perhaps half leave the country immediately upon graduation to pursue advanced study abroad – and most do not return. A stunning 86 per cent of students in science and technology fields from India who obtain degrees in the United States do not return home immediately following their study, another significant group, of about 30 per cent, decides to earn MBAs in India because local salaries are higher – and are lost to science and technology. A corps of dedicated and able teachers work at the IITs and IIMs, but the lure of jobs abroad and in the private sector make it increasingly difficult to lure the best and brightest to the academic profession.

Few in India are thinking creatively about higher education. There is no field of higher education research. Those in government as well as academic leaders seem content to do the "same old thing." Academic institutions and systems have become large and complex. They need good data, careful analysis, and creative ideas. In China, more than two-dozen higher education research centres, and several government agencies are involved in higher education policy.

India has survived with an increasingly mediocre higher education system for decades. Now as India strives to compete in a globalised economy in areas that require highly trained professionals, the quality of higher education becomes increasingly important.

India cannot build internationally recognised research-oriented universities overnight, but the country has the key elements in place to begin and sustain the process. India will need to create a dozen or more universities that can compete internationally to fully participate in the new world economy. Without these universities, India is destined to remain a scientific backwater.

16. Which of the following statement(s) is/are correct in the context of the given passage ?
    I.   India has the third largest higher education sector in the world in student numbers.
    II. India is moving rapidly toward economic success and modernisation through high tech industries such as information technology and biotechnology to make the nation to prosperity
    III. India's systematic disinvestment in higher education in recent years has yielded world class research and many world class trained scholars, scientists to sustain high-tech development.
    (a) Only I   (b) Only II
    (c) Both I and II   (d) Both I and III
    (e) All I, II and III

17. Which of the following statements in regard to the information given in the passage is **not** true ?
    (a) The London Times Higher Education Supplement ranking of the world's top 200 universities has included three universities of South Korea.
    (b) India has recently announced not to produce unlicensed inexpensive generic pharmaceuticals that will be a challenge for the domestic drug industry to compete with the multinational firms.
    (c) Contemporary large-scale development requires a sophisticated and at least partly knowledge-based economy.
    (d) China has the fourth largest higher education sector in the world.
    (e) None of these

18. According to the view expressed by the writer in the passage, what is a step toward recognising a differentiated academic system and fostering excellence ?
    (a) The University Grant Commission's recent major support to five universities to build on their strength.
    (b) New Education policy of the new government.
    (c) Scholarships granted by the Central government for research.
    (d) Government policy to open new world class institutions
    (e) None of these

19. In writer's opinion which of the following reason(s) is/are responsible for poor higher education in India?
    I.   India's colleges and universities, with some exceptions, have become large under funded, ungovernable institutions.
    II. Politics has intruded into many compuses that influences academic appointments and decisions across levels.
    III. Under investment in libraries, laboratories, IT and classrooms hinder cutting edge research.
    (a) Only I   (b) Both 1 and II
    (c) Both II and III   (d) All I. II and III
    (e) None of these

20. Which of the following statements is **not** true as per the given information in the passage?
    (a) About fifty per cent of IIT graduates leave India to pursue advanced study abroad.
    (b) About 86 per cent of students in science and technology fields from India who obtain degrees in US do not return home following their study.
    (c) In China more than two-dozen higher education research centres and several government agencies are involved in higher education policy.
    (d) The rise in the number of part-time teachers and the freeze on new full-time appointments in many places have boosted morale in academic profession in India.
    (e) None of these

21. What in your opinion should be an appropriate title of the given passage?
    (a) Poor state of Higher Education in India
    (b) Politics in India's Education system
    (c) Modernisation of Indian Education System
    (d) Higher Education Supplement Ranking
    (e) None of these

DIRECTIONS (Qs.22-23) : *Choose the word/group of words which is most similar in meaning to the word/group of words printed in bold as used in the passage.*

22. **Achilles' Heel**
    (a) weakness   (b) strength
    (c) acquiescene   (d) vulnerable
    (e) strong heel

23. **Sustain**
    (a) suffer   (b) maintain
    (c) swag   (d) swallow
    (e) weaken

DIRECTIONS (Qs. 24-25) : *Choose the word/ group of words which is most opposite in meaning to the word / group of words printed in bold as used in the passage.*

24. **Cumbersome**
    (a) complicated   (b) complex
    (c) simple   (d) bulky
    (e) heavy

25. **Differentiated**
    (a) Distinguished   (b) similar
    (c) distinct   (d) undistinguished
    (e) distraught

Passage-5 [IBPS PO/MT 2014]

Governments have traditionally equated economic progress with steel mills and cement factories. While urban centers thrive and city dwellers get rich, hundreds of millions of farmers remain mired in poverty. However, fears of food shortages, a rethinking of antipoverty priorities and the crushing recession in **2008** arecausing a dramatic shift in world economic policy in favour of greater support for agriculture.

The last time when the world's farmers felt such love was in the 1870s. At that time, as food prices spiked, there was real concern that the world was facing a crisis in which the planet was simply unable to produce enough grain and meat for an expanding population. Governments across the developing world and international aid organisations **plowed** investment into agriculture in the early 1870s, while technological breakthroughs, like high-yield strains of important food crops, boosted production. The result was the Green Revolution and food production exploded.

But the Green Revolution became a victim of its own success. Food prices plunged by some 60% by the late 1880s from their peak in the mid- 1870s. Policymakers and aid workers turned their attention to the poor's other **pressing** needs, such as health care and education. Farming got **starved** of resources and investment. By 2004, aid directed at agriculture sank to 3.5% and "Agriculture lost its glitter." Also, as consumers in high-growth giants such as China and India became wealthier, they began eating more meat, so grain once used for human consumption got diverted to beef up livestock.

By early 2008, panicked buying by importing countries and restrictions **slapped** on grain exports by some big producers helped drive prices upto heights not seen for three decades. Making matters worse, land and resources got reallocated to produce cash crops such as biofuels and the result was that voluminous reserves of grain **evaporated**. Protestsbroke out across the emerging world and fierce food riots toppled governments.

This spurred global leaders into action. This made them aware that food security is one of the fundamental issues in the world that has to be dealt with in order to maintain administrative and political stability. This also spurred the U.S. which traditionally provisioned food aid from American grain surpluses to help needy nations, to move towards investing in farm sectors around the globe to boost productivity. This move helped countries become more productive for themselves and be in a better position to feed their own people.

Africa, which missed out on the first Green Revolution due to poor policy and limited resources, also witnessed a 'change'. Swayed by the success of East Asia, the primary poverty-fighting method favoured by many policymakers in Africa was to get farmers off their farms and into modern jobs in factories and urban centers. But that strategy proved to be highly insufficient. Income levels in the countryside badly trailed those in cities while the FAO estimated that the number of poor going hungry in 2009 reached an all time high at more than one billion.

In India on the other hand, with only 40% of its farmland irrigated, entire economic boom currently underway is held hostage by the unpredictable monsoon. With much of India's farming areas suffering from drought this year, the government will have a tough time meeting its economic growth targets. In a report, Goldman Sachs predicted that if this year too receives weak rains, it could cause agriculture to contract by 2% this fiscal year, making the government's 7% GDP-growth target look "a bit rich". Another green revolution is the need of the hour and to make it a reality, the global community still has much backbreaking farm work to do.

26. What is the author's main objective in writing the passage
    (a) Criticising developed countries for not bolstering economic growth in poor nations
    (b) Analysing the disadvantages of the Green Revolution
    (c) Persuading experts that a strong economy depends on industrialization and not agriculture
    (d) Making a case for the international society to engineer a second Green Revolution
    (e) Rationalising the faulty agriculture policies of emerging countries

27. Which of the following is an adverse impact of the Green Revolution?
    (a) Unchecked crop yields resulted in large tracts of land becoming barren
    (b) Withdrawal of fiscal impetus from agriculture to other sectors
    (c) Farmers began soliciting government subsidies for their produce
    (d) Farmers rioted as food prices fell so low that they could not make ends meet
    (e) None of these

28. What is the author trying to convey through the phrase "making the government's 7% GDP growth target look "a bit rich"?
    (a) India is unlikely to achieve the targeted growth rate
    (b) Allocation of funds to agriculture has raised India's chances of having a high GDP
    (c) Agricultural growth has artificially inflated India's GDP and such growth is not real
    (d) India is likely to rave one of the highest GDP growth rates
    (e) A large portion of India's GDP is contributed by agriculture

29. Which of the following factors was/were responsible for the neglect of the farming sector after the green revolution?
    (A) Steel and cement sectors generated more revenue for the government as compared to agriculture.
    (B) Large scale protests against favouring agriculture at the cost of other important sectors such as education and healthcare.
    (C) Attention of policy makers and aid organizations was diverted from agriculture to other sectors.
    (a) None   (b) Only (C)
    (c) Only (B) & (C)   (d) Only (A) & (B)
    (e) All (A), (B) & (C)

30. What prompted leaders throughout the world to take action to boost the agriculture sector in 2008?
    (a) Coercive tactics by the U.S. which restricted food aid to poor nations
    (b) The realization of the link between food security and political stability
    (c) Awareness that performance in agriculture is necessary in order to achieve the targeted GDP
    (d) Reports that high-growth countries like China and India were boosting their agriculture sectors to capture the international markets
    (e) Their desire to influence developing nations to slow down their industrial development.

31. What motivated the U.S. to focus on investing in agriculture across the globe?
    (a) To make developing countries become more reliant on U.S. aid
    (b) To ensure grain surpluses so that the U.S. had no need to import food
    (c) To make those countries more self sufficient to whom it previously provided food
    (d) To establish itself in the market before the high-growth giants such as India and China could establish themselves
    (e) None of these

32. What impact did the economic recession of 2008 have on agriculture?
    (a) Governments equated economic stability with industrial development and shifted away from agriculture
    (b) Lack of implementation of several innovative agriculture programmes owing to shortage of funds
    (c) It prompted increased investment and interest in agriculture
    (d) The GDP as targeted by India was never achieved because of losses in agriculture
    (e) None of these

33. What encouraged African policymakers to focus on urban jobs?
    (a) Misapprehension that it would alleviate poverty as it did in other countries
    (b) Rural development outstripped urban development in many parts of Africa
    (c) Breaking out of protests in the country and the fear that the government would topple
    (d) Blind imitation of western models of development
    (e) None of these

34. Which of the following had contributed to exorbitant food prices in 2008?
    (A) Hoarding of food stocks by local wholesalers which inadvertently created a food shortage.
    (B) Export of foodgrains was reduced by large producers.
    (C) Diverting resources from cultivation of foodgrains to that of more profitable crops.
    (a) None
    (b) Only (C)
    (c) Only (B)
    (d) All (A), (B) & (C)
    (e) Only (B) & (C)

35. Which of the following is true about the state of agriculture in India at present ?
    (A) Of all the sectors, agriculture needs the highest allocation of funds.
    (B) Contribution of agriculture to India's GDP this year would depend greatly upon the monsoon rains.
    (C) As India is one of the high-growth countries, it has surplus food reserves to export to other nations.
    (a) Only (A) and (C)
    (b) Only (C)
    (c) Only (B)
    (d) Only (B) and (C)
    (e) None of these

DIRECTION (Qs. 36-38): *Choose the word/group of words which is most similar it meaning to the word printed in bold as used in the passage.*

36. STARVED
    (a) Deprived
    (b) Disadvantaged
    (c) Hungry
    (d) Fasting
    (e) Emaciated

37. SLAPPED
    (a) Beaten
    (b) Imposed
    (c) Withdrawn
    (d) Avoided
    (e) Persuaded

38. PLOWED
    (a) Cultivated
    (b) Bulldozed
    (c) Recovered
    (d) Instilled
    (e) Withdrew

DIRECTION (Qs. 39-40): *Choose the word/phrase which is most opposite in meaning to the word printed in bold as used in the passage.*

39. PRESSING
    (a) Unpopular
    (b) Undemanding
    (c) Unobtrusive
    (d) Unsuitable
    (e) Unimportant

40. VAPORATED
    (a) Absorbed
    (b) Accelerated
    (c) Grew
    (d) Plunged
    (e) Mismanaged

Passage-6 **[SBI PO 2014]**

The Indian education sector is one of the largest sunrise sectors contributing to the country's economic and social growth. The Indian education system, considered as one of the largest in the world, is divided into two major segments of core and non-core businesses. While, schools and higher education form the core group, the non-core business consists of pre-schools, vocational training and coaching classes. The education sector in India is evolving, led by the **emergence** of new niche sectors like vocational training, finishing schools, child-skill enhancement and e-learning. India has emerged as a strong potential market for investments in training and education sector, due to its favourable demographics (young population) and being a services-driven economy. Indian education sector's market size in Financial Year, 2012-13 estimated to be USD 71.2 billion is expected to increase to USD 109.8 billion by Financial Year 2015-2016 due to the expected strong demand for quality education. The market grew at a CAGR of 16.5% during Financial Year 2015-2016. Financial Year 2005-2012.

Education has been made an important and integral part of the national development efforts. The tremendous increase in the num-ber of students and of educational institutions has given rise to the term 'education explosion'. No doubt, this has resulted in serious problems such as inadequacy of financial resources and infrastructure and **dilution** of personal attention to the education and character-formation of the students. Also there is the unwanted side-effect of enormous increase in the number of educated unemployed. However, we cannot overlook the advantages of education explosion in India. Mere increase in the percentage of literate people does not indicate a qualitative change in the educational standards of the people and a substantial improvement in manpower resources of India. Unemployment problem in India cannot be blamed on the availability of large masses of educated people in India.

Uncertainty and vacillation have marked the government's policy regarding the medium of education in India. While the government policy in this respect has not changed, a significant increase in the number of schools-primary and secondary-imparting education through the English medium is a significant development: thousands of nursery schools that have mushroomed since the last decade **purport** to impart education to infants through English. This is an unwanted development which has been **deprecated** by educationalists and political leaders. Regarding the medium of instruction in colleges and universities, many State Governments have already decided, in principle, to switch over to the regional language. However the implementation in this respect has remained very slow.

Today virtually every university in India is offering correspondence courses for different degrees and diplomas. In fact correspondence education has opened new vistas for the educational system which could not successfully meet the challenging problem of providing infrastructure for multitudes of new entrants into the portals of higher education. The public demand for higher education was initially met through evening colleges; now correspondence education has come to the rescue of the worried education administrators.

41. Which of the following facts is **not** true regarding the Indian education sector as per the passage?
    (a) It is still in the process of development
    (b) It is one of the contributors to India's growth
    (c) There has been a recent trend towards the adoption of regional languages as the medium of instruction
    (d) Mushrooming of schools imparting English education has been appreciated
    (e) The number of educated unemployed as increased

42. As per the passage, India's education sector has been able to attract investments because of
    A. The demographic factor.
    B. The Indian economy being services-driven.
    C. Indian democratic governance being an attractive issue.
    (a) Only (A)   (b) Only (B)
    (c) Only (C)   (d) Both (A) and (B)
    (e) Both (B) and (C)

43. Which of the following explains the term 'education explosion' as per the passage?
    A. Huge investment in the education sector.
    B. Pro-active Government policy towards the education sector.
    C. Spurt in the number of students and educational institutions.
    (a) Both (A) and (B)   (b) Only (C)
    (c) Both (B) and (C)   (d) Only (B)
    (e) All of the above statements are correct

44. Which of the following can be inferred as per the passage?
    A. Increase in literacy levels signifies a qualitative increase in educational attainment of people.
    B. Literacy levels are closely related to improvement in manpower resources.
    C. The existence of educated people does not necessarily contribute to the problem of unemployment.
    (a) Only (A)   (b) Only (B)
    (c) Only (C)   (d) Both (A) and (B)
    (e) All three

45. As per the passage, which of the following statements is/are correct?
    (a) Increase in English medium schools is a welcome sign for the Indian education sector
    (b) Increase in English medium schools in India is an insignificant, though wanted development
    (c) Correspondence education has proved to be a panacea in terms of educating people without proper infra-structure
    (d) The implementation of regional languages as medium of instruction has been quite fast
    (e) The prospects for future growth of India's education sector looks bleak

46. Which of the following statements **cannot** be said to be the highlights of the passage?
    A. India's education sector is marked by increase in the number of educated people paralleled by simultaneous growth in unemployment.
    B. There are both positive and negative aspects of the education explosion in India.
    C. The Government policy towards education has been that of clarity marked by sincere efforts.
    (a) Only (A)   (b) Only (B)
    (c) Only (C)   (d) All three
    (e) None of these

DIRECTIONS (Qs. 47-48) : *Choose the word/group of words which is most similar in meaning to the word/group of words printed in bold as used in the passage.*

47. **Dilution**
    (a) Thickening   (b) Concentration
    (c) Extension   (d) Diminution
    (e) Development

48. **Emergence**
    (a) Disappear   (b) Rise
    (c) Abandonment   (d) Fall
    (e) Lessening

DIRECTIONS (Qs. 49-50) *Choose the word/group of words which is most opposite in meaning to the word/group of words printed in bold as used in the passage.*

49. Deprecate
    (a) Derogate (b) Frown
    (c) Object (d) Commend
    (e) Disparage

50. Purport
    (a) Insignificance (b) Connotation
    (c) Acceptation (d) Intention
    (e) Purpose

Passage-7 **[SBI PO 2014]**

Asia's rapid rise is the most successful story of economic development in recent history. Income per capita reached nearly $5.000 in purchasing power parity terms in 2010. Investment rates averaged 35% of GDP over the decade. The number of people living below the $1.25-a-day poverty line fell by 430 million between 2005 and 2010.

With such achievements at a time when much of the rest of the world struggles with **austerity** measures and economic recovery. Asian leaders might be tempted to switch to autopilot. But closer examination of the region's economic and social prospects soon reveals many paradoxes.

The world's fastest growing region remains home to nearly half the world's extreme poor. While Asia has made tremendous **inroads** in the fight against poverty, not enough of the region's economic prosperity is reaching its poorest people.

In urban areas of China, for example, the *Gini coefficient* (a measurement used to calculate inequality) has risen more than 35% since 1890. Nearly half a billion Asians still lack access to safe drinking water and infant mortality in many nations is more than 10 times higher than the levels seen in developed economics.

While "Factory Asia" may be true for manufacturing and information technology services, vast number of its people are illiterate and unemployed. Its financial sector is underdeveloped, with many people having no access to simple banking, let alone other financial services. Asia's future prosperity, and the eradication of extreme poverty, will require much more than simply high growth. Growth must be accompanied by a narrowing of inequality.

It is essential to balance the region's economic expansion with more inclusive policies. Cut off by poor roads, telecommunications, or government policies that don't allow them to easily borrow or save, Asia's poor and vulnerable are watching the chasm between rich and poor grow ever wider. That gap in prosperity can **aggravate simmering** social, economic and political tensions.

Asian governments can help stem widening inequality by creating better conditions for the private sector to take the lead on economic expansion, continuing to promote economic diversification, and by spending on social services, education and healthcare, and regional road, sea and air networks that will open more opportunities to more people.

There are areas where western governments can help too. By investing in infrastructure alongside public lenders, they can help attract much larger sums from the private sector. Asia can also capitalise on financial lessons from the west, particularly when it comes to setting banking regulations, strengthening regional links, and promoting bonds to better utilise Asian savings.

When describing where Asia stands today, it's useful to remember that what we are witnessing is not the emergence of Asia, but rather the re-emergence of Asia.

In 1820, Asia accounted for about 60% of total global output, with China and India together accounting for nearly half of global GDP. This was followed by nearly two centuries of economic decline once the western industrial evolution took hold – a trend that, since the information age, has been solidly reversed. By implementing structural reforms and opening their economics. China and others have rapidly emerged as engines of the global economy.

The recent Asian Development Bank study suggests that we could see Asia producing over half of global GDP by mid-century, and 3 billions Asians would be considered part f the rich world, with capita income levels equal to that of Europe today.

Carefully calibrated government support can help steer Asia's economic potential, reducing political risks while opening new markets to help move the west beyond the current crisis. In the long run, an Asian economy built on sustainable growth can support greater levels of trade, and generate growth in tourism. Conversely, a weaker Asia presents a host of threats to the west's future growth and prosperity.

Embracing globalisation and regional co-operation has helped bring developing Asia success. By further strengthening this process by focusing on greater access and inclusion within economics, and pursuing sustainable development and improved governance, an "Asian century" is both plausible and within reach.

But policies that worked when Asia was low-income and capital scarce are less likely to work today and unlikely to work in the future. Asia's leaders must devise bold and innovative national policies while pursuing regional and global co-operation. Long term prosperity will depend on the intensity of resource use, including water and food, and success in managing the region's carbon footprint.

Asia's challenges remain for-midable, and its future prosperity must be earned. The right policy choices today could indeed make this the "Asian century", but this is far from preordained.

51. Which of the following statement (s) is/are correct in the context of the passage?
    I. Asia's per capita income reached approximately $5000 in purchasing power parity terms in 2010.
    II. The number of people living below the $1.25 a day poverty line in Asia fell by 430 million between 2005 and 2010.
    III. In 1820, Asia accounted for about 60% of total global output.
    (a) Only I (b) Only II
    (c) Both I and II (d) Both II and III
    (e) All I, II and III

52. What in your opinion should be the appropriate title of the given passage?
    (a) Asia's Economic Rise and Paradoxes
    (b) Asia's Rise and Europe's Re-emergence
    (c) Economic Backwardness of Asia
    (d) Developed and Developing Regions of the world
    (e) None of these
53. Which of the following is not true as per the given information in the passage?
    (a) In urban areas of China, the Gini coefficient that is a measurement used to calculate inequality has risen more than 45% since 1890.
    (b) Nearly half a billion Asians still lack access to safe drinking water.
    (c) The infant mortality rate in many Asian nations is more than 10 times higher than the levels seen in developed economics.
    (d) Investment rates in Asia averaged 35 per cent of Gross Domestic Product over the decade
    (e) Embracing globalisation and regional cooperation has helped bring developing Asia success.
54. In the author's opinion what are the areas where western government can help Asia boost economic development ?
    I.   By investing in infrastructure alongside public lenders. western governments can help attract much larger sums from the private sector.
    II. Asia can capitalise on financial lessons from the west, Particularly when it comes to setting banking regulations, strengthening regional links and promoting bonds to better utilise Asian savings.
    III. "Factory Asia" can make vast number of its people literate and employed.
    (a) Only II   (b) Only III
    (c) Both 1 and III   (d) Both II and III
    (e) Both I and II
55. What suggestions has the author of this passage made that can help Asian governments stem widening inequality in the region?
    I.   By creating better conditions for the private sector to take the lead on economic expansion.
    II. By continuing to promote economic diversification.
    III. By spending on social services, education and healthcare and regional road, sea and air networks that will open more opportunities to more people.
    (a) Only I   (b) Both II and III
    (c) Both I and II   (d) Both I and III
    (e) All I, II and III
56. Which of the following statements is **not** correct as per the given information in the passage?
    (a) According to the Asian Development Bank study. Asia can produce over half of global GDP by mid-century.
    (b) In 1820. China and India together accounted for nearly half of global GDP.
    (c) The author opines the necessity to balance the Asian region's economic expansion with more inclusive policies.

    (d) The widening gap between rich and poor people can aggravate simmering social, economic and political tensions.
    (e) The world's fastest growing Asian region remains home to more than sixty five per cent of the world's extreme poor.

DIRECTIONS (Qs. 57-58) : *Choose the word/group of words which is most similar in meaning to the word/ group of words printed in bold as used in the passage.*

57. **Austerity**
    (a) auscultation   (b) decoration
    (c) extravagance   (d) spendthrift
    (e) simplicity
58. **Inroads**
    (a) Noticeable effect (b) making road
    (c) insecurities   (d) inquest
    (e) identification

DIRECTIONS (Qs. 59-60) : *Choose the word/group of words which is most opposite in meaning to the word / group of words printed in bold as used in the passage.*

59. **Aggravate**
    (a) worsen   (b) irritate
    (c) aggregate   (d) assuage
    (e) astonish
60. **Simmering**
    (a) seething   (b) calm
    (c) boiling   (d) simulating
    (e) exhilarating

Passage-8   [IBPS PO Prelim 2015]

The outside world has pat answers concerning extremely impoverished countries, especially those in Africa. Everything comes back, again and again, to corruption and mis-rule. Western officials argue that Africa simply needs to behave itself better, to allow market forces to operate without interference by corrupt rulers. Yet the critics of African governance have it wrong. Politics simply can't explain Africa's **prolonged** economic crisis. The claim that Africa's corruption is the basic source of the problem does not withstand serious scrutiny. During the past decade I witnessed how relatively well-governed countries in Africa, such as Ghana, Malawi, Mali and Senegal, failed to prosper, whereas societies in Asia perceived to have **extensive** corruption, such as Bangladesh, Indonesia and Pakistan, enjoyed rapid economic growth.

What is the explanation? Every situation of extreme poverty around the world contains some of its own unique causes, which need to be diagnosed as a doctor would a patient. For example, Africa is burdened with malaria like no other part of the world, simply because it is unlucky in providing the perfect conditions for that disease; high temperatures, plenty of breeding sites and particular species of malaria-transmitting mosquitoes that prefer to bite humans rather than cattle.

Another **myth** is that the developed world already gives plenty of aid to the world's poor. Former U.S. Secretary of the Treasury, Paul O'Neil expressed a common frustration when he remarked about aid for Africa : "We've spent trillions of dollars on these problems and we have damn near nothing to show for it". O'Neil was no foe of foreign aid. Indeed, he wanted to fix the system so that more U.S. aid could be justified. But he was wrong to believe that vast flows of aid to Africa had been **squandered**. President Bush said in a press conference in April 2004 that as "the greatest power on the face of the earth, we have an **obligation** to help the spread of freedom. We have an obligation to feed the hungry". Yet how does the U.S. fulfill its obligation? U.S. aid to farmers in poor countries to help them grow more food runs at around $200 million per year, far less than $1 per person per year for the hundreds of millions of people living in subsistence farm households.

From the world as a whole, the amount of aid per African per year is really very small, just $30 per sub-Saharan African in 2002. Of that **modest** amount, almost $5 was actually for consultants from the donor countries, more than $3 was for emergency aid, about $4 went for servicing Africa's debts and $5 was for debt-relief operations. The rest, about $12, went to Africa. Since the "money down the drain" argument is heard most frequently in the U.S., it's worth looking at the same calculations for U.S. aid alone. In 2002, the U.S. gave $3 per sub-Saharan African. Taking out the parts for U.S. consultants and technical cooperation, food and other emergency aid, administrative costs and debt relief, the aid per African came to grand total of 6 cents.

The U.S. has promised repeatedly over the decades, as a signatory to global agreements like the Monterrey Consensus of 2002, to give a much larger proportion of its annual output, specifically upto 0.7% of GNP, to official development assistance. The U.S. failure to follow through has no political fallout domestically, of course, because not one in a million U.S. citizens even knows of statements like the Monterrey Consensus. But no one should underestimate the salience that it has around the world. Spin as American might about their nation's generosity, the poor countries are fully aware of what the U.S. is not doing.

61. The passage seems to emphasize that the outside world has
    (a) correct understanding about the reasonable aid provided by the USA to the poor countries
    (b) definite information about what is happening in under developed countries
    (c) stopped extending any financial aid to under developed countries
    (d) misconceptions about the aid given to the poor nations by developed countries
    (e) None of these

62. According to the Westerners the solution to eradicate poverty of African nations lies in
    (a) corruption
    (b) improving their own national behaviour
    (c) mis-rule
    (d) prolonged economic crisis
    (e) None of these

63. The author has given the example of Bangladesh, Indonesia and Pakistan in support of his argument that
    (a) corruption is the major culprit in the way of prosperity
    (b) mis-governance hampers the prosperity of nations
    (c) despite rampant corruption, nations may prosper
    (d) developed nations arrogantly neglect under developed countries.
    (e) None of these

64. The author has mentioned Ghana as a country with
    (a) reasonably good-governance
    (b) corrupt leadership
    (c) plenty of natural resources
    (d) rapid economic growth
    (e) None of these

65. The cases of malaria in Africa are mainly due to
    A. high temperature.
    B. climatic conditions conducive for breeding.
    C. malaria carries liking for human blood in preference to that of cattle.
    (a) None of these   (b) Only B and C
    (c) Only A and C   (d) Only A and B
    (e) All the three

DIRECTIONS (Qs. 66-68) : *Choose the word/group of words which is most nearly the same in meaning to the word/group of words printed in bold as used in the passage.*

66. **OBLIGATION**
    (a) lip sympathy   (b) true sympathy
    (c) self pity
    (d) conditional responsibility
    (e) moral binding

67. **SQUANDER**
    (a) use economically   (b) spend wastefully
    (c) siphon judiciously   (d) donate generously
    (e) None of these

68. **MODEST**
    (a) humble   (b) sufficient
    (c) meagre   (d) sober
    (e) unpretentious

DIRECTIONS (Qs. 69-70) : *Choose the word/group of words which is most opposite in meaning of the word given in bold as used in the passage.*

69. **MYTH**
    (a) reality   (b) mystery
    (c) misery   (d) misconception
    (e) exaggeration

70. **EXTENSIVE**
    (a) intensive   (b) abominable
    (c) inherent   (d) rampant
    (e) negligible

Passage-9

A spate of farmer sucides linked to harassment by recovery agents employed by Micro Finance Institutions (MFIs) in Andhra Pradesh **spurred** the state government to bring in regulation to protect consumer interests. But, while the Bill has brought into sharp focus the need for consumer protection, it tries to micro-manage MFI operations and in the process it could **scuttle** some of the crucial benefits that MFIs bring to farmers, says the author of Microfinance India, State of the Sector Report 2010. In an interview he points out that prudent regulation can ensure the original goal of the MFIs–social uplift of the poor.

Do you feel the AP Bill to regulate MFIs is well thought out ? Does it ensure fairness to the borrowers and the long-term health of the sector ?

The AP bill has brought into sharp focus the need for customer protection in four critical areas First is pricing. Second is tender's liability — whether the Lender can give too much loan without assessing the customer's ability to pay. Third is the structure of loan repayment – whether you can ask money on a weekly basis from people who don't produce weekly incomes. Fourth is the practices that attend to how you deal with defaults.

But the Act should have looked at the positive benefits that institutions could bring in, and where they need to be regulated in the interests of the customers. It should have brought only those features in.

Say, you want the recovery practices to be consistent with what the customer can really **manage**. If the customer is aggrieved and complains that somebody is harassing him, then those complaints should be investigated by the District Rural Development Authority.

Instead what the Bill says is that MFIs cannot go to the customer's premises to ask for recovery and that all transactions will be done in the Panchayat office. With great difficulty, MFIs brought services to the door of people. It is such a relief for the customers not to be spending time out going to banks or Panchayat offices, which could be 10 km away in some cases. A facility which has brought some relief to people is being shut. Moreover, you are practically telling the MFI where it should do business and how it should do it.

Social responsibilities were in-built when the MFIs were first conceived. If MFIs go for profit with loose regulations, how are they different from moneylenders?

Even among moneylenders there are very good people who take care of the customer's circumstance, and there are really bad ones. A large number of the MFIs are good and there are some who are **coercive** because of the kind of prices and processes they have adopted. But Moneylenders never got this organised. They did not have such a large footprint. An MFI brought in organisations, it mobilized the equity, it brought in commercial funding. It invested in systems. It appointed a large number of people. But some of then **exacted** a much higher price than they should have. They wanted to break even very fast and greed did take over in some cases.

Are the for-profit MFIs the only ones harassing people for recoveries ?

Some not-for-profit outfits have also adopted the same kind of recovery methods. That may be because you have to show that you are very efficient in your recovery methods and that your portfoilo is of a very high quality if you want to get commercial funding from a bank.

In fact, among for-profits there are many who have sensible recovery practices. Some have fortnightly recovery, some have monthly recovery. So we have differing practices. We just describe a few dominant ones and assume every for-profit MFI operates like that.

How can you introduce regulations to ensure social upliftment in a sector that is moving towards for -profit models ?

I am not really concerned whether someone wants to make a profit or not. The bottom-line for me is customer protection. The first area is fair practices. Are you telling your customers how the loan is structured ? Are you being transparent about your performance ? There should also be a lender's lilability attached to what you do. Suppose you lend excessively to a customer without assessing their ability to service the loan, you have to take the hit.

Then there's the question of limiting returns. You can say that an MFI cannot have a return on assets more than X, a return on equity of more than Y. Then suppose there is a privately promoted MFI, there should be a regulation to ensure the MFI cannot access equity markets till a certain amount of time. MFIs went to markets perhaps because of the need to grow too big too fast. The government thought they were making profit off the poor, and that's an indirect reasons why they decided to clamp down on MFIs. If you say an MFI won't go to capital market, then it will keep political compulsions **under rein**.

71. Which of the following best explains 'Structure of loan repayment' in the context of the first question asked to the author ?
    (a) Higher interest rate
    (b) Payment on weekly basis
    (c) Giving loan without assessing ability to pay
    (d) Method of dealing with defaults
    (e) Total amount of loan

72. The author is of the view that _____
    (a) the bill to regulate MFIs is not needed
    (b) the bill neglects the interests of the customers
    (c) the positive aspects of MFIs should also be considered.
    (d) most of the MFIs are not good.
    (e) MFIs must be told what and where they should do business

73. One of the distinct positive feature of MFIs is that _____.
    (a) they brought services to the door of people
    (b) they dealt with defaulters very firmly
    (c) they provided adequate customer protection
    (d) they are governed by the local people
    (e) they have highly flexible repayment plan

74. What is the difference between MFIs and moneylenders ?
    (a) There is no difference.
    (b) A large number of money lenders are good whereas only a few MFIs are good
    (c) Money lenders gave credit at lower rate of interest than that of MFIs
    (d) MFIs adopted a structure and put a process in place, which was not the case with moneylenders
    (e) Moneylender appointed large number of local people as against more outside people in MFIs

75. Which of the following is positive outcome of the AP Bill to regulate MFIs ?
    (a) The banks have started this service in remote areas
    (b) It highlighted some areas of customer protection
    (c) It highlighted the bad practices being followed by moneylenders
    (d) MFIs is invested in systems and brogurh in commercial funding.
    (e) It will help convert MFIs into small banks

76. The author is recommending ____ .
    (a) Not-for profit MFIs
    (b) For-profit MFIs
    (c) Stoppage of commercial funding to MFIs
    (d) Customer satisfaction irrespective of 'Not-for profit' or 'for profit' MFIs
    (e) Public sector promoted MFIs

77. Why did MFIs go to the equity markers ?
    (a) To repay the loan
    (b) To lower interest rate
    (c) There were political compulsions
    (d) To become a public sector institution
    (e) To grow very fast

78. Which of the following has **not** been indicated as one of the features of air practices for customer protection ?
    (a) Providing information about loan structuring.
    (b) MFIs should also be held liable for some of their actions
    (c) Not to raise money from capital market
    (d) MFIs should also inform public about their own performance also
    (e) To provide credit as per the rational assessment of their ability to service the loan

79. Which of the following could possibly be most plausible reason for banning recovery by going to customer's premises ?
    (a) To protect the family members
    (b) To protect the customer from harassment and coercion
    (c) To reduce the undue expenses of MFIs is resulting in lower interest rates.
    (d) To account systematically the money recovered in the books of accounts
    (e) To keep Panchayat office out of these transactions

DIRECTIONS (Qs. 80-83) : *Choose the word which is most nearly the same in meaning as the word/group of words printed in bold.*

80. **manage**
    (a) afford
    (b) assess
    (c) thrust
    (d) administer
    (e) use

81. **exacted**
    (a) perfected
    (b) demanded
    (c) estimated
    (d) corrected
    (e) accurate

82. **scuttle**
    (a) delay
    (b) mix
    (c) shuffle
    (d) destroy
    (e) smoothen

83. **spurred**
    (a) agitated
    (b) instigated
    (c) reflected
    (d) disapproved
    (e) prompted

DIRECTIONS (Qs. 84-85) : *Choose the word or group of words which is most opposite in meaning of the word printed in bold.*

84. **under rein**
    (a) under wrap
    (b) without target
    (c) let loose
    (d) no cloud
    (e) under cloud

85. **coercive**
    (a) gentle
    (b) promoting
    (c) progressive
    (d) natural
    (e) opinionated

Passage-10 [IBPS PO Main 2015]

Mobile technology is transforming the global banking and payment industry by providing added convenience to existing bank customers in developed markets, and by offering new services to the unbanked customers in emerging markets. While consumers and governments are keen to adopt mobile technology for government-to-person (G2P) payments, intermediaries are creating barriers as they end up losing a good source of income. Any new product for the G2P market needs to consider the incentives and motivations of all parties involved in the current value chain. As banks, mobile network operators (MNOs), NGOs and for-profit firms build new services to seize the opportunity to reach the large unbanked population, they must take time to understand the needs of customers. Even within a country, there are distinct differences in customer needs in urban and rural areas, and across segments. This has the potential to unlock a large **untapped** market. This opportunity has attracted several new players ranging from MNOs and start-ups to companies from adjacent industries such as retail, each trying its own business model to succeed in this new world. The **influx** of so many players and services has created confusion for customers, lack of coordination among players and limited scale for a single company. History tells us that after the initial stage of confusion, the dust eventually settles down as a few winners emerge.

86. What does the author mean by 'unbanked customer'?
    (a) Not having access to the services of a bank.
    (b) A person who buys goods or services from a financial institution.
    (c) A customer of a specified kind with whom one has to deal.
    (d) Both 2 and 3
    (e) Other than given options.

87. Which of the following is possibly the most appropriate title for the passage?
    (a) Progress on banking
    (b) Banking in the future
    (c) Mobile banking
    (d) Integration between e-commerce firms and banks
    (e) Instant banking

88. Which of the following is most SIMILAR in meaning of the word given in bold as used in the passage? UNTAPPED
    (a) Final
    (b) Fresh
    (c) Concluding
    (d) Latest
    (e) Last

89. Which of the following is most OPPOSITE in meaning of the word given in bold as used in the passage? INFLUX
    (a) Invasion
    (b) Enlargement
    (c) Advance
    (d) Incline
    (e) Ebb

90. Which of the following is/are true according to the passage?
    (a) With each passing day, banking is becoming narrower.
    (b) Smart users today have round-the-clock access to their bank accounts and carry their back in their pockets.
    (c) Only limited customers can avail all services of bank.
    (d) All of the above
    (e) None of these

Passage-11

It is a strange that, according to his position in life, an extravagant man is admired or despised. A successful businessman does nothing to increase his popularity by being careful with his money. He is expected to display his success, to have smart car, an expensive life, and to be lavish with his hospitality. If he is not so, he is considered mean and his reputation in business may even suffer in consequence. The paradox remains that if he had not been careful with his money in the first place, he would never have achieved his present wealth. Among the two income groups, a different set of values exists.

The yaung clerk who makes his wife a present of a new dress when the hadn't paid his houserent condemned as extravagant. Carefulness with money to the point of meanness is applauded as a virtue. Nothing in his life is considered more worthy than paying his bills. The ideal wife for such a man separaters her housekeeping money into joyless little piles- so much for rent, for food, for the children's shoes; she is able to face the milkman with equanimity and never knows the guilt of buying something she can't able to face the milkman with equanimity and never knows the guilt of buying something she can't really afford. As for myself, I fall into neither of these categories. If I have money to spare I can be extravagant, but when, as is usually the case, I am hard up, then I am then meanest man imaginable.

91. In the opinion of the writer, a successful businessman:
    (a) is more popular if he appears to be doing nothing.
    (b) should not bother about his popularity.
    (c) must be extravagant before achieving success.
    (d) is expected to have expensive tastes.
    (e) None of these

92. The phrase lavish with his hospitatlity signifies
    (a) miserliness in dealing with his friends.
    (b) considerate ness in spending on guests and strangers.
    (c) extravagance in entertaining guests.
    (d) indifference in treating his friends and relatives.
    (e) none of these

93. We understand from the passage that
    (a) all mean people are wealthy
    (b) wealthy people are invariably successful.
    (c) carefulness generally leads to failure.
    (d) thrift may lead to success.
    (e) none of these

94. It seems that low paid people should
    (a) not pay their bills promptly.
    (b) not keep their creditors waiting.
    (c) borrow money to meet their essential needs
    (d) feel guilty if they overspend
    (e) none of these

95. The word paradox means:
    (a) statement based on facts.
    (b) that which brings out the inner meaning.
    (c) that which is contrary to received opinion.
    (d) statement based on the popular opinion.
    (e) none of these

96. How does the housewife, described by the writer, feel when she saves money?
    (a) is content to be so thrifty.
    (b) wishes life were less burdensome.
    (c) is still troubled by a sense of guilt.
    (d) wishes she could sometimes be extravagant.
    (e) none of these

97. Which of the following is opposite in meaning to the word applauded in the passage?
    (a) Humiliated   (b) Decried
    (c) Cherished   (d) Suppressed
    (e) None of these

98. The statement she is able to face the milkman with equanimity implies that:
    (a) she is not upset as she has been paying the milkman his dues regularly.
    (b) she loses her nerve at the sight of the milkman who always demands his dues.
    (c) she manages to keep cool as she has to pay the milkman who always demands his dues.
    (d) she remains composed and confident as she knows that she can handle the milkman tactfully.
    (e) none of these

99. As far as money is concerned, we get the impression that the writer:
    (a) is incapable of saving anything
    (b) is never inclined to be extravagant
    (c) would like to be considered extravagant
    (d) doesn't often have any money to save
    (e) none of these

100. Which of the following would be the most suitable title for the passage?
    (a) Extravagance leads to poverty
    (b) Miserly habits of the poor.
    (c) Extravagance in the life of the rice and the poor.
    (d) Extravagance is always condemnable.
    (e) None of these

DIRECTIONS (Qs. 101-110): *Read the following information and answer the questions that follows:*

[SBI PO Main 2015]

Passage-12

True, it is the function of the army to maintain law and order in abnormal times. But in normal times there is another force that compels citizens to obey the laws and to act with due regard to the rights of others. The force also protects the lives and the properties of law abiding men. Laws are made to secure the personal safety of its subjects and to prevent murder and crimes of violence. The are made to secure the property of the citizens against theft and damage to protect the rights of communities and castes to carry out their customs and ceremonies, so long as they do not conflict with the rights of other. Now the good citizen, of his own free will obey these laws and he takes care that everything he does is done with due regard to the rights and well-being of others. But the bad citizen is only restrained from breaking these laws by fear of the consequence of his actions. And the necessary steps to compel the bad citizen to act as a good citizen are taken by this force. The supreme control of law and order in a state is in the hands of a Minister who is responsible to the State Assembly and acts through the Inspector General of Police.

101. The expression 'customs and ceremonies' means
    (a) fairs and festivals.
    (b) habits and traditions.
    (c) usual practices and religious rites.
    (d) superstitions and formalities.
    (e) None of these

102. A suitable title for the passage would be :
    (a) the function of the army.
    (b) laws and the people's rights.
    (c) the fear of the law and citizen's security.
    (d) the functions of the police.
    (e) None of these

103. Which of the following is not implied in the passage?
    (a) Law protects those who respect it.
    (b) Law ensures people's religious and social rights absolutely and unconditionally.
    (c) A criminal is deterred from committing cirmes only for fear of the law.
    (d) The forces of law help to transform irresponsible citizens into responsibile ones.
    (e) None of these

104. According to the writer, which one of the following is not the responsibility of the police?
    (a) To protect the privileges of all citizens.
    (b) To check violent activities of citizens.
    (c) To ensure peace among citizens by safeguarding individual rights.
    (d) To maintain peace during extraordinary circumstances.
    (e) None of these

105. Which of the following reflects the main thrust of the passage.
    (a) It deals with the importance of the army in maintaining law and other.
    (b) It highlights role of the police as superior to that of the army.
    (c) It discusses the roles of the army and the police in different circumstances.
    (d) It points to the responsibility of the Minister and the Inspector General of Police.
    (e) None of thesess

106. "They are made to secure the property of citizens against theft and damage", means that the law :
    (a) helps in recovering the stolen property of the citizens.
    (b) assist the citizens whose property has been stolen or destroyed.
    (c) initiate process against offenders of law.
    (d) safeguard people's possessions against being stolen or lost.
    (e) None of thesess

107. Out of the following which one has the opposite meaning to the word 'restrained' in the passage?
    (a) Promoted   (b) Accelerated
    (c) Intruded   (d) Inhibited
    (e) None of thesess

108. Which one of the following statement is implied in the passage?
    (a) Peaceful citizens seldom violate the law, but bad citizens have to be restrained by the police.
    (b) Criminals, who flout the law, are seldom brought to book.
    (c) The police hardly succeed in converting bad citizens into good citizens.
    (d) The police check the citizens, whether they are good or bad, and stop them from violating the law.
    (e) None of thesess

109. Which of the following statement expresses most accurately the idea contained in the first sentence?
    (a) It is the job of the army to ensure internal peace at all times.
    (b) It is the police that should always enforce law and order in the country.
    (c) Army and the police ensure people's security through combined operations.
    (d) It is in exceptional circumstances that the army has to ensure peace in the country.
    (e) None of thesess

110. The last sentence of the passage implies that
    (a) The Inspector General of Police is the sole authority in matters of law and order.
    (b) In every State maintenance of public peace is under the overall control of the responsible Minister.
    (c) A Minister and a responsible State, Assembly exercise direct authority in matters pertaining to law and order.
    (d) The Inspector General of Police is responsible to the State Assembly for maintaining law and order.
    (e) None of thesess

Passage - 13

A recent report in News Week says that in American colleges, students of Asian origin outperform not only the minority group students but the majority whites as well. Many of these students must be of Indian origin, and their achievement is something we can be proud of. It is unlikely that these talented youngsters will come back to India and that is the familiar brain drain problem. However recent statements by the nation's policy-makers indicate that the perception of this issue is changing. 'Brain bank' and not 'brain drain' is the more appropriate idea, they suggest since the expertise of indians abroad is only deposited in other places and not lost.

This may be so, but this brain bank, like most other banks, is one that primarily serves customers in its neighborhood. The skills of the Asians now excelling in America's colleges will mainly help the U.S.A.. No matter how significant, what non-resident Indians do for India and what their counterparts do for other Asian lands is only a by-product.

But it is also necessary to ask, or be remained, why Indians study fruitfully when abroad. The Asians whose accomplishments News Week records would have probably has a very different tale if they had studied in India. In America they found elbow room, books and facilities not available and not likely to be available here. The need to prove themselves in their new country and the competition of an international standard they faced there must have cured mental and physical laziness. But other things helping them in America can be obtained here if we achieve a change is social attitudes, specially towards youth.

We need to learn to value individuals and their unique qualities more than conformity and respectability. We need to learn the language of encouragement to add to our skill in flattery.

111. Among the many groups of students in American colleges, Asian students.
    (a) are often written about in magazines like News Week.
    (b) are most successful academically
    (c) have proved that they are as good as the whites.
    (d) have only a minority status like the blacks.
    (e) None of these

112. The student of Asian origin in America include :
    (a) a fair number from India.
    (b) a small group from India.
    (c) persons from India who are very proud.
    (d) Indians who are the most hard working of all.
    (e) None of thesess

113. In general, the talented young Indians studying in America:
    (a) have a reputation for being hard working
    (b) have the opportunity to contribute to India's development.
    (c) can solve the brain drain problem because of recent changes in policy.
    (d) will not return to pursue their careers in India.
    (e) None of thesess

114. There is talk now of the 'brain bank' This idea :
    (a) is a solution to the brain drain problem
    (b) is a new problem caused parly by the brain drain
    (c) is a new way of looking at the role of qualified Indians living abroad.
    (d) is based on a plan to utilize foreign exchange remittances to stimulate research and development.
    (e) None of thesess

115. The brain bank has limitations like all banks in the sense that:
    (a) a bank's services go mainly to those near it.
    (b) small neighbourhoods banks are not visible in this age of multinationals.
    (c) only what is deposited can be withdrawn and utilized.
    (d) no one can be forced to put his assets in a bank.
    (e) None of thesess

116. The author feels that what non-resident Indians do for India:
    (a) will have many useful side effects.
    (b) will not be their main interest and concern.
    (c) can benefit other Asian countries as a by-product.
    (d) can American colleges be of service to the world community.
    (e) None of thesess

117. The performance of Indians when they go to study in the West :
    (a) shows the fruits of hardwork done by school teachers in India.
    (b) should remind us that knowledge and wisdom are not limited by the boundaries of race and nation.
    (c) is better than people in the West expect of non-whites.
    (d) is better than what it would have been if they had studied in India.
    (e) None of thesess

118. The high level of competition faced by Asian students in America.
    (a) helps them overcome their lazy habits.
    (b) makes them lazy since the facilities there are good.
    (c) makes them worried about failing.
    (d) helps them prove that they are as good as whites.
    (e) None of thesess

119. The author feels that some of the conditions other than the level of facilities that make the West attractive.
    (a) are available in India but young people do not appreciate them.
    (b) can never be found here because we believe in conformity.
    (c) can be created if our attitudes and values change.
    (d) can also give respectability to our traditions and customs.
    (e) None of thesess

120. One of the ways of making the situation in India better would be
    (a) to eliminate flattery from public life.
    (b) to distinguish between conformity and respectability.
    (c) to give appreciation and not be tightfisted.
    (d) to encourage people and no merely flatter them.
    (e) None of thesess

Passage - 14

As the government prepare to empty its filling candidates and heads for the hot and dusty plans to solicit votes. It is visibly **exuding** optimism about the economy. According to its non-elected representatives, all the lead indicators seem to be showing signs of a revival with the first glimmer of some incipient growth pushing through the enveloping groom. Steel, cement, auto, fast moving consumer goods (such as soaps and detergents), food items, beverages, volume' of goods moved by the railways have all shown some improvement in January after having shrunk in the previous two months.

But before we start congratulating the government for its excellent economic management, let's hit the pause button for a moment. How much of the Indian economy's resilience is owed to governmental intervention? Ok, is there a strategy at all? One of the economy's mainstays for over a decade has been service. This contributes to over 50% of the country's GDP and has been providing enormous growth impulse over the past few years. If you were to listen to the government representatives, it would seem as if they had foreseen the coming age of services and had designed that structure. The truth is somewhat different. There are many reasons behind the extraordinary growth of services.

One of the reasons is the kind of elaborate rent-seeking structures erected by the government in the manufacturing sector. Any person wanting to set-up a manufacturing facility in India still has to fill a large number of outstretched palms, making the operations costly from day one.

Here's another unique aspect of the economy for which politicians routinely take credit. One of the saving graces for the Indian economy during this episode of the downturn is the safety net expected to be provided by Indian consumers, even as the international economy winds down and **eschews** consumption of goods made in India.

This has had a **deleterious** impact on Indian exports, leading many exporters to scale down their operations and restructure their businesses. Fortunately, for the planners and the administrators, the impact of the global slowdown is likely to be cushioned, to a large extent, by the gigantic Indian domestic market, which will continue consuming and providing the growth push to the economy.

Again, it's not as if some wise person in government woke up one morning and presciently decreed that hence forth the country would focus only on the domestic markets. The government has always felt that exports should be the **apposite** strategy for economic growth, just like some of the other emerging countries.

Guess what? Exporters also have to manufacture and that is quite an endurance test in India. Plus, the intricate structure built around promoting exports also worked as a huge deterrent. The government also did not quite see exports as an alternative, viable economic growth model till the Southeast Asian success story burst on to the scene. Hence, till then exports did not quite get the required push. So, no grand design here too.

Unlike in USA and various other European economies, where the government provides unemployment benefits as part of their social contract, Indians have to fend for themselves. In the current downturn, for example, many Indians-especially in the urban and semi-urban settlements-are wary of spending because of uncertainties surrounding their jobs. This has impacted consumption but, conversely, is bound to improve the savings rate.

The credit, therefore, should go to the Indian citisen who, despite the varous hurdles and inconveniences, is using his ingenuity to improve his lot at all times. This collective strength has not been forged by some steely policy push, but has developed by default, almost in line' with Charles Darvins's theory of survival.

121. According to the author, one of the reasons behind services flourishing in our country is
    (a) financial support provided by the government
    (b) funding by theele
    (c) availability of a pool of experts from developed countries in this sector
    (d) availability of young working population
    (e) Other than those given as options

122. Which of the following is most nearly the opposite in meaning to the word 'Exuding' as used in the passage?
    (a) Excluding   (b) Displaying
    (c) Percolating   (d) Closing
    (e) Concealing

123. Which of the following is most nearly the same in meaning to the word 'Apposite' as used in the passage?
    (a) Appropriate   (b) Opposite
    (c) Further   (d) Soft
    (e) Believable

124. According to the author, one of the reasons why India's economy managed to sail through the economic downturn was
    A.   There was demand for Indian goods from domestic consumers even when internationally it had declined.
    B.   The politicians had foreseen the trouble and could prepare the country to efficiently deal with it.
    C.   It was least affected by the economic downturn.
    (a) Only B   (b) Only C
    (c) A and B   (d) Only A
    (e) A and C

125. Which of the following is the central theme of the passage?
    (a) Social contract-A Must in Every Country
    (b) Hurdles Created by the government for the Common Man
    (c) Government's Campaign to Once Again Regain Confidence of the Masses
    (d) Economic Growth-A Result of Natural Forces rather than the government
    (e) Service Industry-The Backbone of Every Economy across the Globe

126. The author attributes the improvement (or maintenance of) the economic condition of the country to
    A.   The government, as it could foresee a dwindle in the economy and could take suitable measures to tackle it.
    B.   Appropriate policies to push people to spend more.
    C.   The Economy for it is surviving on its own either through consumption or saving.
    (a) Only B   (b) Only C
    (c) A and B   (d) Only A
    (e) A and C

127. Which of the following is most nearly the same in meaning to the word 'Eschews' as used in the passage?
    (a) Faces   (b) Avoids
    (c) Accepts   (d) Bestows
    (e) Ridicules

128. Which of the following is most nearly the opposite in meaning to the word 'Deleterious' as used in the passage?
    (a) Positive   (b) Harmful
    (c) Disastrous   (d) Zilch
    (e) Additional

129. Which of the following correctly explains the phrase 'Wary of' as used in the passage regarding spending behaviour of citizens?
    (a) Careless   (2) Miserly
    (c) Upset about   (d) Cautious about
    (e) Fearless in

130. Which of the following is **not true** in the context of the passage?
    (a) Traditionally the government did not believe exports to be providing a boost to the economy.
    (b) Most unemployed Indians today reap the benefits provided under social contracts.
    (c) The author is a firm believer of the fact that the government has played the smallest role in supporting the economy of the country.
    (d) The government is portraying a rosy picture of the economy to gain people's confidence.
    (e) All the given statements are true.

Passage-15   [SBI PO Main 2016]

Right through history, imperial powers have clung to their possessions to death. Why, then, did Britain in 1847 give up the jewel in its crown, India? For many reasons. The independence struggle exposed the hollowness of the white man's burden. Provincial self-rule since 1835 paved the way for full self-rule. Churchill resisted independence, but the Labour Government of Atlee was anti-imperialist by ideology. Finally, the Royal Indian Navy Mutiny in 1846 raised fears of a second Sepoy Mutiny, and convinced British waverers that it was safer to withdraw gracefully. But politico-military explanations are not enough. The basis of empire was always money. The end of empire had much to do with the fact that British imperialism had ceased to be profitable. World War II left Britain victorious but deeply indebted, needing Marshall Aid and loans from the World Bank. This constituted a strong financial case for ending the no longer-profitable empire.

Empire building is expensive. The US is spending one billion dollar a day in operations in Iraq that fall well short of fullscale imperialism. Through the centuries, empire building was costly, yet constantly undertaken because it promised high returns. The investment was in armies and conquest. The returns came through plunder and taxes from the conquered. No immorality was attached to imperial loot and plunder. The biggest conquerors were typically revered (hence titles like Alexander the Great, Akbar the Great, and Peter the Great). The bigger and richer the empire, the more the plunderer was admired. This mindset gradually changed with the rise of new ideas about equality and governing for the public good, ideas that culminated in the French and the American Revolutions. Robert Clive was impeached for making a little money on the side, and so was Warren Hastings. The white man's burden came up as a new moral rationale for conquest. It was supposedly for the The Princeton Review CAT sample paper 12 good of the conquered. This led to much muddled hypocrisy. On the one hand, the empire needed to be profitable. On the other hand, the white man's burden made brazen loot impossible.

An additional factor deterring loot was the 1857 Sepoy Mutiny. Though crushed, it reminded the British vividly that they were a tiny ethnic group who could not rule a gigantic subcontinent without the support of important locals. After 1857, the British stopped annexing one princely state after another, and instead treated the princes as allies. Land revenue was fixed in absolute terms, partly to prevent local unrest and partly to promote the notion of the white man's burden. The empire proclaimed itself to be a protector of the Indian peasant against exploitation by Indian elites. This was denounced as hypocrisy by nationalists like Dadabhai Naoroji in the 18th century, who complained that land taxes led to an enormous drain from India to Britain. Objective calculations by historians like Angus Maddison suggest a drain of perhaps 1.6 percent of Indian Gross National Product in the 18th century.

But land revenue was more or less fixed by the Raj in absolute terms, and so its real value diminished rapidly with inflation in the 20th century. By World War II, India had ceased to be a profit centre for the British Empire. Historically, conquered nations paid taxes to finance fresh wars of the conqueror. India itself was asked to pay a large sum at the end of World War I to help repair Britain's finances.

But, as shown by historian Indivar Kamtekar, the independence movement led by Gandhiji changed the political landscape, and made mass-taxation of India increasingly difficult. By World War II, this had become politically impossible. Far from taxing India to pay for World War II, Britain actually began paying India for its contribution of men and goods. Troops from white dominions like Australia, Canada and New Zealand were paid for entirely by these countries, but Indian costs were shared by the British government. Britain paid in the form of non-convertible sterling balances, which mounted swiftly. The conqueror was paying the conquered, undercutting the profitability on which all empire is founded. Churchill opposed this, and wanted to tax India rather than owe it money.

But he was overruled by Indian hands, who said India would resist payment, and paralyze the war effort. Leo Amery, Secretary of State for India, said that when you are driving in a taxi to the station to catch a life-or-death train, you do not loudly announce that you have doubts whether to pay the fare. Thus, World War II converted India from a debtor to a creditor with over one billion pound in sterling balances. Britain, meanwhile, became the biggest debtor in the world. It's not worth ruling over people who are afraid to tax.

(The topic of the Passage asked in the exam was based on African banks)

131. Which of the following was NOT a reason for the emergence of the 'white man's burden' as a new rationale for empire building in India?
    (a) The emergence of the idea of the public good as an element of governance.
    (b) The decreasing returns from imperial loot and increasing costs of conquest.
    (c) The weakening of the immorality attached to an emperor's looting behaviour.
    (d) A growing awareness of the idea of equality among peoples.
    (e) None of these

132. Which of the following best expresses the main purpose of the author?
    (a) To present the various reasons that can lead to the collapse of an empire and the granting of independence to the subjects of an empire.
    (b) To point out the critical role played by the 'white man's burden' in making a colonizing power give up its claims to native possessions.
    (c) To highlight the contradictory impulse underpinning empire building which is a costly business but very attractive at the same time.
    (d) To illustrate how erosion of the financial basis of an empire supports the granting of independence to an empire's constituents.
    (e) None of these
133. What was the main lesson the British learned from the Sepoy Mutiny of 1857?
    (a) That the local princes were allies, not foes.
    (b) That the land revenue from India would decline dramatically.
    (c) That the British were a small ethnic group.
    (d) That India would be increasingly difficult to rule. The Princeton Review CAT sample paper 13
    (e) None of these
134. Which of the sfollowing best captures the meaning of the 'white man's burden', as it is used by the author?
    (a) The British claim to a civilizing mission directed at ensuring the good of the natives.
    (b) The inspiration for the French and the American Revolutions.
    (c) The resource drain that had to be borne by the home country's white population.
    (d) An imperative that made open looting of resources impossible.
    (e) None of these
135. Why didn't Britain tax India to finance its World War II efforts?
    (a) Australia, Canada and New Zealand had offered to pay for the Indian troops.
    (b) India had already paid a sufficiently large sum during World War I.
    (c) It was afraid that if India refused to pay, Britain's war efforts would be jeopardised.
    (d) The British empire was built on the premise that the conqueror pays the conquered.
    (e) None of these

Passage -16

Emerging markets account for more than half of world GDP on the basis of purchasing power according to the International Monetary Fund (IMF). In the1890s it was about a third and in the late 1890s 30% of countries in the developing world managed to increase their output per person faster than America did, thus achieving what is called 'catch-up growth'. That catching up was somewhat lackadaisical. The gap closed at just 1.5% a year.

Some of this was due to slower grower in America, most was not. The most impressive growth was in four of the biggest emerging economies Brazil, Russia, India and China (BRICS). These economies have grown in different ways and for different reasons. The remarkable growth of emerging markets in general and the BRICS in particular transformed the global economy in many ways. Some wrenching commodity prices soared and the cost of manufacturers and labour sank. A growing and vastly more accessible pool of labour in emerging economies played a part in both wage stagnation and rising income inequality in rich ones. Global poverty rates tumbled. Gaping economic imbalances fuelled an era of financial vulnerability and laid the ground work for global crisis. The shift towards the emerging economies will continue. But its most tumultuous phase seems to have more or less reached its end. Growth rates have dropped, the nature of their growth is in the process of changing too and its new mode will have lesser direct effects on the rest of the world. The likelihood of growth in other emerging economies having an effect in the near future comparable to that of the BRICS in the recent past is low. The emerging giants will grow larger and their ranks will swell but their tread will no longer shake the Earth as it once did.

After the 1890s there followed 'convergence with a vengeance'. China's pivot towards liberalization and global markets came at a propitious time in terms of politics, business and technology. Rich economies were feeling relatively relaxed about globalization and current account deficits. America's booming and confident was little troubled by the growth of Chinese industry or by off-shoring jobs to India. And the technology etc., necessary to assemble and maintain complex supply chains were coming into their own, allowing firms to spread their operations between countries and across oceans. The tumbling costs of shipping and communication sparked 'globalization's second unbounding' (the fiat was the simple ability to provide consumers in one place with goods from another). As longer supply chains infiltrated and connected places with large and fast growing working-age populations, enormous quantities of cheap new labour became accessible. In 2007 China's economy expanded by an eye-popping 14.2%. India managed 10.1% growth, Russia 8.5% and Brazil 6.1%. The IMF now reckons there will be a slowdown in growth. China will grow by just 7.6% in 2013 India by 5.6% and Russia and Brazil by 2.5%. Other countries have impressive growth potential. 'Next 11' (N 11) which includes Bangladesh, Indonesia, Mexico, Nigeria and Turkey. But there are various reasons to think that this N11 cannot have an impact on the same scale as that of the BRICS. The first is that these economies are smaller. The N11 has a population of just over 1.3 billion, less than half that of the BRICS. The second is that the N11 is richer now than the BRICS were back in the day. The third reason that the performance of the BRICS cannot be repeated is the very success of that performance. The world economy is much larger than it used to be twice as in real terms as it was in 1892 according to IMF figures. But whether or not the world can build remarkable era of growth will depend in large part on whether new giants tread a path towards greater global co-operation or stumble in times of tumult and in the worst case fight. (The topic of the Passage asked in the exam was based on Brain drain in China)

136. According to the passage which of the following is a reason for the author's prediction regarding N11 countries?
   (a) N11 countries are poorer, have less resources than BRICS countries and do not have much scope to grow
   (b) The size of these countries is too great to fuel a high rate of growth as expected by BRICS countries
   (c) The world economy is so large that the magnitude of growth from these countries will have to be huge to equal the growth of BRICS
   (d) These economies are agricultural and have not opened up their economies yet so their scope of growth is greater than that of BRICS
   (e) Other than those given as options

137. What is the author's view of globalization's second unbounding?
   (a) It proved beneficial since it created a large number of jobs and tremendous growth in crossborder trade
   (b) It disturbed the fragile balance of power among BRICS nations and caused internal strife
   (c) It caused untold damage to America's economy since it restricted the spread of American firms off-shore
   (d) It proved most beneficial for the agricultural sector creating huge employment opportunities
   (e) Citizens in advanced countries became much better off than those in emerging economies

138. What do the comparative statistics of 2007 and 2013 for BRICS countries published by the IMF as cited in the passage indicate?
   (a) BRICS economies are contributing less to global growth
   (b) As the population of these countries grows its growth rate is falling
   (c) The financial practices followed by these countries will continue to pay rich dividends
   (d) These countries are creating global financial imbalances to the detriment of smaller developing economies like Africa
   (e) IMF forecasts of growth rate for these countries have not been fulfilled

139. What effect did rise in economies of BRICS have on the global economy?
   (a) It helped stabilize the globle economy and insulate it from the fall out of the global financial crisis
   (b) Labour became more highly skilled and wages rose alarmingly reducing the off-shoring of jobs to developing countries
   (c) Though worldwide poverty rates tumbled, the gap between the rich and the poor in rich economies increased
   (d) The cost of living and level of inflation in these countries were maintained at low levels
   (e) All the given options are effects of the rise in BRICS economies

140. What does the phrase "their ranks will swell but their tread will no longer shake the Earth as it once did" convey in the context of the passage?
   (a) While many countries will try and achieve the same rate of growth as BRICS they will not succeed
   (b) The growth of BRICS countries has changed the world's economy in ways that any further growth will not have such a disruptive effect on the world economy
   (c) Developing countries have strengthened their fiscal systems in such a way that they will not be shaken to such an extent again
   (d) Poverty may increase as the gap between the rich the poor increase but it will never reach the same levels as prior to the crisis
   (e) Citizens in advanced countries became much better off than those in emerging economies

141. Which of the following best describes 'catch up growth'?
   (a) Emerging economies tried but failed to catch up with America which always grew at a higher growth rate
   (b) The size of emerging economies and their purchasing power has caught up with and now exceeds as rich countries together
   (c) The growth of the America economy determines the growth of emerging economies
   (d) In the latter half of the 1890s some emerging economies out did America in terms of output per person
   (e) None of the given statements describes catch up growth

142. Which of the following can be said about 'convergence with a vengeance'?
   A. After the 1890s advanced economies like America were open to the idea of free trade and globalization.
   B. There were huge technological advances which were conducive to allowing business to spread their area of operations.
   C. Rich economies felt threatened by the competition from China.
   (a) Only A   (b) Only B
   (c) Only C   (d) A and B
   (e) B and C

143. What is the author's main objective in writing this passage?
   A. To urge emerging economies to deal with growth which can be disruptive maturely and without conflict.
   B. To point out that while the period of growth of BRICS was disruptive this disruption has almost come to a close.
   C. To criticize advanced economies for their handling of growth and promoting competition and conflict in certain regions.
   (a) A and B   (b) Only A
   (c) Only C   (d) All A, B and C
   (e) B and C

Passage -17

Globalization is the objective trend of economic development in the world today, featured by free flow and optimized allocation of capital, technology, information and service in the global context. It is the inevitable result of the development of productive forces and advances of science and technology, especially the revolution of information technology since the 1880s and 1890s.

The influence of globalization on countries at different stages of development is entirely different. The "dividends" derived from globalization are not fairly distributed. The developed countries have apparent advantages in capital, technology, human resources and administrative expertise and in setting the "rules of the game". They are usually the biggest beneficiaries of globalization. The developing countries on the other hand are on the whole in an unfavorably position. Developing countries can obtain some foreign investment, advanced technologies and management expertise, but at the same time they are the most vulnerable to the negative impacts of globalization and lack the ability to effectively fend off and reduce the risks and pitfalls that come along with globalization. In the 1890s, especially in recent years, the gap between the North and the South has further widened. The economic sovereignty and economic security of the developing countries are confronted with enormous pressure and stern challenges. Some least-developed countries are even on the brink of being marginalized by globalization. Therefore, in participation of globalization, developing countries should always be on alert and try by all means to exploit the advantages and avoid all kinds of risk and harm.

In the past 20-odd years, China has maintained an annual growth rate of over 9.3% on average. China is now the 6th largest economy and the 5th largest trading nation in the world. More than 200 million people have been lifted out of poverty. The above accomplishments were achieved against the backdrop of a volatile international situation. The reason why China was so successful in such a short period of time and in a constantly changing international environment is because China has found its own road of development i.e, to base what we do on the realities of China while sticking to the basic system of socialism, reforms should be carried out to solve the problems of incompatibility between the productive forces and the relations of production, and between economic base and the superstructure, so as to achieve self-perfection of socialism. Every country is different from the other.

It opens not only to developed countries, but also to developing countries, not only in economic field, but also in all areas of social development. At the same time, it is not a blind opening, but a self-conscious one, not a disorganized opening but a systematic one. China's opening proceeds and deepens in a gradual and step by step fashion. It started from the 4 special economic zones, to coastal cities, then to capital cities of inland provinces and now it has reached an unprecedented stage of all-round opening demonstrated by China's accession to the World Trade Organization. During its opening-up, China paid special attention to give full play to its comparative advantages to actively conduct international cooperation and competition. For instance, China has fully exploited its advantages of low cost of labour to attract foreign investment and technology to push economic development and better efficiency and quality of economic growth. These measures have brought the Chinese economy increasingly integrated with the world economy.

China has learnt many lessons and accumulated rich experiences in dealing with globalisation from its practice of reform and opening-up. To adopt opening-up policy. It opens not only to developed countries, but also to developing countries, not only in economic field, but also in all areas of social development. At the same time, it is not a blind opening, but a self-conscious one, not a disorganized opening but a systematic one. China's opening proceeds and deepens in a gradual and step by step fashion. It started from the 4 special economic zones, to coastal cities, then to capital cities of inland provinces and now it has reached an unprecedented stage of all-round opening demonstrated by China's accession to the World Trade Organization. During its opening-up, China paid special attention to give full play to its comparative advantages to actively conduct international cooperation and competition.

China's participation in Globalization is by no means a one-way street. When the world economic growth remains weak, China's economy is one of the few bright spots. As World Bank Report on Global Development Finance 2003 published in early April pointed out that China's fast growth "helped to drive the recovery in East Asia. Together with policy stimulus in other countries, China's performance lifted the region to growth of 6.7 % in 2002, up from 5.5% in 2001. China has also provided the world with the largest rising market. When more than 1.25 billion people become well-off, the demand on everything will be enormous. Just to give you an example, in the coming 10 years alone, China will import US$ 2 trillion of goods from the outside world. It goes without saying that we are also facing many challenges. For instance, with the accession to the WTO, China is faced with growing pressure from international competition. China's enterprises have to cope with fiercer competition not only at international market, but at home market as well. Nevertheless, opening the country to the outside world is China's basic and long-term state policy. China is committed to opening still wider to the outside world in an all-directional and multi-tiered way, with an even more active approach.

144. Why the "dividends" derived from globalization are not fairly distributed?

    (a) Apprehension in embracing and seizing the opportunities presented by globalization

    (b) Failing to adopt reforms to keep up with the steps of the changing world.

    (c) Political disadvantage due to inactivity in the developing countries.

    (d) Due to the lack of a just and equitable international economic order

    (e) None of these.

145. What reason author has given for China's achievement in such a short span of time?

    (a) Signficant modifications in the basic system of socialism.

    (b) Framing their models on Chinese characteristics rather than relying on plagiarism.

    (c) As they gave much more impetus on advancement in technology, human resources and administrative expertise

    (d) Their responsible approach as they remained vigilant against various risks, especially financial risks.

    (e) None of these

146. Which of the following is the most suitable term for the nature of Chinese opening to the outside world?
    (a) Progressive   (b) Self conscious
    (c) Comprehensive   (d) Discerning
    (e) Selective

147. How according to author China is contributing to World Economy?
    (a) By giving the road development to other developing countries so that they can follow the same path.
    (b) By providing a huge market to the World to supply the needs of billion uplifted Chinese population.
    (c) By new advancements in technology and human resources.
    (d) Focusing their attention to conduct international cooperation and competition.
    (e) None of these.

148. Which of the following statement(s) is/ are true in context of the passage?
    (i) Developing countries are raising their concern over China's commitment to even more active approach towards opening to World.
    (ii) Developing countries are usually the most active propellers of globalization.
    (iii) China's rise is a threat for the developing countries like America.
    (a) Only (ii)   (b) Both (i) and (iii)
    (c) Both (i) and (ii)   (d) Only (i).
    (e) All of the above

149. What is the challenge that is faced by China?
    (a) Need to fulfill the enormous demands of more than a billion Chinese people who have recently escaped from poverty.
    (b) Adapting to the model adopted by the other countries so as to not get isolated.
    (c) Growing pressure from the international market.
    (d) Opening the country to the outside world
    (e) None of these

150. Which of the following statement is false?
    (a) Low cost of labour in China is key to attract foreign investment.
    (b) Achieving self-perfection of socialism is a reason for China's incredible growth
    (c) Developing country can suffer economically due to globalization.
    (d) China is facing a much fiercer competition at home compared to international markets.
    (e) None of these.

Passage - 18   **[IBPS PO Main 2016]**

The finance ministry on Monday said the Union budget would be growth-oriented, implicitly signaling that it will address the investment crisis in the Indian economy. "Given the fiscal constraints and other parameters under which the government has to function, the effort of the government is to present a budget which is growth-oriented, that maintains the momentum of growth and tries to develop on it," economic affairs secretary Shaktikanta Das said in an interview with DD News uploaded on YouTube on Monday.

According to Das, the budget will also detail new measures to support ongoing programmes such as Start-up India, Standup India, Make In India, Digital India and the Skill mission – all of which have a strong focus on creating jobs. Finance minister ArunJaitley will be presenting his third budget on 29 February at a time when private investment has dried up and the exchequer has had to incur higher expenditure due to implementation of the One Rank One Pension scheme for the armed forces and the recommendations of the Seventh Pay Commission. That may cramp the government's ability to accelerate public investment to revive economic growth while sticking within the confines of its fiscal deficit targets. Some parts of the government believe that the emphasis should be on growth and not fiscal consolidation. Other parts, and the Reserve Bank of India, believe the finance minister should adhere to his fiscal commitments made in the last budget.

Without revealing whether the government will digress from the path of fiscal consolidation, Das said the government's priority is to take a balanced view on "the expenditure requirement to keep our growth momentum and to what extent we can borrow'. Care Ratings chief economist MadanSabnavis said the government has to increase its allocation for public investment on infrastructure to stimulate growth. "I expect government to spend ₹ 10,000-20,000 crore additional amount on infrastructure. Given nominal GDP (gross domestic product) is not expected to expand significantly, the leeway for the government to spend more may not be there while keeping fiscal deficit within 3.7-3.9% of GDP. So I don't expect a big-bang push for infrastructure spending given the fiscal constraint," he said.

The finance ministry revealed more contours of its budget when minister of state for finance JayantSinha, also in an interview to DD News, said the four pillars of the budget will be poverty eradication, farmers' prosperity, job creation and a better quality of life for all Indian citizens. 'This budget will be a forward looking budget that will ensure that India will continue to be a haven of stability and growth in a very turbulent and choppy global economic environment," he added.

The government has been contemplating tax incentives to companies in the manufacturing sector, including tax deductions on emoluments paid to new employees, to encourage firms to step up hiring and create jobs under its Make in India initiative. The government published suggestions that it has received internally from various government departments and other stakeholders on the mygov.in website, seeking further ideas and comments from the public. Suggestions being considered by the government include financial incentives, tax incentives under the Income Tax Act, 1861, and subsidies for equipping employees with job skills, and upgrading and improving employment exchanges. Another suggestion is to expand the scope of the tax deduction currently available to companies that add at least 10% to their workforce in a year by lowering the threshold. This incentive is available only in cases of employees who earn less than '6 lakh a year.

151. What is the main objective of the government to create the Union Budget?
    (a) It should meet the requirements of the society.
    (b) It should be under some fiscal constraints.
    (c) It should be growth oriented.
    (d) It should meet the requirements of a developed country.
    (e) It should change the momentum of growth.

152. Where is it expected to invest by government to stimulate growth?
    (a) On infrastructure
    (b) On governments plans.
    (c) On fiscal management
    (d) On manufacturing sector
    (e) On social development.

153. What does this mean that India will continue to be a "haven of stability"?
    (a) That new budget will make India stable forever.
    (b) The four pillars of budget will lead to make stability.
    (c) India will continue towards stability even in disturbed economic environment.
    (d) The budget will remain unchanged even in turbulent and choppy economic environment.
    (e) None of the above

154. Why is the government providing tax incentive to companies in manufacturing sector?
    (a) For better infrastructure.
    (b) For tax deductions on emoluments paid to new employees,
    (c) To create new job opportunities and to initiate project 'Make in India'
    (d) to create new job opportunities and to initiate project Standup India.
    (e) to encourage firms to step up hiring new skilled employees

155. Which one of the following is NOT the suggestion considered by the government?
    (a) To expand the scope of tax deduction to companies that add at least 10% to their workforce in a year.
    (b) To upgrade and improve employment exchange.
    (c) To provide incentive to employees who earn less than Rs.6 lakh a year.
    (d) Subsides to train employees with job skills.
    (e) Tax penalty for high income people.

Passage-19
[IBPS PO Main 2016]

The alarm bells should start ringing any time now. An important component of the economy has been sinking and needs to be rescued urgently. This critical piece is 'savings' and, within this overall head, household savings is the one critical subcomponent that needs close watching and nurturing.

While it is true that one of the primary reasons behind the current economic slowdown is the tardy rate of capital expansion - or, investment in infrastructure as well as plant and machinery - all attempts to stimulate investment activity are likely to come to naught if savings do not grow. Without any growth in the savings rate, it is futile to think of any spurt in investment and, consequently, in the overall economic growth. If we source all the investment funding from overseas, it might be plausible to contemplate investment growth without any corresponding rise in savings rate. But that is unlikely to happen.

Within the overall savings universe, the subcomponent 'household savings' is most critical. It provides the bulk of savings in the economy, with private corporate savings and government saving contributing the balance. The worrying factor is the near-stagnation in household savings over the last eight years or so. What's even more disconcerting is the fact that household savings remained almost flat during the go-go years of 2004-08.

This seems to be counter-factual. There are many studies that show that there is a direct relationship between overall economic growth and household savings. So, at a time when India's GDP was growing by over 9% every year, the household savings rate stayed almost constant at close to 23% of GDP. There was, of course, an increase in absolute terms, but it remained somewhat fixed as a proportion of GDP.

What is responsible for this contradictory movement? The sub-group on household savings, formed by the working group on savings for the 12th Plan set up by the Planning Commission and chaired by RBI deputy governor SubirGokarn, has this to say, "...a recent study had attributed the decline in the household saving ratio in the UK during 1895-2007 to a host of factors such as declining real interest rates, looser credit conditions, increase in asset prices and greater macroeconomic stability."

While recognising that one of the key differences in the evolving household saving scenario between the UK and India is the impact of demographics (dependency ratio), anecdotal evidence on increasing consumerism and the entrenchment of (urban) lifestyles in India, apart from the easier availability of credit and improvement in overall macroeconomic conditions, is perhaps indicative of some 'drag' on household saving over the last few years as well as going forward." India has another facet: a penchant for physical assets (such as bullion or land). After the monsoon failure of 2009, and the attendant rise in price levels that has now become somewhat deeply entrenched, Indians have been stocking up on gold. Consequently, savings in financial instruments dropped while those in physical assets shot up. This is also disquieting for policy planners because savings in physical assets stay locked in and are unavailable to the economy for investment activity. There is a counter view that higher economic growth does not necessarily lead to higher savings. According to a paper published by Ramesh Jangili (Reserve Bank of India Occasional Papers, Summer 2011), while economic growth doesn't inevitably lead to higher savings, the reciprocal causality does hold true. "It is empirically evident that the direction of causality is from saving and investment to economic growth collectively as well as individually and there is no causality from economic growth to saving and (or) investment."

Whichever camp you belong to, it is beyond doubt that savings growth is a necessary precondition for promoting economic growth. The Planning Commission estimates that an investment of $1 trillion, or over 50 lakh crore, will be required for the infrastructure sector alone. And, a large part of this critical investment will have to be made from domestic savings.

156. What is the main concern of the author behind saying that 'the alarm bells should start ringing anytime now'?

    (a) The current economic growth is slowing down due to regular failure of monsoon.

    (b) Due to power shortage industrial growth could not touch the target.

    (c) Household savings are sinking and they require to be revamped.

    (d) Due to a sharp decline in real interest rates people have lost their enthusiasm to invest in govt schemes.

    (e) All the above

157. What is/are the primary reasons behind the current economic slowdown?

    (A) Slow rate of capital expansion

    (B) Tardy investment in infrastructure as well as plant and machinery

    (C) A rapid increase in the cases of corruption, and decreased FDI

    (a) Only (A)   (b) Both (A) and (B)

    (c) Either (A) or (C)   (d) Both (B) and (C)

    (e) All (A), (B) and (C)

158. How is household savings related to overall economic growth? Give your answer in the context of the passage?

    (A) Overall economic growth is directly related to household savings.

    (B) Overall economic growth is inversely proportional to household savings.

    (C) There is no specific relationship between overall economic growth and household savings.

    (a) Only (C)   (b) Only (B)

    (c) Only (A)   (d) Either (A) or (B)

    (e) Either (A) or (C)

159. What was/were the reason(s) of drop in savings in financial instruments after 2009?

    (a) Rise in price level of gold

    (b) Decrease in real interest rates on savings in financial instruments

    (c) Investment in physical assets, particularly land

    (d) Only (a) and (c)

    (e) Only (b) and (c)

160. Which of the following is/are the reasons of a drag on household savings in India over the last few years?

    (a) Increasing consumerism

    (b) Entrenchment of urban lifestyle

    (c) Easier availability of credit

    (d) Improvement in overall macroeconomic conditions

    (e) All the above

Passage-20

Job performance is affected by a number of factors. Motivation alone does not lead to increase in performance. Ability and technology **moderates** the relationship between motivation and performance. The higher the levels of ability and motivation, the higher the level of performance will be. However, increasing motivation beyond an optimal level tends to produce a dysfunctional result because it is accompanied by an increasing level of anxiety. A high level of anxiety often disrupts performances.

The relationship between satisfaction and performance is not clear. Satisfaction may or may not lead to high performance depending on the perceived availability of valued outcomes and the perceived expectancy that a person's effort and performance will lead to receiving the valued rewards. If the person expects that his performance will lead to increased rewards which he values, the level of his motivational effort will increase, if he anticipates less, his motivational effort will be lower.

The relationship between job dissatisfaction and poor performance seems to be clearer than that between satisfaction and performance. Dissatisfaction leads to poor performance by means of **apathy,** absenteeism, turnover, sabotage, and strike. In addition, high performers are more vulnerable to job dissatisfaction because they tend to expect more from their jobs than low performers.

Job satisfaction is more closely related to the decision to join and remain in an organisation than to the motivation to produce. The motivation to produce largely depends on the availability of valued outcomes (valence), the perceived instrumentality of performance for receiving incentive rewards, and the perceived expectancy that effort leads to performance. The task of satisfying employees is much easier than the task of motivating them because the former can be achieved by rewarding them while the latter requires such additional constraints as establishing performance-reward contingencies and designing motivating work systems.

161. The individual's decision to remain in the organisation depends on

    (a) relationship between satisfaction and performance

    (b) the level of anxiety induced by the job

    (c) his level of motivation

    (d) the level of job satisfaction

    (e) None of these

162. Which of the following tasks is easier according to the passage?

    (a) Satisfying employees

    (b) Motivating the employees

    (c) Increasing the ability level of employees

    (d) Reducing the anxiety level of employees

    (e) None of these

163. Which of the following statement/s is/are **true** in the context of the passage?

    (A) Ability leads to performance.

    (B) Job satisfaction certainly leads to higher performance.

    (C) High anxiety adversely affects performance.

    (a) (A) and (B) only   (b) (B) and (C) only

    (c) (A) and (C) only   (d) (A) only

    (e) (B) only

164. Which of the following combination of factors affects job performance?

    (a) Job satisfaction and Motivation

    (b) Motivation and Ability

    (c) Job Satisfaction and Ability

    (d) Job Satisfaction, Motivation and Ability

    (e) None of these

165. The task of motivating employees is difficult due to
    (a) apathy and lack of enthusiasm of employees
    (b) difficulty in establishing relationship between satisfaction and performance
    (c) difficulty in monitoring ability level of employees
    (d) unavailability of attractive rewards in organisations
    (e) difficulty in designing a motivating work system

Passage-21

Now, the question arises: what is the secret of the longevity and imperishability of Indian culture? Why is it that such great empires and nations as **Babylon, Assyria, Greece, Rome** and **Persia** could not **last** more than the footprints of a camel on the shifting sands of the deserts, while India, which faces the same ups and downs, the same mighty and cruel hand of time, is still alive and with the same halo of glory and splendour? The answer is given by Prof JB Pratt of America. According to him, Hindu religion is **"self-perpetuating and self-renewing."** Unlike other religions, "not death, but development" has been the fate of Hinduism. Not only Hindu religion but the whole culture of the Hindus has been growing, changing, and developing in accordance with the needs of the times and circumstances without losing its essentially imperishable spirit. The culture of the Vedic ages, of the ages of the Upanishads, the various philosophical systems, the Mahabharata, the Smritis, the Puranas, various scholarly commentators, the medieval saints, and the age of modern reformers is the same in spirit and yet very different in form. Its basic principles are so broad-based that they can be adapted to almost any environment of development.

166. Which of the following combinations of periods of Indian culture is **incorrect** as mentioned in the passage?
    (a) The Puranas, the Mahabharata, the medieval saints
    (b) The Smritis, the modern reformers, the Vedas
    (c) The Upanishads, the philosophical system, the Smritis
    (d) The Puranas, the Ramayana, the Mahabharata
    (e) The modern reformers, the Vedas, the medieval saints

167. What changes has the spirit of Indian culture undergone during the long period of history right from the Vedic age down to the present time?
    (a) The prevalence of moral values was eclipsed at certain periods of time.
    (b) The spirit of Indian culture has remained unchanged from the ancient times down to the present.
    (c) Materialism was the hallmark of Indian culture during certain periods of time
    (d) There is no such thing as any spirit of Indian culture
    (e) During certain periods authoritarian values dominated over democratic values.

168. "... could not last more than the footprints of a camel on the shifting sands of the deserts". What does this expression mean as used in the passage?
    (a) It lost itself in desert.
    (b) It was transient.
    (c) It lacked solidity.
    (d) It was limited only to desert area.
    (e) It lacked cohesion.

169. What is the characteristic quality of the basic principles of Indian culture?
    (a) They are static.
    (b) They derive their strength from the genius of people.
    (c) They believe in the purity of Indian culture.
    (d) They can be adapted to almost any environment.
    (e) They project the glimpses of ancient civilization.

170. What, according to JB Pratt, is the secret of the longevity and imperishability of Indian culture?
    (a) It has its origin in the remote past.
    (b) It stems from the minds and hearts of its sages.
    (c) It is founded on religion.
    (d) It is founded on universal moral values.
    (e) It is self-perpetuating and self-renewing.

Passage-22

Comfort is now one of the causes of its own spread. It has now become a physical habit, a fashion, an ideal to be pursued for its own sake. The more comfort is brought into the world, the more it is likely to be valued. To those who have known comfort, discomfort is a real torture. The fashion which now **decrees** the worship of comfort is quite as imperious as any other fashion. Moreover, enormous material interests are bound up with the supply of the means of comfort. The manufacturers of furniture, of heating apparatus, of plumbing fixtures cannot afford to let the love of comfort die. In modern advertisements they have found a means for compelling it to live and grow. A man of means today, who builds a house, is in general concerned primarily with the comfort of his future residence. He will spend a great deal of money on bathrooms, heating apparatus, padded furnishings, and having spent he will regard his house as perfect. His counterpart in an earlier age would have been primarily concerned with the impressiveness and magnificence of his dwelling with beauty, in a word, rather than comfort. The money our contemporary would spend on baths and central heating would have been spent on marble staircases, frescoes, pictures and statues. I am inclined to think that our present passion for comfort is a little exaggerated. Though I personally enjoy comfort, I have lived most happily in houses **devoid of** everything that Anglo-Saxons deem **indispensable**. Orientals and even South Europeans who know not comfort and live very much as our ancestors did centuries ago seem to go on very well without our elaborate apparatus and padded luxuries. However, comfort for me has a justification; it facilitates mental life. Discomfort handicaps thought; it is difficult to use the mind when the body is cold and aching.

171. How do people manage to keep the love of comfort alive?
    (a) By pumping in more comfort goods in the market
    (b) By sacrificing high profit on comfort goods
    (c) By targeting youths in the sales campaign
    (d) By appealing to the emotionality of people
    (e) None of these

172. What is the author's prediction about comfort?
    (a) The value of comfort will increase.
    (b) People will value more spirituality thus reducing the value of comfort.
    (c) People will desire simple lifestyle.
    (d) The advertisements will play down the comfort aspect of goods.
    (e) None of these

173. What was the characteristic of affluent men of an earlier age?
    (a) He used to put higher premium on comfort.
    (b) He was relying much on advertisements.
    (c) He believed more in simple and cheaper things.
    (d) He was more qualitative in his emphasis rather than being quantitative.
    (e) His emphasis was on beauty.
174. What change according to the author has taken place in the attitude towards comfort?
    (a) It is taken for granted in the modern way of living.
    (b) It has become now an ideal to be pursued for its own sake.
    (c) It is now believed that discomfort handicaps thought.
    (d) It is thought that comfort helps body and mind to function effectively.
    (e) None of these
175. Why would manufacturers of various devices not permit comfort to die?
    (a) They want to manufacture more and more comfort goods.
    (b) Manufacturers are mainly interested in creating new things.
    (c) Manufacturers' emphasis is on producing beautiful things.
    (d) Their prosperity is closely linked with the people's desire for comfort.
    (e) None of these

Passage-23

Employment exchanges — one of the surviving bastions of babudom — face the prospect of becoming irrelevant in an era of reform. Even in the heart of the nation's capital, the premises are often dilapidated structures with dirty passages and manned by surly staff. Not surprisingly, job-seekers hardly throng these exchanges. Paradoxically, when jobs are getting scarce due to pressure of liberalisation, job-seekers are **spurning** an institution intended to help them **secure** placements. The reasons are simple enough. Employment exchanges still concentrate on government and public sector placements, which are fast losing ground in the labour market. For most government jobs, the eligibility criterion is still registration with the employment exchanges. But what is the use of going through the formalities of registration when government jobs themselves are dwindling? The placement effected by all the 939-odd exchanges in the country in 2001 was of the order of 1.69 lakh against annual registration levels of 60 lakh. As there are too few jobs when compared to the number of job-seekers, the accumulated backlog of registrations is close to 4.16 crore. The latter of course doesn't indicate unemployment levels as those registered with the employment exchanges are not necessarily unemployed.

How can the employment exchanges be revamped? The thinking in the Union labour ministry is to transform them into employment promotion and guidance centres. The plan includes modernisation, changing the mindset of the staff and making them into an effective instrument for monitoring and coordinating various employment generation schemes. This objective calls for developing a better database on the fast changing employment situation with a comprehensive coverage of new economic establishments. For instance, the various economic censuses are an important source of information on the changing employment profile of, say, the nation's capital. Far from being a bureaucrat-dominated city, Delhi over the years has become more of an industrial metropolis. According to the fourth economic census, manufacturing accounted for 40 per cent of jobs in the capital. The employment exchanges in the capital thus have their work cut out notably, to shift the focus away from government and public sector jobs more towards placements in the private sector, especially in manufacturing and services, including the **burgeoning** retail trade sector. By doing so, they will better reflect the **imperatives** of economic reform and remain relevant in today's times.

176. Which of the following revamped role can be entrusted to employment exchanges?
    (a) Conducting economic surveys
    (b) To conduct vocational training programme for the unemployed
    (c) To modernise registration process through the Internet
    (d) To reduce the number of exchanges
    (e) None of these
177. What can be inferred about the employment exchanges outside Delhi?
    (a) The registration in them would be much less.
    (b) Their condition will be worse.
    (c) Their condition will be better.
    (d) They focus more on manufacturing sector.
    (e) None of these
178. Choose the word that is **same** in meaning as the word **"secure"** as used in the passage.
    (a) fasten   (b) safe
    (c) obtain   (d) reassure
    (e) lock
179. In order to remain relevant, which of the following should be the focus of employment exchanges?
    (a) To make efforts to increase their registration
    (b) To shift attention to jobs in private sector
    (c) To shift focus on jobs in manufacturing in public sector organisations
    (d) To reform exchanges by recruiting trained staff
    (e) To obtain more grants from government
180. Which of the following is not true in the context of the passage?
    (a) Those who register with the employment exchanges inform them if they are able to get the job on their own.
    (b) The annual placement arranged by employment exchanges is less than 3% of the registration.
    (c) For government jobs, registration with employment exchanges is required.
    (d) In Delhi, over the years more industries have started.
    (e) All the above are true

Passage-24

We have inherited the tradition of secrecy about the budget from Britain where also the system has been strongly attacked by eminent economists and political scientists including Peter Jay. Sir Richard Clarke, who was the originating genius of nearly every **important** development in the British budgeting techniques during the last two decades, has spoken out about the abuse of budget secrecy: "The problems of long-term tax policy should surely be **debated** openly with the facts on the table. In my opinion, all governments should have just the same **duty** to publish their expenditure policy. Indeed, this obligation to publish taxation policy is really essential for the control of public expenditure in order to get realistic taxation implications." Realising that democracy **flourishes** best on the principles of open government, more and more democracies are having an open public debate on budget proposals before introducing the appropriate Bill in the legislature. In the United States the budget is conveyed in a message by the President to the Congress, which comes well in advance of the — date when the Bill is introduced in the Congress. In Finland the Parliament and the people are already discussing in June the tentative budget proposals which are to be introduced in the Finnish Parliament in September. Every budget contains a cartload of figures in black and white - but the dark figures represent the **myriad** lights and shades of India's life, the contrasting tones of poverty and wealth, and of bread so dear and flesh and blood so cheap, the deep tints of adventure and enterprise and man's ageless struggle for a brighter morning. The Union budget should not be an annual **scourge** but a part of presentation of annual accounts of a partnership between the Government and the people. That partnership would work much better when the nonsensical secrecy is replaced by openness and public consultations, resulting in fair laws and the people's acceptance of their moral duty to pay.

181. How do the British economists and political scientists react to budget secrecy? They are
    (a) in favour of having a mix of secrecy and openness.
    (b) indifferent to the budgeting techniques and taxation policies.
    (c) very critical about maintenance of budget secrecy.
    (d) advocating not disclosing in advance the budget contents.
    (e) None of these

182. The author seems to be in favour of
    (a) maintaining secrecy of budget
    (b) judicious blend of secrecy and openness
    (c) transparency in budget proposals
    (d) replacement of public constitution by secrecy
    (e) None of these

183. Which of the following statements is definitely TRUE in the context of the passage?
    (a) The British Government has been religiously maintaining budget secrecy.
    (b) Budget secrecy is likely to lead to corrupt practices.
    (c) Consulting unjustifiable taxes with public helps make them accept those taxes.
    (d) There should be no control on public expenditure in democratic condition.
    (e) None of these

184. From the contents of the passage, it can be inferred that the author is
    (a) authoritarian in his approach.
    (b) a democratic person.
    (c) unaware of India's recent economic developments.
    (d) a conservative person.
    (e) None of these

185. Which of the following statement(s) is/are definitely False in the context of the passage?
    A Transparency helps unscrupulous elements to resort to corrupt practices.
    B Open approach of Government is a sign of healthy democracy.
    C People's acceptance of their moral duties can best be achieved through openness and public consultations.
    (a) Only A   (b) Only B
    (c) Only C   (d) A and B
    (e) B and C

Passage-25

The happy man is the man who lives objectively, who has free affections and wide interests, who secures his happiness through these interests and affections and through the fact that they in turn make him an object of interest and affection to many others. To be the recipient of affection is a potent cause of happiness, but the man who demands affection is not the man upon whom it is **bestowed**. The man who receives affection is, speaking broadly, the man who gives it. But it is useless to attempt to give it as a calculation, in the way in which one might lend money at interest, for a calculated affection is not genuine and is not felt to be so by the recipient.

What then can a man do who is unhappy because he is encased in self ? So long as he continues to think about the causes of his unhappiness, he continues to be self-cantered and therefore does not get outside it. It must be by genuine interest, not by simulated interests adopted merely as a medicine. Although this difficulty is real, there is nevertheless much that he can do if he has rightly diagnosed his trouble. If for example, his trouble is due to a sense of sin, conscious or unconscious, he can first persuade his conscious mind that he has no reason to feel sinful, and then proceed, to plant this rational conviction in his unconscious mind, concerning himself meanwhile with some more or less neutral activity. If he succeeds in **dispelling** the sense of sin, it is possible that genuine objective interests will arise spontaneously. If his trouble is self-pity, he can deal with it in the same manner after first persuading himself that there is nothing extraordinarily unfortunate in his circumstances.

If fear is his trouble, let him practise exercises designed to give courage. Courage has been recognized from time immemorial as an important virtue, and a great part of the training of boys and young men has been devoted to producing a type of character capable of fearlessness in battle. But moral courage and intellectual courage have been much less studied. They also, however, have their technique. Admit to yourself every day at least one painful truth, you will find it quite useful. Teach yourself to feel that life would still be worth living even if you were not, as of course you are, immeasurably superior to all your friends in virtue and in intelligence. Exercises of this sort prolonged through several years will at last enable you to admit facts without **flinching** and will, in so doing, free you from the empire of fear over a very large field.

186. Who according to the passage is the happy man?
    (a) Who is encased in self
    (b) Who has free affection and wide interests
    (c) Who is free from worldly passions
    (d) Who has externally centred passions
    (e) None of these

187. Which of the following statements is **NOT TRUE** in the context of the passage ?
(a) The happy man has wide interests.
(b) Courage has been recognised as an important virtue.
(c) Unhappy man is encased in self.
(d) A man who suffers from the sense of sin must tell himself that he has no reason to be sinful.
(e) Issue of intellectual courage has been extensively studied.

188. Which of the following, according to the passage, has not been studied much ?
(a) Feeling of guilt and self-pity
(b) The state of mind of an unhappy man
(c) How to get absorbed in other interests
(d) Moral and intellectual courage
(e) None of these

189. What should a man do who is suffering from the feeling of self-pity ?
(a) He should control his passions and emotions.
(b) He should persuade himself that everything is alright in his circumstances.
(c) He should seek affection from others.
(d) He should develop a feeling of fearlessness.
(e) He should consult an expert to diagnose his trouble.

190. What happens to a man who demands affection ?
(a) His feelings are reciprocated by others.
(b) He tends to take a calculated risk.
(c) He becomes a victim of a vicious circle.
(d) He takes affection for granted from others.
(e) None of these

Passage-26

In the second week of August 1998, just a few days after the incidents of bombing the US embassies in Nairobi and Dar-es-Salaam, a high-powered, brain-storming session was held near Washington D.C. to discuss various aspects of terrorism. The meeting was attended by ten of America's leading experts in various fields such as germ and chemical warfare, public health, disease control and also by the doctors and the law-enforcing officers. Being asked to describe the horror of possible bio-attack, one of the experts narrated the following **gloomy** scenario.

A culprit in a crowded business centre or in a busy shopping mall of a town empties a test tube containing some fluid, which in turn creates an unseen cloud of germ of a dreaded disease like anthrax capable of inflicting a horrible death within 5 days on any one who inhales it. At first 500 or so victims feel that they have mild influenza which may recede after a day or two. Then the symptoms return again and their lungs start filling with fluid. They rush to local hospitals for treatment, but the panic-stricken people may find that the medicare services run quickly out of drugs due to excessive demand. But no one would be able to realise that a terrorist attack has occurred. One cannot deny the possibility that the germ involved would be of contagious variety capable of causing an epidemic. The meeting concluded that **such attacks,** apart from causing immediate human tragedy, would have dire long-term effects on the political and social fabric of a country by way of ending people's trust on the competence of the government.

The experts also said that the bombs used in Kenya and Tanzania were of the old-fashioned variety and involved quantities of high explosives, but new terrorism will prove to be more deadly and probably more **elusive** than hijacking an aeroplane or a gelignite of previous decades. According to Bruce Hoffman, an American specialist on political violence, old terrorism generally had a specific manifesto - to overthrow a colonial power or the capitalist system and so on. These terrorists were not shy about planting a bomb or hijacking an aircraft and they set some limit to their brutality. Killing so many innocent people might turn their natural supporters off. Political terrorists want a lot of people watching but not a lot of people dead. "Old terrorism sought to change the world while the new sort is often practised by those who believe that the world has gone beyond redemption", he added.

Hoffman says, "New terrorism has no long-term agenda but is ruthless in its short-term intentions. It is often just a **cacophonous** cry of protest or an outburst of religious **intolerance** or a protest against the West in general and the US in particular. Its **perpetrators** may be religious fanatics or diehard opponents of a government and see no reason to show restraint. They are simply intent on **inflicting** the maximum amount of pain on the victim."

191. In what way would the new terrorism be different from that of the earlier years?
A   More dangerous and less baffling
B   More hazardous for victims
C   Less complicated for terrorists
(a) A and C only
(b) B and C only
(c) A and B only
(d) All the three
(e) None of these

192. What could be the probable consequences of bio-attacks, as mentioned in the passage?
A   Several deaths
B   Political turmoil
C   Social unrest
(a) A only   (b) B only
(c) C only   (d) A and B only
(e) All the three

193. According to the author of the passage, the root cause of terrorism is
A   Religious fanaticism
B   Socio-political changes in countries
C   The enormous population growth
(a) A only   (b) B only
(c) C only   (d) A and B only
(e) All the three

194. The phrase **"such attacks"**, as mentioned in the last sentence of the second paragraph, refers to
(a) the onslaught of an epidemic as a natural calamity
(b) bio-attack on political people in the government
(c) attack aimed at damaging the reputation of the government
(d) bio-attack manoeuvred by unscrupulous elements
(e) None of these

195. Which of the following statements is **true** about new terrorism?
(a) Its immediate objectives are quite tragic.
(b) It has farsighted goals to achieve.
(c) It can differentiate between the innocent people and the guilty.
(d) It is free from any political ideology.
(e) It advocates people in changing the socio-political order.

Passage-27

After "Liberalization", "Globalization" and the consequent change in the new international economic order as well as new information technology order, a new catchphrase is being coined: 'A New Health Order'. Talking about setting it up is the theme of the WHO-sponsored international conference on primary health and medical care, currently being held at Milan in Italy. While much has been said and written on establishing the "new order", little has actually been done. Will the conference at Milan too swear by the "new health order", go home and then forget about it, while the present medical and healthcare set-up in poor countries further **entrenches** itself? This does not have to be the fate of the radical resolutions that will undoubtedly be passed at Milan. Unlike creating a new world economic or information order, establishing a new health set-up is essentially a matter for individual countries to accomplish. No conflict of international interests is involved. But this advantage is, at least until it begins to take concrete shape, only theoretical. The million-dollar question is whether individual third-world governments are able and willing to **muster** the will, the resources, the administrative and other infrastructure to carry out what it is entirely within their power to attain and implement.

The dimensions of the problem are known and the solutions broadly agreed on. The present medical and healthcare system is urban-based, closely geared to drugs, hospitals and expensively trained apathetic doctors. The bulk of the population in poor countries, who live in rural areas, are left untouched by all this and must rely on traditional healers. The answer is to turn out medical health personnel sufficiently, but not expensively, trained to handle routine complaints and to get villagers to pay adequate attention to cleanliness, hygienic sanitation, garbage disposal and other elementary but **crucial** matters. More complicated ailments can be referred to properly equipped centres in district towns, cities and metropolises. Traditional healers, whom villagers trust, can be among these intermediate personnel. Some third-world countries, including India, have **launched** or are preparing elaborate schemes of this nature. But the experience is not quite happy. There is **resistance** from the medical establishment which sees them as little more than licensed quackery but is not prepared either to offer **condensed** medical courses such as the former licentiate course available in this country and now unwisely scrapped. There is the question of how much importance to give to indigenous system of medicine. And there is the difficult matter of striking the right balance between preventive healthcare and curative medical attention. These are complex issues and the Milan conference would perhaps be more fruitful if it were to discuss such specific subjects.

196. The author is doubtful whether.......
(a) an individual country can set up a new health order.
(b) the Milan conference would pass radical resolutions.
(c) under-developed countries have the capacity to organize their resources.
(d) traditional healers could be trained as intermediate health personnel.
(e) the problem has been understood at all.

197. The author has reservations about the utility of the Milan Conference because ....
(a) it is expected only to discuss but not decide upon anything.
(b) earlier conferences had failed to reach any decisions.
(c) the medical profession is opposed to a new health order.
(d) while "new orders" are talked and written about, not much is actually done.
(e) None of these

198. It can be inferred from the contents of the passage that the author's approach is ....
(a) sarcastic   (b) constructive
(c) indifferent   (d) fault-finding
(e) hostile

199. What does the author suggest for the cure of the cases involving complications?
(a) Treating such cases at well-equipped hospitals in district places
(b) Training such victims in preliminary hygiene
(c) Training semi-skilled doctors to treat such cases
(d) Issuing licenses to semi-skilled doctors to treat such cases
(e) None of these

200. For a new health order, the author recommends all of the following EXCEPT
(a) motivating villagers to pay attention to cleanliness
(b) setting up well equipped centres in district towns
(c) discontinuing the present expensive medical courses
(d) training traditional healers to function as medical health personnel
(e) striking a balance between preventive healthcare and curative medical attention

Passage-28

It is an old saying that knowledge is power. Education is an instrument which imparts knowledge and, therefore, indirectly controls power. Therefore, ever since the dawn of civilization persons in power have always tried to supervise or control education. It has been the **hand-maid of the ruling class**. During the Christian era, the ecclesiastics controlled the institution of education and diffused among the people the gospel of the Bible and religious teachings. These gospels and teachings were no other than a philosophy for the maintenance of the existing society. It taught the poor man to be meek and to earn his bread with the **sweat of his brow**, while the priests and the landlords lived in luxury and fought duels for the slightest offence. During the Renaissance, education passed more from the clutches of the priest into the hand of the prince. In other words it became more secular. It was also due to the growth of the nation-state and powerful monarchs who united the country under their rule. Thus, under the control of the monarch, education began to devise and preach the **infallibility** of its masters, the monarch or king. It also invented and supported fantastic theories like the Divine Right Theory and that the king can do no wrong etc. With the advent of the industrial revolution education took a different turn and had to please the new masters. It now no longer remained the privilege of the baron class but was thrown open to the new rich merchant class of society. Yet education was still confined to the few elite. The philosophy which was in vogue during this period was that of **'Laissez Faire'** restricting the function of the State to a mere keeping of law and order while, on the other hand, in practice the law of the jungle prevailed in the form of free competition and the survival of the fittest.

201. What does the theory of Divine Right of king stipulate?
   (a) That kings are gods.
   (b) They have the right to be worshipped like gods by their subjects.
   (c) That the right of governing is conferred upon kings by god.
   (d) That the rights of kings are divine and therefore sacred.
   (e) None of these

202. What does the word "infallibility" mean?
   (a) That every man is open to error
   (b) That some divine power is responsible for determining the fate of men
   (c) The virtue of not making any mistake
   (d) Sensitivity
   (e) None of these

203. What did the ruling class in the Christian era think of the poor man?
   (a) That he is the beloved of god
   (b) That he deserves all sympathy of the rich
   (c) That he should be strong
   (d) That he is meant for serving the rich
   (e) None of these

204. Who controlled the institution of education during the Christian era?
   (a) The church and the priests
   (b) The monarchs
   (c) The secular leaders of society
   (d) The common people
   (e) None of these

205. Why have persons in power always tried to supervise or control education?
   (a) Because they wanted to educate the whole public.
   (b) Because they wanted to deprive the common man of the benefits of education.
   (c) Because it involved a huge expenditure on the state exchequer.
   (d) Because it is an instrument of knowledge and therefore power.
   (e) None of these

Passage-29

An independent, able and upright judiciary is the hallmark of a free democratic country. Therefore, the process of judicial appointments is of vital importance. At present, on account of the Supreme Court's last advisory opinion, the role of the executive and its interference in the appointment of judges is minimal, which, **in the light of our previous experience**, is most welcome. However, there is a strong demand for a National Judicial Commission on the ground of wider participation in the appointment process and for greater transparency. The composition, the role and the procedures of the proposed National Judicial Commission, must be clearly spelt out, **lest** it be a case of jumping **from the frying pan into the fire**.

Recently, there has been a lively debate in England on the subject. A judicial commission has been proposed but there are not many takers for that proposal. In the paper issued this month by the Lord Chancellor's Department on judicial appointments, the Lord Chancellor has said, "I want every vacancy on the Bench to be filled by the best person available. Appointments must and will be made on merit, irrespective of ethnic origin, gender, marital status, political affiliation, sexual orientation, religion or disability. These are not mere words. They are firm principles. I will not tolerate any form of discrimination."

At present, there are hardly any persons from the ethnic minorities manning the higher judiciary and so far not a single woman has made it to the House of Lords. The most significant part of the Lord Chancellor's paper is the requirement that "allegations of professional misconduct made in the course of consultations about a candidate for judicial office must be specific and subject to disclosure to the candidate". This should go a long way in ensuring that principles of natural justice and fair play are not **jettisoned** in the appointment process, which is not an uncommon phenomenon.

206. According to the passage, there has been a demand for a National Judicial Commission to
   (a) clear the backing of court cases.
   (b) make judiciary see eye to eye with executive.
   (c) wipe out corruption at the highest places.
   (d) make the appointment process of judges more broad based and clear.
   (e) safeguard the interest of natural justice and fair play in judicial pronouncement.

207. Which of the following could be in the author's mind when he says 'in the light of our previous experience'?
   (a) Not having enough judges from backward communities.
   (b) Interference of the executive in the appointment of judges.
   (c) Professional misconduct of judges.
   (d) Delay that occurred in the judicial appointments.
   (e) None of these

208. The role and procedure of the National Commission must be spelt out clearly
   (a) because executive wing will depend on it heavily.
   (b) because judges will take judicial decisions on the basis of it.
   (c) it will be represented by a cross-section of the society.
   (d) it will bring a qualitative change in the interpretation of law.
   (e) None of these

209. What, according to the author, is the typical characteristic of an independent democratic country?
 (a) Objective process of judicial appointments.
 (b) Supreme Court's advisory opinion on legal matters.
 (c) Responsible, free and fair judiciary.
 (d) Lively and frank debate in the society on the role of judiciary.
 (e) None of these

210. Which of the following according to the author is the most welcome thing?
 (a) The negligible role to be played by the executive in the appointment of judges.
 (b) Coordinating role played by the executive in the appointment of judges.
 (c) The appointment of judges from the ethnic minority classes.
 (d) Appointment of judges purely on the basis of merit.
 (e) None of these

DIRECTION (Q. 211) : *Read the following passages divided into number of paragraphs carefully and answer the questions that follows.*

Passage-1

The function of business is to increase the wealth of the country and the value and happiness of life. It does this by supplying the material needs of men and women. When the nation's business is successfully carried on, it renders public service of the highest value.

Passage-2

Education should not stop when the individual has been prepared to make a livelihood and to live in modern society. Living would be mere existence were there not appreciation and enjoyment of the riches of art, literature and science.

Passage-3

Through advertising manufacturers exercise a high degree of control over consumers' desires. However, the manufacturer assumes enormous risks in attempting to predict what consumers will want and in producing goods in quantity and distributing them in advance of final selection by the consumers.

Passage -4

It is often the case that our friends share beliefs and attitudes similar to ours. Indeed, this may have been one reason for becoming friends in the first place. For example, non-smokers tend, by and large, to have non-smoking friends and supporters of the same football team may have this common feature as one basis for their liking of each other.

Passage -5

Honest people in one nation find it difficult to understand the viewpoints of honest people in another. Foreign ministries and their ministers exist for the purpose of explaining the viewpoints of one nation in terms understood by the ministries of another. Some of their most important work lies in this direction.

Passage-6

Rationalism has been defined as the mental attitude which **unreservedly** accepts the supremacy of reason and aims at establishing a system of philosophy and ethics verifiable by experience and independent of all arbitrary assumptions or authority. This definition of rationalism was framed at the inauguration of the Rationalist Press Association (RPA) in London in the year 1899.

Passage-7

In today's world where teachers have a busy schedule, it is noticed that only a few teachers have time for the student's learning experiences. One thing which is lacking in almost all classrooms is teachers motivating students to do better. What happens is that teachers would like to give attention to the students who have high intelligence and who are academically good. A larger portion of the student population is neglected. Teachers blame them for not trying to do their best.

Passage-8

Due to the development of individualism and permissiveness, social norms have become slack and parents and teachers are unable to play their traditional role of shaping the character of their children and people. The growing complexity of society due to technological development and the **slackness** of social norms as a result of the growth of individualism and permissiveness are the two causes of the moral crisis of our time.

Passage-9

Marx, the founder of communism, had predicted the failure and eventual overthrow of capitalism because of what he **regarded** as its inherent contradiction. He visualised that capitalism would maintain the wages of labour at a low subsistence level, while progressively increasing its productivity by the employment of technologically advanced means of production. During the last many decades the real wages of workers in advanced capitalist countries have gradually and progressively increased. The prediction of Marx has not been borne out by history.

Passage-10

Literature is a medium through which a person can convey his ideas towards or protest against different norms of society. Those works that deal with a moral issue are of particular importance in literature. They are written with a particular purpose in mind. A literary work with a moral issue will live on to be reinterpreted by different generations. These works involve the reader for he forms his own moral judgement towards the issue.

Passage-11

The phenomena of child labour is quite complex. Children work because they belong to poor families who cannot survive without the benefit of the income which accrues to the family on account of child labour. Any attempt to abolish it through legal recourse would, under the circumstances, not be practical. The only alternative is to ban child labour in hazardous areas and to regulate and **ameliorate** the conditions of work in other areas. Many developing countries including India have accepted this approach.

Passage-12

In recent years our society has shown readiness to **address** the educational and developmental needs of adolescents. Be it the Government or people in the community, there is a realisation that something needs to be done to build on the energy and enthusiasm of this crucial section of the population. Growing social unrest, violence, crime and increasing visibility of the young has contributed to this readiness.

Passage-13

Recently a study was made on the popularity of TV programmes and viewers' perception about their quality. The study of attitudes towards prime-time television programmes showed that programmes with identical ratings in terms of numbers of people watching them received highly **divergent** marks for quality from their viewers. This additional piece of information could prove valuable for advertisers who might be well advised to spend their advertising money for programmes that viewers **feel** are of high quality.

Passage-14

Econometric models like the computable general equilibrium model are mostly valuable in policy formulation as they give some insight into how trade policy changes will affect the sectoral composition of output and employment. They are not in themselves designed to provide direct inputs but really to serve as background as to the sectors that will be most favourably or most unfavourably affected by policy. Besides, they render valuable help in policy matters regarding free trade. Free trade has distinct benefits. These benefits are well accepted all over. However, there is a growing opposition to free trade. There is an increasing perception among certain groups of how international trading systems impact, especially how they affect low-wage workers and also have a degrading environmental impact. Yet it is difficult to accept that is the reason for any kind of protectionist move in the most advanced countries.

211. The passage - 1 best supports the statement that
    (a) all businesses which render public service are successful.
    (b) human happiness is enhanced only by the increase of material wants.
    (c) the value of life is increased only by the increase of wealth.
    (d) the material needs of men and women are supplied by well-conducted business.
    (e) business is the only field of activity which increases happiness.

212. The passage -2 best supports the statement that true education
    (a) is focused on the routine problems of life.
    (b) prepares one for a full enjoyment of life.
    (c) deals chiefly with art, literature and science.
    (d) is not possible for one who does not enjoy scientific literature.
    (e) disregards practical ends.

213. The passage -3 best supports the statement that manufacturers
    (a) can eliminate the risk of over-production by advertising.
    (b) completely control buyers' needs and desires.
    (c) must depend upon the final consumers for the success of their undertakings.
    (d) distribute goods directly to the consumers.
    (e) can predict with great accuracy the success of any product they put on the market.

214. The passage -4 best supports the statement that
    (a) most of the people live in similar conditions.
    (b) adversity brings the people of differing views together.

(c) liking others is the inherent characteristic of people.
(d) people always try to rest on their laurels.
(e) birds of a feather flock together.

215. The Passage -5 best supports the statement that
    (a) people of different nations may not consider matters in the same light.
    (b) it is unusual for many people to share similar ideas.
    (c) suspicion prevents understanding between nations.
    (d) the chief work of foreign ministries is to guide relations between nations united by a common cause.
    (e) the people of one nation must sympathise with the viewpoints of the people of other nations.

216. The Passage-6 best supports the statement that
    (a) Ethics do not constitute a part of philosophy.
    (b) One has to accept certain beliefs to find the final truth.
    (c) Rationalism is not a set of beliefs which is devoid of verification.
    (d) Mental attitude is independent of all assumptions.
    (e) Only RPA can establish philosophy of Rationalism.

217. Which of the following words is most nearly the **SAME** in meaning as the word **unreservedly** as used in the passage 6?
    (a) Conditionally (b) Fully
    (c) Partially (d) Collectively
    (e) Unilaterally

218. In the passage 7, the author would like the teachers to
    (a) motivate bright students to enhance their academic achievements.
    (b) improve their own academic standards to motivate students.
    (c) keep their schedule busy by carrying out various duties.
    (d) encourage and give planned learning experiences to all students.
    (e) encourage good students to help poor students.

219. In the passage 7, according to the author, why are teachers not in a position to perform their expected role?
    (a) Majority of the students neglect classroom teaching.
    (b) The students are very busy and have less time to learn.
    (c) Intelligent students are after the teacher, seeking their help in studies.
    (d) They are forced to spend more time in motivating good students.
    (e) None of these

220. In the passage 8 according to the author, which of the following is one of the outcomes of the present crisis of our time?
    (a) Inability of parents and teachers to develop value base of children
    (b) More than expected growth of science and technology
    (c) Increasing social cohesiveness IN SPITE OF violence and disturbances
    (d) Emergence of new social norms which obstruct growth of individualism
    (e) None of these

221. In the passage 9, which of the following supports the statement "the prediction ... borne out by history"?
    (a) Capitalism has just survived but not taken firm roots.
    (b) The salaries of the employees have gone up in advanced countries.

(c) Technological development has not taken place in capitalist countries.
(d) The salaries of all the employees have gone down in all the countries.
(e) There is no increase in the productivity of workers.

222. In the passage 10, why does the author consider write-ups 'that deal with a moral issue' more important in literature?
(A) They are open for rethinking by coming generations.
(B) They are written with a specific approach.
(C) They help the reader in forming or consolidating his values and approaches.
(a) Only A   (b) Both A and B
(c) Both A and C   (d) Only C
(e) None of these

223. In the passage 10, the first sentence of the paragraph implies...
(a) literature is not one of the best media of expression for a society.
(b) society does not observe the same standard for all its members.
(c) only literature allows individuals to express their different views.
(d) society can change its value system after it reinterprets literature.
(e) None of these

224. In the passage 11, according to the paragraph, abolishing child labour through legal means is most likely to result into...
(a) dragging/pushing the family of the child in acute economic stress.
(b) shortage of labour in other areas of work.
(c) regulation of services of adult workers.
(d) betterment of working conditions of adult labourers.
(e) better understanding of reality.

225. In the passage 11, what can be inferred about the policy being followed about child labour in India?
(A) Giving economic benefits to the families of child labourers.
(B) Reducing/controlling child labour in unhealthy areas of work.
(C) Monitoring and improving working conditions for children.
(a) Only A and B   (b) Only B and C
(c) Only A and B   (d) Only B
(e) None of these

226. In the passage 12, which of the following is not a likely cause of readiness shown by people towards adolescents?

(a) Increase in crime
(b) Growing violence
(c) Equality of opportunity
(d) Physical presence of youth
(e) Increased social unrest

227. In the passage 13, which of the following inferences can best be drawn from the above paragraph?
(a) The number of viewers decided the quality of the programmes.
(b) The viewers' perception about the quality of programmes is significant for advertisers.
(c) The poor quality programmes have very few viewers.
(d) Advertisers can derive benefit from the information about viewers' perception of quality of programmes.
(e) None of these

228. In the passage 13, which of the following can be inferred from the contents of the paragraph?
A. Advertisement can have some effect on the viewers' buying habits.
B. Money spent on advertising with high quality programmes yields more profits.
C. Different programmes with equal number of viewers can be rated differently as far as quality is concerned.
(a) Only A   (b) Only B
(c) Only A and B   (d) Only B and C
(e) None of these

229. In the passage 14, the author of the passage seems to be
(a) in favour of use of econometric models but against free trade.
(b) in favour of free trade but neutral regarding econometric models.
(c) against both free trade as well as econometric models.
(d) indifferent about both free trade and econometric models.
(e) in favour of both econometric models and free trade.

230. In the passage 14, which of the following statements is definitely true in the context of the passage?
A. Despite the advantages of free trade, it is not whole-heartedly acclaimed by most advanced countries.
B. Policy formulation should be solely dependent on econometric models.
C. Reasons for model protectionist approach by advanced countries are not given in the passage.
(a) Only A   (b) Only B
(c) Only C   (d) A and B only
(e) B and C only

Answer Key

1	(d)	30	(b)	59	(a)	88	(b)	117	(d)	146	(c)	175	(d)	204	(a)
2	(e)	31	(c)	60	(b)	89	(e)	118	(d)	147	(b)	176	(b)	205	(d)
3	(b)	32	(c)	61	(d)	90	(e)	119	(c)	148	(a)	177	(e)	206	(d)
4	(a)	33	(a)	62	(b)	91	(d)	120	(c)	149	(c)	178	(c)	207	(b)
5	(d)	34	(e)	63	(c)	92	(c)	121	(a)	150	(d)	179	(b)	208	(e)
6	(b)	35	(c)	64	(a)	93	(d)	122	(e)	151	(c)	180	(a)	209	(c)
7	(d)	36	(a)	65	(e)	94	(d)	123	(a)	152	(a)	181	(c)	210	(a)
8	(e)	37	(b)	66	(e)	95	(c)	124	(d)	153	(c)	182	(b)	211	(d)
9	(e)	38	(a)	67	(b)	96	(a)	125	(d)	154	(c)	183	(e)	212	(b)
10	(e)	39	(b)	68	(a)	97	(b)	126	(b)	155	(e)	184	(b)	213	(c)
11	(d)	40	(c)	69	(a)	98	(a)	127	(b)	156	(c)	185	(a)	214	(e)
12	(e)	41	(d)	70	(e)	99	(d)	128	(a)	157	(b)	186	(b)	215	(a)
13	(c)	42	(d)	71	(b)	100	(c)	129	(d)	158	(a)	187	(e)	216	(c)
14	(b)	43	(b)	72	(c)	101	(c)	130	(b)	159	(c)	188	(d)	217	(b)
15	(c)	44	(c)	73	(a)	102	(d)	131	(b)	160	(e)	189	(b)	218	(d)
16	(c)	45	(c)	74	(d)	103	(b)	132	(d)	161	(d)	190	(c)	219	(e)
17	(d)	46	(c)	75	(b)	104	(c)	133	(c)	162	(a)	191	(b)	220	(a)
18	(a)	47	(d)	76	(d)	105	(c)	134	(a)	163	(c)	192	(e)	221	(b)
19	(d)	48	(b)	77	(e)	106	(d)	135	(c)	164	(b)	193	(a)	222	(c)
20	(d)	49	(d)	78	(d)	107	(b)	136	(e)	165	(e)	194	(d)	223	(e)
21	(a)	50	(d)	79	(b)	108	(d)	137	(a)	166	(d)	195	(a)	224	(a)
22	(a)	51	(e)	80	(a)	109	(d)	138	(a)	167	(b)	196	(c)	225	(b)
23	(b)	52	(a)	81	(b)	110	(b)	139	(c)	168	(b)	197	(d)	226	(c)
24	(c)	53	(a)	82	(d)	111	(c)	140	(b)	169	(d)	198	(b)	227	(d)
25	(d)	54	(e)	83	(e)	112	(a)	141	(d)	170	(e)	199	(a)	228	(d)
26	(d)	55	(e)	84	(c)	113	(d)	142	(b)	171	(a)	200	(c)	229	(e)
27	(b)	56	(e)	85	(a)	114	(c)	143	(b)	172	(e)	201	(e)	230	(a)
28	(c)	57	(e)	86	(a)	115	(a)	144	(d)	173	(e)	202	(c)		
29	(b)	58	(a)	87	(c)	116	(b)	145	(b)	174	(b)	203	(d)		

Hints & Explanations

22. (a) **Achilles heel (Noun)** = a weak point or fault in somebody's character which can be attacked by other people.

23. (b) **Sustain (Verb)** = to make something continue for sometime without becoming less; maintain.
    Look at the sentence:
    She managed to sustain everyone's interest until the end of her speech.

24. (c) **Cumbersome (Adjective)** = large and heavy; difficult to carry; bulky; complex; complicated.
    Look at the sentence:
    Government should ease the cumbersome legal procedures.

25. (d) **Differentiated (Adjective)**
    = distinguished; to be the particular thing; important.
    Look at the sentence:
    I think grey hair makes you look very differentiated.

30. (b) The realization of the link between food security and political stability.

31. (c) To make those countries more self sufficient to whom it previously provided food.

32. (c) It prompted increased investment and interest in agriculture.

33. (a) Misapprehension that it would alleviate poverty as it did in other countries.

36. (a) The meaning of the word **Starve (Verb)** as used in the passage is : keep deprived of : to not give something that is needed.

Hence, the words **starved** and **deprived** are synonyms.

37. (b) The meaning of the word **Slap (Verb)** as used in the passage is : impose : to order especially in a sudden or an unfair way, that something must happen or somebody must do something.

Hence, the words **slapped** and **imposed** are synonyms.

38. (a) The meaning of the word **Plow (Verb)** as used in the passage is : to invest a large amount of money in a company or project : to cultivate.

Hence, the words **plowed** and **cultivated** are synonyms.

39. (b) The meaning of the word **Pressing (Adjective)** as used in the passage is : urgent, serous, insistent, needing to be dealt with immediatley.

Hence, the words **pressing** and **undemanding** are antonyms.

40. (c) The meaning of the word **Evaporate (Verb)** as used in the passage is : to disappear, especially by gradually becoming less and less.

Hence, the words **evaporated** and **grew** are antonyms.

41. (d) It is mentioned in the last few lines of the second last paragraph that many state governments have decided in principle to switch over to the regional language as the medium of instruction in colleges and universities. However the implementation in this regard has been slow.

42. (d) It is mentioned in the last few lines of the first paragraph that India has emerged as a strong potential market for investments in training and education sector due its favorable demographics (young population) and being a service driven economy.

43. (b) The meaning of education explosion is mentioned in the second paragraph. It means a tremendous rise in the number of educational institutions and students.

44. (c) Option (c) can be inferred from the last few lines of the second paragraph where it says that unemployment problem in India cannot be blamed on the availability of large masses of educated people in India.

45. (c) Option (c) can be inferred from the first few lines of the last paragraph where it says that correspondence education has opened new vistas for the education system which could not be met earlier because of the challenges of providing necessary infrastructure for it.

46. (c) Option (a) and (b) are clearly mentioned in the paragraphs. There is tota contradiction to pint (c) in the first few lines of the second last paragraph where

it says that uncertainty and vacillation have marked the government policy towards medium of education in India.

47. (d) Dilution means weakening in force, content or value. Diminution means reduction in size, content , importance.

48. (b) Emergence means the process of coming into existence, prominence, visibility.

49. (d) Deprecate means to express disapproval. Commend means to praise, approve.

50. (d) Purport as used as a verb means to claim, profess pretend falsely. Intention in general is clear as expressed.

57. (e) **Austerity (Noun)** = simplicity; a situation when people do not have much money to spend because there are bad economic conditions.

Look at the sentence:

War was followed by many years of austerity.

58. (a) **Inroads (Noun)** = something that is achieved, especially by reducing the success of something else.

Look at the sentence:

Tax rises have made some inroads into the country's national debt.

59. (a) **Aggravate (Verb)** = to make a bad/unpleasant situation worse; worsen

Assuage (Verb) = to make an unpleasant situation less severe.

60. (b) **Simmering (Adjective)** = to be filled with a strong feeling especially anger which you have difficulty in controlling; seething.

Calm = peaceful.

123. (a) 'Apposite' and 'Appropriate' both have a meaning 'Suitable', hence they are synonyms to each other.

124. (d) Passage clearly suggests that indian market is a very big domestic market and therefore there was a demand for Indian goods from domestic consumers even when it had declined internationally. That's why author said that India's economy managed to sail through the economic downturn.

125. (d) The central theme of the passage is Economic Growth - A Result of Natural Forces rather than the Government.

126. (b) The author attributes the improvements of the economic condition of the country to the economy for it is surviving on its own either throgh consumption or saving.

127. (b) 'Eschews' means 'Nothing to do with'. 'Avoid also means the same. Hence, both of the words are synonyms.

128. (a) 'Deleterious' means 'Harmful' or ' Negative'. So its antonym will be 'Positive'.

129. **(d)** 'Wary of' has been used in the passage in the context of 'being cautious about'. So, option (d) is suitable choice.

130. **(b)** Statement (b) is not true. There is nothing like social contracts in India that one can reap the benefits provided under the scheme.

144. **(d)** In the 2nd paragraph of the passage it has been stated that how the developing countries are lacking in the infrastructure and expertise because of which they always need to be alert therefore option (d) is the correct choice for the given question. It clearly states that the developed countries have apparent advantages in capital, technology, human resources and administrative expertise and in setting the "rules of the game". They are usually the biggest beneficiaries of globalization. The developing countries on the other hand are on the whole in an unfavourably position. It shows lack of a just and equitable international economic order. Other options in relation to dividends derived from globalization are not fairly distributed are not correct in the given context.

145. **(b)** The third paragraph clearly states—The reason why China was so successful in such a short period of time and in a constantly changing international environment is because China has found its own road of development. This is implied in option (b) that China created its own model of development without following others. Other options are partially true and option (e) is ruled out.

146. **(c)** Comprehensive means including or dealing with all or nearly all elements or aspects of something most suitably describes the Chinese opening to the outside world. Therefore option (c) comprehensive is the most suitable choice. Options (a) and (b) are one of the aspects. Other options are ruled out.

147. **(b)** In the sixth paragraph it is mentioned that, China has also provided the world with the largest rising market. When more than 1.25 billion people become well-off, the demand on everything will be enormous. Just to give you an example, in the coming 10 years alone, China will import US$ 2 trillion of goods from the outside world. Therefore option (b) is the correct answer while other options like (a) is not true at all. Option (c) is partially true. Option (d) is not relevant and option (e) is completely ruled out.

148. **(a)** It is given in the 2nd paragraph of the passage that developing countries are the one that are the biggest beneficiaries. Therefore statement (ii) is correct. Statements (i) and (iii) are incorrect. So option (a) is the correct choice for the given question.

149. **(c)** In the last paragraph of the passage it is clearly mentioned that, "China is faced with growing pressure from international competition." Therefore option (c) best expresses the desired answer. Option (a) is partially correct but not true in the given context. Option (b) is not mentioned and option (d) is not a challenge.

150. **(d)** It is not mentioned in the last paragraph of the passage that, China faces fiercer competition at home compared to international markets. Therefore option (d) is the correct choice. Other options are true while option (e) is ruled out.

151. **(c)** With an interview given by economic affairs secretary Shaktikanta Das it is clearly mentioned that government has to work under some fiscal constraints and it is making efforts to present a growth oriented budget. Fiscal constraints are characteristics and not an objective and hence option (b) is wrong.

152. **(a)** In the fifth passage it is said by economist Madan Sabnav is the government has to increase its allocation for public investment on infrastructure to stimulate growth.

153. **(c)** The new budget is based on four pillars: poverty eradication, farmers' prosperity, job creation and a better quality of life for all Indian citizens. The new budget will ensure that India will continue towards stability even in disturbed and choppy situations.

154. **(c)** In the second last passage it is mentioned that the government has been providing tax incentives to companies in the manufacturing sector, including tax deductions on emoluments paid to new employees, to encourage firms to step up hiring and create jobs under its Make in India initiative.

155. **(e)** The government has considered various suggestions which includes a, b, c and d. The option (e) is not mentioned anywhere in the passage.

156. **(c)** In the opening paragraph it is clearly mentioned that, 'This critical piece is 'savings' and, within this overall head, household savings is the one critical subcomponent that needs close watching and nurturing.' Therefore the main concern behind the alarm bells is option (c). Option (a) is a regular phenomenon. Option (b) is not the main concern as it is a temporary problem. Option (d) is not mentioned. Option (e) is ruled out.

157. **(b)** In the opening line of the second paragraph it is sated that, 'while it is true that one of the primary reasons behind the current economic slowdown is the tardy rate of capital expansion - or, investment in infrastructure as well as plant and machinery - all attempts to stimulate investment activity are likely to come to naught if savings do not grow.' Therefore option (b) is the only correct choice.

158. (a) In the second paragraph it is said that, 'Without any growth in the savings rate, it is futile to think of any spurt in investment and, consequently, in the overall economic growth.' Therefore, option (a) overall economic growth is directly related to household savings is correct.

159. (c) It is mentioned in the passage that, 'India has another facet: a penchant for physical assets (such as bullion or land). After the monsoon failure of 2009, and the attendant rise in price levels that has now become somewhat deeply entrenched, Indians have been stocking up on gold. Consequently, savings in financial instruments dropped while those in physical assets shot up.' Threrefore option (c) is correct.

160. (e) It is clearly mentioned in the passage that, 'While recognising that one of the key differences in the evolving household saving scenario between the UK and India is the impact of demographics (dependency ratio), anecdotal evidence on increasing consumerism and the entrenchment of (urban) lifestyles in India, apart from the easier availability of credit and improvement in overall macroeconomic conditions, is perhaps indicative of some 'drag' on household saving over the last few years as well as going forward.' Therefore option (e) is the correct answer.

191. (b) "New terrorism has no long-term agenda but is ruthless in its short-term intentions". This statement from the passage supports (B). While, in the light of passage, (C) also seems suitable.

192. (e) Bio-attack will result in several deaths which will lead to political turmoil creating social unrest.

193. (a) 'Religious intolerance' as cited in the last paragraph stands behind terrorism.

196. (c) Go through the last line of the first paragraph.

197. (d) While much had been said and written on establishing " new order", little has actually been done.

199. (a) More complicated ailments can be referred to properly equipped centres in district towns, cities etc.

204. (a) During the Christian era, the ecclesiastics controlled the institution of education.

Para Jumbles

SENTENCE OR WORD REARRANGEMENT

In this type of questions, basically, you are given a paragraph or sentence - but the sentences (in case of paragraph) or words (in case of sentence) are not in the right order. It's up to you to untie this knot and rearrange the sentences or words so that they logically make sense.

Sentences or words rearrangement questions are included in BANK exams as they

❖ Help students relate events in a logical manner

❖ Sequence sentences based on English usage skills

HOW TO TACKLE THESE TYPES OF QUESTIONS?

To tackle these types of questions, you have to know three things-

❖ Theme of the paragraph that might be created on un-jumbling the sentences

❖ Initiating sentence, which starts the paragraph

❖ Links have to be found between two sentences. Once a link of this type is created, it becomes easy to eliminate irrelevant choices.

HOW TO SAVE TIME WHILE SOLVING THESE QUESTIONS?

It is very important to read selectively and search for transition words or other keywords.

The best way is to establish a link between any two (or more) statements. Once a link is found, you get to know which statements will come together. Then, look in the options. Select the option with those statements together.

EXAMPLE 1.

A. 1971 war changed the political geography of the subcontinent

B. Despite the significance of the event there has been no serious book about the conflict

C. Surrender at Dacca aims to fill this gap

D. It also profoundly altered the geo-strategic situation in South-East Asia

(a) ACBD   (b) CADB

(c) BADC   (d) ADBC

Explanation : We can see that sentence A is most likely the starting sentence. Now that we know A is the starting sentence we can eliminate choice (b) and (c) as they start with C and B respectively.

This narrows down our possibilities to option (a) and option (d).

Now we can see in option (a), C follows sentence A but the gap spoken of in sentence C has no correlation with political geography of the subcontinent spoken of in sentence A , so we can rule out Option (a).

Therefore answer has to be option (d), as we can also see it elaborates on the change mentioned in sentence A.

EXAMPLE 2.

A. Thus begins the search for relief: painkillers, ice, yoga, herbs, even surgery

B. Most computer users develop disorders because they ignore warnings like tingling fingers, a numb hand or a sore shoulder

C. They keep pointing and dragging until tendons chafe and scar tissue forms, along with bad habits that are almost impossible to change

D. But cures are elusive because repetitive stress injuries present a bag of ills that often defy easy diagnosis.

(a) BDAC   (b) BADC

(c) BCAD   (d) ABCD

Explanation : Here we can make out that sentence B will be the starting sentence as it introduces the subject matter which is 'computer users and related problems'.

Option (d) automatically gets eliminated as it starts with sentence A.

Option (a) can be rule out as there is no correlation between sentence B and sentence D. Sentence B talks of warnings whereas sentence D talks of cures for illness and hence no correlation exists. This narrows down possibilities to options (b) and (c). In option (b), sentence C follows sentence B which doesn't make much sense. So, option (b) can also be ruled out. We are left with option (c) which is the correct answer.

EXAMPLE 3.

A. If you are used to having your stimulation come from outside, your mind never develops its own habits of thinking and reflecting

B. Marx thought that religion was the opiate, because it soothed people's pain and suffering and prevented them from rising in rebellion

C. If Karl Marx was alive today, he would say that television is the opiate of the people.

D. Television and similar entertainments are even more of the opiate because of their addictive tendencies.

(a) BACD   (b) ADBC

(c) BDCA   (d) CBDA

Explanation: Sentence B has Marx (short form) and sentence C has Karl Marx (Full form). So C will come before B. Now in given options (a), (b) and (c) we can clearly see, B is placed before C and hence we reject option (a), (b) and (c) which leaves us with only option (d) which is the correct option.

EXAMPLE 4.

A. Then two astronomers-the German, Johannes Kepler, and the Italian, Galileo Galilei-started publicly to support the Copernican theory, despite the fact that the orbits it predicted did not quite match the ones observed.

B. His idea was that the sun was stationary at the centre and that the earth and the planets move in circular orbits around the sun.

C. A simple model was proposed in 1514 by a Polish priest, Nicholas Copernicus.

D. Nearly a century passed before this idea was taken seriously.

(a) CDBA   (b) CBDA
(c) BCAD   (d) CADB

Explanation: Answer is option (b) as we can see that in sentence D it says ' nearly a century has passed ' so we have to keep the timeline in consideration here also while sequencing the sentences and only in option (b) the timeline fits correctly.

EXERCISE

DIRECTION (Qs. 1-20): *Arrange sentences A, B, C and D between sentences 1 & 6 to form a logical refrence of the six sentences.*

1. 1. Whenever technology has flowered, it has put man's language-developing skills into overdrive
   A. Technical and technoid terms are spilling into the mainstream almost as fast as junk-mail is slapped into e-mail boxes.
   B. The era of computers is no less.
   C. From the wheel with its axle to the spinning wheel with its bobbins, to the compact disc and its jewel-box, inventions have trailed new words in their wake.
   D. "Cyberslang is huge, but it's parochial, and we don't know what will filter into the larger culture" said Tom Dalzell, who wrote the slang dictionary *Flappers 2 Rappers*.
   6. Some slangs already have a pedigree.
   (a) BCAD   (b) CBAD   (c) ABCD
   (d) DBCA   (e) None of these

2. 1. Until the MBA arrived on the scene the IIT graduate was king
   A. A degree from one of the five IIT's was a passport to a well-paying job, great prospects abroad and, for some, a decent dowry to boot.
   B. From the day he or she cracked the joint entrance exam, the IIT student commanded the awe of neighbours and close relatives.
   C. IIT students had, meanwhile, also developed their own special culture, complete with lingo and attitude, which they passed down.
   D. True, the success stories of IIT graduates are legion and they now constitute the cream of the Indian diaspora.
   6. But not many alumni would agree that the IIT undergraduate mindset merits a serious psychological study, let alone an interactive one.
   (a) BACD   (b) ABCD   (c) DCBA
   (d) ABCD   (e) None of these

3. 1. Some of the maharajas, like the one at Kapurthala, had exquisite taste
   A. In 1902, the Maharaja of Kapurthala gave his civil engineer photographs of the Versailles palace and asked him to replicate it, right down to the gargoyles.
   B. Yeshwantrao Holkar of Indore brought in Bauhaus aesthetics and even works of modern artists like Brancusi and Duchamp.
   C. Kitsch is the most polite way to describe them.
   D. But many of them, as the available-light photographs show, had execrable taste.
   6. Like Ali Baba's caves, some of the palaces were like warehouses with the downright ugly next to the sublimely aesthetic.
   (a) BACD   (b) BDCA   (c) ABCD
   (d) ABDC   (e) None of these

4. 1. There, in Europe, his true gifts unveiled
   A. Playing with Don Cherie, blending Indian music and jazz for the first time, he began setting the pace in the late 70s for much of present-day fusion is.
   B. John McLaughlin, the legendary guitarist whose soul has always had an Indian stamp on it, was seduced immediately.
   C. Fusion by Gurtu had begun.
   D. He partnered Gurtu for four years, and 'nurtured' him as a composer.
   6. But for every experimental musician there's a critic nestling nearby.
   (a) ABCD   (b) BCAD   (c) ADBC
   (d) ABDC   (e) None of these

5. 1. India, which has two out of every five TB patients in the world, is on the brink of a major public health disaster.
   A. If untreated, a TB patient can die within five years.
   B. Unlike AIDS, the great curse of modern sexuality, the TB germ is air-borne, which means there are no barriers to its spread.
   C. The dreaded infection ranks fourth among major killers worldwide.

D. Every minute, a patient falls prey to the infection in India, which means that over five lakh people die of the disease annually.
6. Anyone, anywhere can be affected by this disease.
(a) CADB   (b) BACD   (c) ABCD
(d) DBAC   (e) None of these

6. 1. Buddhism is a way to salvation.
A. But Buddhism is more severely analytical.
B. In the Christian tradition there is also a concern for the fate of human society conceived as a whole, rather than merely as a sum or network of individuals.
C. Salvation is a property, or achievement of individuals.
D. Not only does it dissolve society into individuals, the individual in turn is dissolved into component parts and instants, a stream of events.
6. In modern terminology, Buddhist doctrine is reductionist.
(a) ABCD   (b) CBAD   (c) BDAC
(d) ABCD   (e) None of these

7. 1. The problem of improving Indian agriculture is both a sociological and an administrative one.
A. It also appears that there is a direct relationship between the size of a state and development.
B. The issues of Indian development, and the problems of India's agricultural sector, will remain with us long into the next century.
C. Without improving Indian agriculture, no liberalisation and delicensing will be able to help India.
D. At the end of the day, there has to be a ferment and movement of life and action in the vast segment of rural India.
6. When it starts marching, India will fly.
(a) DABC   (b) CDBA   (c) ACDB
(d) ABCD   (e) None of these

8. 1. Good literary magazines have always been good because of their editors.
A. Furthermore, to edit by committee, as it were, would prevent any magazine from finding its own identity.
B. The more quirky and idiosyncratic they have been, the better the magazine is, at least as a general rule.
C. But the number of editors one can have for a magazine should also be determined by the number of contributions to it.
D. To have four editors for an issue that contains only seven contributions, is a bit silly to start with.
6. However, in spite of this anomaly, the magazine does acquire merit in its attempt to give a comprehensive view of the Indian literary scene as it is today.
(a) ABCD   (b) BCDA   (c) ABDC
(d) CBAD   (e) None of these

9. 1. It's the success story of the Indian expatriate in the US which today hogs much of the media coverage in India.
A. East and West, the twain have met quite comfortably in their person, thank you.
B. Especially in its more recent romancing the -NRI phase.
C. Seldom does the price of getting there - more like not getting there - or what's going on behind those sunny smiles get so much media hype.
D. Well groomed, with their perfect Colgate smiles, and hair in place, they appear the picture of confidence which comes from having arrived.

6. The festival of feature films and documentaries made by Americans of Indian descent being screened this fortnight, goes a long way in filling those gaps.
(a). ACBD   (b) DABC   (c) BDAC
(d) ABCD   (e) None of these

10. 1. A market for Indian art has existed ever since the international art scene sprang to life.
A. But interest in architectural conceits is an unanticipated fallout of the Festivals of India of the '80s' which were designed to increase exports of Indian crafts.
B. Simultaneously, the Indian elite discarded their synthetic sarees and kitsch plastic furniture and a market came into being.
C. Western dealers, unhappy in a market afflicted by violent price fluctuations and unpredictable profit margins, began to look East, and found cheap antiques with irresistible appeal.
D. The fortunes of the Delhi supremos, the Jew Town dealers in Cochin and myriad others around the country were made.
6. A chain of command was established, from the local contacts to the provincial dealers and up to the big boys, who entertain the Italians and the French, cutting deals worth lakhs in warehouse worth corers.
(a) BCAD   (b) DCBA   (c) ACBD
(d) CABD   (e) None of these

11. 1. Making people laugh is tricky.
A. At times, the intended humour may not simply not come off.
B. Making people laugh while trying to sell them something is a tougher challenge, since the commercial can fall flat on two grounds.
C. There are many advertisements which do amuse but do not even begin to set the cash thrills ringing.
D. Again, it is rarely sufficient for an advertiser simply to amuse the target audience in order to reap the sales benefit.
6. There are indications that in substituting the hard sell for more entertaining approach, some agencies have rather thrown out the baby with the bath water.
(a) CDBA   (b) DBAC   (c) BADC
(d) DCBA   (e) None of these

12. 1. Picture a termite colony, occupying a tall mud hump on an African plain.
A. Hungry predators often invade the colony and unsettle the balance.
B. The colony flourishes only if the portion of soldiers to workers remain roughly the same, so that the queen and the workers can be protected by the soldiers, and the queen and the soldiers can be serviced by workers.
C. But its fortunes are presently restored, because the immobile queen walled in well below ground level, lays eggs not only large enough numbers, but also in the varying proportions required.
D. The hump is alive with worker termites and solider termites going about their distinct kind of business.
6. How can we account for her mysterious ability to respond like this to events on the distant surface.
(a) BADC   (b) DBAC   (c) ADBC
(d) BDCA   (e) None of these

13. 1. According to recent research, the critical period for developing language skills is between the ages of three and five and a half years.
    A. The read-to child already has a large vocabulary and a sense of grammar and sentence structure.
    B. Children who read in these years have a far better chance of reading well in school, indeed, of doing well in all subjects.
    C. And the reason is actually quiet simple.
    D. This correlation is far and away the highest yet found between home influences and school success.
    6. Her comprehension of language is therefore is very high.
    (a) DACB   (b) ADBC   (c) ABCD
    (d) BDCA   (e) None of these

14. 1. High-powered outboard motors were considered to be one of the major threats to the survival of Beluga whale.
    A. With these. hunters could approach belugas within hunting range and profit from its inner skin and blubber.
    B. To escape an approaching motor, Belugas have learned to drive to the ocean bottom and stay there for up to 20 minutes, by which time the confused predator has left.
    C. Today however, even with much more powerful engines, it is difficult to come close because the whales seem to disappear suddenly just when you thought you had them in your sights.
    D. When the first outboard engines arrived in the early 1930's. one came across 4 and 8 HP motors.
    6. Belugas seem to have used their well- known sensitivity to noise to evolve an 'avoidance' strategy to outsmart hunters and their powerful technologies.
    (a) DACB   (b) CDAB   (c) ADBC
    (d) BDAC   (e) None of these

15. 1. The reconstruction of history by post- revolutionary science texts involve more than a multiplication of historical misconstructions.
    A. Because they aim quickly to acquaint the student with the contemporary scientific community thinks it knows textbooks treat the various experiments, concepts, laws and theories of the current normal science as separately and as nearly seriatim as possible.
    B. Those misconstruction render revolutions invisible; the arrangement of the still visible material in science texts implies a process that, if it existed, would deny revolutions a functions.
    C. But when combined with the generally unhistorical air of science writing and with the occasional systematic misconstruction, one impression is likely to follow.
    D. As pedagogy this technique of presentation is unexceptionable.
    6. Science has reached its present state by series of individual discoveries and inventions that, when gathered together, constitute the modern body of technical knowledge.
    (a) BADC   (b) ADBC   (c) DACB
    (d) CBDA   (e) None of these

16. 1. Security inks exploit the same principle that causes the vivid and constantly changing colours of a film of oil on water.
    A. When two rays of light meet each other after being reflected from these different surfaces, they have each traveled slightly different distances.
    B. The key is that the light is bouncing off two surface, that of the oil and that of the water layer below it.
    C. The distance the two rays determines which wavelengths, and hence colours, interfere constructively and look bright.
    D. Because light is an electromagnetic wave, the peaks and troughs of each ray then interfere either constructively, to appear bright, or destructively, to appear dim.
    6. Since the distance the rays travel changes with the angle as you look at the surface, different colours look bright from different viewing angles.
    (a) ABCD   (b) BADC
    (c) BDAC   (d) DCAB

17. 1. Commercially reared chicken can be unusually aggressive, and are often kept in darkened sheds to prevent them pecking at each other.
    A. The birds spent far more of their time - up to a third - pecking at the inanimate objects in the pens, in contrast to birds in other pens which spent a lot of time attacking others.
    B. In low light conditions, they behave less belligerently, but are more prone to opthalmic disorders and respiratory problems.
    C. In an experiment, aggressive head-pecking was all but eliminated among birds in the enriched environment.
    D. Altering the birds' environment, by adding bales of wood-shavings to their pens, can work wonders.
    6. Bales could diminish aggressiveness and reduce injuries; they might even improve productivity, since a happy chicken is a productive chicken.
    (a) DCAB   (b) CDBA   (c) DBAC
    (d) BDCA   (e) None of these

18. 1. The concept of a 'nation-state' assumes a complete correspondence between the boundaries of the nation and the boundaries of those who live in a specific state. *(CAT 2000)*
    A. Then there are members of national collectivities who live in other countries, making a mockery of the concept.
    B. There are always people living in particular states who are not considered to be (and often do not consider themselves to be) members of the hegemonic nation.
    C. Even worse, there are nations which never had a state or which are divided across several states.
    D. This, of course has been subject to severe criticism and is virtually everywhere a fiction.
    6. However, the fiction has been, and continues to be, at the basic nationalist ideologies.
    (a) DBAC   (b) ABCD   (c) BACD
    (d) DACB   (e) None of these

19. 1. In the sciences, even questionable examples of research fraud are harshly punished. *(CAT 2000)*
    A. But no such mechanism exists in the humanities-much of what humanities researchers call research does not lead to results that are replicable by other scholars.
    B. Given the importance of interpretation in historical and literary scholarship, humanities researchers are in a position where they can explain away deliberate and even systematic distortion.

C. Mere suspicion is enough for funding to be cut off ; publicity guarantees that careers can be effectively ended.

D. Forgeries which take the form of pastiches in which the forger intersperses fake and real parts can be defended as mere mistakes or aberrant misreading.

6. Scientists funding data have no such defences.

(a) BDCA   (b) ABDC   (c) CABD
(d) CDBA   (e) None of these

20. 1. Horses and communism were, on the whole, a poor match.

A. Fine horses bespoke the nobility the party was supposed to despise.

B. Communist leaders, when they visited villages, preferred to see cows and pigs.

C. Although a working horse was just about tolerable, the communists were right to be wary.

D. Peasants from Poland to the Hungarian Pustza preferred their horse to party dogma.

6. "A farmer's pride is his horse; his cow may be thin but his horse must be fat," went a Slovak saying.

(a) ACDB   (b) DBCA   (c) ABCD
(d) DCBA   (e) None of these

DIRECTIONS (Qs. 21 to 35) : *Five sentences are given below, labeled A, B, C, D and E. They need to be arranged in a logical order to form a coherent paragraph/passage. From the given options, choose the most appropriate one.*

---

21. A. It is demanding that any party it backs should establish a working group on violence against women and children in the assembly.

B. In the run-up to the January 28 polls, for instance, members of Women Action for Development (WAD) are organising camps in all constituencies.

C. Ironically, Manipur has many activist groups led by women.

D. True empowerment will only happen when women enter the assembly in good numbers.

E. Conflict Widows' Forum is a group made up of women who have lost their husbands to civil violence in the state.

(a) DBCEA   (b) CBADE   (c) BDCEA
(d) CBEAD   (e) None of these

22. A. Fortunately, global wealth and technology allow us to better prepare for and respond to natural disasters.

B. It does not necessarily mean that volcanoes and quakes are getting worse — but rather that there are more of us living in areas where we might be affected by a disaster, and we have more to lose.

C. As global populations have grown and people have crowded into risk zones — like earthquake areas and flood plains — the toll of natural disasters has grown as well.

D. According to the Center for Research on Epidemiology of Disasters, the number of catastrophic events has more than doubled since the 1980s.

E. The Red Cross estimates that the economic damage from disasters rose fivefold, to $629 billion, from 1985 to 2005.

(a) CDBEA   (b) BCDEA   (c) CDEBA
(d) CADEB   (e) None of these

23. A. That may be beyond us, but as long as there are tears and suffering, so long our work will not be over.

B. The service of India means the service of the millions who suffer.

C. That future is not one of ease or resting but of incessant striving so that we may fulfil the pledges we have so often taken and the one we shall take today.

D. It means the ending of poverty and ignorance and disease and inequality of opportunity.

E. The ambition of the greatest man of our generation has been to wipe every tear from every eye.

(a) BDCEA   (b) CBDEA   (c) CDEBA
(d) CEABD   (e) None of these

24. A. So that his place shall never be with those cold and timid souls who neither know victory nor defeat.

B. Who strives valiantly; who errs, who comes short again and again, because there is no effort without error and shortcoming; but who does actually strive to do the deeds.

C. It is not the critic who counts; not the man who points out how the strong man stumbles, or where the doer of deeds could have done them better.

D. Who knows great enthusiasms, the great devotions; who spends himself in a worthy cause; who at the best knows in the end the triumph of high achievement, and who at the worst, if he fails, at least fails while daring greatly,

E. The credit belongs to the man who is actually in the arena, whose face is marred by dust and sweat and blood.

(a) EBDAC   (b) CEDBA   (c) DBAEC
(d) CEBDA   (e) None of these

25. A. The recent communal violence in Hyderabad and in Bareilly a month ago has remained on the sidelines of national attention.

B. In both cities, the present round of violence was preceded by mobilisations and speeches, primarily by Hindu fundamentalist groups.

C. Fortunately, there was no death in the violence in Bareilly, while in Hyderabad only three people were killed.

D. Yet, the scale, planning and causes behind the riots indicate a certain change in the morphology of the typical riot, a change which needs to be identified and understood if we want to keep religious sectarianism and violence in check.

E. Communal violence has become so endemic to the polity of India that it has ceased to attract much attention outside its immediate area of impact, or unless it crosses very high levels of fatality and barbarity.

(a) EACDB   (b) ABEDC   (c) EABCD
(d) ABCDE   (e) None of these

26. A. That too was historic.

B. The word that immediately rolled off of every tongue after the presidential election was "historic"; and rightly so.

C. It would have been unimaginable forty years ago.

D. The fact that the country has become civilized enough to accept this outcome is a considerable tribute to the activism of the 1960s and its aftermath.

E. The two candidates in the Democratic primary were a woman and an African-American.

(a) BCDAE (b) BCDEA (c) BEDAC
(d) BEACD (e) None of these

27. A. The revolution began as an attack on despotism.
 B. Already by 1762 Rousseau was implying in his "Social Contract" that there was no meaningful difference between the authority of a despot and that of a monarch
 C. As usual, regular usage soon diluted the original rigor of the expression's meaning.
 D. Montesquieu has defined its spirit as "The rule of one, according to no law".
 E. Obeying no law, authority was arbitrary and its animating spirit was fear.
 (a) ABDCE (b) AEDCB
 (c) ADECB (d) ADEBC

28. A. On the whole, we have not arrived at any general consensus over the nature and causes of fascism in our time.
 B. Historians, sociologists, social psychologists, and political theorists have been debating this question since Mussolini's seizure of power in 1922.
 C. However, with limited success.
 D. What is the 'true' nature of fascism?
 E. Is it something radically new to political experience, a unique creation of the 20th century; or is it merely old tyranny possessed of new, more efficient techniques for gaining and holding power?
 (a) ABCDE (b) DEABC (c) DEBCA
 (d) ADEBC (e) None of these

29. A. Those who don't recognize wisdom latent in the foolishness?
 B. There is always a knowing wink in these tales, but who is being laughed at?
 C. In an imaginary East European scene, these paragons of scholarship and righteousness are shown to be fools.
 D. The wise men of Chelm may be among the most familiar folk characters in the Jewish tradition.
 E. The fools who don't realize they are fools?
 (a) DCEAB (b) AEDCB (c) BDCEA
 (d) DCBEA (e) None fo these

30. A. In addition to being one of Mr. De Palma's signature set pieces — a deft and dazzling aria of surveillance, suspense and partial nudity — this sequence seems especially designed to beguile critics who have covered the annual carnival of cinematic indulgence and bureaucratic intransigence that is Cannes.
 B. The loot in question is a serpentine diamondstudded gold brassiere that adorns the otherwise naked torso of a willowy model named Veronica (Rie Rasmussen), who strolls up the famed red carpet at the Palais des Festivals on the arm of the French filmmaker Regis Wargnier.
 C. *Femme Fatale,* the breathtakingly convoluted new thriller from Brian De Palma, opens with a daring jewel heist carried out in the middle of the Cannes International Film Festival.
 D. If this conjures up an image of diamonds tastefully stashed in a velvet drawstring bag, think again.

 E. Veronica is abruptly summoned to the ladies room — whose sparkling cleanliness is a notably unrealistic touch — for some heavy-breathing sex with Laure Ash (Rebecca Romijn-Stamos), a thief posing as a member of the paparazzi.
 (a) CBDAE (b) CBDEA (c) CDBEA
 (d) CDAEB (e) None of these

31. A. At the critical moment, a canopy conceals the act of anointment, by a priest not a civil official.
 B. The conferring of state headship is an exclusive Anglican ritual, steeped in the Henrician Reformation.
 C. The Queen is serene and vulnerable, flanked by fussing bishops and ranks of hereditary peers, symbolising the legitimacy of inherited office.
 D. Succession is sanctioned and blessed by God, with a staged cry of assent from the congregation.
 E. The Queen's 1953 coronation, to be reprised many times on television this weekend, now seems medieval in its costumes and ritual.
 (a) BDACE (b) EBCAD (c) BECAD
 (d) ECBAD (e) None of these

32. A. Logic suggests that Japanese food should not do well in North Indian fish-hating markets.
 B. But sushi is all the rage because teenagers love it.
 C. Over the last decade, new restaurants have opened and turned the conventional wisdom on its head.
 D. Similarly, the fast food chains which survive on wheat (pizzas, pasta, hamburger buns, etc.) should all flop in the rice-loving South.
 E. My guess is that the differences will be ironed out as the new generation comes of age.
 (a) ECABD (b) ABDEC (c) CABED
 (d) EABDC (e) None of these

33. A. Two and a half years ago, her father received the grim news that he was suffering from the early symptoms of Alzheimer's.
 B. She is focusing on her other career as a successful children's book author.
 C. Her latest, *What's Happening to Grandpa?* is a touching, compassionate story about a young girl who learns that her grandfather is suffering from Alzheimer's disease.
 D. As an author, she has taken up the challenge of tackling subjects that kids often don't understand and parents don't know how to talk about.
 E. Sadly, this book - like her past two children's best-sellers *What's Heaven?* and *What's wrong with Timmy?* — stems from a firsthand family drama.
 (a) BDCEA (b) BEDCA (c) ABEDC
 (d) ABCDE (e) None of the above

34. A. He also mentions the existential burdens on his brother with as much delicacy as the subject will permit.
 B. Many will be disappointed that there is little introspective dwelling on his relationship with Hillary.
 C. Even from the early part of his life, he seems to have inspired extraordinary loyalty from his friends, most of whom he managed to involve in his presidency.
 D. They will be disappointed because his early life in Arkansas is particularly well told.

E.   The early life contains description of his troubled family life with an abusive stepfather, the dilemmas of his mother.
(a) ABEDC   (b) BEDAC   (c) ABCDE
(d) BDEAC   (e) None of these

35. (A) The driving force of the 'nuclear renaissance' is a claim that nuclear power, once up and running, is a carbon free energy source. The assertion is that a functioning nuclear reactor creates no greenhouse gases and thus contributes nothing to global warming or chaotic weather.
(B) The frequently repeated notion that nuclear power is a carbon free energy source is simply untrue.
(C) At every stage of the cycle greenhouse gases are released into the atmosphere from burning diesel, manufacturing steel and cement and, in the circumpolar regions of the planet, by disturbance of the tundra, which releases large amounts of methane, a particularly potent greenhouse gas.
(D) That part is almost true, but the claim ignores the total environmental impact of nuclear energy, which includes a long and complicated chain of events known in the industry as the 'nuclear cycle' which begins with finding, mining, milling and enriching uranium, then spans through plant construction and power generation to the reprocessing and eventual storage of nuclear waste, all of which creates tons of CO_2.
(E) Even the claim that a functioning nuclear power facility is CO_2– free challenged by the face that operating plant requires an external power source to run, and that electricity is almost certain to come from a fossil-fuelled plant.
(a) DCEB   (b) EBCD   (c) DEBC
(d) EDCB   (E) None of these

DIRECTIONS (Qs. 36-40): *Rearrange the following six sentences (A), (B), (C), (D), (E) and (F) in the proper sequence to form a meaningful paragraph; then answer the questions given below them.*

(SBI PO 2014)

(A) As a consequence, even if it is plausible that ambient air pollution plays a role for the onset and increasing frequency of respiratory allergy, it is not easy to prove this conclusively.
(B) Another factor clouding the issue is that laboratory evaluations do not reflect what happens during natural exposure when atmospheric pollution mixtures are inhaled.
(C) Interpretation of studies are confounded by the effect of cigarette smoke. exposure to indoor pollutants and to outdoors and indoors allergens.
(D) However, despite evidence of a correlation between the increasing frequency of respiratory allergy and the increasing trend in air pollution, the link and interaction is still speculative.
(E) Allergic respiratory diseases such as hay fever and bronchial asthma have indeed become more common in the last decades in all industrialized countries and the reasons for this increase are still debated.
(F) Several studies have shown the adverse effects of ambient air pollution on respiratory health.

36. Which of the following should be the **LAST** sentence after rearrangement?
(a) A   (b) B   (c) C
(d) D   (e) E

37. Which of the following should be the **FIRST** sentence after rearrangement?
(a) A   (b) B   (c) C
(d) D   (e) E

38. Which of the following should be the **THIRD** sentence after rearrangement?
(a) A   (b) B   (c) C
(d) D   (e) E

39. Which of the following should be the **FOURTH** sentence after rearrangement?
(a) A   (b) B   (c) C
(d) D   (e) E

40. Which of the following should be the **SECOND** sentence after rearrangement?
(a) A   (b) B   (c) C
(d) D   (e) E

DIRECTIONS (Qs. 41-45): *Rearrange the following six sentences (A), (B), (C), (D), (E) and (F) in the proper sequence to form a meaningful paragraph; then answer the questions given below them.*

(IBPS PO/MT Prelim 2015)

(A) Two of the best-performing major economies in 2014 were China and Brazil, with growth estimated at 7.5% and 10.5% resepectively.
(B) Despite that limp growth, major US stock market indexes are up between 11% and 20% for the year.
(C) Even knowing where economies are headed sometimes it is of no help to an investor.
(D) It is hard to anticipate the direction of financial markets.
(E) But as of December, stock markets of both nations were in the red for the year.
(F) By contrast, the US economy is likely to have expanded at only about 2.6% for the year.

41. Which of the following would be the **SECOND** sentence?
(a) A   (b) C   (c) D
(d) E   (e) F

42. Which of the following would be the **FOURTH** sentence?
(a) A   (b) B   (c) C
(d) E   (e) F

43. Which of the following would be the **FIFTH** sentence ?
(a) A   (b) B   (c) C
(d) D   (e) F

44. Which of the following would be the **FIRST** sentence ?
(a) B   (b) C   (c) D
(d) E   (e) F

45. Which of the following would be the **SIXTH (LAST)** sentence ?
(a) A   (b) B   (c) C
(d) D   (e) E

DIRECTIONS (Qs. 46-50) : *Rearrange are following six sentences (A), (B), (C), (D), (E) and (F) in the proper sequence to form a meaningful paragraph; then answer the questions given below them.*

(IBPS PO/MT Main 2015)

(A)   There are a number of item in the atomic energy programme which are being made indigenously.

(B)   Given the overall energy situation in India, the use of nuclear power in some measure is inescapable even while thermal and hydro power continue to be the dominant elements.

(C)   However, commercial aspects of exploiting nuclear capabilities, especially for power-generation programmes, have been recently given high priority.

(D)   Atomic energy programmes have been subject to severe restrictions for every obvious reason as the Department of Atomic energy is becoming self-reliant in areas in which only a few countrices have such capability.

(E)   Even to meet these nuclear power requirements, India critically requires a commercia level power-generation capability, with its commensurate safety and nuclear waste management arrangements.

(F)   Thus, in Indian context energy security is also crucial, perhaps much more than it is for the U.S.A. because India imports a good part of its crude oil requirements, paying for it with precious foreign exchange.

46.   Which of the following will be the FIFTH sentence after rearrangement ?
(a)   (A)   (b)   (B)   (c)   (C)
(d)   (D)   (e)   (E)

47.   Which of the following will be the THIRD sentence after rearrangement ?
(a)   (A)   (b)   (B)   (c)   (C)
(d)   (D)   (e)   (E)

48.   Which of the following will be the SECOND sentence after rearrangement ?
(a)   (A)   (b)   (B)   (c)   (C)
(d)   (D)   (e)   (E)

49.   Which of the following will be the FIRST sentence after rearrangement ?
(a)   (A)   (b)   (B)   (c)   (C)
(d)   (D)   (e)   (E)

50.   Which of the following will be the FOURTH sentence after rearrangement ?
(a)   (A)   (b)   (B)   (c)   (C)
(d)   (D)   (e)   (E)

DIRECTIONS (Qs. 51 - 55): *Given below are six sentences i.e. A, B, C, D, E and F, which have been presented in a wrong order. Arrange them in order to form a meaningful paragraph and then answer the questions given below.*

(SBI PO Prelim 2015)

(A)   Some others, like the European nations, have a low birth rate and a low death rate.

(B)   Many others have a high birth rate with a low death rate.

(C)   Different countries show different patterns of growth.

(D)   Some have high birth rate and still have a high death rate.

(E)   Compared to this is Europe the growth rate is low.

(F)   The developing countries show the most rapid growth rate.

51.   Which will the LAST sentence in the Para?
(a)   A   (b)   B   (c)   C
(d)   D   (e)   E

52.   Which will be the FIRST sentence in the Para?
(a)   E   (b)   D   (c)   C
(d)   B   (e)   A

53.   Which will come at SECOND place in the para?
(a)   A   (b)   B   (c)   C
(d)   D   (e)   E

54.   Which sentence will come at FIFTH place in the Para?
(a)   F   (b)   D   (c)   B
(d)   A   (e)   C

55.   Which will be the THIRD sentence in the Para?
(a)   B   (b)   A   (c)   D
(d)   F   (e)   E

DIRECTIONS (Qs. 56-60): *There are six sentences marked S_1, S_6, P, Q, R, S. The positions of S_1 and S_6 are fixed as the first and last sentence of the passage. You are required to choose one of the five alternatives given below every passage which would be most logical sequence of the sentences in the passage.*

(SBI PO Main 2015)

56. S_1 :   There are numerous kinds of superstitions in different parts of the country.
S_6 :   A dog's howling predicts death– this is a typical superstition.
P :   But people go on respecting it through force of blind custom.
Q :   Most of them have a bearing on 'luck'–good or bad.
R :   Superstitions usually hae their origin in fear and ignorance.
S :   Nobody remembers now how a superstition first started in remote ages.
The proper sequence should be
(a)   QPRS   (b)   RSPQ   (c)   RSQP
(d)   QSPR   (e)   PRSQ

57. S_1 :   A spider's web, after a shower of rain, is a very beautiful thing.
S_6 :   They are also feared because their bites may have unpleasant effects like a rash on the skin.
P :   This party explains why spiders are thoroughly disliked.
Q :   But no poet has ever sung of the beauty of the spiders, for most spiders are not beautiful.
R :   On the contrary, most of them are rather unattractive, if not ugly!
S :   Poets have sung about the beauty of the spider's webs, comparing the water drops on them to ropes of pearls.
The proper sequence should be
(a)   SPQR   (b)   QSRP   (c)   QRSP
(d)   SQRP   (e)   PQRS

58. S_1 :   Unhappiness and discontent spring not only form poverty.
S_6 :   We suffer from sickness of spirit and hence we should discover our roots in the internal.
P :   Man is a strange creature fundamentally different from other animals.
Q :   If they are undeveloped and unsatisfied, he may have all the comforts of the wealth, but will still feel that life is not worthwhile.
R :   He has far horizons invariable hopes, spiritual powers.
S :   What is missing our age is the soul, there is nothing wrong with the body.
The proper sequence should be
(a)   PRQS   (b)   SPRQ   (c)   SPQR
(d)   PRSQ   (e)   QSRP

59. S_1 : On vacation in Tangier, Morocco, my friend and I sat down at a street cafe.

S_6 : Finally a man walked over to me and whispered, " Hey buddy .... This guy is your waiter and he wants your order."

P : At one point, he bent over with a big smile, showing me a single gold tooth and dingy fez.

Q : Soon I felt the presence of someone standing alongside me.

R : But this one wouldn't budge.

S : We had been cautioned about beggars and were told to ignore them.

The proper sequence should be

(a) SQRP   (b) SQPR   (c) QSRP

(d) QSPR   (e) PRQS

60. S_1 : In 1934, William Holding published a small volume of peoms.

S_6 : But Lord of the flies which came out in 1954 was welcomed as 'a most absorbing and instructive tale'.

P : During the World War II (1939-45) he joined the Royal Navy and was present at the sinking of the Bismarck.

Q : He returned to teaching is 1945 and gave it up in 1962, and is now a full-time writer.

R : In 1939, he married and started teaching at Bishop Wordsworth's School in Salisbury.

S : At first his novels were not accepted.

The proper sequence should be

(a) RPQS   (b) RPSQ   (c) SRPQ

(d) SQPR   (e) RQPS

DIRECTIONS (Qs. 61-65): *Rearrange the following Six sentences (A), (B), (C), (D), (E) and (F) in the proper sequence to form a meaningful paragraph and then answer the questions given below.*

(IBPS PO/MT Prelim 2016)

A. It is the only country in the world that is carbon negative, which means it produces more oxygen than it consumes.

B. Bhutan, sandwiched between the two most populous nations on Earth, suffers for their sins.

C. So far, so good. But then, two things happened.

D. Carbon sinks, 70% forest cover, powered almost entirely by mountain streams—Bhutan is a poster child for green living.

E. Glaciers are beginning to melt, flash floods and heavy rains—and even droughts—are common, and temperatures are climbing.

F. One, India and China got richer.

61. Which of the following should be the First sentence of the given paragraph?

(a) E   (b) D   (c) C

(d) B   (e) A

62. Which of the following should be the Third sentence of the given paragraph?

(a) A   (b) B   (c) C

(d) D   (e) E

63. Which of the following should be the LAST sentence of the given paragraph?

(a) A   (b) C   (c) B

(d) D   (e) E

64. Which of the following should be the Fourth sentence of the given paragraph?

(a) F   (b) C   (c) B

(d) E   (e) D

65. Which of the following should be the Second sentence of the given paragraph?

(a) B   (b) D   (c) A

(d) C   (e) E

66. If sentence (B) "The Finance Ministry's warning to potential investors in bitcoin and other cryptocurrencies has come at a time when a new, seemingly attractive investment area has opened up that few have enough information about." is the first sentence, what is the order of other sentences after rearrangement?

(A) One of the main reasons for this volatility is speculation and the entry into the market of a large number of people lured by the prospect of quick and easy profits.

(B) The Finance Ministry's warning to potential investors in bitcoin and other cryptocurrencies has come at a time when a new, seemingly attractive investment area has opened up that few have enough information about.

(C) A number of investors, daunted by the high price of bitcoin, have put their money into less well-established and often spurious cryptocurrencies, only to lose it all.

(D) Investment in bitcoin and other cryptocurrencies increased tremendously in India over the past year, but most new users know close to nothing of the technology, or how to verify the genuineness of a particular cryptocurrency.

(E) The price of bitcoin, the most popular of all cryptocurrencies, not only shot up by well over 1000% over the course of the last year but also fluctuated wildly.

(F) The government's caution comes on top of three warnings issued by the Reserve Bank of India since 2013.

(a) CDEFA   (b) EAFDC   (c) DCAEF

(d) ECDAF   (e) FEDAC

67. If sentence (C) "Clinical trials involving human subjects have long been a flashpoint between bioethicists and clinical research organisations (CROs) in India." is the first sentence, what is the order of other sentences after rearrangement?

(A) Such over-volunteering occurs more frequently in bioequivalence studies, which test the metabolism of generics in healthy subjects.

(B) Landmark amendments to the Drugs and Cosmetics Act in 2013 led to better protection of vulnerable groups such as illiterate people, but more regulation is needed to ensure truly ethical research.

(C) Clinical trials involving human subjects have long been a flashpoint between bioethicists and clinical research organisations (CROs) in India.

(D) The big problem plaguing clinical research is an over-representation of low-income groups among trial subjects.

(E) While CROs have argued that more rules will stifle the industry, the truth is that ethical science is often better science.

(F) Sometimes CROs recruit them selectively, exploiting financial need and medical ignorance; at other times people over-volunteer for the money.

(a) ABDFE   (b) BDEAF   (c) DFAEB
(d) BEDFA   (e) DFABE

68. If sentence (A) "The fresh round of economic sanctions imposed unanimously by the UN Security Council on North Korea is a predictable response to mounting international frustration over the nuclear stand-off. " is the first sentence, what is the order of other sentences after rearrangement?

(A) The fresh round of economic sanctions imposed unanimously by the UN Security Council on North Korea is a predictable response to mounting international frustration over the nuclear stand-off.

(B) Despite the crippling nature of the curbs, there is some good news on this imbroglio.

(C) The measures come days after the U.S., echoing suspicions in other countries, charged the North Korean government with the world-wide 'WannaCry' cyber attacks in May.

(D) As on previous occasions, Beijing and Moscow were able to impress upon the Security Council the potentially destabilising and hence counterproductive impact of extreme measures.

(E) The sanctions include an 89% curb on refined petroleum imports into North Korea, stringent inspections of ships transferring fuel to the country, and the expulsion of thousands of North Koreans in other countries within two years.

(F) This is significant given the intercontinental ballistic missile that Pyongyang launched in November.

(a) CEBDF   (b) BDCEF   (c) CFEBD
(d) BEDFC   (e) DFCBE

69. If sentence (C) "Kolkata-based Bandhan Bank has filed papers with the SEBI for an initial public offering that is estimated to raise at least Rs. 2500 crore." is the first sentence, what is the order of other sentences after rearrangement?

(A) The microlender, which was one of the entities to receive a banking licence from RBI in 2015, on Monday said it has filed a draft red herring prospectus with the market regulator.

(B) It consists of a fresh issue of up to 9.76 crore shares and an offer for sale of up to 1.40 crore shares by the IFC and 75.65 lakh shares by IFC FIG investment company.

(C) Kolkata-based Bandhan Bank has filed papers with the SEBI for an initial public offering that is estimated to raise at least Rs. 2500 crore.

(D) The proposed IPO is for 11.92 crore shares.

(E) Bandhan Bank's MD said that the public offering will strengthen its capital base and help in its expansion.

(F) "With IPO, the bank will also comply with the regulatory requirement of listing on the stock exchanges," he added.

(a) ABDFE   (b) ADBEF   (c) DFAEB
(d) BEDFA   (e) DAFEB

70. If sentence (C) "The job of enrolling Aadhaar is stretching bank resources even as they grapple with stressed assets and pushing credit offtake in the early months of 2018." is the first sentence, what is the order of other sentences after rearrangement?

(A) The problem is more acute for the banks where the Reserve Bank of India has initiated prompt corrective action (PCA) to improve their financial health.

(B) "The selection process of branches that will offer Aadhaar enrolment is not random and has to be such that it provides coverage in every district where the bank is present.

(C) The job of enrolling Aadhaar is stretching bank resources even as they grapple with stressed assets and pushing credit offtake in the early months of 2018.

(D) A senior executive of a state-run lender said all commercial banks have been asked by the Unique Identification Authority of India (UIDAI) to facilitate Aadhaar seeding by opening enrolment centres in one out of every ten branches.

(E) Once the selection is done, the banks have to allocate officers and employees, to offer this service. The process has already begun and many bank branches have started this service," the executive said.

(F) As banks have been included in the central government's Aadhaar enrolment drive, they are having to allocate staff, otherwise engaged in different activities, towards Aadhaar enrolment.

(a) BDAEF   (b) EFBAD   (c) DABFE
(d) ABEFD   (e) FDBEA

71. If sentence (C) "The first note was introduced on November 30, 1917, with the photo of King George V." is the first sentence, what is the order of other sentences after rearrangement?

(A) Even as it has gone through these travails, the Re. 1 note has retained many of its unique distinctions, including being called a 'coin' in legal speak.

(B) The last hundred years - the first note was introduced on November 30, 1917, with the photo of King George V -have been all but tumultuous for this creation.

(C) The first note was introduced on November 30, 1917, with the photo of King George V.

(D) Its genesis lies in the World War I where the inability to mint coins forced the then colonial authorities to shift to printing Re. 1 notes in 1917.

(E) The Reserve Bank website says its issuance was discontinued first in 1926 on "cost benefit considerations".

(F) It got reintroduced in 1940, only to be discontinued in 1994 again.

(a) DBAEF   (b) EFBAD   (c) DBEFA
(d) ABEFD   (e) FDBEA

72. If sentence (C) "The United States has suspended its USD 255 million military aid to Pakistan for now, the White House has confirmed, saying the fate of such assistance will depend on Islamabad's response to terrorism on its soil." is the first sentence, what is the order of other sentences after rearrangement?

(A) The confirmation comes on the same day when US President Donald Trump accused Pakistan of giving nothing to the US but "lies and deceit" and providing "safe haven" to terrorists in return for USD 33 billion aid over the last 15 years.

(B) "The president has made clear the US expects Pakistan to take decisive action against terrorists and militants on its soil, and that Pakistan's actions in support of the South Asia Strategy will ultimately determine the trajectory of our relationship, including future security assistance," he said.

(C) The United States has suspended its USD 255 million military aid to Pakistan for now, the White House has confirmed, saying the fate of such assistance will depend on Islamabad's response to terrorism on its soil.

(D) "The United States does not plan to spend the USD 255 million in FY 2016 in Foreign Military Financing for Pakistan at this time," a senior administration official told PTI on conditions of anonymity.

(E) Earlier in the day, US President Donald Trump, in his first tweet of the New Year, blasted the Pakistan leadership by saying that they have given America "nothing but lies and deceit" despite having received more than USD 33 billion in last 15 years.

(F) The US administration continues to review Pakistan's level of cooperation, the official said.

(a) DABEF   (b) EFBAD   (c) DBEFA
(d) ADBFE   (e) FDBEA

73. If sentence (C) "Victoria Beckham once tweeted, "Airport is my runway!" When I am at the airport all set for a vacation, I have a sinking feeling in my stomach." is the first sentence, what is the order of other sentences after rearrangement?

(A) Meanwhile I, in my corduroy trousers and T-shirt, look as if I have fallen off the laundry cart.

(B) My travel companions look like they have stumbled off the Paris Fashion Week ramp.

(C) Victoria Beckham once tweeted, "Airport is my runway!" When I am at the airport all set for a vacation, I have a sinking feeling in my stomach.

(D) Sadly, no one in my group seems to have any regard for the imported or even the aviation giant.

(E) Jessica Alba also wore a sentence sweatshirt with a jacket thrown over it carelessly, and she made it to the top-whatever list of best-dressed travellers!

(F) My trousers are phoren and the grey tee has an Airbus logo.

(a) BAFDE   (b) EFBAD   (c) BFAED
(d) ADBEF   (e) FDAEB

74. If sentence (C) "If law-making is a long and tedious process, it appears that unmaking existing laws is an equally arduous task." is the first sentence, what is the order of other sentences after rearrangement?

(A) In the latest round, 235 outdated Acts and nine pre-Independence Ordinances have been repealed.

(B) These pieces of legislation may have been relevant and necessary at the time they were introduced, but in the absence of a periodic review they continue to burden the statutory corpus.

(C) If law-making is a long and tedious process, it appears that unmaking existing laws is an equally arduous task.

(D) How else does one explain the fact that until three years ago, a huge number of obsolete Acts remained in the law books despite losing their relevance and utility?

(E) These laws are archaic mainly because the social, economic and legal conditions that required their enactment does not obtain today; they are also not in tune with the progress of democracy since Independence.

(F) It has been only in the last three years that nearly 1,800 obsolete laws have been repealed.

(a) ABFDE   (b) EFBAD   (c) DFABE
(d) ADBEF   (e) DAEBF

75. If sentence (C) "There are occasions when not only the accused but the criminal justice system itself is on trial." is the first sentence, what is the order of other sentences after rearrangement?

(A) It has framed charges against them for conspiracy, murder and other offences, including under the provisions of the Unlawful Activities (Prevention) Act.

(B) The Anti-Terrorism Squad of the Maharashtra police and the NIA have come to varying conclusions on the culpability of Abhinav Bharat members.

(C) There are occasions when not only the accused but the criminal justice system itself is on trial.

(D) By overruling the National Investigation Agency's finding that key members of a Hindu right-wing group called Abhinav Bharat were not involved in the explosion that killed at least six persons and wounded over a hundred in the Maharashtra town, the Special Court in Mumbai has chosen to let the evidence decide their guilt or innocence.

(E) The ATS chargesheet claims it was primarily a conspiracy.

(F) The case relating to the Malegaon blast of 2008 is one such.

(a) FAEDB   (b) EFBAD   (c) DABEF
(d) ADFEB   (e) FDABE

76. If sentence (C) "The Central government has been working hard to address India's twin balance sheet problem, but it hasn't had much to show in the form of results." is the first sentence, what is the order of other sentences after rearrangement?

(A) This, according to a research report released by CARE Ratings, puts India fifth among significant economies with the most NPAs.

(B) The RBI stated further that it expects NPAs to continue to rise to as high as 11.1% of total outstanding loans by September 2018, so the end to the bad loans mess seems nowhere near.

(C) The Central government has been working hard to address India's twin balance sheet problem, but it hasn't had much to show in the form of results.

(D) According to the report released last week, gross non-performing assets (NPAs) in the banking system as a whole rose to 10.2% at the end of September, from 9.6% at the end of March.

(E) The Financial Stability Report released by the Reserve Bank of India, for one, suggests that India is still far away from solving the troubles ailing its banks and large business corporations.

(F) The bad loans problem has also not spared private sector banks - these lenders have seen their asset quality deteriorate at a faster pace than public sector banks.

(a) EDABF (b) FEBAD (c) BADEF
(d) EDFAB (e) EDBAF

77. If sentence (C) "The struggle to keep the Internet freely accessible to all got a welcome shot in the arm on Tuesday." is the first sentence, what is the order of other sentences after rearrangement?

(A) The Telecom Regulatory Authority of India (TRAI) finally came out with clear guidelines in favour of Net neutrality that are consistent with its earlier stand on Facebook's Free Basics proposal.

(B) After consultation papers issued in May 2016 and this January, the regulator reiterated that there cannot be discriminatory treatment of websites on the Internet by service providers.

(C) The struggle to keep the Internet freely accessible to all got a welcome shot in the arm on Tuesday.

(D) This, in a nutshell, means that service providers such as telecom companies cannot stand in the way of a consumer's access to content that would otherwise be provided to her without any undue hindrance.

(E) Quite notably, TRAI's decision comes in the wake of international focus on the U.S. Federal Communications Commission's decision to scrap regulations on service providers imposed during the Obama administration.

(F) In particular, TRAI warned providers against the practice of blocking certain websites and tinkering with content speeds.

(a) EDABF (b) DABFE (c) BADEF
(d) ABFDE (e) AFEDB

78. If sentence (C) "In the 15 years since it's inauguration in December 2002, the Delhi Metro has become a mundane, everyday part of the Delhiite's life." is the first sentence, what is the order of other sentences after rearrangement?

(A) Parts of central Delhi have witnessed an urban renewal that would not have been possible without the metro.

(B) As it winds its way around the many elevated corridors and deep tunnels beneath the city, the ways in which it has changed life around it are not immediately evident.

(C) In the 15 years since it's inauguration in December 2002, the Delhi Metro has become a mundane, everyday part of the Delhiite's life.

(D) Special women's compartments in every train have added to the feeling of being in a 'safe' space.

(E) And some far-flung suburbs have witnessed the kind of development that would have been inconceivable without the network effect.

(F) In a city notorious for its aggression, the metro gave women a chance to stay out late - at least as late as the metro timings allowed.

(a) EAFDB (b) BFDAE
(c) BADEF (d) ABFDE
(e) ADBEF

79. If sentence (C) "The country's top food regulator i.e. the Food Safety and Standards Authority of India (FSSAI) plans to upgrade 15 laboratories across the country." is the first sentence, what is the order of other sentences after rearrangement?

(A) Once upgraded, the 15 labs will have the authority to certify their findings, which can be used as the basis for punitive action.

(B) India has more than 250 food-testing laboratories, of which about 150 are run by either the state or central governments, but none has the standing that would mean its findings are immediately and completely accepted by all stakeholders, including food companies.

(C) The country's top food regulator i.e. the Food Safety and Standards Authority of India (FSSAI) plans to upgrade 15 laboratories across the country.

(D) Currently, after primary testing at local labs, the sample is sent to an appellate authority in case of discrepancies.

(E) There's more work to be done, though, as enumerated in a recent report on the regulator by the government auditor, the Comptroller and Auditor General of India (CAG) that revealed serious gaps in the organisation's processes.

(F) That's the gap FSSAI's new network of laboratories will be looking to fill.

(a) DAFEB (b) BAFDE (c) BADEF
(d) AEFDB (e) DABFE

80. If sentence (C) "Stock market investors have had a good year." is the first sentence, what is the order of other sentences after rearrangement?

(A) Two straight years of good rains and a pay raise for government staff has fuelled hopes of higher domestic consumption in 2018 and kept the markets going.

(B) The benchmark Sensex has crossed 34,000, gaining around 28%.

(C) Stock market investors have had a good year.

(D) A sluggish economy, disappointing investment in capacity building and lacklustre corporate earnings have also not impeded the steady rise in stock prices.

(E) Investors shrugged off changes such as the currency note ban in November 2016 and the July implementation of the Goods and Services Tax (GST) which disrupted businesses.

(F) Domestic institutional investors invested a record Rs. 91,000 crore in Indian stocks this year betting that the economy will see a cyclical recovery the next fiscal year.

(a) DAFEB (b) BAFDE (c) BEDAF
(d) AEFDB (e) DAEFB

81. If sentence (C) "The decision to use Aadhaar as proof of identity in the annual collation of data on teachers employed in higher education has led to an uncomfortable discovery: nearly a tenth of them turned out to be ghost teachers." is the first sentence, what is the order of other sentences after rearrangement?

(A) Around 130,000 teachers were found to be fake.

(B) The human resource development (HRD) ministry in 2017 told colleges and universities across India that while furnishing data they need to give the Aadhaar number of the faculty members to authenticate their presence.

(C) The decision to use Aadhaar as proof of identity in the annual collation of data on teachers employed in higher education has led to an uncomfortable discovery: nearly a tenth of them turned out to be ghost teachers.

(D) The bad news is that the country has just found out that understaffing in higher education institutes is far greater than what has been estimated so far.

(E) While the good news is that this will lead to a focus on improving the quality of teaching,

(F) India has about 1.4 million teachers in colleges and universities.

(a) DFAEB   (b) BAFDE   (c) BEDAF
(d) AFEDB   (e) DAEFB

82. If sentence (C) "The Reserve Bank of India will shortly issue new Rs 10 notes under the Mahatma Gandhi series." is the first sentence, what is the order of other sentences after rearrangement?

(A) With chocolate brown colour as the base, the new note will bear the picture of Konark Sun Temple.

(B) The central bank has already printed around 1 billion pieces of the new Rs 10 note.

(C) The Reserve Bank of India will shortly issue new Rs 10 notes under the Mahatma Gandhi series.

(D) The change in design in the old Rs 10 note was last made in 2005.

(E) The design received the go-ahead from the government last week, said the two of the people cited earlier.

(F) In August last year, RBI had introduced the new Rs 200 and Rs 50 notes under the Mahatma Gandhi series.

(a) DFAEB   (b) AEFDB   (c) FEDAB
(d) BDEFA   (e) BAEDF

83. If sentence (C) "The continuing failure of the Myanmar government to act decisively and urgently to protect civilians from the raging crossfire between the security forces and insurgents is shocking." is the first sentence, what is the order of other sentences after rearrangement?

(A) The latest flare-up began last Friday when militants suspected to be from the Arakan Rohingya Salvation Army attacked military and police outposts.

(B) That should have served as a caution against an excessive counter-insurgency operation, a real possibility given the history of systematic persecution of the Muslim minorities in Rakhine.

(C) The continuing failure of the Myanmar government to act decisively and urgently to protect civilians from the raging crossfire between the security forces and insurgents is shocking.

(D) Most of the victims are women and children, according to the UN's International Organisation for Migration, which has called for additional aid to cope with Dhaka's refugee situation.

(E) The military crackdown that followed has been widely condemned as disproportionate and the government accused of being an onlooker.

(F) The recent clashes in the western State of Rakhine have claimed over 70 lives and forced thousands of Rohingya to flee across the border into Bangladesh, in a rapidly deteriorating humanitarian crisis.

(a) DAFEB   (b) FDABE   (c) FEDBA
(d) BDEAF   (e) BEDFA

84. If sentence (C) "The success of the first developmental flight of GSLV Mark III will enable indigenous launching up to 4 tonne class of communication satellites in the future." is the first sentence, what is the order of other sentences after rearrangement?

(A) Next developmental launch is in first half of 2018.

(B) ISRO has been providing commercial launch services for earth observation satellites and small satellites onboard the Polar Satellite Launch Vehicle (PSLV) through Antrix Corporation Limited since 1999.

(C) The success of the first developmental flight of GSLV Mark III will enable indigenous launching up to 4 tonne class of communication satellites in the future.

(D) The successful launch of GSLV Mark III is a step ahead in building credibility in launching.

(E) Some more launches of GSLV-MK III will be needed before GSLV MK III gets recognised internationally as a vehicle for transportation to space.

(F) ISRO has just completed one launch of GSLV-MK III.

(a) BDFAE   (b) FBEDA   (c) FEDBA
(d) AEDBF   (e) BFADE

85. If sentence (C) "The Central Government is the competent authority to initiate disciplinary proceedings against IAS officers for misconducts while working in the affairs of Government of India." is the first sentence, what is the order of other sentences after rearrangement?

(A) The Central Government is also the competent authority in respect of disciplinary proceedings initiated by the State Government where subsequent to inquiry, a major penalty has been proposed.

(B) The Central Government also considers proposals for sanction for prosecution against IAS Officers for offences under P.C. Act, 1988, subsequent to completion of investigation and filing of chargesheet.

(C) The Central Government is the competent authority to initiate disciplinary proceedings against IAS officers for misconducts while working in the affairs of Government of India.

(D) Department of Post and Telegraph in exercise of powers conferred under sub-rule 3 of the Rule 16 of the All India Services (Death-cum-retirement Benefits) Rules 1958 has prematurely retired, in public interest, 4 (four) IAS officers since 2014.

(E) There are 36 disciplinary proceeding against IAS officers (State and Central cases) currently in progress at various stages.

(F) In the past one year 8 cases for prosecution sanction have been granted by the Central Government.

(a) AEDBF   (b) FADBE   (c) FEDBA
(d) AEBFD   (e) BFADE

86. If sentence (C) "The country's largest telecommunications services provider, Bharti Airtel and Samsung, India's number one smartphone and consumer electronics brand have partnered to bring in a range of affordable 4G smartphone options to customers." is the first sentence, what is the order of other sentences after rearrangement?
    - (A) For instance, for Galaxy J2 which is available for Rs 6,990, the company will give a cashback of Rs 1,500 making the effective price of the smartphone at Rs 5,490.
    - (B) All devices will come bundled with Airtel's special recharge pack of Rs 199 that offers 1GB data/day and unlimited calling to enable best-in-class experience on India's leading smartphone network, the companies said.
    - (C) The country's largest telecommunications services provider, Bharti Airtel and Samsung, India's number one smartphone and consumer electronics brand have partnered to bring in a range of affordable 4G smartphone options to customers.
    - (D) Four top models from Samsung's Galaxy J-series range - J2 (2017), J5 Prime, J7 Prime, and J7 Pro - will be available with attractive cashback offers, bringing down the effective price of the device and making them affordable for customers.
    - (E) "The Rs 1,500 cashback will be disbursed to customers over 24 months. At the end of 12 months, customers who have done recharges (in any denomination of their choice) worth Rs 2,500 will be eligible for the first instalment of Rs 300," Airtel said.
    - (F) Similarly, Samsung Galaxy J7 Pro that costs Rs 19,900, would be offered at Rs 18,400 with the cashback offer.
    - (a) DBAFE   (b) FAEBD   (c) DFEAB
    - (d) ABEFD   (e) ABDEF

87. If sentence (C) "There are many reasons to welcome the bill outlawing *talaq-e-biddat*, or instant triple talaq, called the Muslim women (protection of the rights on marriage) bill." is the first sentence, what is the order of other sentences after rearrangement?
    - (A) By showing that the practice was not supported by the Quran, the court pointed out that what was bad in theology was bad in law.
    - (B) That is, pronouncing *talaq* three times successively would have no legal effect on the marriage.
    - (C) There are many reasons to welcome the bill outlawing *talaq-e-biddat*, or instant triple talaq, called the Muslim women (protection of the rights on marriage) bill.
    - (D) The movement against it was headed by, among others, women from the minority community, who welcomed the Supreme Court judgment in August 2017 that made instant triple talaq illegal.
    - (E) The judgment, while preventing the violation of rights, was also a step towards gender justice.
    - (F) Instant divorce, the moment the husband pronounced '*talaq*' three times in succession, was a cruel practice, one of the various rules in most religions that cause women suffering.
    - (a) DBAEF   (b) FAEBD   (c) FDBAE
    - (d) ABEFD   (e) AFEBD

88. If sentence (C) "When talks turn to how India has done for itself in 50 years of independence, the world has nothing but praise for our success in remaining a democracy." is the first sentence, what is the order of other sentences after rearrangement?
    - (A) On other fronts, the applause is less loud.
    - (B) Life expectancy has increased.
    - (C) When talks turn to how India has done for itself in 50 years of independence, the world has nothing but praise for our success in remaining a democracy.
    - (D) Industry, which was barely a fledging, has grown tremendously.
    - (E) In absolute terms, India hasn't done too badly, of course.
    - (F) So has literacy.
    - (a) DEFBA   (b) FAEDB   (c) FABED
    - (d) AEBFD   (e) AFEBD

89. If sentence (C) "Under pressure from the government, State Bank of India is understood to be reviewing its minimum balance requirement which is currently Rs 3,000 in urban centers." is the first sentence, what is the order of other sentences after rearrangement?
    - (A) The move follows reports that the bank made Rs 1,772 crore in fees by imposing penalties for non-maintenance of minimum balance between April and November 2017.
    - (B) The bank is also changing the requirement from monthly average balance to quarterly average balance.
    - (C) Under pressure from the government, State Bank of India is understood to be reviewing its minimum balance requirement which is currently Rs 3,000 in urban centers.
    - (D) According to sources, the bank is looking at bringing down the minimum balance requirement to around Rs 1,000 but is yet to take a call.
    - (E) However, following public backlash the bank brought down the minimum balance requirement to Rs 3,000 in metros, Rs 2,000 in semi-urban and Rs 1,000 in rural centres.
    - (F) SBI had originally increased the minimum balance requirement to Rs 5,000 in June.
    - (a) DABEF   (b) BAEFD   (c) FABED
    - (d) AEFDB   (e) BADFE

90. If sentence (C) "Every state has a constitution, since every state functions on the basis of certain rules and principles." is the first sentence, what is the order of other sentences after rearrangement?
    - (A) It has often been asserted that the US has a written constitution,
    - (B) In fact, however, many parts of the British constitution exist in written form, whereas important aspects of the American constitution are wholly unwritten.
    - (C) Every state has a constitution, since every state functions on the basis of certain rules and principles.
    - (D) This is true only in the sense that, in the US, there is a formal document called the constitution, whereas there is no such document in Great Britain.
    - (E) but that the constitution of Great Britain in unwritten.
    - (F) Every state, in short has a written constitution, but in some, real constitution operates behind the façade of a nominal constitution.
    - (a) DABEF   (b) AEDBF   (c) FABED
    - (d) AEBFD   (e) BADEF

ANSWER KEY

1	(b)	10	(c)	19	(c)	28	(c)	37	(e)	46	(a)	55	(b)	64	(a)	73	(a)	82	(e)
2	(a)	11	(c)	20	(c)	29	(d)	38	(d)	47	(b)	56	(d)	65	(c)	74	(c)	83	(b)
3	(d)	12	(b)	21	(d)	30	(c)	39	(c)	48	(c)	57	(d)	66	(b)	75	(e)	84	(a)
4	(d)	13	(d)	22	(c)	31	(d)	40	(e)	49	(d)	58	(a)	67	(d)	76	(a)	85	(d)
5	(a)	14	(a)	23	(b)	32	(a)	41	(b)	50	(e)	59	(c)	68	(a)	77	(d)	86	(a)
6	(b)	15	(a)	24	(d)	33	(a)	42	(d)	51	(e)	60	(a)	69	(b)	78	(b)	87	(c)
7	(d)	16	(b)	25	(a)	34	(d)	43	(e)	52	(c)	61	(b)	70	(e)	79	(e)	88	(d)
8	(b)	17	(d)	26	(b)	35	(a)	44	(c)	53	(d)	62	(c)	71	(c)	80	(c)	89	(e)
9	(c)	18	(a)	27	(c)	36	(a)	45	(b)	54	(a)	63	(e)	72	(d)	81	(d)	90	(b)

Hints & Explanations

1. (b) Sentence C is the only which makes sense as the 1st sentence because it is an example of the claim made in sentence 1 thus, consolidates it. Following it is B, which gives another category of example for sentence 1 and then is A which explains all this and the last is D, which is linked to sentence 6.

2. (a) Sentence 1 and B are linked as they refer to IIT graduates. Next comes A which refers to the degree from the IIT as well as its prospects, this is followed by C which is linked to D and sentence number 6 which are about the culture success stories and the IIT undergraduate mindset.

3. (d) Sentence number 1 is followed by A as they both refer to the Maharaja of Kapurthala. Sentence B logically follows A as it is a particular example of the exquisite taste of a Maharaja. This is followed by D and then by C in a logical sequence before linking C to sentence number 6.

4. (d) The sequence ABDC stands out as the only logical sequence as A is directly links the sentence number 1 in which there is given the unveiling of the two gifts, this is followed by B, which gives the proper noun for the pronoun used in the first two sentence and then D and C logically follow as C is a logical sequence of D and both talk about Gurtu.

5. (a) Sentence C explains sentence number 1 and is followed by A which gives more details. D also gives more details and therefore, follows A whereas B links to sentence number 6 and comes before it thus, the logical sequence is CADB.

6. (b) Sentence C is the sequence of sentence number 1 as it explains the word salvation, this is followed by B which introduces Christianity and its principles about salvation which is the theme. Then is A, which compares Christian tradition and Buddhism which is the logical sequence of B. This is followed by D which precedes sentence number 6 in the sequence.

7. (d) The only logical sequence that comes across is ABCD which can be explained in context of sentences between 1 and 6 which they appear, as each sentence follows to each other in a logical sequence and sentence D precedes sentence number 6. As the last part of D and the first part of sentence 6 refers to rural area.

8. (b) Sentence B follows sentence number 1, as B refers to the editors of the good literacy magazines given in sentence 1. C logically follows B which again refer to the editors and D directly links to the number of editors referred to in C. The last choice is A which is giving a different choice all together, however, it is in sequence with sentence number 6.

9. (c) Sentence number 1 is logically followed by B as B refers to the NRI phase of the Indian expatriate in the US. This is followed by D explaining the expatriates and then by A which talks about the media image of NRIs and last by C which is altogether in a sequence before ending with sentence number 6.

10. (c) The first choice will be A as it follows sentence number 1 and then comes sentence C which is in sequence of A, explaining the reason for exports of Indian crafts. This is followed by B which mentions event that occurred alongwith those mentioned in C simultaneously in the same era. This will then be followed by D, which explains the fortunes being made by people dealing in Antiques.

11. (c) Sentence number 1 and B are linked together through trying to make people laugh and then is followed by A which is one of the two grounds mentioned in B, this

is then followed by D which is the second ground. The last choice is C which is an adequate precursor of sentence number 6.

12. (b) Sentence D picturises the termite colony mentioned in sentence number 1 and thus, naturally follows it. This is followed by B which also explains a little bit about the colony and then is followed by A and lastly by C, which is linked to A through the restoration of balance that had been unsettled in sentence A.

13. (d) The most logical sequence in this is BDCA, as sentence B logically follows 1, referring to the ages of 3 and 5½ years. This is followed by D which talks on the co-relation between developing language skills and the given age and then by C which gives the reason which has been explained in A.

14. (a) Sentence D explains the kind of outboard engines mentioned in sentence number 1 and thus, logically follows sentence number 1. This is followed by A, which explains why these motors are a major threat and then by C, which talks of the situation today. The last part of the logical sequence is B, which explains why the Belugas cannot be found even with outboard motors having more powerful engines.

15. (a) Both sentence B and sentence number 1 refer to historical mis-constructions, thus, sentence B follows the sentence number 1. This is followed by A, which explains B and then by D, which talks about the theory of teaching. Lastly, the sentence in the logical sequence is C, which talks about the impression which is most likely to follow in pedagogy is combined with the generally unhistorical air of science writing and occasional systematic misconstruction.

16. (b) Sentence B is the first choice as it explains the principle given in sentence number 1, this is followed by A which further clarifies it and then by D, which is again a further clarification of the principle and last is C, which is the logical conclusion of the principle.

17. (d) In sentence B, the low light conditions refer to the darken sheds in sentence number 1, thus, sentence B follows sentence number 1. A logical sequence to it is D and then it is followed by C, which talks about the enriched environment of bales of wood-shavings mentioned in D. The last choice is A which gives the conclusion of adding the bales of wood.

18. (a) Sentence D follows sentence number 1 as it talks about criticism of the statement given in sentence number 1. B follows it, which talks of the people living in particular states, not members of the nation state or hegemonic nation. This is followed by A and then by C, which is a culmination of the different types of states mentioned.

19. (c) CABD comes across the most logical sequence as the four sentences follow each other in a sequence. The sentence C talks about the cut off funding for research as given in sentence 1, followed by sentence A which

explains that no such funds are cut in humanity, this is followed by B which is an explanation of A and then is followed by D, which is the perfect precursor to sentence number 6.

20. (c) Sentence A is the first choice as it shows why horses and communism were a poor match, this is followed by B which shows the result of the poor match of horses and communism. Then is followed by C and then by D of which, sentence number 6 is a natural extension.

21. (d) The 'It' in A refers to the forum in E. EA forms a mandatory pair and this helps rule out option (b). Option (a) can be ruled out because C does not follow B; however, B can be used to substantiate C – as done in option (d). Option (c) can be ruled out for the same reason as B is cited as an example and it follows C. Option (d) is the answer as C should start the sequence as the word 'Ironically' cannot otherwise be logically justified.

22. (c) (E-B) is a mandatory pair as statement B gives the correct inference that should be made from the data in statement E. Statements D & E should also come together as they both present data pertaining to natural disasters. Statement A begins a new idea and therefore has to come in the end.

23. (b) (E-A) is a mandatory pair as is (B-D). Statement C starts talking about a new idea that of taking a pledge. It could come either at the end or the beginning. However, statement C starts with 'that future'. This reference does not make sense if we put statement C at the end of the paragraph. Therefore, statement C has to begin the paragraph.

24. (d) (C-E) is a mandatory pair as it builds upon the idea through contrast. 'It is not the critic who counts…' in statement C and 'the credit belongs to the man who is actually in the arena' in statement E. Statements B and D should also come together as they build on the idea of the man in the arena. (D-A) is another mandatory pair as the conclusion in statement A is based on statement D.

27. (c) The paragraph begins with statement A. Statements D and E discuss the definition and hence have to come together. Similarly, B describes the idea which begins in C. The 'dilution' in C is followed by B which gives an example of this dilution. 'Already by 1762………there was no meaningful difference between the authority of a despot and that of a monarch'.

28. (c) The paragraph should begin with sentence A or D. On comparing sentences A and D, it is found that sentence A is not suitable as an introductory sentence because it expresses a conclusion. Sentence D and E should go together followed by sentences B and C. Sentence A should follow sentence C as it is concluding sentence in the paragraph. So, option (c) is the correct answer.

29. (d) Sentences A, B or E cannot be introductory sentence of the paragraph. Since sentence C mentions - '…these paragons of…' it cannot be the first sentence of paragraph. The paragraph should begin with sentence D followed by sentence C. Sentences B, E and A should follow DC in order to make the paragraph coherent. So, option (d) is the correct answer.

30. (c) Sentence C is the first sentence of the paragraph as suggested by given options. It talks about a jewel heist carried out during an important event. Sentence D should follow sentence C which is its logical continuation. Sentence B should follow D because it gives more details of the heist. Sentences E and A should follow sentence B in order to make the paragraph coherent. So, option (c) is the correct answer.

31. (d) A quick review of all options reveals that no other sentence except E is fit to be the introductory sentence of this paragraph. This eliminates options (a) and (c) as they begin with sentence B. Sentence E should be followed by C because it focuses on the details of Queen's coronation. Next, sequence BAD is a logical continuation of ideas expressed in sentences E and C. Sentence B tells that conferring of state headship is an exclusive Anglican ritual; sentence A tells what happens in the ritual and sentence D states how the ritual concludes. Option (d) presents right sequence of sentences in the paragraph and is the correct answer.

32. (a) In this paragraph, E should be the introductory sentence as it is a general statement while other sentences are examples. Next, sentences C, A and B form a logical sequence. Sentence C includes the fact that conventional wisdom has been turned over by new restaurants. Sentence A supports its preceding sentence by arguing that Japanese food should not do well in North Indian markets. Sentence B presents a contrasting fact that Sushi is a favourite among teenagers. Options (b), (c) and (d) are incorrect as they do not contain sequence CAB. Option (a) presents correct sequence of sentences and is the correct answer.

33. (a) Sentence B is about what the author is focusing on. Sentence D is about challenge that she has taken up. Sentence C tells about her latest title. Sentence E is about how it has been inspired by her life and sentence A describes an instance. So, option (a) is the correct answer.

34. (d) Sentences B and D make a pair. Next, sentence E mentions aspects of his early life and sentence A continues this. Sentence C should be the concluding sentence of the sequence as it talks about his relationship with his friends. So option (d) is the correct answer.

35. (a) Since Statement A talks about nuclear power, the most suitable part next to it will be Statement D, which carries forward the topic and talks about nuclear cycle. Next in series will be Statement C as it talks about effects of nuclear cycle. Next most suitable option will be Statement E as it talks about CO_2 which is a greenhouse gas. The last option is Statement B which is the concluding statement.
Hence, the correct answer is option (a). DCEB

61. (b) DACFBE will be the right order and it will be:

66. (b) The first sentence talks about the fact that only few investors have idea about bitcoins and other cryptocurrencies (which seems an attractive investment area), so, the finance ministry has warned the potential investors about it. Sentence E will follow the first sentence because it says that 'bitcoin not only shot up well over by 1000%......' which justifies 'attractive investment area' and forms a link. Now, we are left with only option (b) and (d) to choose from. When we consider the sentence F, we can see that this line seems to be a part somewhere in the middle of the paragraph, also, the first line starts with a warning, therefore, it must justify the consequences of the investment in bitcoins and other cryptocurrencies which is justified by sentence C. Hence, option (b) is the correct choice.

67. (d) After reading all the sentences carefully, we see that sentence A and F should go one after another as both talk about 'over-volunteer'. Moreover, sentence A will follow sentence F because of the presence of the word 'such' which signifies that the subject of the sentence has already been discussed in the previous sentence. So, we have option (c), (d) and (e) to choose from. Considering sentence D which talks about 'a big problem', we find that it can't be the second sentence as no problem of any sort has been dealt in the first sentence, so, option (c) and (e) gets eliminated. Hence, by elimination method, we can conclude that option (d) is the correct choice.

68. (a) After reading all the sentences carefully, we see that sentence B and E should go one after another as both talk about 'curb'. Moreover, sentence B will follow sentence E because of the presence of 'the crippling nature of the curb' which signifies that the curb has already been discussed in the previous line. So, we have only option (a) and (c) to choose from. Sentence E will follow sentence C because the first line deals with 'economic sanction' making ACEB form a link. Hence, option (a) is the correct choice.

69. (b) Sentence A will follow the first sentence because it talks about the 'microlender' i.e. the subject (Bandhan bank) of the first sentence and thus, forms a link. We have only two options which start with sentence A viz. (a) and (b). Sentence D should come before the sentence B as it talks about the whole proportionate of the proposed IPO whereas, sentence B talks about its distribution. Hence, option (b) is the correct choice.

70. (e) After reading all the sentences carefully, we see that sentence F is the only option that will follow the first sentence and will form a correct link as the first sentence i.e. sentence C talks about the 'bank resources' and so does the sentence F. Hence, option (e) is the correct choice.

71. (c) Sentence D will follow the first sentence as it talks about genesis i.e. the origin or source of the note, the history of which has been dealt in the first sentence. No other sentence except sentence D will form a correct sequence. So, we have option (a) and (c) to choose from. Sentence A which talks about the travails (which have been discussed in sentence E and F) which the coin has gone through and despite these, it has maintained its unique distinctions should be the concluding line as it gives an overview of the entire passage. Hence, the correct option is (c).

72. (d) The first sentence i.e. the sentence C talks about suspension of the military aid by the US that was given to Pakistan and so, the second sentence should be a sentence that talks about the suspension or anything related to it in a little detail, therefore, sentence A is the only sentence that appears to be the second sentence as it talks about the confirmation of the suspension. No other sentence forms a direct co-relation with the first sentence as sentence A. Hence, the correct option is (d).

73. (a) When we read all the sentences carefully, we see that all the sentences except sentence E are the lines said by Victoria Beckham, whereas, sentence E is a different sentence which talks about what Jessica Alba said, therefore, this should be the last sentence as all other sentence except E co-relate with each other and form a sequence. We have only one option ending with sentence E, therefore, option (a) is the correct choice.

74. (c) After reading all the sentences carefully, we see that the second part of the first sentence appears to be sarcastic and therefore, it must be followed by a sentence that connects to the mockery made in it. Sentence D appears to be the best sentence to follow the first sentence among all other sentences because it shows the writer's frustration and his question mark on the system. So, we have only options (c) and (e) to choose from. Sentence F talks about what happened in last three years which the writer is concerned about in sentence D and so, D & F form a sequence. Hence, option (c) is the answer.

75. (e) It is clear from the first sentence that there are many incidences when a question mark is put on the criminal justice system apart from the accused. When we read all the sentences carefully, we see that sentence F makes a direct connection i.e. 'Malegaon blast of 2008 is one such' with the first sentence due to the

presence of the word 'such' which means the sentence is talking about something that has been discussed previously. So, we have options (a) and (e) to choose from. Sentence A can't follow sentence F as it says 'It has framed.......' because nothing in this context has been discussed in the first two sentences. Hence, we are left with option (e) which is the answer.

76. (a) After reading all the sentences carefully, we can see that sentence D and A are complementing each other because sentence D talks about a report on NPA and sentence A is starting with 'This (which has been discussed in the previous sentence)' and it also talks about NPA i.e. it is explaining how the percentage of NPA (discussed in sentence D) has put India fifth among significant economies with the most NPAs. So, we should look for the option in which sentence D is followed by sentence A. We have only option (a) where we see sentence A after D. Hence, option (a) is the answer.

77. (d) When we read all the sentences carefully, we see that sentence A is an independent sentence and clearly follows the first sentence because the first sentence exhibits that something good related to the free access of Internet has been done on Tuesday and sentence A talks about the clear guidelines that TRAI has come up with in the same context i.e. Net neutrality so, we have option (d) and (e) to choose from. Sentence F can't follow sentence A because it talks about the warning given to the providers about which nothing has been discussed in the previous two sentences, also, the use of 'In particular....' makes it out of the context as far as sentence A is concerned and therefore, it is eliminated and option (d) is the answer.

78. (b) The first sentence introduces Delhi Metro and therefore, the second sentence should be the one which goes in its continuation. After reading all the sentences, we see that only sentence B appears to be the continuing part of the first sentence because all other sentences are independent and do not make a direct link with the first sentence, so, we have option (b) and (c) to choose from. We also see that sentence F and D are complementing each other as both talk about women safety and thus, they should be together. From the option (b) and (c), only in option (b), F and D are together. Hence option (b) is the answer.

79. (e) The first sentence talks about the plan made by FSSAI about the upgradation of 15 laboratories. The second sentence should be the one which explains the urge for the upgradation i.e. the reason behind the plan and we have sentence D which states the current situation pertaining to the testing at local labs and thus, it forms link with the first line, so we have option (a) and (e) to choose from. Sentence F talks about the gap about which nothing have been discussed in the previous sentences and therefore, option (a) gets eliminated and we have option (e) as our answer.

80. (c) Sentence B will follow the first sentence as it explains the reason why stock market investors have had a good year and thus, these two sentences are making a

direct link with each other. So, we have option (b) and (c) to choose from. Now, let us talk about the last line i.e. the concluding line. Option (b) and (c) have sentence E and F respectively as the last line and after reading both of these, we can easily conclude that sentence F will be the last line as it talks about the future i.e. what the economy is likely to see whereas sentence E appears to be a part somewhere in the middle of the passage. Hence, the correct choice is option (c).

81. (d) After reading all the sentences carefully, we see that only sentence A make a coherent link with the first sentence as it explains the 'uncomfortable discovery' mentioned in the first sentence, therefore, we will look for the option starting with the sentence A. The only option which we have is option (d), hence, it is the answer.

82. (e) In this question, we can easily find the correct choice just by finding the direct link between two or three sentences. Here, sentence A, D and E talk about the design and detailing of the new Rs 10 note and hence, they should be in continuation. Looking at the options, we see that only option (e) is the one where these three sentences are in a sequence, thereby making it the correct choice.

83. (b) After reading all the sentences carefully, we see that sentence F and D make a complementary pair and thus, should go together. Moreover, sentence D should follow sentence F because it talks about the victims who are women and children (as stated in sentence F i.e. " ...western state of Rakhine have claimed over 70 lives..."). Only in option (b), sentence D is followed by sentence F, hence, it is the correct choice.

84. (a) After reading all the sentences carefully, we see that sentence F and A are coherent and should go together, so we have option (a) and (e) to choose from as sentence F and A are together only in these two options. However, option (e) will be eliminated as sentence D can't follow sentence A because both of these are independent sentences and do not make a link, so, we are left with option (a) which is our answer. We have solved it by elimination method.

85. (d) In this question, after reading each and every sentence carefully, we see that sentence D appears to be different from all other sentences so, it must be the last line because it is not making a direct link with any other given sentences and therefore, it can't be substituted anywhere in the middle of the paragraph. We have only one option ending with sentence D, hence, option (d) is the correct choice.

86. (a) The first sentence discusses the partnership between Airtel and Samsung and therefore, it must be complemented with a sentence which starts with the idea of benefits which the customers will get after the partnership. All other sentences apart from sentence D explain the monetary benefits which the customers will get, hence, they can't be the second sentence so, the second sentence will be sentence D. We have option (a) and (c) to choose from. Further, sentence B, A and F are making a correct sequence and therefore, they must go together. Hence, option (c) will be eliminated and our answer will be option (a).

87. (c) After reading all the sentences carefully, we see that sentence A and E talk about the judiciary, thereby, making a coherent link and so, they must go together. On this basis, we have only option (a) and (c) to choose from. Moreover, after further analysis of sentence F (present in option (a) after sentence E), we can conclude that sentence F can't be the last line of the paragraph because it is making a link with sentence D thus, option (a) gets eliminated and we have option (c) as the answer.

88. (d) After reading all the sentences carefully, we see that sentence B and F are making complementary pair. Moreover, sentence F will follow sentence B due to the presence of the word 'So has...'. Looking at the options, we see that sentence B is followed by sentence F in only one option i.e. option (d), hence, the correct choice is option (d). We have solved it by the elimination method.

89. (e) In this question, after reading all the sentences carefully, we see that sentence A, B or D could be the second sentence as all of these seem to be making a direct link with the first sentence. So, in this type of questions, we should try to find the complementary pair of sentences or the concluding line in order to eliminate wrong options and find the correct choice. Here, we see that sentence E starts with 'However...'which indicates that it may be the concluding line. It must be kept in mind that sentences starting with 'Finally', 'However', 'Therefore', 'Thus' and 'So' etc. most of the time are the concluding lines. In this question, sentence E will be the last line as all other sentences except E seem to be a part somewhere in the middle of the passage. We, have only one option ending with sentence E, therefore, the correct choice is option (e).

90. (b) After reading all the sentences carefully, we see that sentence E is second part of sentence A because sentence A ends with a comma and sentence E starts with a small letter, therefore, E should follow A. Considering this, we have option (b) and (d) to choose from. Moreover, sentence F is the concluding line as it summarises the entire paragraph thus, it must be the last line so, we are left with only option (b) which is the correct choice. This question has been solved by elimination as well as by finding the complementary pair of sentences.

CHAPTER 5

Odd Sentence

'Sentence Exclusion' or 'Odd Sentence'

'Sentence Exclusion' or 'Odd Sentence' is a recent addition to banking competitive exams. Many aspirants are not well acquainted with these types of questions. In fact, odd sentence is nothing but a new way of presenting the old concept of Parajumbles. Aspirants are advised not to attempt questions without understanding the concept properly as it could be counter-productive.

In these types of questions, four sentences are given; out of which three of them when arranged in a logical sequence form a coherent paragraph, but one of them does not fit into the sequence. You have to choose the sentence which does not fit into the sequence.

Hence, to deal with the odd sentence, the aspirants should strategize in the following way -

1. Spot the sentence that is most likely to start a paragraph, that sentence which introduces an idea, or a concept, and which is not abrupt often starts a paragraph.

2. Now you have to establish a connecting link; here the parajumbles come into the picture. The sentence that is taking the idea forward on similar lines will come next in the sequence. Also, check whether the subjects in the sentences are linked or not.

3. Now repeat the step 2, see if there is some coherence to the paragraph that is formed after the logical arrangement of the sentences.

4. The sentence that is left from fitting into the sequence is your answer.

Keep in mind that the subject matter of odd sentence may be very similar to that of the other sentences but you have to see if it is logically related. Aspirants are advised not to make any haste while attempting this question because a little haste may cost you a question. So, if you are not convinced of the logical connectivity, you should not mark the answer. For this, develop your reading habit and practise a lot.

Here we give some examples which will make things clear:

Example 1: (d). The computer took 45 hours of non-stop computation.

(c) Charles Babbage proposed the first general mechanical computer, the Analytical Engine in 1837.

(a) This is not really surprising, because with eleven items of clothing the number of possible combinations is given by multiplying 11,10,9,8 and so on, which gives over 39 million combinations.

(b) Someone once used the IBM computer to work out the number of ways of getting dressed with eleven items of clothing.

Answer : (c) b is the opening sentence, since it introduces the narrative. d will follow b, as it tells the chronology of the event. That is what happened next. This will be followed by a. Since a begins with the reflective pronoun, that indicates the action that happened in d. Anyways, the statement in 'c' does not relate to the passage, hence, an odd sentence.

Example 2 : (d) When briefing Kennedy, Eisenhower emphasized that the communist threat in Southeast Asia required priority.

(a) ohn F. Kennedy, Democratic victor in the election of 1960, was at 43, the youngest man ever to win the presidency.

(b) On television, in a series of debates with opponent Richard Nixon, he appeared able, articulate and energetic.

(c) In the campaign, he spoke of moving aggressively into the new decade, for "the New Frontier is here whether we seek it or not".

Answer: (d) The statement 'd' just looks odd as it does not make a coherent paragraph with the other three sentences.

Example 3: (c) One day, a 17-year old shepherd boy came to visit his brothers and asked, "Why don't you stand up and fight the giant?"

(d) We all know the story of David and Goliath, in which there was a giant who was bullying and harassing the children in the village.

(b) But David said, "Okay! Let's go to the town and buy some eatables".

(a) The brothers were terrified and they replied, "Don't you see he is too big to hit?"

Answer : (b) The sentence beginning with David saying that they should go to the town and buy some eatables does not fit into the above paragraph, hence, may be excluded.

EXERCISE

DIRECTIONS (Qs. 1-40): *Four sentences are given below a, b, c and d. Of these, three statements are in logical order and form a coherent paragraph/ passage. From the given options, choose the option that does not fit into the sequence.*

1. (a) The list of horrors goes on.
   (c) And one in every five is malnourished.
   (d) Nobody has been able to figure out a way to reduce the speed that is at the root of India's over-population problems: a baby born every second.
   (b) Foods with a high content of absorbable micronutrients are considered the best means for preventing micronutrient deficiencies.

2. (b) In fact, it suites the purpose of the politicians, they can drag the people into submission by appealing to them in the name of religion.
   (a) In order to inculcate, the unquestioning belief, they condemn the other states which do not follow their religion.
   (d) The emergence of the theocratic states, where all types of crimes are committed in the name of religion of the Middle Ages is dangerous.
   (c) Monarchy thus entails not only a political-administrative organization but also a "court society".

3. (d) It was something I knew that it would give me a chance to be my own boss.
   (b) Today I have 800 on my staff, office and members.
   (c) Although if you work for an ad agency in the 1960s, evidently it isn't there either.
   (a) I was sick of working for others.

4. (d) Fire ripped through another pipeline in southern Nigeria, killing at least 40 people.
   (b) Fuel is supplied not only to homes, but also to a variety of businesses and commercial establishments without any difficulty.
   (a) The explosion was the third in two weeks.
   (c) Police were deployed to stop villagers from stealing fuel from other pipelines.

5. (d) You would be very surprised indeed to find it hot.
   (b) Cold, of course.
   (c) Rivers are the most obvious and significant feature of the landscape.
   (a) When you go bathing in a river or a pond, do you expect the water to be hot or cold?

6. (b) In a number of cases, the drivers have refused to carry passengers according to the meter reading despite it being in working condition.
   (a) Refusal to carry commuters to their respective destinations is another common complaint which has been lodged with the call centres.
   (d) The most shocking is the complaints about misbehaviour by the rickshaw drivers with the passengers.
   (c) It's hard to reconcile the image of the paan-chewing driver greeting you with `Good morning'.

7. (b) Finish specialists recommended a chewing gum containing xylitol - a natural sweetener present in birch, maple, corn and straw - to be used several times a day by young children.
   (c) Chewing gum is a new solution that "may work for parents whose children suffer from chronic ear infections.
   (a) Sugared gums can with heavy use cause tooth decay, gum disease and cavities.
   (d) After Finish studies showed that xylitol is effective in preventing cavities, a team of researchers decided to investigate its effects on a very similar type of bacteria which causes ear infections.

8. (d) The CEO's leadership role also entails being ultimately responsible for all day-to-day management decisions.
   (a) The chief executive had done an excellent job in welding a group of motley and successful companies into one profitable company.
   (b) It is not surprising that company had been sitting on a cash hoard of about $24 billion year after year without any attempt to use it for growth or development.
   (c) The chief executive of the General Electric Company in England once told me that he was very happy when there were no problems in any of his many divisions.

9. (d) Businesses often feel that since they have a lot of market muscle and in such a dominant position, maintenance will be enough.
   (b) IBM fell behind on the concept of "connectivity" and has suffered as a result.
   (a) In recent years, however, even mighty IBM found that market domination was not enough if you fall behind on concept.
   (c) IBM has been well known through most of its recent history as one of the world's largest computer companies.

10. (b) In the past, the customised tailoring units were localised to the township or city and catered exclusively to domestic demand.
    (a) Traditionally, Indians preferred custom-made clothing and the concept of ready-to-wear is a relatively recent one.
    (d) This is contrary to the popular notion that Indian men do not spend as much as women on clothing.
    (c) The customised tailoring outfits have always been a major source of clothing for domestic market.

11. (a) Michael Hofman, a poet and translator, accepts this sorry fact without approval.
    (c) He acknowledges too - in fact, he returns to the point often - the best translators of poetry always fail at some level.
    (b) Poetry typically follows some type of pattern while prose does not follow any formal patterns of verse.
    (d) In terms of the gap between worth and rewards, translators come somewhere near nurses and street cleaners.

12. (b) Reservation should not exceed 50% for the civil services for want of balance and efficiency.
    (a) A common form of caste discrimination in India has been the practice of untouchability.
    (c) The number of aspirants to the civil services in India is very large and they come from various socio-economic backgrounds.
    (d) These aspirants come from both reserved and unreserved category.

13. (d) Almost a century ago, when the father of the modern automobile industry, Henry Ford, sold the first Model T car, he decided that only the best would do for his customers.
    (a) In October 2012, Toyota announced a recall of 7.43 million vehicles worldwide to fix malfunctioning power window switches, the largest recall since that of Ford Motor Company in 1996.
    (b) And for over 90 years, this philosophy has endured in the Ford Motor company.
    (c) Thus a vehicle is ready for the customers only, if it passes the Ford 'Zero Defect Programme'.

14. (a) Because, if the manager's subordinates are inefficient and ineffective and are not helped to increase their efficiency and effectiveness, the task may not be achieved.
    (b) This must be just as true as the responsibility for achieving his prescribed tasks.
    (c) Dealing with employees who don't respect you or your authority can eventually make your job unbearable.
    (d) It is often and that one of the prime responsibilities of a manager is the training and development of his staff.

15. (b) Over the last decade, Australia and India have set up Test cricket's most absorbing rivalry.
    (d) Every champion needs a counterpoint; legacies, defined referentially, draw from the dynamic between world-beater and contender.
    (c) It was tough but India outperformed most of the teams in all three departments of the game in the last two years.
    (a) India, thanks to its natural style of calm aggressive cricket, its distinctive ability to play at the level of the opposition, and the confluence of some of the finest cricketers in the contemporary game, fulfilled this role of contender.

16. (c) Early in August, as his jeep wound its way through the piles of burning tyres that angry protestors had used to barricade the road from Srinagar airport into the city, former Chief Minister Farooq Abdullah, turned to a journalist sitting next to him with a smile on his face.
    (b) "So," he said, "Are you here to write another article about how I don't know how to run a government?"
    (a) More likely than not, Dr. Abdullah's leadership - or that of Jammu and Kashmir National Conference President, his son Omar Abdullah - will soon be put to the test.
    (d) The three time chief minister of Jammu & Kashmir asserted that only dialogue can bring peace in the valley.

17. (a) A nation has gone against its historical record.
    (d) The single undeniable aspect of Obama's legacy is that he demonstrated that a black man can become president of the United States.
    (b) Risen above its worst prejudices in one, emotional incandescent moment.
    (c) Well, at least partly, and for a while Americans have voted in larger numbers than they have in decades, perhaps ever.

18. (d) This is the time of the year when people go out and shop for their winter wear.
    (b) But it seems economic recession has hit the fashion industry as well.
    (a) We haven't seen exclusive fashion shows from big designers this winter.
    (c) Winters for the past two years have been among the warmest, during December to March, in north India that heavily impacted sales of winter clothing by almost 30%.

19. (b) After all, a story told on the large screen inevitably differs from that told on the small screen.
    (c) This critical difference has an impact on viewership in terms of age, income and occupation.
    (a) In this, the age of multimedia, we have to train ourselves to understand that as a rule, the medium is the message.
    (d) In any play you've got to know what's going on around you so you can hear your cue to give a line or move in the scene.

20. (d) The size of the carbon footprint of nations in the developing world has again come in for serious international discussion.
    (c) The failed mission of Copenhagen is the immediate cause of the resumption of this debate.
    (b) While the main triggers of the debate are economic, social and cultural factors also have a major role to play.
    (a) There are both natural and human sources of carbon dioxide emissions.

21. (b) For pure vegetarians India is a heaven.
    (a) These are also prepared using different methods of cooking like baking, boiling, frying etc.
    (c) Indians like their vegetable curries real hot 'n' spicy and so add a number of spices to make them really exotic.
    (d) In factory farms around the world, animals are very often treated as commodities just to be exploited for profit.

22. (a) But it's true that Chinese people were well aware about green tea from ancient time.
    (d) We came to know about this green tea very late.
    (b) If I had said that tea is a healthy drink some years before the introduction of green tea, I might have been ridiculed.
    (c) Plain tea doesn't contain any sugar or calories, but many bottled iced teas on the market are loaded with both.

23. (c) Environment Education Unit of Centre for Science and Environment has always been working towards providing easy-to-understand reading material.

(d) Their new publication on this subject is an attempt to lend teachers a helping hand.

(a) It unfolds in two sections: Climate Change: how to make sense of it all, and Natural Resources: how to share and care.

(b) During the past century, human activities have released large amounts of carbon dioxide and other greenhouse gases into the atmosphere.

24. (d) A famous Japanese rock garden is at Ryoan-ji in NorthWest Kyoto, Japan.

(c) A rock garden can also turn an otherwise awkward spot, like a hard-to-mow slope, into a showcase for your more delicate plants.

(b) The garden is 30 meters long from East to West and 10 meters from North to South.

(a) There are no trees, just 15 irregularly shaped rocks of varying sizes, some surrounded by moss, arranged in a bed of white gravel/sand that is raked every day.

25. (a) When they gathered together, the Buddha was completely silent and some speculated that perhaps the Buddha was tired or ill.

(b) It is said that Gautama Buddha gathered his disciples one day for a Dharma talk.

(d) The Buddha silently held up and twirled a flower and twinkled his eyes; several of his disciples tried to interpret what this meant, though none of them was correct.

(c) Emperor Ashoka built the first temple near Bodhi tree during the 3rd Century BCE, almost 300 years after Buddha's period (566-486 B.C.E).

26. (a) The band has gone through several drummers over the years, though Travis has held the position since 1989 and is the longest-serving.

(b) 'Judas Priest' are an English heavy metal band from Birmingham, England, formed in 1969.

(d) The core line-up consists of lead vocalist Rob Halford, guitarist Glenn Tipton, bassist Ian Hill, and drummer Scott Travis.

(c) Pop music is a slow and melodious form of music, where you can relax while listening to the refreshing songs sung by mega pop stars.

27. (a) In the past year, CBI has registered 170 cases but most of these relate to middlemen.

(c) Overall, it is proposed to train nearly 550 investigators and prosecutors in these eminent national institutions over the next three years.

(d) This is the job only half done as the agency has not been able to find any incriminating documents against the political class so far.

(b) CBI has made some headway by identifying 121 impersonators after scanning details of over 9.5 lakh medical students.

28. (a) In urban-poor households, it is used for both lighting and cooking.

(c) A recent report by the CEEW shows how shifting from kerosene to alternatives such as solar-assisted solutions for lighting and LPG for cooking could be economically beneficial for both the government as well as households.

(d) The CEEW's analysis of National Sample Survey Office data highlights that kerosene is predominantly used as a lighting fuel in rural India.

(b) LPG is used for cooking in many countries for economic reasons, for convenience or because it is the preferred fuel source.

29. (a) The income-tax department is reportedly on an overdrive to nab tax evaders.

(d) This is extremely unfortunate and will result in harassment of the middle class.

(b) It occurs whenever there is a change of national currency.

(c) Punitive action against non-disclosure should be in consonance with the existing income tax law.

30. (a) Trading or investment ideas come in many ways -from stock brokers, investment advisors, media and in most cases from the man next door who just got rich by following a friend's `tip.'

(b) Numerous canteens across the country may soon turn quiet at the lunch hour if the Securities and Exchange Board of India (Sebi) has its way in regulating the flow of stock tips on social media.

(d) Sebi, which wants to protect your wellbeing, may unintentionally be preventing you from getting rich.

(c) The BSE is the world's 11th largest stock exchange with an overall market capitalization of $1.43 Trillion as of March, 2016.

31. (c) There is no bottle of ink waiting to be typed over on to my writing pad.

(d) I always read storybooks, newspapers, magazines, and any other material that I find interesting in my free time.

(b) While it is true that I do most of my writing by hand, this does not mean that I will use any pencil or pen that comes to hand.

(a) Being one of the clumsiest humans on earth, I am unable to fill or refill or empty a fountain pen of its ink without getting the said ink, black, blue or blue-black, all over my hands or onto my coat-sleeves or shirt front.

32. (a) This message was primarily aimed at China, a country with which India has had differences on the issue of Pakistan-sponsored terrorism against India.

(c) China portrays itself as a Third World country that pursues "an independent foreign policy of peace."

(d) China had recently put a technical hold once again at the United Nations and prevented Azhar from being designated a global terrorist, despite JeM being a UN-proscribed terror group.

(b) The Prime Minister's focus, by and large, remained on the issue of terrorism.

33. (a) Many Indian MNCs with global footprints need linguists to help them in foreign land.

(b) As the global marketplace expands, the need of personnel who can communicate in foreign language will increase.

(d) But learning a foreign language is fast becoming a necessary job skill in its own right.

(c) According to the American Community Survey, more than one in 5 individuals over the age of 5 (21%) speak a language other than English at home.

34. (d) It must be appreciated that there is an imperative need for such special legislations as the normal laws are not adequate to deal with the situation.

(a) An important issue which has come up in this context relates to the need for special legislation to cope with the situation.

(b) Any discussion on human rights is incomplete without reference to the security and terrorist threats facing the country.

(c) But it remains to be seen if the demonetisation really reduced corruption and whether black money hoarders were truly affected by the policy.

35. (c) Else India will continue to be placed in no-win situations, on the outside looking in, as at present.

(b) Asean's decision to tighten its integration should serve as a wake-up call to India's policy makers.

(a) The success of regional trade agreements where India is not a party should prod the Centre to quickly move forward with domestic economic reforms.

(d) The World Trade Organization (WTO) is the only global international organization dealing with the rules of trade between nations.

36. (a) In this particular case FBI has asked Apple to help them crack into one particular phone, not develop a generic backdoor into Apple's encryption.

(b) This could help authorities unearth terror plots and save lives.

(c) In these exceptional circumstances, a channel must be available for security agencies to access data on devices used by terrorists.

(d) Even if it is argued that terrorism is employed by revolutionaries as a 'tactic', such means cannot justify the end.

37. (a) Ambedkar became part of the Constituent Assembly, was assigned the task of preparing the first draft of the Constitution.

(b) He then joined Nehru's Cabinet as India's first law minister, but quit later over the question of the Hindu Code Bill.

(d) At that point of time Ambedkar wasn't sure he would be part of the Constitution making body.

(c) The Constitution applies to the State of Jammu and Kashmir with certain exceptions and modifications as provided in article 370 and the Constitution (Application to Jammu and Kashmir) Order, 1954.

38. (c) Most heartening is that India is now the 26th easiest place to get an electricity connection, up 25 places from last year.

(d) That the Bank in its Doing Business 2017 report now ranks India 130 among 190 countries, just one notch higher than last year, is therefore likely to be taken as a signal of the snail's pace of economic reform.

(a) As proof of its commitment to economic renewal, the Narendra Modi government had set itself the target of breaking into the top 50 in the World Bank's annual ranking of countries on ease of starting and operating a for-profit enterprise.

(b) After the Modi government came the inflation had come down to around 5% while revised gross domestic product (GDP) data was pointing to a growth at 7.4% and will help India better even China.

39. (d) However, it is vulnerable to deliberate abuse, accidental bungling, and occasional failures.

(b) Stories of such anomalies are not rare in the criminal justice system of the United States.

(c) In every nation the justice system strives to be perfect.

(a) The United States joins other nations in sending a clear message: we will not allow Iran to have a nuclear weapon.

40. (a) The recent announcement of Rs 11,300 crore for the Swachh Bharat Mission (SBM) in the 2016-17 budget reiterates this.

(c) There is an urgent need to build greater momentum around a broader understanding of what will make India truly Swachh.

(d) Nearly 17 months have passed since Prime Minister Narendra Modi launched the Swachh Bharat Abhiyan on October 2, 2014.

(b) The effects of poor environmental sanitation are numerous and they include human disease, poor overall human health and economic disadvantages as well as social disadvantages.

DIRECTIONS (Qs. 41-47) : *Four sentences are given below labeled (a), (b), (c) and (d). Of these, three sentences need to be arranged in a logical order to form a coherent paragraph/ passage. From the given options, choose the one that does not fit the sequence.*

---

41 (a) Nostalgia and wonder are the two emotions that dominate visitors' minds when they view the quaint collection of artwork harking back to an idyllic Bangalore, in Fernandes' small gallery, aPaulogy.

(b) Thus nostalgia works at several levels, and as humans think that the condition of their lives is improving as they head into the future, a part of their mind also harks back to a supposedly simpler time when life was more peaceful.

(c) Nostalgia can exist only when there is a linear conception of time and modernity, with its notion of progress, is deeply intertwined with the concept of nostalgia.

(d) And Fernandes' work satiates that hunger for nostalgia an old Bangalorean would have.

(e) None of these

42. (a) With footage including wallowing hippos, galloping herds of antelope and lunching hyenas, it really shows the potential of drones in wildlife filmmaking.

(b) So whether it's an aerial shot of surfers riding giant waves off the coast of Oahu, Hawaii or an eerie journey through ice caves in Alaska, we've rounded up six of the best videos filmed by drones around the world.

(c) By using a drone, he gives you a rare look at the shape of the waves coming in, the flow of the surfers around the bay and the motion of the barrels as they break.

(d) A state-of-the-art video being the one created by photographer Will Burrard-Lucas using his "BeetleCo pter" - this stunning film takes a drone on a safari in the Serengeti.

(e) None of these

43. (a) If that's what it is, there's little wonder Britain is no longer capable of marching into somebody else's country and forcing the indigenous population to wear ill-fitting suits and make us all a fried breakfast.

    (b) I should think that when the English Spirit of Cricket waddles self-deprecatingly into view looking down at the ground, the Australian Spirit of Cricket spits, readjusts its box and growls, "Strewth, what happened to you mate? Did you blow all the housekeeping money at the pie stall?"

    (c) Andrew Strauss went to Radley and all I can say is that is the sort of sharp practice they are teaching in English public schools these days.

    (d) And that to me is what was truly galling about England's final-session shenanigans on Sunday – the complete schoolboy amateurishness of it.

    (e) None of these

44. (a) According to Amnesty International: "In August [2012], despite the failure of Mexican authorities to meet human rights conditions set by the US Congress as part of the Merida initiative, the US State Department recommended that Congress release the 15% of funds subject to the conditions."

    (b) The Americas must follow the progressive lead of countries such as Uruguay and Bolivia in exploring alternatives to a military response to the war on drugs, which has been an unmitigated failure of violence, corruption and oppression.

    (c) It is undeniable that the US dishes out extravagant amounts of military aid to Mexico with a scandalous lack of oversight as to how it is used.

    (d) This aid may have since been spent on equipment and training of the same security services that prosecutors are now accusing of the extrajudicial execution of students, many of whom are teenagers.

    (e) None of these

DIRECTIONS (Qs. 45-47): *Five sentences related to a topic are given below. Four of them can be put together to form a meaningful and coherent short paragraph. Identify the odd one out. Choose its number as your answer and key it in.*

45. (a) The poets in question have, like other poets, various faults.

    (b) But they were, at best, engaged in the task of trying to find the verbal equivalent for states of mind and feeling.

    (c) And this means both that they are more mature, and that they wear better, than later poets of certainly not less literary ability.

    (d) Poetry comes from the heart and not from random philosophical concepts.

    (e) It is not a permanent necessity that poets should be interested in philosophy, or in any other subject.

46. (a) The opening words of James Joyce's Ulysses seem initially to come from the realist world.

    (b) However, the appearances are going to be deceptive, and they become more so as we go through the novel.

    (c) Joyce, after all, was a grand master.

    (d) Its stylistic deviations become more obvious, even though they are at base founded in remarkably accurate history.

    (e) The primary modernist technique here lies in Joyce's making of allusions, which lead us to feel the presence of underlying conceptual or formal structures.

47. (a) The planet is tidally locked to its star, much as the moon is to Earth, and has one face in permanent daylight, the other in darkness.

    (b) Given the world's size and mass, researchers suspect it is rocky, like the inner planets of our solar system.

    (c) It orbits 1.4m miles from its star, far closer than Mercury, which is never less than 36m miles from the sun.

    (d) Red dwarfs are by far the most common type of star in the Milky Way but because of their low luminosity, individual red dwarfs cannot easily be observed.

    (e) Because the red dwarf is so small, and the planet is on such a close orbit, astronomers should find it fairly easy to detect and study any atmosphere the world has.

DIRECTIONS (Qs. 48-52) : *Five statements are given below, labelled a, b, c, d and e. Among these, four statements are in logical order and form a coherent paragraph/passage. From the given options, choose the option that does not fit into the theme of the passage.*

(SBI PO Main 2016)

48. (a) Dinets first observed the behaviour in 2007 when he spotted crocodiles lying in shallow water along the edge of a pond in India with small sticks or twigs positioned across their snouts.

    (b) The behaviour potentially fooled nest-building birds wading in the water for sticks into thinking the sticks were floating on the water.

    (c) The crocodiles remained still for hours and if a bird neared the stick, they would lunge.

    (d) Crocodiles are way clever than thought about generally.

    (e) To see if the stick-displaying was a form of clever predation, Dinets and his colleagues performed systematic observations of the reptiles for one year at four sites in Louisiana, including two rookery and two non-rookery sites.

49. (a) The competitive pressures in the environment have radically altered the context in which human Resource services are delivered in Indian organizations.

    (b) The HR competencies, in other words, differentiate outstanding performers from average performers in the HR function.

    (c) The traditional role of HR, based on the image of a transaction and administrative oriented HR practitioner providing services to a set of customers, is undergoing change.

    (d) With the focus moving towards integrating HR into strategic planning of the organization, another dimension is added to the picture of HR service deliver.

    (e) This change in focus calls for HR professionals taking up the emerging roles of advocate, business partner, and change agent in new organizational structures that are radically different from the past.

50. (a) Every campaign leader known how to pick up and kiss a child in the crowds, how to hug an old widow, how to chant with the pundits, and show abeyance to the Mullahs.
     (b) Did anyone hit at "quality" for infrastructure amenities, education, health and finally governance.
     (c) Politics is still a game of money, mind and manipulations.
     (d) False promise are not entirely a sin, but let these be redeemed by true, professional, and quality governance, that shows at the end of the tenure.
     (e) Many Asian countries have transformed their work culture, and up-scaled their economies.

51. (a) The emerging web services paradigm offers the promise of new efficiencies and improve integration designed to enhance collaboration between internal and external applications.
     (b) For example web services can serve as a bridge between an e-procurement application and an internal inventory system.
     (c) Although, web services are relatively nascent and adoption rates currently low, it is critical for ERP vendors to begin taking steps to prepare for their rapidly maturing initiative.
     (d) As items are purchased through e-procurement application, a web service specific to inventory reduction can be invoked to adjust inventory levels.
     (e) As soon as re-order points are hit, a Web services, the cycle time between buying and replenishment can be greatly reduced and the potential for errors virtually eliminated.

52. (a) Much of the modern use of metals happens behind closed doors of corporations, under the veil of trade secrets.
     (b) He chooses to restrict his analysis to metals and metalloids, which could face more critical constraints because many of them are relatively rare.
     (c) Even if we can find out how certain metals are used, it may not always be possible to determine the proportions they are used in.
     (d) The authors compromise was to account for the use of 80% of the material that is made available each year through extraction and recycling.
     (e) Their compromise was to account for the use of 80% of the material that is made available each year through extraction and recycling.

DIRECTIONS (Qs. 53-57) : *Five statements are given below, labelled a, b, c, d and e. Among these, four statements are in logical order and form a coherent paragraph/passage. From the given options, choose the option that does not fit into the theme of the passage.*

(IBPS PO Main 2016)

53. (a) The reference was to China, a country that has been courting Pakistan for several years through a number of means including assistance in its nuclear programme.
     (b) After the Uri attacks, Pakistan's special Kashmir envoy MushahidHussain Syed declared that the US was a waning power, suggesting that Pakistan was seeking out other allies.
     (c) The most important concern relates to the possible conflict in Pakistan between votaries of economic development and supporters of militancy.
     (d) This corridor—which includes road, rail and port infrastructure—is expected to allow China to avoid the vulnerable Indian Ocean route currently used to transport oil from the Gulf.
     (e) Of late, there has been much talk of the China-Pakistan Economic Corridor (CPEC) that stretches from the autonomous region of Xinjiang to the Gwadar port.

54. (a) India recently ratified the Paris Agreement, assuring it a seat at the 55/55 table
     (b) ratification by at least 55 countries and accounting for at least 55% of global greenhouse gas (GHG) emissions was required for the agreement to come into force
     (c) where countries will negotiate the mechanisms and provisions under the agreement.
     (d) With the ratification, India has demonstrated leadership in climate negotiations but left some with concerns about signing an agreement without realizing its full implications.
     (e) There are certain targets India wants to achieve and to achieve that there is a need to allocate mitigating burden among states and also prioritize adaptation efforts.

55. (a) Corporate Social Responsibility has entered India's legal corridors.
     (b) Given the need for proper legal help for a diverse section of society even the PM, in his address at the Bar Council's centenary celebrations earlier this year, urged lawyers to take on more pro bono cases.
     (c) Top law firms and lawyers are doing pro bono so that they can give back to society.
     (d) In India, traditionally, pro bono legal work was carried out by lawyers who had dedicated themselves to helping society.
     (e) There are a number of socially aware and generous souls who are increasingly lending their expertise for pro bono work.

56. (a) A look at the historical data on forecasts made by the IMF in its World Economic Outlook (WEO) reports seems to suggest that optimism bias may be the bigger culprit.
     (b) The large negative forecast errors in the recession years skewed the historical averages.
     (c) Over the past few years, the growth forecasts made by the International Monetary Fund (IMF) have displayed one consistent pattern
     (d) the forecasts are rosy at the start of the year, then revised downwards towards the end of the year, and the actual estimates of real growth turn out to be even lower.
     (e) Has predicting the fate of the global economy become more difficult in a volatile post-crisis world, or does the IMF suffer from an inherent optimism bias?

57. (a) India has 13 of the 20 most polluted cities in the world, according to the World Health Organization.

    (b) The government should redouble its efforts to combat climate change, which will naturally slash not just greenhouse-gas emissions but particulates as well.

    (c) Every year, more than half a million people are estimated to die prematurely because of air pollution.

    (d) While air quality tends to worsen around this time of year as millions of Indians light firecrackers to celebrate the Diwali festival, the problem isn't limited by season or geography.

    (e) This week, air pollution in New Delhi has been truly off the charts: Tiny particulates, which are especially deadly, topped 999 micrograms per cubic meter—40 times what is considered safe and beyond what the scale was designed to measure.

DIRECTIONS (Qs. 58-62) : *Five statements are given below, labelled a, b, c, d and e. Among these, four statements are in logical order and form a coherent paragraph. From the given options, choose the option that does not fit into the theme of the paragraph.*

58. (a) This can be seen in the growing importance cities are receiving in the distinct "worlds" of government, business, think tanks, academia and civil society.

    (b) After years of ambivalence, urbanization is increasingly being embraced, or at least acknowledged, in India.

    (c) Each of these "worlds" is populated by experts in specific "fields" within the urban realm such as planning, environment, transport, housing, finance and health.

    (d) sustainability is at the core of the "New Urban Agenda". A substantial portion is dedicated to various "transformative commitments for sustainable urban development"

    (e) The multiple "fields" within these parallel "worlds" typically operate as silos and do not interact with the other "fields" and "worlds".

59. (a) It is often said that the urgent and the immediate are not the same as important.

    (b) Therefore, one should not be surprised that the Indian corporate sector has kept its calls for lower interest rates and a competitive exchange rate on an auto-replay mode.

    (c) Indeed, they are in conflict with one another.

    (d) All the urgent and the immediate commentary on the decision by the newly constituted monetary policy committee (MPC) of the Reserve Bank of India (RBI) has already come out.

    (e) RBI has released the minutes of the MPC meeting too. The bulk of it has been seen earlier in the press release that followed the meeting.

60. (a) Notwithstanding the good monsoon this year after back-to-back drought years, most commentators agree that the rural economy and the agricultural sector may not be out of distress.

    (b) Recent attempts by Rahul Gandhi to mobilize farmers during his Kisan Yatra might not revive the fortunes of the Congress party in Uttar Pradesh, but they did contribute to bringing the issues of farmers and agriculture to the political mainstream.

    (c) It is also worth mentioning that most of them were seen as leaders of dominant farming communities or caste groups that benefited from rising profitability and price support.

    (d) Given that almost half of the total workers in the country are still engaged in farming and the majority of households in rural areas are still dependent on agriculture, directly or indirectly, issues confronting the farming community are naturally an important electroral plank.

    (e) More so in an environment where rural areas, and the agricultural sector in particular, have been in some distress in recent years.

61. (a) Dyn is a part of the backbone of the Internet, since it is one of the companies that provides domain name services or DNS to Internet users, and translates simple English-based commands like "livemint.com" typed into a browser into the actual numeric addresses that the Internet's computers use to identify each website.

    (b) Security firm Flashpoint has said that it believes that seemingly innocuous items such as video recorders, webcams, closed-circuit security cameras and the like were taken over by malware, and then, without their owners' knowledge, were used to help execute the massive cyber attack

    (c) This outage was astonishing in its ferocity, especially since it co-opted the much vaunted Internet of Things (IoT) into the attack.

    (d) It claims that hundreds of thousands of such devices were co-opted into the attack by being infected with malware.

    (e) This malware, called Mirai, was released by an anonymous hacker named Anna-senpai some weeks ago.

62. (a) The mathematician Richard K. Guy is arguably best known for discovering a glider. Assuming that's an intriguing-enough opening, let me explain. In 1970, the British mathematician John Conway invented a board game called, simply, "Life".

    (b) Life happens on a grid of squares that stretch in every direction (imagine an infinite chessboard). Each square, or cell, is either alive or dead (or call it black or white, filled or empty).

    (c) Now, this is not a game in the conventional sense: there's no way to "win", nor do you play against an opponent. In fact, Life doesn't even need a player as it proceeds. You just set up an initiale state and then watch what happens.

    (d) To start, you choose a certain number of cells to be live-at random, or in a pattern, whatever. Each cell now evolves according to a set of rules that considers its eight neighbours (left, right, above, below, and on the four corners).

    (e) This is the endlessly fascinating question Conway's game raises, and this is why it was and remains today a much discussed favourite among mathematicians and computer scientists.

ANSWER KEY

1	(b)	8	(d)	15	(c)	22	(c)	29	(b)	36	(d)	43	(b)	50	(e)	57	(b)
2	(c)	9	(c)	16	(d)	23	(b)	30	(c)	37	(c)	44	(b)	51	(c)	58	(d)
3	(c)	10	(d)	17	(d)	24	(c)	31	(d)	38	(b)	45	(d)	52	(b)	59	(b)
4	(b)	11	(b)	18	(c)	25	(c)	32	(c)	39	(a)	46	(c)	53	(c)	60	(c)
5	(c)	12	(a)	19	(d)	26	(c)	33	(c)	40	(b)	47	(d)	54	(e)	61	(a)
6	(c)	13	(a)	20	(a)	27	(c)	34	(c)	41	(a)	48	(d)	55	(a)	62	(e)
7	(a)	14	(c)	21	(d)	28	(b)	35	(d)	42	(c)	49	(b)	56	(e)		

Hints & Explanations

1. (b) Statement b is just out of context; hence, excluded.

2. (c) The monarchy does not find mention in the paragraph, so, excluded as an odd sentence.

3. (c) The sentence stating working for an ad agency can not be a part of the paragraph.

4. (b) Statement b just looks odd in the paragraph. Hence, should be the answer.

5. (c) Statement c does not connect with other three sentences, so, excluded.

6. (c) The statement about the paan-chewing driver greeting you with 'Good morning' does not fit into the passage.

7. (a) Sentence a seems to be out of context, hence is the odd one.

8. (d) 'd' stating CEO's leadership role seems to be unfit in the paragraph, hence, should be excluded.

9. (c) 'c' is the odd sentence which does not fit into the arranged paragraph, hence, is the answer.

10. (d) The statement denoting that Indian men do not spend as much as women on clothing seems to be out of context.

11. (b) 'The difference between prose and poetry' has no mention in other sentences; hence, b is an odd sentence.

12. (a) Sentence a does not match with the core issue of the paragraph, so, excluded.

13. (a) The statement a seems to be unfit into the paragraph; so, excluded.

14. (c) Sentence c does not match with the paragraph; hence, excluded.

15. (c) Statement c does not seem to belong to the paragraph; so, it is excluded.

16. (d) Statement d is not the part of the conversation between the chief minister and reporter.

17. (d) The statement which talks of Obama's legacy does not seem to be the part of the paragraph.

18. (c) Statement c talks of the winter season and not winter wear; hence, is the odd sentence.

19. (d) Statement d does not match with other three sentences so, it is excluded.

20. (a) Sentence a talks of the sources of carbon dioxide emissions which does not fit into the paragraph.

21. (d) Statement d seems to be odd in the paragraph.

22. (c) Sentence c talks of the demerits of the tea which is not the issue in the paragraph.

23. (b) Statement b seems to be out of context, hence, excluded.

24. (c) Statement c seems not to be so close to the paragraph, so, excluded.

25. (c) Statement c talks of Ashoka building the first temple near Bodhi tree which is out of context.

26. (c) Statement about pop singers is not relevant to the paragraph; so, excluded.

27. (c) Proposing to train investigators and prosecutors seems to be out of context.

28. (b) LPG does not find mention in the other three sentences; hence, is an odd sentence.

29. (b) Statement b talks of change in national currency which is irrelevant to the paragraph.

30. (c) Statement c talks of Bombay Stock Exchange which is not relevant to the paragraph.

31. (d) This sentence mentions writer's hobbies which is not relevant to other sentences.

32. (c) Sentence c addresses China's foreign policy while other sentences discuss the terrorism issue with India.

33. (c) Statement c about individuals speaking a language other than English at home is out of context.

34. (c) Statement c talks of demonetization while others discuss handling terrorism by making legislations.

35. (d) Statement d is about WTO whereas all three sentences talk of ASEAN.

36. (d) Statement d does not match with other three sentences which discuss FBI and international terrorism.

37. (c) Statement c talks of Article 370 which is not relevant to the paragraph.

38. (b) Statement b focuses on inflation and GDP while other sentences discuss the ease of doing business.

39. (a) Statement a warning Iran about its nuclear ambitions is not relevant to the paragraph.

40. (b) Statement b talks of the effects of poor environmental sanitation which is not relevant here.

41. (a) Options (c) and (b) should go together as the deep intertwining between modernity and nostalgia mentioned in option (c) is explained in option (b). Also, options (d) and (b) should go together as 'that hunger' mentioned in option (d) refers to the harking back of the human mind to 'a supposedly simpler time' in the past 'when life was more peaceful' in option (b). Option (a) does not fit into the sequence as it talks about the reaction of observers of the artist's work rather than how the work evokes such a reaction. So, it is the correct answer.

42. (c) Options (b), (d) and (a) make a coherent sequence. Option (b) should be the first sentence as it is about filming of videos by drones around the world. Next, option (d) is about one such video recorded on a safari in the Serengeti. Option (a) should follow option (d) as it continues the idea by giving details of what the video contains. Option (c) does not fit into this sequence as it is about waves and surfers. So, option (c) is the correct answer.

43. (b) Options (d), (c) and (a) make a coherent sequence. Sentence (d) criticizes England's trickeries and amateurishness in the final session. Sentence (c) continues this idea by giving an example and questioning the practice in English public schools. Sentence (a) should follow (c) as it mentions the consequence of the situation. Option (b) is the odd as it compares England's and Australia's spirit of cricket. So, option (b) is the correct answer.

44. (b) Options (c), (a) and (d) make a coherent sequence. Option (c) mentions that the US dishes out military aid to Mexico without bothering about how it is used. Option (a) continues the same idea. Option (d) talks about the possibility of the aid being spent on extrajudicial executions. Option (b) does not fit into this sequence as it mentions that America should look at alternatives to a military response. So, option (b) is the correct answer.

45. (d) Sentences a, b, c and e form a paragraph which is about poets. The correct sequence of sentences is abce. Sentence d does not fit in this sequence as it talks about the origin of poetry. So option (d) is the correct answer.

46. (c) Sentences a, b, d and e form a paragraph and their correct sequence is abde. Sentence a mentions name of the novel so it should be the first sentence of the sequence. Sentences b and d make a pair because the pronoun 'Its' mentioned in sentence d refers to 'the novel' in sentence b. Sentence e mentions the word 'here', so it should follows sentence d as it makes the paragraph coherent. Sentence c is an opinion about James Joyce, so, it is the odd one out.

47. (d) Sentences a, b, c and e form a paragraph and their correct sequence is abce. Sentence d is odd one out as it talks about Red dwarfs whereas the paragraph is about a particular planet.

48. (d) Option (d) does not fit into the theme of the passage as the given passage delineates the systematic observations of reptiles. It does focus on the nature of crocodiles particularly.

49. (b) Option (b) is odd one out into the theme of the passage. The passage tells about the changing role of HR in the context of radically altered environment and not about HR competencies.

50. (e) The passage depicts about the strategies followed by politicians during the election campaign. It does not pay attention upon economies.

51. (c) Option (c) does not fit into the theme of the passage.

52. (b) Option (b) is odd one out, all other options describes the modern uses of metals while option (b) is related to analysis of metals.

53. (c) This option deviates from main line of thought which is centered round China-Pak developing relationship.

54. (e) This option deviates from the Paris Agreement and India's ratification.

55. (a) Logically Corporate Social Responsibility does not fit with pro bono cases.

56. (e) This statement differs from IMF's optimism bias.

57. (b) The statement differs as the logical sequence talks about pollution in Indian cities.

58. (d) Only option (d) is not a part of the coherent paragraph as other options form an opening to an article the option (d) talks about the sustainability of "New Urban Agenda" which is not yet mentioned.

59. (b) Only option (b) is not a part of the coherent paragraph as the reason for the call made by the Indian corporate sector for lower interest rates and a competitive exchange rate on an auto-replay mode is not given and thus, is redundant in this paragraph and does not fit into the theme of the paragraph.

60. (c) Option (c) is the one that doesn't fit the theme of the paragraph properly as from the other options it can be concluded that paragraph is an introductory part of the article while option (c) is not the part of this paragraph, it can be indicated by 'most ot them' as we don't know anything about them.

61. (a) Option (a) is the one which is not a part of the coherent paragraph as we can see the other options are talking about the effects and the shock that is caused by the malware option (a) is just defining a term Dyn hence is the correct choice.

62. (e) Option (e) is correct as it does not fit into the theme of the paragraph.

Cloze Test

CLOZE TEST

Cloze tests are common on all bank exams. They usually require you to choose the correct choice out of four possibilities.

A cloze test (also cloze deletion test) is an exercise, test, or assessment consisting of a portion of text with certain words removed (cloze text), where the participant is asked to replace the missing words. Cloze tests require the ability to understand context and vocabulary in order to identify the correct words or type of words that belong in the deleted passages of a text.

Example ▶ 1 : A language teacher may give the following passage to students:

Today, I went to the _________ and bought some milk and eggs. I knew it was going to rain, but I forgot to take my _________, and ended up getting wet on the way _________.

Explanation : Students would then be required to fill in the blanks with words that would best complete the passage. Context in language and content terms is essential in most, if not all, cloze tests. The first blank is preceded by "the"; therefore, a noun, an adjective or an adverb must follow. However, a conjunction follows the blank; the sentence would not be grammatically correct if anything other than a noun were in the blank. The words "milk and eggs" are important for deciding which noun to put in the blank; "market" is a possible answer; depending on the student, however, the first blank could either be store, supermarket, shop or market while umbrella or raincoat fit the second.

Example ▶ 2 : I saw a man lay his jacket on a puddle for a woman crossing the street. I thought that was very ______.

Explanation : Given the above passage, students' answers may then vary depending on their vocabulary skills and their personal opinions. However, the placement of the blank at the end of the sentence restricts the possible words that may complete the sentence; following an adverb and finishing the sentence, the word is most likely an adjective. Romantic, chivalrous or gallant may, for example, occupy the blank, as well as foolish or cheesy.

HOW TO TACKLE A CLOZE TEST

*   Read the text through trying to understanding the general meaning.

*   Look at each missing word gap and try to imagine what the correct word should be.

*   Decide which part of speech (adjective, noun, gerund, etc.) needs to be used to fill each gap.

*   Read the text again, trying to fill a gap as you come to it by imagining what the correct answer should be.

*   Read the text another time, this time choose the correct answer from the five answers given.

*   If you are unsure of any given answer, try reading the sentence with each of the possibilities.

*   Try to eliminate the obvious false choices.

*   Always think about the overall meaning of the text (i.e., whether the text is negative, positive, etc.) to make sure that your answer choice fits the context.

*   Trust your intuition. If you feel a word is right instinctively, it probably is correct.

EXERCISE

DIRECTIONS (Qs. 1-200): *In the following passage, there are blanks, each of which has been numbered. These numbers are printed below the passage and against each, five words are suggested, one of which fits the blank appropriately. Find out the appropriate word in each case.*

Passage - 1

Studies **1** the impact of computer models to support policy-making processes in organisations have **2** that client involvement in the model-building process is often a **3** for effective model-building. One important reason is that the process of model-building is frequently more important than the resulting model. Model-building itself is largely a **4** process about the problem. Most **5** about the characteristics of an ill-structured problem are gained during the **6** process of designing a computer model, rather than after the model is finished. Another important reason is that most information in an organisation **7** in the mental models of organisation members. To support policy-making in an organisation, it is this knowledge which needs to be **8** and represented in the model. An important topic in client-oriented or **9** model building thus becomes the **10** of relevant knowledge contained in the mental models of participants.

1. (a) evaluating (b) focussing (c) projecting (d) advocating (e) directing
2. (a) devised (b) exhibited (c) convinced (d) attributed (e) indicated
3. (a) support (b) valuation (c) prerequisite (d) material (e) blueprint
4. (a) valuable (b) durable (c) tedious (d) learning (e) critical
5. (a) thinking (b) insights (c) planning (d) appreciation (e) opinion
6. (a) elongated (b) concentrated (c) iterative (d) evolving (e) consummate
7. (a) resides (b) follows (c) settles (d) lies (e) committed
8. (a) extended (b) bisected (c) subjected (d) captured (e) attributed
9. (a) revolving (b) interactive (c) dogmatic (d) accentuated (e) formative
10. (a) demarcation (b) formation (c) proliferation (d) association (e) elicitation

Passage - 2

The social **11** of the Web lifestyle and work style are enormous. A lot of people **12** that computers and the Internet will depersonalize experience, creating a world that is less warm. But these are unfounded as we know that some people were **13** afraid that the telephone would reduce face-to-face contact and will **14** society to fall apart. But the **15** actually came true. Just as the phone and e-mail have increased contact between people living in different communities and between people on the go, the PC and the Internet give us **16** way to communicate. They do not take any away. In reality, the ability to use the Internet to redefine **17** in our communities is strengthening personal and cultural **18**. The Web lifestyle is about broadening **19**, not narrowing them. Community building is going to be one of the biggest growth areas on the Web. It dramatically increases the number of communities you can bond to because of its ability to **20** groups of like-minded people independent of geography or time zones.

11. (a) groups (b) needs (c) factor (d) teaching (e) implications
12. (a) accept (b) dare (c) fear (d) propose (e) reject
13. (a) strongly (b) initially (c) always (d) never (e) possibly
14. (a) let (b) decay (c) develop (d) cause (e) destroy
15. (a) opposite (b) found (c) finding (d) different (e) negative
16. (a) cheaper (b) economical (c) another (d) second (e) many
17. (a) groups (b) ethics (c) culture (d) bonds (e) boundaries
18. (a) distances (b) connections (c) differences (d) implications (e) suggestion
19. (a) horizons (b) values (c) nations (d) means (e) status
20. (a) reduce (b) focus (c) prepare (d) connect (e) develop

Passage - 3

The study of accountancy is **21** in demand in the view of **22** of greater complexity in our business organisation. Formerly a **23** of day-to-day income and expenditure was more than **24**. A business organisation today has to **25** a clear account of the **26** it uses, the amounts that are owing to it, the amount that it owes to others, the profit or loss it has made and the **27** it employs. Without a scientific **28** of accounting no businessman can be fully **29** of his real **30** position and run his organisation.

21. (a) progressing (b) getting (c) powering (d) moving (e) growing
22. (a) demand (b) growth (c) status (d) position (e) slackness
23. (a) mixture (b) map (c) measure (d) record (e) transaction
24. (a) sufficient (b) anticipated (c) expected (d) required (e) necessary
25. (a) gather (b) observe (c) maintain (d) organize (e) assimilate

26.   (a) manpower   (b) infrastructure
    (c) money   (d) resources
    (e) capabilities
27.   (a) capital   (b) strength
    (c) authority   (d) strategies
    (e) principles
28.   (a) way   (b) plan
    (c) system   (d) goal
    (e) purpose
29.   (a) ignorant   (b) alert
    (c) prepared   (d) vigilant
    (e) aware
30.   (a) administrative   (b) financial
    (c) capacity   (d) business
    (e) hierarchical

Passage - 4

The weaker sections of the rural population are mostly from the socially and economically backward and **31** sections of the village community. Because of their **32** and financial difficulty, they are not readily **33** to change their work habits and adopt modern technology. **34** sure about the traditional methods, they are **35** to take to **36** equipment and techniques which require some time to get accustomed for **37** work. After holding a number of group meetings with rural people **38** to different vocations and spread over the entire country, we can safely say that persons in the villages are not **39** for training to improve upon their traditional and hereditary **40** of working.

31.   (a) depressed   (b) different
    (c) rich   (d) privileged
    (e) forward
32.   (a) ability   (b) dependence
    (c) illiteracy   (d) number
    (e) majority
33.   (a) discarding   (b) feeling
    (c) bending   (d) undertaking
    (e) willing
34.   (a) Making   (b) Having
    (c) Quite   (d) Being
    (e) Not
35.   (a) forced   (b) reluctant
    (c) bound   (d) prepared
    (e) curious
36.   (a) farming   (b) traditional
    (c) improved   (d) powerful
    (e) old
37.   (a) routine   (b) monotonous
    (c) excessive   (d) wasteful
    (e) effective
38.   (a) accruing   (b) helping
    (c) enabling   (d) belonging
    (e) referring
39.   (a) eager   (b) capable
    (c) indifferent   (d) antagonistic
    (e) unwilling
40.   (a) theories   (b) techniques
    (c) desires   (d) hours
    (e) policies

Passage - 5

In the past, it was thought learning knowledge took place in school and for some also in further education. Then, it was a matter of **41** practical skills at work at the beginning of a career, and with a bit of luck, that **42** it. Now, things have changed. Global competition is **43** the shelf life of products and the knowledge and skills that **44** behind them. The pace of change can be **45**. Knowledge that was at the leading edge one minute can become **46** the next. Therefore, it is **47** rather than knowledge that is the key. Successful organizations have to learn, adapt and change continuously as do the **48** within them. This is **49** in the rapid growth of knowledge workers. It is **50** all levels of organizations.

41.   (a) fostering   (b) projecting
    (c) acquiring   (d) manipulating
    (e) culminating
42.   (a) for   (b) was
    (c) from   (d) with
    (e) may
43.   (a) replacing   (b) retailing
    (c) rotating   (d) re- regulating
    (e) reducing
44.   (a) lie   (b) profess
    (c) exhibit   (d) manifest
    (e) express
45.   (a) analytical   (b) absorbing
    (c) interesting   (d) frightening
    (e) valuable
46.   (a) critical   (b) obsolete
    (c) modern   (d) devastating
    (e) lamentable
47.   (a) durability   (b) reactivity
    (c) activity   (d) Proactivity
    (e) capacity
48.   (a) systems   (b) managements
    (c) processes   (d) individuals
    (e) units
49.   (a) echoed   (b) supported
    (c) adjusted   (d) provided
    (e) developed
50.   (a) directing   (b) providing
    (c) affecting   (d) questioning
    (e) projecting

Passage - 6

The tea plant, a native of Southern China, was known **51** very early times in Chinese botany and medicine. It is **52** in the classics **53** the various names of Tou, Tseh, Chung, Kha and Ming and was **54** praised for possessing the virtues of **55** fatigue, delighting the soul, strengthening the will and repairing the eyesight. It was not only administered as an internal dose, but often **56** externally in the form of paste to **57** rheumatic pains. The Taoists claimed it **58** an important **59** of the elixir of immortality. The Buddhists used it extensively to prevent drowsiness during **60** long hours of meditation.

51.   (a) to   (b) after
    (c) from   (d) beyond
    (e) behind

52. (a) taken   (b) resorted
    (c) awarded   (d) alluded
    (e) introduced
53. (a) under   (b) between
    (c) among   (d) besides
    (e) like
54. (a) rarely   (b) loosely
    (c) under   (d) severely
    (e) highly
55. (a) absorbing   (b) relieving
    (c) avoiding   (d) resolving
    (e) recognising
56. (a) inserted   (b) developed
    (c) conceived   (d) controlled
    (e) applied
57. (a) recuperate   (b) alleviate
    (c) conceal   (d) indicate
    (e) slow
58. (a) to   (b) also
    (c) although   (d) as
    (e) hardly
59. (a) ingredient   (b) aspect
    (c) offshoot   (d) outcome
    (e) discovery
60. (a) that   (b) these
    (c) their   (d) our
    (e) remote

Passage - 7

Man has always considered himself to be the ruler of his planet. This **61** and the attendant superiority feeling has made him look down **62** other creatures who co-exist with human on this earth. The so-called civilized human race has **63** and ill-treated small and large animal species and birds in an attempt to prove his **64**. It is common knowledge that **65** number of animals have been **66** for centuries under the **67** of conducting scientific experiments or for sports. Till recently, in the **68** of scientific experiments, monkeys and frogs have been **69** to dissection and **70** in the laboratory.

61. (a) pleasure   (b) fact
    (c) achievement   (d) force
    (e) arrogance
62. (a) in   (b) upon
    (c) with   (d) for
    (e) into
63. (a) criticised   (b) devalued
    (c) protected   (d) abused
    (e) enlarged
64. (a) supremacy   (b) wisdom
    (c) cleverness   (d) instinct
    (e) possession
65. (a) tall   (b) plenty
    (c) countless   (d) diverse
    (e) numerous
66. (a) tortured   (b) exposed
    (c) treated   (d) vanished
    (e) extinct
67. (a) projection   (b) criticism
    (c) pretext   (d) game
    (e) study

68. (a) matter   (b) set
    (c) scheme   (d) virtue
    (e) name
69. (a) confined   (b) subjected
    (c) condemned   (d) allied
    (e) performed
70. (a) cruelty   (b) deformation
    (c) study   (d) vivisection
    (e) proliferation

Passage - 8

In **71** of constitutional guarantees relating to equality of opportunity and various other guarantees of equality before the law, the social and economic **72** of women, especially of poor women in India, is well-known. We are referring mainly to the poor rural women who have little or no assets and who **73** the bulk of the female population in rural areas. It is not as if only poor rural women get less wages or suffer from social **74** because they belong to a particular community. Even at higher levels of the socio-economic hierarchy among the well-to-do groups, women are not **75** to men. Among the economically **76** sections of society, women's proper place is **77** to be the home. In rural areas, women of **78** status families normally do not go out to work. In the **79** value system, there is a gradation of economic activities, which is **80** in the socio-economic status of the family.

71. (a) support   (b) spite
    (c) contrast   (d) wake
    (e) view
72. (a) condition   (b) prosperity
    (c) progress   (d) deprivation
    (e) value
73. (a) constitute   (b) deploy
    (c) measure   (d) define
    (e) exploit
74. (a) status   (b) service
    (c) indifference   (d) ignorance
    (e) discrimination
75. (a) dedicated   (b) accountable
    (c) equal   (d) responsible
    (e) antagonistic
76. (a) marginal   (b) significant
    (c) well-off   (d) affordable
    (e) dependable
77. (a) entitled   (b) decided
    (c) indicated   (d) debated
    (e) considered
78. (a) economic   (b) appropriate
    (c) ample   (d) higher
    (e) social
79. (a) unequal   (b) prevailing
    (c) appropriate   (d) commendable
    (e) deplorable
80. (a) reflected   (b) exempted
    (c) barred   (d) considered
    (e) neglected

Passage - 9

The urgent need of the hour is to **81** up the moral **82** of our society in general and of our student community in particular, if we want to save ourselves and our society from the present **83** of mass indiscipline and **84** of basic human values, which has become a **85** phenomenon. We must, therefore, **86** and practise the most **87** basic human values like cooperation, tolerance, patriotism, generosity, truth, justice and excellence — the ideals which are universal in nature and which are **88** in themselves and which are worthy of **89** for their own sake. These ideals are both personally as well as socially **90.**

81. (a) give   (b) stand
    (c) jack   (d) climb
    (e) tone
82. (a) fibre   (b) enactment
    (c) reconstruction   (d) situation
    (e) appreciation
83. (a) polarisation   (b) degradation
    (c) chaos   (d) provocation
    (e) sentiments
84. (a) calamity   (b) focus
    (c) realisation   (d) erosion
    (e) criticism
85. (a) durable   (b) universal
    (c) perpetual   (d) segmental
    (e) prolific
86. (a) incorporate   (b) induce
    (c) implicate   (d) inculcate
    (e) involve
87. (a) absorbing   (b) cherished
    (c) introspective   (d) famous
    (e) productive
88. (a) distinctive   (b) appreciated
    (c) formative   (d) helping
    (e) end
89. (a) evolving   (b) spreading
    (c) esteem   (d) wisdom
    (e) popularity
90. (a) desirable   (b) manageable
    (c) redundant   (d) valnerable
    (e) possible

Passage - 10

In the decade since reforms were introduced, India has achieved substantial success in the sphere of macroeconomics. Overall growth rate has been **91** except for the last couple of years. It bears pointing out that we have now come to view a 6 per cent **92** rate as a slowdown! This is a far cry from pre-reforms rate of growth of 3 per cent. The price level has by and large remained **93** both as measured by the WPI and CPI. India's **94** of payments position has been comfortable, Exports, while **95** some sluggishness this fiscal, have been growing. Imports, in spite of **96** liberalisation, have not gone out of hand. The is amply reflected in the comfortable current account deficits (CAD); the CAD-to-GDP ratio has remained way below the crisis **97** that it had achieved in 1991. The rupee has weathered external turbulence rather well even when East Asia was experiencing **98** difficulties.

However, the one unambiguous Achilles' heel of the reforms has been the **99** state of government finances. One of the two crises that India faced in 1990-91 was the unsustainable imbalance between government revenues and **100.**

91. (a) pulsating   (b) shocked
    (c) commendable   (d promotable
    (e) dipped
92. (a) production   (b) consumption
    (c) index   (d) growth
    (e) progress
93. (a) moderate   (b) lukewarm
    (c) shaky   (d) considerate
    (e) obstinate
94. (a) ledger   (b) balance
    (c) equilibrium   (d intention
    (e) idea
95. (a) demonstrated   (b) exercising
    (c) rejecting   (d) display
    (e) exhibiting
96. (a) substantial   (b) exemplary
    (c) indicative   (d) conservative
    (e) destructive
97. (a) rationalisation   (b) handling
    (c) management   (d) proportions
    (e) ration
98. (a) crisis   (b) overcoming
    (c) severe   (d) enjoyable
    (e) wailing
99. (a) critical   (b) vulnerable
    (c) prone   (d) attackable
    (e) easygoing
100. (a) surplus   (b) measurement
     (c) thinking   (d) incomes
     (e) expenditure

Passage - 11

Economic backwardness of a region is **101** by the co-existence of unutilized or underutilized **102** on the one hand, and **103** natural resources on the other. Economic development essentially means a process of **104** change whereby the real per capita income of an economy **105** over a period of time. Then, a simple but meaningful question arises: what causes economic development? Or what makes a country developed? This question has absorbed the **106** of scholars of socio-economic change for decades. Going through the **107** history of developed countries like America, Russia and Japan, man is essentially found as **108** in the process of economic development. Japan, whose economy was **109** damaged from the ravages of the Second World War, is the clearest example of our time to **110** its kingpin role in economic development.

101. (a) developed   (b) cured
     (c) improved   (d) enhanced
     (e) characterised
102. (a) sources   (b) finances
     (c) funds   (d) manpower
     (e) industries
103. (a) exhaustive   (b) unexploited
     (c) abundant   (d) indefinite
     (e) unreliable

104. (a) upward   (b) drastic
     (c) negligible   (d) incredible
     (e) sudden
105. (a) diminishes   (b) degenerates
     (c) increases   (d) succumbs
     (e) stabilizes
106. (a) plans   (b) attempts
     (c) attention   (d) resources
     (e) strategy
107. (a) existing   (b) glorious
     (c) ancient   (d) economic
     (e) discouraging
108. (a) pivotal   (b) neutral
     (c) insignificant   (d) enchanted
     (e) vicious
109. (a) increasingly   (b) always
     (c) gradually   (d) deliberately
     (e) badly
110. (a) enlighten   (b) validate
     (c) negate   (d) underestimate
     (e) belittle

Passage - 12

The latest stage of the continuing **111** between India and the United States on the nuclear issue is now punctuated with pleasing diplomatic observations. Our latest round of talks with the American Deputy Secretary of State is "positive and encouraging". The US Deputy Secretary of State remarked that "none of us are pleased to have any clouds over the **112"**. We in India know that these clouds have **113** towards the subcontinent from the West. The US can easily disperse the clouds if it wants. But the economic sanctions are still in place. The US is only **114** trying to come to terms with the fact that the nuclear weapons are not the **115** of the Permanent Members of the Security Council. If they do not recognize India as a nuclear power, then what is it that they are **116** to? India will not **117** by their de-recognising the nuclear tests. Both sides can happily close **118** eyes and agree to **119** what has happened. The fact that India is a sovereign nation, entitled to take decisions beneficial for its own security, has not been altered by the tests. The US has come round to **120** that India has some say in this matter.

111. (a) adversaries   (b) negotiations
     (c) strifes   (d) strategies
     (e) disputes
112. (a) relationship   (b) struggle
     (c) matter   (d) talks
     (e) countries
113. (a) formed   (b) eclipsed
     (c) reined   (d) covered
     (e) floated
114. (a) spontaneously   (b) generously
     (c) grudgingly   (d) gracefully
     (e) willingly
115. (a) threats   (b) creations
     (c) properties   (d) monopoly
     (e) possessions

116. (a) prepared   (b) objecting
     (c) pointing   (d) clinging
     (e) planning
117. (a) gain   (b) differ
     (c) flourish   (d) suffer
     (e) develop
118. (a) their   (b) our
     (c) naked   (d) inward
     (e) both
119. (a) imitate   (b) undo
     (c) cherish   (d) reiterate
     (e) ignore
120. (a) expecting   (b) suspecting
     (c) accepting   (d) advocating
     (e) rejecting

Passage - 13

Bret Bonson loved animals **121** on a family owned Zoo. He had grown up caring for antelope, deer and wildcats. He was **122** at times stubbornly protective. Once, when a tiger cub was born with a deformed leg, the local veterinarian and Bret's parents **123** the animal would never live a full life. Even so, the boy bottle-fed the cub and cared for it. **124** Bret's mothering, the cub died, but Bret's mothering **125** lived on.

He worked at a Safari park where, in 1980, he trained his first African elephant and found his true **126**. From the beginning Bonson was **127** by elephants. They have the **128** force to uproot trees and can outrun the fastest human sprinter. But they also have **129** fine motor skills. The same trunk that could **130** the front end of an automobile or fracture.

121. (a) created   (b) constructed
     (c) built   (d) erected
     (e) raised
122. (a) methodically   (b) carefully
     (c) fiercely   (d) suitably
     (e) actually
123. (a) believed   (b) valued
     (c) expressed   (d) imagined
     (e) exhibited
124. (a) Until   (b) Unless
     (c) Instead   (d) Despite
     (e) Although
125. (a) belief   (b) instinct
     (c) love   (d) passion
     (e) care
126. (a) companion   (b) attitude
     (c) calling   (d) friend
     (e) abode
127. (a) absorbed   (b) alarmed
     (c) attacked   (d) attached
     (e) awed
128. (a) empowered   (b) brute
     (c) tall   (d) high
     (e) exhibited
129. (a) domestic   (b) durable
     (c) devastating   (d) delicately
     (e) dubious

130. (a) hoist   (b) puncture
    (c) disturb   (d) attack
    (e) deflate

Passage - 14

Gandhiji once said, "I would say that if the village perishes, India will perish too. India will be **131** more India. Her own mission in the world will get **132**. The **133** of the village is possible only when it is no more **134**. Industrialisation on a mass scale will **135** lead to passive or active exploitation of the villagers as the problem **136** competition and marketing come in. Therefore, we have to **137** on the village being self-contained, manufacturing mainly, for use. Provided this character of the village industry is **138** there would be no objection to villagers using even the modern machines and tools that they can make and **139** to use. Only, they **140** not be used as a means of exploitation of others."

131. (a) certainly   (b) scarcely
    (c) much   (d) no
    (e) any
132. (a) lost   (b) extension
    (c) elevated   (d) flourished
    (e) jeopardy
133. (a) rehabilitation   (b) pruning
    (c) revival   (d) devastation
    (e) atonement
134. (a) denuded   (b) exploited
    (c) contaminated   (d) populated
    (e) ruined
135. (a) passionately   (b) surprisingly
    (c) scarcely   (d) never
    (e) necessarily
136. (a) forming   (b) enhancing
    (c) between   (d) of
    (e) with
137. (a) concentrate   (b) ponder
    (c) imagine   (d) ensure
    (e) decide
138. (a) regained   (b) neglected
    (c) maintained   (d) thwarted
    (e) abolished
139. (a) prepare   (b) afford
    (c) hesitate   (d) propose
    (e) plan
140. (a) can   (b) could
    (c) need   (d) would
    (e) should

DIRECTIONS (Qs. 141-150) : *In the following passage there are blanks, each of which has been numbered. These numbers are printed below the passage and against each, five words are suggested, one of which fits the blank appropriately. Find out the appropriate word in each case.*

(IBPS PO/MT 2013)

Traditional bank architecture is based on bank branches. These branches ensure the physical **(141)** of a customer's savings. A customer may go there to deposit and withdraw money, **(142)** loans and **(143)** in other financial transactions. In the past two decades banking architecture has changed the Automated Teller Machine (ATM) has been a big **(144)** and credit and debit cards have created new financial spaces. **(145)** the bank branch has remained the bedrock of the banking system after all a person needs a bank account in a branch before he can operate a debit or ATM card. This may be about to change as technocrats now **(146)** cell phones as the new architecture of virtual banks. This has the potential to make branches **(147)**. Cell phone banking looks especially relevant for India, since it can penetrate the countryside cheaply and **(148)**. The world over cell phones are spreaing at a **(149)** rate and in India alone new cell phone connection are growing at the rate of six million a month a rate of customer **(150)** that no bank can dream of.

141. (a) Knowledge   (b) security
    (c) presence   (d) confidentiality
    (e) guarantee
142. (a) negotiate   (b) advance
    (c) credit   (d) disburse
    (e) sanction
143. (a) pursue   (b) interact
    (c) operate   (d) enable
    (e) engage
144. (a) drawback   (b) hurdle
    (c) consequence   (d) luxury
    (e) innovation
145. (a) Despite   (b) Although
    (c) Even   (d) Yet
    (e) Until
146. (a) View   (b) realize
    (c) Display   (d) engineer
    (e) assess
147. (a) essential   (b) obsolete
    (c) extant   (d) retreat
    (e) expired
148. (a) moderately   (b) occasionally
    (c) compulsorily   (d) indiscriminately
    (e) effectively
149. (a) phenomenal   (b) gradual
    (c) proportionate   (d) competitive
    (e) projected
150. (a) discount   (b) base
    (c) expansion   (d) satisfaction
    (e) relationship

DIRECTIONS (Qs. 151-160) : *In the following passage there are blanks, each of which has been numbered. These numbers are printed below the passage and against each, five words are suggested, one of which fits the blank appropriately. Find out the appropriate word in each case.*

(SBI PO 2014)

Women **(151)** up half the world's population and yet represent a staggering 70% of the world's poor. We live in a world in which women living in poverty face gross **(152)** and injustice from birth to death. From poor education to poor nutrition to **(153)** and low pay employment, the sequence of discrimination that a woman may suffer during her entire life is unacceptable but all too common. Millennium Development Goal 3 is to promote gender equality and empower women. This MDG is critical for **(154)** poverty and improving prospects for women. But how can women break gender based stereotypes to minimise discrimination and **(155)** gender based violence when they are trapped in societies with socio-cultural practices which routinely discriminate them from having equal opportunities in education, health and livelihood? These women are invisible and the **(156)** in their way prevent them from accessing the most basic human rights and needs. The outlook is bleak.

Women make up 70% of the world's working hours and **(157)** only 10% of the world's income and half of what men earn. This leads to greater poverty, slower economic growth and a **(158)** standard of living. In developing countries, millions of women also die each year as a result of gender-based **(159)**. This deep-rooted gender discrimination creates a bleak outlook for women in developing countries. For millions of girls living in poverty, it is often those closest to them who work against the child's interests and their immediate environment is often **(160)** and sometimes, down-right harmful. Parents arrange marriages when you are a child. Neighbours say, if you are a girl, you must limit your activities to your home. Friends say, it is OK not to go to school.

151. (a) made   (b) make
    (c) look   (d) has made
    (e) complete
152. (a) equality   (b) affection
    (c) inequality   (d) support
    (e) justice
153. (a) vulnerable   (b) weakness
    (c) vulnerability   (d) specific
    (e) weakest
154. (a) tackle   (b) tackling
    (c) fight   (d) tackled
    (e) fought
155. (a) increase   (b) support
    (c) weak   (d) reduce
    (e) influencing
156. (a) obstacles   (b) make
    (c) pleasantries   (d) pebbles
    (e) encouragements
157. (a) earns   (b) carried
    (c) spend   (d) earn
    (e) spends
158. (a) slow   (b) slower
    (c) low   (d) lowest
    (e) lower
159. (a) violence   (b) violent
    (c) virulent   (d) corruption
    (e) violation
160. (a) functional   (b) natural
    (c) artificial   (d) dysfunctional
    (e) disfunctional

DIRECTIONS (Qs. 161-170) : *In the following passage there are blanks, each of which has been numbered. These numbers are printed below the passage and against each five words are suggested, one of which fit the blank appropriately. Find out the appropriate word in each case.*

(IBPS PO/MT Prelim 2015)

Economic backwardness of a region is **(161)** by the coexistence of unutilized **(162)** on the one hand and **(163)** natural resources on the other. Economic development essentially means a process

of **(164)** change whereby the real per capita income of an economy **(165)** over a period of time. Then a simple but meaningful question arises; what causes economic development? Or what makes a country developed? This question has absorbed the **(166)** of scholars of socio-economic changes for decades. Going through the **(167)** history of developed countries like America, Russia and Japan, man is essentially found as **(168)** in the process of economic development. Japan, whose economy was **(169)** damaged from the ravages of the 2nd world War, is the example of our time to **(170)** kingdom role in economic development.

161. (a) Developed   (b) Cured
    (c) Improved   (d) Enhanced
    (e) Characterized
162. (a) Source   (b) Finance
    (c) Funds   (d) Manpower
    (e) Industries
163. (a) Exhaustive   (b) Unexploited
    (c) Abundant   (d) Indefinite
    (e) Unreliable
164. (a) Upward   (b) Drastic
    (c) Negligible   (d) Incredible
    (e) Sudden
165. (a) Diminishes   (b) Degenerates
    (c) Increases   (d) Succumbs
    (e) Stabilizes
166. (a) Plans   (b) Attempts
    (c) Attention   (d) Resources
    (e) Strategy
167. (a) Existing   (b) Glorious
    (c) Ancient   (d) Economic
    (e) Discouraging
168. (a) Pivotal   (b) Neutral
    (c) Insignificant   (d) Enchanted
    (e) Vicious
169. (a) Increasingly   (b) Always
    (c) Gradually   (d) Deliberately
    (e) Badly
170. (a) Enlighten   (b) Validate
    (c) Negate   (d) Underestimate
    (e) Belittle

DIRECTIONS (Qs. 171-175): *Fill in the blank with most appropriate words from the given options.*

(IBPS PO/MT Main 2015)

Tibet **(171)** up images of a mystic land. Snow-capped mountain peaks pierce the blue sky and fierce chilly winds sweep the rolling grasslands. Maroon-robed Buddhist monks pray in remote monasteries and **(172)** horsemen pound the rugged earth. People in this high plateau perform punishing rituals like prostrating hundreds of miles in tattered clothes on pilgrimage. Spirits, spells and flying apparitions are part of the Tibetan world. In short, Tibet remains an exotica. Such images are largely the result of books by Western travellers and explorers in the last century, which helped in keeping the mystique alive. And when the Communist rulers took over Tibet in the 1950s and began **(173)** Chinese language and culture on the people, Tibet's own history started to **(174)** in the background. Thus, the only books available in English to Tsering Wangmo Dhompa as a young girl growing up in India and Nepal as a refugee **(175)** those written by Westerners, and so she came to view the country as a forbidden land, a place where fantasy and fable collaborated against a dramatic backdrop of mountains, black magic and people with strange customs and appearances.

171. (a) makes   (b) conjures
     (c) puts   (d) toil
     (e) appoints

172. (a) sturdy   (b) wobbly
     (c) handsome   (d) herculean
     (e) beautiful

173. (a) implementing   (b) evading
     (c) imposing   (d) experimenting
     (e) all of these

174. (a) amplify   (b) Stretch
     (c) die   (d) recede
     (e) increase

175. (a) are   (b) have been
     (c) was   (d) were
     (e) are

DIRECTIONS (Qs. 176–180): *Fill in the blanks with appropriate word:-*

(SBI PO Prelim 2015)

Let children learn to judge their own work. A child **(176)** to talk does not learn **(177)** being corrected all the time **(178)** corrected too much, he will **(179)** talking. He notices a thousand times a day the difference between the **(180)** he uses and the language those around him use.

176. (a) endeavouring   (b) learning
     (c) experimenting   (d) experiencing
     (e) preparing

177. (a) In   (b) on
     (c) By   (d) to
     (e) From

178. (a) unless   (b) being
     (c) until   (d) if
     (e) so

179. (a) stop   (b) halt
     (c) avoid   (d) shun
     (e) giveup

180. (a) speech   (b) language
     (c) talk   (d) skill
     (e) virtue

DIRECTIONS (Qs. 181-190): *In the following passage there are blanks, each of which has been numbered. These numbers are printed below the passage and against each, four words are suggested, one of which fits the blank appropriately. Find out the appropriate word in each case.*

(SBI PO Main 2015)

Delinking of jobs **(181)** degrees is one of the salient **(182)** of our education **(183)**. There has been a steep **(184)** in **(185)** in the academic field in recent years. There is a **(186)** of degree holders in the country. As a result, university degrees have lost their value and charm while the number of students in colleges and universities of the country has been steadily **(187)**. Consequently, thousands of graduates and postgradutes come out of these institutions and stand in **(188)** waiting to get some **(189)** jobs **(190)** in the country.

181. (a) to   (b) with
     (c) from   (d) by
     (e) None of these

182. (a) factors   (b) features
     (c) reasons   (d) methods
     (e) None of these

183. (a) process   (b) system
     (c) procedures   (d) policy
     (e) None of these

184. (a) fall   (b) rise
     (c) down   (d) decrease
     (e) None of these

185. (a) evaluation   (b) assessment
     (c) result   (d) competence
     (e) None of these

186. (a) flood   (b) growth
     (c) increase   (d) slope
     (e) None of these

187. (a) falling   (b) diminishing
     (c) rising   (d) growing
     (e) None of these

188. (a) lines   (b) long
     (c) rows   (d) queues
     (e) None of these

189. (a) managerial   (b) nice
     (c) prestigious   (d) available
     (e) None of these

190. (a) vacate   (b) posted
     (c) created   (d) available
     (e) None of these

DIRECTIONS (Qs. 191-195) : *In the following passage there are blanks, each of which has been numbered. These numbers are printed below the passage and against each five words/ phrases are suggested, one of which fits the blank appropriately. Find out the appropriate word/phrase in each case.*

(SBI PO Prelim 2016)

Twenty years from now, nearly 60% of the world's population will live in urban areas. The impact of urbanization might not all be positive on India as urban expansion is happening at a much faster rate than infrastructure expansion.

Sustainability issues need to be **(191)** so that eco nomic development is not at the **(192)** of public health. Some urban services that ought to be in **(193)** in a city like water, electricity, transport etc. need special consideration.

TERI has put together a detailed report that **(194)** sustainability in the provision of basic urban services in Indian cities.

Inadequate public transport is a major reason for the proliferation of private vehicles on the road. Respiratory illness in children living in urban areas is on the rise with more cases of Asthma being **(195)** because of pollution. The future of cities of Indian dreams depends on whether we can build better cities today.

191. (a) Speculated   (b) Believed
     (c) Imagined   (d) Considered
     (e) Understand

192. (a) Payment   (b) Rate
   (c) Costs   (d) Charge
   (e) Expense
193. (a) Abundance   (b) Large
   (c) Functional   (d) Vicinity
   (e) Location
194. (a) Bring   (b) Emphasizes
   (c) Speculates   (d) Postulates
   (e) Requests
195. (a) Produced   (b) Develop
   (c) Composed   (d) Resulted
   (e) Reported

(DIRECTIONS (Qs. 196-200): *In the following passage, you have a brief passage. In the following passage, some of the words have been left out. First read the passage over and try to understand what it is about. Then fill in the blanks with the help of the alternatives given.*

(SBI PO Prelim 2016)

Big ideas come from tackling **(196)** problems. When one is confronted with an overwhelming task, it's pieces. Business jargon is full of phrases about that, like "pilot projects" and "low-hanging fruit." They have their place, but in the repertory of management **(197)**, they should share their place with bold approaches to big challenges. Much of today's most valuable management knowledge came from wrestling with such issues. The most complicated workplace in the middle of the last century was the automobile assembly plant. Drawn to its complexity where Peter F. Drucker, W. Edwards Deming, and Taiichi Ohno, among others. The work they and their disciples did, applied in industry after industry, is the basis of the best that we know about operations, managing people, innovation, organizational design, and much more.

The most complex workplaces are tertiary care hospitals. These vast **(198)** employ tens of thousands of people who, under one roof, do everything from neurosurgery to laundry. Each patient – that is to say, each "job" — calls on a different set of people with a different constellation of **(199)**; even when the two patients have the same diagnosis, success may be **(200)** differently.

196. (a) small   (b) big
   (c) irrelevant   (d) buildings
   (e) minor
197. (a) weakness   (b) strength
   (c) power   (d) practice
   (e) symptom
198. (a) houses   (b) institute
   (c) demagogue   (d) forts
   (e) enterprises
199. (a) barbarity   (b) talent
   (c) skills   (d) unskilled
   (e) barbaric
200. (a) managed   (b) officious
   (c) delivered   (d) measured
   (e) postponed

DIRECTIONS (201-215): *In the following passage, there are blanks, each of which has been numbered. These numbers are printed below the passage and against each, five words are suggested, one of which fits the blank appropriately. Find out the appropriate word in each case.*

Agriculture has always been celebrated as the primary sector in India. Thanks to the Green Revolution, India is now _(201)_ **(self-addressed for)** production. Indian agriculture has been _(202)_ **(growing and using technologically)** as well. Does that mean everything is looking bright for Indian agriculture? A superficial analysis of the above points would tempt one to say yes, but the _(203)_ **(the study is different)**. The reality is that Indian farmers have to face extreme poverty and financial crisis, which is _(204)_ **(understanding them for)** suicides. What are the grave adversities that drive the farmers to commit suicide? At a time when the Indian economy is _(205)_ **(up for performing)** to take on the world?

Indian agriculture is _(206)_ **(dominantly about the)** nature. Irrigation facilities that are currently available, do not cover the entire cultivable land. If the farmers are at the _(207)_ **(leniency of land)** for timely water for their crops, they are at the mercy of the government for _(208)_ **(alternating irrigation facility)**. Any failure of nature directly affects the _(209)_ **(destination of farmers)**. Secondly, Indian agriculture is largely an unorganized sector, there is no _(210)_ **(unorganized planning)**, farmers work on lands of uneconomical sizes, institutional finances are not available and minimum purchase prices of the government do not, in reality, reach the poorest farmer. Added to this, the cost of agricultural inputs have been steadily rising over the years, farmers margins of profits have been _(211)_ **(causing the irrigation)** rise in inputs is not complemented by an increase in the purchase price of the agricultural produce. Even today, in several parts of the country agriculture, is a seasonal occupation. In many districts, farmers get only one crop per year and for the remaining part of the year, they find it _(212)_ **(feasible to increase livelihood)**. The farmers normally resort to borrowing from money lenders, in the absence of institutionalized finance. Where institutional finance is available, the ordinary farmer does not have a chance of availing it because of the procedures involved in disbursing the finance. This calls for removing the elaborate formalities for obtaining the loans. The institutional finance, where available is mostly availed by the medium or large land owners, the small farmers do not even have the awareness of the existence of such facilities. The money lender is the only source of finance to the farmers. Should the crops fail, the farmers fall into a debt trap and crop failures piled up over the years give them no other option than ending their lives. Another disturbing trend has been observed where farmers commit suicide or deliberately kill a family member in order to avail relief and benefits announced by the government to support the families of those who have committed suicide so that their families could at least benefit from the Government's relief programs. What then needs to be done to prevent this sad state of affairs? There cannot be one single solution to end the woes of farmers. Temporary measures _(213)_ **(through donation)** would not be the solution. The governmental efforts should be _(214)_ **(mentioning the measures)** of the small farmers wherein the relief is not given on a drought to drought basis, rather they are taught to overcome their difficulties through their own skills and capabilities. Social responsibility also goes a long way to help the farmers. The general public, NGOs, Corporates and other organizations too can play a part in helping farmers by _(215)_ **(rectifying their fields)** and families and helping them to rehabilitate.

201. (a) perfect about   (b) rely to food
   (c) self-sufficient in food   (d) dependent to food
   (e) no change
202. (a) longing to greenery
   (b) making technological advancement
   (c) creating marginal
   (d) producing grains
   (e) no change
203. (a) reality suggests the same
   (b) demand is same

(c) reality is bright
(d) truth is far from it
(e) no change

204. (a) driving them to (b) bringing them for
(c) drived them to (d) attracting them in
(e) no change

205. (a) thought of alleviate up
(b) imagined for elevation
(c) supposed to be gearing up
(d) gradually steeping up at
(e) no change

206. (a) dominating over the
(b) making up to
(c) looking at
(d) predominantly dependent on
(e) no change

207. (a) profit of crops (b) mercy of monsoons
(c) help of landlords (d) need of having facilities
(e) no change

208. (a) alternative irrigation facilities
(b) alteration in the facility
(c) irrigation facility alteration
(d) facility to alter
(e) no change

209. (a) right of the farmers (b) fortunes of the farmers
(c) decision of the farmers (d) nature of the farmers
(e) no change

210. (a) intellectual cultivation
(b) thoughful cultivation

(c) true approach
(d) systematic planning in cultivation
(e) no change

211. (a) curtailing as the availability
(b) broadening because the approach
(c) narrowing because the price
(d) resulting in the occupation
(e) no change

212. (a) far more easier to love a luxury life
(b) difficult to make both ends meet
(c) annoying to control occupation
(d) convenient to increase output
(e) no change

213. (a) through monetary relief
(b) through retreating monsoons
(c) through deliberate meditation
(d) through NGOs, irrigation
(e) no change

214. (a) ignoring the need
(b) targeted at improving the entire structure
(c) depending upon the need of
(d) detecting the crisis engraved
(e) no change

215. (a) raising the marginal cost of the inputs
(b) giving them fertilizers at high cost
(c) motivating NGOs
(d) adopting drought affected villages
(e) no change

ANSWER KEY

No.	Ans	No.	Ans	No.	Ans	No.	Ans	No.	Ans	No.	Ans	No.	Ans	No.	Ans	No.	Ans	No.	Ans
1	(a)	23	(d)	45	(d)	67	(c)	89	(c)	111	(b)	133	(a)	155	(d)	177	(c)	199	(c)
2	(e)	24	(a)	46	(b)	68	(e)	90	(a)	112	(a)	134	(c)	156	(a)	178	(d)	200	(d)
3	(c)	25	(c)	47	(d)	69	(b)	91	(c)	113	(e)	135	(b)	157	(d)	179	(a)	201	(c)
4	(d)	26	(c)	48	(d)	70	(d)	92	(d)	114	(c)	136	(e)	158	(e)	180	(b)	202	(b)
5	(b)	27	(a)	49	(a)	71	(b)	93	(a)	115	(d)	137	(d)	159	(a)	181	(c)	203	(d)
6	(c)	28	(c)	50	(c)	72	(a)	94	(b)	116	(c)	138	(a)	160	(d)	182	(b)	204	(a)
7	(d)	29	(e)	51	(c)	73	(a)	95	(e)	117	(d)	139	(c)	161	(e)	183	(b)	205	(c)
8	(d)	30	(b)	52	(e)	74	(e)	96	(a)	118	(a)	140	(b)	162	(d)	184	(a)	206	(d)
9	(b)	31	(a)	53	(a)	75	(c)	97	(d)	119	(e)	141	(e)	163	(b)	185	(d)	207	(b)
10	(e)	32	(c)	54	(e)	76	(c)	98	(c)	120	(c)	142	(b)	164	(b)	186	(a)	208	(a)
11	(e)	33	(e)	55	(b)	77	(e)	99	(b)	121	(e)	143	(d)	165	(c)	187	(c)	209	(b)
12	(c)	34	(d)	56	(e)	78	(d)	100	(e)	122	(e)	144	(c)	166	(c)	188	(d)	210	(d)
13	(b)	35	(b)	57	(b)	79	(b)	101	(e)	123	(a)	145	(d)	167	(d)	189	(c)	211	(c)
14	(d)	36	(c)	58	(d)	80	(a)	102	(d)	124	(d)	146	(a)	168	(a)	190	(d)	212	(b)
15	(a)	37	(e)	59	(a)	81	(e)	103	(b)	125	(d)	147	(b)	169	(e)	191	(d)	213	(a)
16	(c)	38	(d)	60	(c)	82	(a)	104	(b)	126	(c)	148	(e)	170	(b)	192	(e)	214	(b)
17	(d)	39	(a)	61	(e)	83	(c)	105	(c)	127	(e)	149	(a)	171	(b)	193	(d)	215	(d)
18	(b)	40	(b)	62	(b)	84	(d)	106	(c)	128	(b)	150	(c)	172	(a)	194	(b)		
19	(a)	41	(c)	63	(d)	85	(b)	107	(d)	129	(d)	151	(b)	173	(c)	195	(e)		
20	(e)	42	(b)	64	(a)	86	(d)	108	(a)	130	(a)	152	(c)	174	(d)	196	(b)		
21	(e)	43	(e)	65	(c)	87	(b)	109	(e)	131	(d)	153	(a)	175	(d)	197	(d)		
22	(a)	44	(a)	66	(a)	88	(a)	110	(b)	132	(d)	154	(b)	176	(b)	198	(e)		

CHAPTER 7

Sentence Completion

In this section, a sentence is given with a blank space that can be filled with multiple options while giving same sense and intended meaning to the situation described in sentence. Student has to mark the option which has correct pair of words to suit the sentence out of five choices. Six option words are given for the blank.

Main requisite for doing well in this particular section requires a rich vocabulary. This knowledge of words should be more from the usage point of view. A student shall be able to recognize how some words, although not synonymous yet highly replaceable.

While reading a book, newspaper or magazine one should always try to find out certain combinations of words. Sometimes a particular word can be attached with only other specific verbs or adjectives.

See the word conclusion it can be used in a certain way with certain verbs only.

Conclusion- Reach a conclusion, draw a conclusion

One will find word 'conclusion' used in this way more often than not in all reading materials used by all.

Some logic also goes in for solving these questions.

See the other word License-

License can be allotted or sanctioned. There are no other verbs that fit so well with process of obtaining a license.

Now have a look at following examples of adjectives which you will find interesting and helpful to solve questions. Have a stock of these and it would work like a support system for you. A list of the combinations has to be formed and revised daily to strengthen the usage based vocabulary application.

See some of the combinations that are usually seen in reading materials.

Technology-current, existing, latest, obsolete, emerging, unmatchable, unbeatable, state of art.

Warning-dire, grim, ominous, stark.

Withdrawal-sudden, imminent, strategic, ignominious.

Slope- Precipitous, steep, gradual.

Recollection -Vivid, faint, hazy.

Shout- muffled, raucous, triumphant.

Suggestion-Constructive, Practical, Outrageous, Preposterous, tentative.

Proof -Conclusive, incontrovertible, irrefutable, tangible

Students should try to locate more of such combinations while reading and note them down in their diaries.

In this section of book such questions of exam level have been given for your practice. These are more or less daily usage words used in day today writings by bank officers, clerks and other professionals and similar words are expected to appear in exam.

EXERCISE

Directions (Qs. 1-50): The following questions consist of a single sentence with one blank only. You are given five or six words as answer choices you have to pick up correct pair in option, which will make the sentence meaningfully complete.

1. Despite slowing loan growth and Central Bank is taking steps to ensure .... liquidity, banks are borrowing record amounts of money from the central bank.
   (1) Sufficient   (2) Abundant
   (3) Unprecedented   (4) Enough
   (5) Mandatory   (6) Redundant
   (a) 1&4   (b) 1&2
   (c) 5&3   (d) 5&4
   (e) 1&3

2. Many banks have decided not to mobilize high cost deposits and have therefore increased their ....on borrowings from the Central Bank.
   (1) Dependency   (2) Reliance
   (3) Faith   (4) Independence
   (5) Future   (6) Trust
   (a) 2&1   (b) 2&6
   (c) 3&5   (d) 6&1
   (e) 3&5

3. Experts said Indian debt yields were .... high and could attract investors in developed Western markets, many of whom could borrow funds at low single digit rates.
   (1) Unprecedently   (2) Illogically
   (3) Irrationally   (4) Alluringly
   (5) Fearfully   (6) Falsely
   (a) 2&1   (b) 1&4
   (c) 3&5   (d) 6&1
   (e) 3&5

4. IIM Calcutta, which ....its final placements on Monday, expects consulting to be strong.
   (1) Kick starts   (2) Kicks off
   (3) Announces   (4) Hosts
   (5) Offers   (6) Pushes
   (a) 2&1   (b) 1&4
   (c) 3&5   (d) 2&3
   (e) 3&5

5. Supreme Court has cancelled many licenses .... by the previous Telecom Minister.
   (1) Distributed   (2) Sanctioned
   (3) Divided   (4) Granted
   (5) Awarded   (6) Utilized
   (a) 2&4   (b) 1&4
   (c) 3&5   (d) 6&1
   (e) 3&5

6. The investigators are also not ....the possibility of a local, most likely a Shia trained terrorist group.
   (1) Ruling out   (2) Pulling out
   (3) Doubting   (4) Putting out
   (5) Leaving   (6) Kicking out
   (a) 2&1   (b) 3&4
   (c) 1&4   (d) 6&1
   (e) 3&5

7. Our understanding is that elections would be held as early as considered ......by all concerned.
   (1) unavoidable   (2) Needed
   (3) Feasible   (4) Demanded
   (5) Grilled   (6) Loathed
   (a) 3&1   (b) 1&4
   (c) 3&5   (d) 6&1
   (e) 3&5

8. The new management came out with a ....that could put back on growth trajectory.
   (1) Plan   (2) Road map
   (3) Strategy   (4) Formula
   (5) Logic   (6) Tool
   (a) 2&3   (b) 1&2
   (c) 3&5   (d) 6&1
   (e) 3&5

9. Timely delivery is a given ....in a courier company.
   (1) Vice   (2) Specialty
   (3) System   (4) Faith
   (5) Virtue   (6) Feature
   (a) 2&1   (b) 1&5
   (c) 3&5   (d) 6&1
   (e) 3&5

10. Tata has urged the Supreme Court to order a ....investigation by an independent agency.
    (1) New   (2) Fresh
    (3) Vital   (4) Re
    (5) Fulsome   (6) Secondary
    (a) 2&1   (b) 1&4
    (c) 3&5   (d) 2&1
    (e) 3&5

11. The two parties released a ....press statement in the evening.
    (1) Combined   (2) Compromised
    (3) Joint   (4) Single
    (5) Fabricated   (6) Handpicked
    (a) 2&1   (b) 1&4
    (c) 3&5   (d) 6&1
    (e) 3&1

12. When the stock market ....is negative .Funding, a critical element for scale, becomes a prized commodity.
    (1) Emotion   (2) Trend
    (3) Sentiment   (4) Feeling
    (5) Curve   (6) Figure
    (a) 2&3   (b) 1&4
    (c) 3&5   (d) 6&4
    (e) 3&5

13. The powers of Centre appear to be a/an ....on the powers of State Government.
    (1) Crouching (2) Infringement
    (3) Invading (4) Cutting
    (5) Brushing (6) Extension
    (a) 2 &3 (b) 1&4
    (c) 1&2 (d) 6&1
    (e) 3&5

14. The economy has been roughly ....for about two years.
    (1) Inclined (2) Flat
    (3) Curved (4) Sphere
    (5) Round (6) Down
    (a) 2 &1 (b) 1&4
    (c) 2&6 (d) 6&1
    (e) 3&5

15. The ....before the board is that if it accepts his demand or not.
    (1) Confusion (2) Dilemma
    (3) Fear (4) Threat
    (5) Opportunity (6) Interest
    (a) 2 &6 (b) 1&2
    (c) 3&5 (d) 6&1
    (e) 3&5

16. Building reputation in market should be seen as a ....agenda for growth.
    (1) Persistent (2) Continuous
    (3) Consistent (4) Urgent
    (5) Jaded (6) Final
    (a) 3 &1 (b) 1&4
    (c) 3&5 (d) 6&1
    (e) 3&5

17. We seek a/an ....for our daughter who is a divorcee and 34 years of age.
    (1) Match (2) Interest
    (3) Alliance (4) Partner
    (5) Permanence (6) Joint
    (a) 3 &1 (b) 2&4
    (c) 3&5 (d) 6&5
    (e) 3&2

18. India has moved a step ....to lifting the ban investments from Pakistan.
    (1) Away (2) Closer
    (3) Near (4) Further
    (5) Back (6) Positive
    (a) 2 &3 (b) 1&4
    (c) 3&5 (d) 6&1
    (e) 3&5

19. As Finance Minister steps in ,will the Economy ....?
    (1) Step in (2) Step up
    (3) Step ahead (4) Step down
    (5) Step off (6) Step on
    (a) 2 &1 (b) 1&4
    (c) 3&5 (d) 2&3
    (e) 3&5

20. Lifting the ban from the investment from the long time enemy Pakistan will be a goodwill ....
    (1) Step (2) Virtue
    (3) Gesture (4) Offer
    (5) Move (6) Threat

    (a) 1 &3 (b) 1&4
    (c) 3&5 (d) 6&1
    (e) 3&5

21. It will take at least five years for the electronic media sector to ....
    (1) Complete (2) Grow
    (3) Flourish (4) Propagate
    (5) Survive (6) Die
    (a) 2 &3 (b) 1&4
    (c) 3&5 (d) 6&1
    (e) 3&5

22. Supreme Court took serious note of the .... on the protesters in Janpath ground done by police.
    (1) Tortures (2) Excesses
    (3) Beatings (4) Charges
    (5) Researches
    (a) 2&3 (b) 1&2
    (c) 3&5 (d) 2&5
    (e) 2&4

23. Indian Army is a well ....army.
    (1) Equipped (2) Trained
    (3) Guided (4) Supported
    (5) Provided (6) Reached
    (a) 2&5 (b) 1&2
    (c) 3&1 (d) 2&3
    (e) 2&4

24. Culprit Officers will .... the action after the decision of High Court.
    (1) See (2) Face
    (3) Read (4) Smell
    (5) Follow (6) Reap
    (a) 1&3 (b) 3&4
    (c) 4&5 (d) 1&2
    (e) 2&4

25. Manoj Tiwari with this century has ....his place in the Indian team for next tour.
    (1) Cemented (2) Stabilized
    (3) Plastered (4) Fixed
    (5) Approved
    (a) 1&2 (b) 1&3
    (c) 1&4 (d) 1&5
    (e) 2&4

26. Rare blue Eagle was ....after 90 years in Indian zoo.
    (1) Spotted (2) Discovered
    (3) Flown (4) Seen
    (5) Brought
    (a) 2&3 (b) 3&4
    (c) 1&2 (d) 1&5
    (e) 4&3

27. The bird is ....found between northeast Pakistan along the base of the Himalayas from Himachal to Bhutan.
    (1) Commonly (2) Usually
    (3) Rarely (4) Seldom
    (5) Often
    (a) 1&4 (b) 2&3
    (c) 3&4 (d) 2&1
    (e) 4&5

28. Centre ………….. an alert about a plan by leader of an outlawed fundamentalist outfit.
    (1) Issued   (2) Declared
    (3) Sounded   (4) Cautioned
    (5) Doubted
    (a) Only (1)   (b) 1 & 2
    (c) 1&2&3   (d) 1&3&4
    (e) All the options

29. Nina Gupta is a familiar …………..in the fashion circles of city.
    (1) Personality   (2) Leader
    (3) Figure   (4) Protagonist
    (5) Name
    (a) 1&5   (b) 1 & 2
    (c) 1&2&3   (d) 1&3&4

30. Company has demanded ……………measures to tackle the problem.
    (1) Adequate   (2) Substantial
    (3) Rational   (4) Enough
    (5) Sure
    (a) Only (1)   (b) 1 & 2
    (c) 2&3   (d) 1&3
    (e) 1&4

31. BBC representative said that their December episode ……………..the country's charm, beauty and wealth along with its idiosyncrasies.
    (1) Announced   (2) Portrayed
    (3) Depicted   (4) Pictured
    (5) Confirmed
    (a) 2&5   (b) 1 & 2
    (c) 2&3   (d) 3&4
    (e) 1&4

32. Wikipedia …………….. access to its widely used, user generated, free source content. No one was able to use it.
    (1) allowed   (2) Blocked
    (3) Blacked out   (4) Increased
    (5) Stopped
    (a) 3&4   (b) 2&5
    (c) 2&3   (d) 1&3
    (e) 3&5

33. Out of the 6.5 million abortions …………...in 2010, 68% were performed by an unqualified person or in unsafe environment.
    (1) Recorded   (2) Registered
    (3) Counted   (4) Performed
    (5) Conducted
    (a) 4&5   (b) 1 & 2
    (c) 1&2   (d) 1&3
    (e) 3&4

34. Mr. John has been ………..for the top job at the ADB bank.
    (1) Shortlisted   (2) Selected
    (3) Appointed   (4) Questioned
    (5) Approved
    (a) 2&3   (b) 1 & 2
    (c) 1&4   (d) 3&5
    (e) 1&2

35. The procedure adopted by the bank authorities was totally ……………..as they did not follow the principles of natural justice.
    (1) Miscalculated (2) Flawed
    (3) Irrational   (4) Accurate
    (5) In place
    (a) Only (1)   (b) 1 & 4
    (c) 2&3   (d) 1&2
    (e) 3&5

36. Delhi High Court directed RBI to respond to the plea of ……………..commissioner of Income tax.
    (1) Appointed   (2) Sacked
    (3) Removed   (4) Selected
    (5) Responsible
    (a) 5&1   (b) 1 & 2
    (c) 2&3   (d) 3&4

37. The High Court withdrew a ……………approval that allowed him to make numerous trips to hospitals in last 4 years.
    (1) Ordered   (2) Pending
    (3) Blanket   (4) Prior
    (5) False
    (a) 3&4   (b) 1 & 2
    (c) 2&3   (d) 1&3
    (e) 3&5

38. You may be ………………to see that many people sleep on the footpaths of Delhi in the bone chilling nights as well.
    (1) Astonished   (2) Surprised
    (3) Annoyed   (4) Angry
    (5) Speech less
    (a) Only (1)   (b) 1 & 2
    (c) 2&3   (d) 1&3
    (e) 2&5

39. The guard showed ……………courage and helped police to nab the robbers.
    (1) Defending   (2) Exemplary
    (3) Highest   (4) Extreme
    (5) Collected   (6) Unprecedented
    (a) 3&5   (b) 2&4
    (c) 2&3   (d) 1&6
    (e) All of the options

40. I …………...my felicitations to all officers and ranks of the National Disaster Relief Force and their families on the occasion of its Raising Day.
    (1) Show   (2) Offer
    (3) Extend   (4) Sign
    (5) Pay   (6) Move
    (a) 2 & 5   (b) 1 & 2
    (c) 2 & 3   (d) 5&6
    (e) 4&5

41. Our Company reserves the right to accept/reject any tender without ……………..any reason thereof.
    (1) Claiming   (2) Assigning
    (3) Notifying   (4) Validating
    (5) Giving   (6) Disclosing
    (a) 5&6   (b) 3&4
    (c) 2&5   (d) 2&4
    (e) 2&6

42. Hence you are requested to appear ....in court on the desired date.
   - (1) Physically
   - (2) In person
   - (3) In self
   - (4) As yourself
   - (5) In front
   - (6) In Proxy
   - (a) 3&5
   - (b) 2&4
   - (c) 1&2
   - (d) 3&4
   - (e) 5&6

43. The Passengers are advised to not to try to ....enter/exit/obstruct the doors of metro trains.
   - (1) Forcefully
   - (2) Intentionally
   - (3) Vehemently
   - (4) Trespass
   - (5) Unintentionally
   - (6) Thrust fully
   - (a) 1&6
   - (b) 2 &5
   - (c) 1&4
   - (d) 6&3
   - (e) 2&3

44. Railways has made it ....for all passengers travelling in AC classes to carry an identity proof during journey to stop misuse of tickets.
   - (1) Mandatory
   - (2) Optional
   - (3) Compulsory
   - (4) Advisable
   - (5) Urgent
   - (6) Implied
   - (a) 3 &4
   - (b) 1&3
   - (c) 2&3
   - (d) 4 &6
   - (e) 5&4

45. A competitive environment is ....for growth.
   - (1) Desired
   - (2) Necessary
   - (3) Mandatory
   - (4) Must
   - (5) Requisite
   - (6) Required
   - (a) 2 &1
   - (b) 2&6
   - (c) 3&5
   - (d) 6&1
   - (e) 3&5

46. Growth in the second quarter will ....to announcement in the Budget regarding the subsidies, tax cuts and new initiatives.
   - (1) Subject
   - (2) Amount
   - (3) Revolve around
   - (4) Yield
   - (5) Prosper
   - (6) Reliable
   - (a) 2 &1
   - (b) 1&4
   - (c) 3&5
   - (d) 6&1
   - (e) 3&1

47. To achieve this, one of the ....policy measures would be to reduce our tarrif barriers.
   - (1) Major
   - (2) Preeminent
   - (3) Prominent
   - (4) Foremost
   - (5) Leading
   - (6) Serious
   - (a) 2 &1
   - (b) 1&4
   - (c) 3&5
   - (d) 3&1
   - (e) 3&5

48. ....of competition in product markets would enable India reap both static efficiency gains and dynamic efficiency gains.
   - (1) Promotion
   - (2) Enhancement
   - (3) Increment
   - (4) Stimulation
   - (5) Simulation
   - (6) Prevention
   - (a) 2 &1
   - (b) 1&4
   - (c) 1&4
   - (d) 6&1
   - (e) 3&5

49. All these conclusions ....from the unit level data in National Statistical Surveys done in last year.
   - (1) Draw
   - (2) Emerge
   - (3) Arise
   - (4) Follow
   - (5) Inject
   - (6) Reach
   - (a) 2 &3
   - (b) 1&4
   - (c) 3&5
   - (d) 6&1
   - (e) 3&5

50. Most of this increase has come due to ....in corporate and public savings.
   - (1) Change
   - (2) Improvement
   - (3) Amalgamation
   - (4) Turnaround
   - (5) Circumspection
   - (6) Speculation
   - (a) 2 &4
   - (b) 6&4
   - (c) 3&5
   - (d) 4&1
   - (e) 3&6

ANSWER KEY

1	(a)	6	(c)	11	(e)	16	(a)	21	(a)	26	(b)	31	(d)	36	(c)	41	(c)	46	(e)
2	(a)	7	(a)	12	(a)	17	(a)	22	(e)	27	(d)	32	(b)	37	(a)	42	(c)	47	(d)
3	(b)	8	(b)	13	(c)	18	(e)	23	(b)	28	(d)	33	(a)	38	(d)	43	(a)	48	(c)
4	(d)	9	(b)	14	(c)	19	(d)	24	(d)	29	(a)	34	(e)	39	(b)	44	(b)	49	(a)
5	(a)	10	(d)	15	(b)	20	(a)	25	(c)	30	(c)	35	(d)	40	(c)	45	(b)	50	(d)

Hints & Explanations

1. (a) Sentence indicates that central bank is taking steps to increase liquidity to a certain level. In the blank - enough, sufficient or abundant can fit. But the correct combination is given only in option (a).

2. (a) Reliance /faith can fit in the blank as sentence discusses dependence on a bank. Other options are not valid with reference to the sentence.

3. (b) This blank is followed by word 'high' which is logical with all the options. But debts cannot be false. Illogical or irrational is also not appropriate as experts must have some base for statement. Only unprecedently and alluringly fit as attraction to investors is also discussed in later part of sentence.

4. (d) Kicks off and announces are appropriate fillers for the blank space in reference to a college starting its placement seasons difference.
Kick start to do 8th to help a process or project start more quickly. The Govt's attempt to kick start the economy has failed.

5. (a) Licenses are granted or sanctioned not distributed or divided. Utilized is out of context. Awarded also fits with license. But it has no valid pair with it.

6. (c) Sentence says that the possibility of a particular terrorist group cannot be ruled out or put out.

7. (a) Elections can be unavoidable or related to feasibility but not grilled/loathed or held on demand.

8. (b) Management is related to planning or a strategy or a road map. Even formula can fit. So we have to search for an option with right combination.

9. (b) Timely delivery is a virtue or specialty that can be linked with a courier company.

10. (d) Investigation can be started with fresh outlook hence can be new or fresh. Other options do not have valid pair.

11. (e) Joint statement by two parties is right expression. 'Combined' can also replace the 'joint'.

12. (a) Stock market has sentiment of investment. But not emotions. Trends in stock markets are also scaled or measured. Feelings can also fit.

13. (c) Conflict of powers between two authorities is discussed where one is infringing/ crouching on the powers of other.

14. (c) Low economic activity is synonym to flat/down.

15. (b) Board is at a point of making a decision but is in dilemma/confusion. Fear or threats do not adjust.

16. (a) Consistent or persistent both give same sense to the sentence.

17. (a) For marriage advertisement - match or alliance are perfect words.

18. (e) Sentence hints for improvement of relationships so closer or near are correct fillers for the blank space.

19. (d) Sentence asks a question that intervention by Finance minister will bring what results for economy. Hence 'step up' or 'step ahead' are correct. Other options are not correct s the meaning differs completely.

20. (a) 'Lifting the ban ' is a step /gesture/move.

21. (a) Sentence is about the growth and future of media.

22. (e) Grammatically with 'On' only Excesses and Charge fits in.

23. (b) With ARMY - equipped and trained are appropriate. Other word which can be correct is 'reached' but no proper pair is given.

24. (d) Other words do not fit in context. Smell, reap are out of context cannot be used for the officers.

25. (c) For next tour - is being stated so fix can come in blank and cemented means to strengthen' so it can also fit in the blank space of sentence referring to a player's selection in team.

26. (b) This pair best represents the idea best as words like 'rare' and '90 years' goes in line with this pair of words. Discovered and invented are wrong. Flown or brought do not fit in either.

27. (d) This pair is appropriate in grammer and context as gives proper sense to the sentence referring to a bird found in a specific area.

28. (d) With alert -sounded and cautioned fit best from the options.

29. (a) A well known 'name' is treated as 'figure'.

30. (c) Problem can be tackled with only 'adequate' measures in 'enough' quantity.

31. (d) Episode is portrayed to 'depict' and 'pictured' for the same purpose.

32. (b) As access is prevented so blocked /stopped can fit.

33. (a) Illegal thing is not recorded or registered. It can be performed or conducted.

34. (e) For a post through different processes - selection or short listing is done.

35. (d) Procedure can only be flawed or miscalculated. Other options raise a conflict in first and second part of the sentence.

36. (c) All options can fit. Only proper option with proper combination has to be selected.

37. (a) Prior /Blanket fits in grammatically and goes well with sentence.

38. (d) By seeing people sleeping on road in winter is annoying or make angry or render someone speechless or surprise so all the options can fit. But the best combination is this.

39. (b) With courage exemplary and extreme are correct. 'Unprecedented' is also good with 'courage' but is not given in the options with correct pair.

40. (c) Felicitations are offered or extended or paid.

41. (c) With 'reason' - 'assign'/notifying/giving/disclosing all are appropriate.

42. (c) Other options are not right in context and do not give desired meaning to the sentence.

43. (a) Forcefully and Thrust fully both carry similar meaning.

44. (b) Railways is authority and has made it mandatory/ compulsory to carry the identity proof with it.

45. (b) In competitive environment growth prospers. So It is necessary/requisite/required. Must is impelling and doubtful.

46. (e) Only subject and revolve around fit in. Other options are out of sync.

47. (d) Major and prominent both carry same sense and gives proper meaning to sentence.

48. (c) Sentence advocates the promotion of or stimulation of the competition.

49. (a) With conclusion - arise or emerge is suitable replacements.

50. (d) Sentence is in positive sense and change /turnaround is in sync with the situation of sentence.

CHAPTER 8

Passage Completion

In this type of questions, a small paragraph will be given with a deleted sentence. This sentence can be at last or at the beginning or in between the passage. A student needs to identify the best sentence which completes the paragraph from the answer options. Even though there are several general principles and some ideas about answering these questions, most of the times a student finds the so called rules may not apply to these questions. In several instances, besides, identifying the author's style, way of thinking, tone will be difficult with just one paragraph. So it requires a lot of concentration to answer the paragraph completion questions.

In a test of English language in Bank Exams for PO, this question type is a new introduction; passage completion plays a very important role as it has a significant role in the verbal section of the test with 5 questions. Once you have spent crucial exam time on these, there is no logic to answer it incorrect. Hence a lot of practice should be done to attempt these questions with accuracy and speed.

It tests the ability of a student to logically connect the different parts of a passage. It also tests certain reasoning skills of the student. Para-completion is nothing else but a test of your comprehension skills. All it asks of you is to complete a missing line from a paragraph. Following tips can be followed while solving these questions-

- Identify the theme of the passage.
- Identify the continuing flow of thought.
- Continue the thread of thought keeping in mind the already discussed matter.
- Try to connect the thoughts of passage.
- Judge your option on location of blank space.
- Relate the missing part with preceding and following sentences.
- Do not introduce new things.
- Do not deviate from the real issue of the passage.
- Judge the passage tone and compare it with the tone of the option.

Sufficient number of good questions is given with detailed solutions to increase your proficiency in this section.

EXERCISE

 In each of the following questions a short passage is given with one of the lines in the passage missing and represented by a blank. Select the best out of the five answer choices given, to make the passage complete and coherent.

1. There are many industries where India has an advantage because of relatively lower Costs of all forms of manpower- whether it is professional or factory labour. However, while this can give initial advantage, it should not be taken for an enduring advantage due to the following reasons. One as products become more sophisticated, labour as cost factor becomes less and less important. Two, the differences in costs are narrowed down through higher level of automation. There, in processes that require large number of cheap labour, the industry is bound to shift its operation along; the line of the ever-declining scale of poorer countries. So a poorer country than India can eventually overtake us with yet cheaper labour. Therefore, when one has established an export market on the basis of cheaper manpower ....

   (a) One has to be vigilant to make sure that one builds up other advantages to compensate for the inevitable loss of this temporary advantage.
   (b) One has to be vigilant to make sure that this advantage should not be given away
   (c) One need not be vigilant as there is no competition in near future
   (d) There is need of caution to see the variations in labour charges of other countries
   (e) There is need to build this cheap labour on regular basis

2. Standards and standardization, quality systems, certification and inspections, measurement systems, testing laboratories, their accreditation and calibration service, production and supply of standard reference materials etc, are all important building blocks. Quality control through the agency of the Export Inspection Agency leaves much to be desired. It is often alleged that EIA is actually playing a retrograde role, although inadvertently. ....
   (I) The list of items subject to compulsory export inspection need to be reviewed and shortened. A trimmer EIA list essential for a modicum of efficiency. (II) EIA should use international agencies to train people and update the equipment available for those limited items. (III) The quality development process need to be professionalized by making use of quality development skills and managerial methods available around the world. Overall, per-export inspection needs to be greatly simplified, both in the interests of speedier clearance and less harassment for the exporters as well as better administration.
   (a) EIA is to be scrapped and new council should be made with following improvements.

   (b) This is happening in absence from a guiding international agency which can suggest a number of measures.
   (c) This needs to be corrected.
   (d) EIA is short of experience and therefore such a negative effect.
   (e) Why was EIA formed in the first place ...?

3. The International Monetary Fund (IMF), the World Bank and the International Trade Organization were conceived at the Breton woods Conference in July, 1944 as institutions to strengthen international economic cooperation and to help create a more stable and prosperous global economy. While the IMF and the World Bank come into existence and started functioning from 1946, the International Trade Organization could not be set up. Instead, the General Agreement on Tariffs and Trade (GATT) was set up in 1947. Through successive round of negotiations, the GATT got transformed into what has come to be known as the World Trade Organization (WTO) that started functioning from January1, 1995. The various institutions have set up to govern international economic relations. While all the institutions work in close coordination with each other.................
   (a) Each of the institutions is independent
   (b) Each of the these institutions works with different focus in different direction
   (c) Each of these institutions has its own specific area of responsibilities
   (d) Each of these institutions has major role to play in each other's work
   (e) Each of these institutions has imprint of its work on other's performance

4. ADB finances principally specific projects in the region. It may make loans to or invest in the projects concerned. It may also guarantee loans granted to the projects. Most of the loans granted are hard loans or tired loans. However, loans form special funds set aside by the ADB up to 10 per cent of its paid-up capital are granted under soft loan term for which purpose it has set up a separate window known as the Asian Development Fund (ADF). Soft loans are normally granted to projects of high development priority requiring longer periods of repayment with lower rates of interest. ADB normally finances foreign exchange cost of the project and the loan in repayable in the currency in which it is made. India has been eligible for assistance both under the ADB and its soft loan window, ADF.................
   However, it has been getting large assistance under the ADB.
   (a) But India does not need any assistance from ADB.
   (b) But India is not a member of ADB
   (c) But India is not interested in ADB aids.
   (d) But India has stayed away from the ADB
   (e) But India is against ADB.

5. In the planned economy of India, foreign capital has been assigned a significant role, although it has been changing over time. In the earlier phase of planning, foreign capital was looked upon as a means to supplement domestic investment. Many concession and incentives were given to foreign investors. Later on, however, the emphasis shifted to encouraging technological collaboration between India entrepreneurs and foreign entrepreneurs. In more recent times, efforts are on to invite free flow of foreign capital ………………………

    (a) It would be instructive in this background to examine the Government's policy towards foreign capital.

    (b) It would be instructive in this background to examine the World Bank's policy towards foreign capital in India

    (c) Let us keep our fingers crossed and look for the next parliamentary session for debate on the issue

    (d) Issue of Foreign capital is fragile and can be discussed only with relevant statistical figures in hand

    (e) New changes are waiting in the line.

6. FDI may actually be harmful to the recipient country if the economy is highly protected and foreign investment takes place behind high tariff walls. This type of investment is generally referred to as the tariff-jumping' variety of foreign investment, whose primary objective is to take advantage of the protected markets in the host country. The longer the Government shields its home market with tariffs………………… and more acute will be the conflict between it and the domestic entrepreneur. In view of this, an appropriate policy framework must respond to two conflicting objectives: the need to liberalize rules governing such investment in view of the growing integration of the world economy, and the need to ensure that such investment has positive effects on the country's economy and does not lead to negative welfare effects.

    (a) The more the foreign countries to apply pressure on India

    (b) The more the foreign money to come in India

    (c) The more the foreigner will come to exploit that protected market

    (d) The more the foreigner to protest against that government

    (e) The more the foreigner will raise the issue on international platform

7. The Indian constitution provides for demarcation of functional responsibilities and finances between the Centre and the States. The provision of public services has been largely entrusted to the States. These mainly relate to law and order, public health, sanitation, water supply and agriculture. The States have to concurrently take certain functions in areas such as education, infrastructure. Their share in combined expenditure (Centre and States) on social services is about 85 per cent, while in the case of economic services; it is about 60 per cent. Thus, the States have the primary responsibility to undertake tasks pertaining to developing social and economic infrastructure. However, their ability to undertake such development functions is critically determined by their financial position. The growing importance of state finances in the macro-economy is evident from the fact……………….. The size of overall development expenditures of the states has always been higher than that of the Centre and the difference has got widened rather significantly in the 1990s.

    (a) That the States have overrun their planned expenditures and lacking freedom of further development

    (b) That the States have reached at the peak of their finances and overtaken Centres in revenues

    (c) That Centre borrows money from the states for its expenditures on educational and social welfare programmes

    (d) That the total expenditures of State governments has even undertaken those of the Centre

    (e) That the total expenditures of State and Center has widened unprecedentedly in 1990s.

8. A budget is a statement containing a forecast of revenues and expenditures for a period of time, usually a year. It is a comprehensive plan of action designed to achieve the policy objectives set by the Government for the coming year. A budget is plan and a budget document is reflection or what Government expects to do in future. While any plan need not be a budget, a budget has to be necessarily a pan. It shows detailed allocation to resources and proposed taxation or other measures for their realization. A budget is, however, not a balanced sheet (exhibiting total assets and liabilities) of the Government on a particular date- is a financial blueprint for action and is, therefore, of great advantage to Government departments, legislatures and citizens. The budget of government expresses its total activity in figures……………………………..

    (a) A budget reflects what the Government is doing or intends to do.

    (b) A budget is a legal document

    (c) A budget is a promise of Government to its people

    (d) A budget is a guideline for State Governments

    (e) A budget is only a plan on papers that have never been achieved

9. For a federal country like India, the budget of the Government of India is the most important instrument for implementing various economic and social objectives. The budgets of state government affect local activities. The Government of India budget influences the whole economy. The latter tries to bring about growth with social justice through its budget; it influences regional, functional and overall distribution of income and wealth through its expenditure (transfer) payments, investments and tax policies. The provisions of grants and loans to State governments and Union Territories and to the private sector and various subsidies (such as for export promotion, food grains distribution, etc.) are some of the elements of Central government budget policy for promoting growth and income distribution. ………………… Its significance lies in its ability to promote the various objectives of a modern state which has assumed the role of a welfare state and of a catalytic agent for promoting growth with social justice.

    (a) A budget in modern times should, therefore not be judged sound or otherwise merely on the basis of its 'deficit' or 'surplus' or 'balanced' position

(b) A budget is therefore not only instrument of implementing the economic and social objectives but it is also about growth with social justice

(c) A budget is a reflection of success or failure of a government

(d) A budget in modern times should, therefore not be judged on its face value

(e) A budget in this turbulence time cannot be judged on basis of monetary indices of 'surplus' or 'deficits'

10. After the East Asia crisis, the World Bank conducted a study on the underlying reasons for the crisis. It was found that at least a major part of the fundamental responsibility was on banks, which had understated their non-performing accounts by as much as 47%. Since this was a study and not an investigation…………….. Nevertheless, the Basel committee on supervision did take cognizance, and issued circulars and directives not only on supervision, but also on Internal Functional Management. It will be remembered by those interested that Basel committee had also acted expeditiously after the Barring Bank's failure, to separate treasury and lending operations from the decision making processes. Bank failures are nothing new in the world, although we in India have been insulated from such traumas for more than two decades.

(a) The findings were not taken note of

(b) The findings were not taken seriously

(c) The findings were not legally binding on any one

(d) The fallout from this revelation was only taken note of

(e) The fallout from this revelation was seriously taken

11. Whether the Government is right in bailing out a private sector bank is an issue that is decided more than by the long term social security policy of the Government, than by economic reasons alone……………….. Nevertheless, in a situation of scarcity of resources, bailing out somebody means the denial of resources to others. The irony of it is that in performing its duties of proper governance to the larger society through the process of bailing out, Government excuses the lack of corporate governance in banks.

(a) Economists world over learnt it hard way during the Great depression

(b) This is elementary principle of economics taught in schools

(c) Reasons are not limited to these two but extend to debts, liquidity & credit ratings issues

(d) It was unexpected and came like a bolt from the blue

(e) Particularly true for the Asian countries like India and China

12. But no depreciation is allowed on Live Stock i.e. Horses. Although the horses are in the nature of fixed assets in the hands of the owner, no depreciation is allowed under Income Tax Act. Instead when the animal dies or becomes permanently useless the entire value of the horse can be written off as revenue loss in the year in which it dies or becomes permanently useless. When the gross income exceeds the total expenditure, it results in net profit which will be taxable at usual rates of tax applicable to the person. …………………..Although the live stock is in the nature of fixed assets of the owners, buy them, maintain them, train

them, and participate in races and Sell them or send them away to studs when they are useless.

(a) But when the gross income is less than the expenditure, then results in loss

(b) But when the gross income is higher than the expenditure, then results in loss

(c) But when the gross income is equal to expenditure then result is loss

(d) But when the gross income is there loss is the result

(e) But when the gross income is increasing then result is becoming evident

13. Aggregation of risks is somewhat quite new to banks in India. While some banks have started thinking in that line by trying to put integrated limits framework and integrated risk policies as well as using CBS solutions for technological integration, the effort required is beyond such requirement. Risk aggregation would mean aggregating the individual risk measures to decide most appropriate assets class that would contain the risk to the desired level dictated by the risk appetite .Capital allocation (about how much) would be based on such strategies………..

(a) Most banks are yet to conceptualize the same in their processes

(b) Most banks have already integrated it in their functioning; it is working over the years satisfactorily.

(c) Which would in long run prove to be the growth impeding

(d) Of risk aggregation which is really a new concept to Indian banks

(e) On expected lines of the regulation conditions laid down in the manual of the bank

14. However, it is possible that the non-resident entity may have a business connection with the resident Indian entity. In such a case, the resident Indian entity could be treated as Permanent Establishment of the non-resident entity. ……………During the last decade or so, India has seen a steady growth of outsourcing of business processes by non residents or foreign companies to IT-enabled entities in India. Such entities are either branches or associated enterprises of the foreign enterprise or an independent India enterprise. The non-resident entity or foreign company will be liable to tax in India only if the IT -enabled BPO unit in India constitutes its Permanent Establishment.

(a) The tax treatment of the Permanent Establishment in such a case is under consideration

(b) How would the profit would be shared is not decided yet?

(c) A lengthy and cumbersome process requiring a lot of application of mind and revenue principles is ahead for the tax department of India

(d) A new trend is seen in last decade.

(e) Indian companies have a lot on stake as competition increases.

15. The Finance Commission is entrusted with periodic review and resolution of Central- State fiscal problems. It was the clear intention of the father of the India Constitution that all matters pertaining to normal Central-State financial adjustment should be scrutinized by the Finance commission………………. An incidental and by no means

insignificant advantage of the appointment of a Finance Commission has generally been to rekindle interest in issues pertaining to financial relations between the Centre and the States and to promote an enlightened national debate on the several facets of India's federal fiscal set-up. The role of the Indian Finance Commission is unique in many ways. It is one of few commissions provided in the constitution.

(a) which was given a pre-eminent role in the resolution of problems in fiscal federalism

(b) Which was constituted with the vision of a modern India with modern facilities

(c) Which was a dream of Father of Nation also

(d) Which was to be unique in its ways and a constitutional body

(e) Which was introduced as a backbone for Indian Economy

16. The art of medicine is the art of healing, not just treating, and not even just curing. Yet it is only when the art and science join hands that healing is best accomplished. The author then adds ...., remember that the practice of medicine is an art, not a trade, a calling, not a business, a calling in which your heart will be exercised equally with your head. This book is rare work of the art of medicine, from a very rare practitioner of the science of medicine.

(a) " mankind depends on science as equally on the art"

(b) " for the mercy's sake let us have little less science and a little more art"

(c) " let us consider science at par with art"

(d) " let us forget what is art and what is science"

(e) " do not blame medicine for it"

17. The thirteen Finance commissions cover a span of more than 60 years during which many conditions have changed. Correspondingly, the approach of the later commissions may be expected to be different in several respects from the earlier ones. Nevertheless, it is possible to discern certain common elements in the thinking of the successive Finance Commissions. Which have come to evolve gradually what may be called 'the Indian Finance Commission's approach to federal finance........ According to this approach, States' share of Central taxes is not allocated strictly on the basis of need. These problems and shortcomings come later in light but have caused what was not accounted at that time.

(a) And it happened to be in that way

(b) There are several inadequacies in the approach of the Finance Commissions

(c) Evolution is a long process and it is a same story for commissions

(d) But they differ completely from them and each time new approach was looked for

(e) This was based on the tax sharing basis principle of commissions

18. The Parihar is, for all practical purposes, a functional, fully fitted out submarine. After this brief ceremony, the submarine is to be towed out for the first time across the naval dockyard and moored in an enclosed pier called Site Bravo ....Over the next few months, it will commence a series of harbour trials. The primary system, a nuclear reactor, generates the heat which drives the secondary system, a steam turbine which spins the submarine's propeller, is to be tested separately. First, the steam turbine is to be jumpstarted with shore based supply. The next significant step will be starting up the submarine's nuclear reactor where Zirconium rods in the core of the submarine's pressurized water reactor will be slowly raised.

(a) It is the advent of new technology in India

(b) It has entered in chain reaction chamber

(c) It is like coming out from maternity ward to nursery

(d) It is unprecedented step to start such a sequence of processes

(e) It is very critical for a nuclear submarine

19. For all those women who perpetually complained about how all cars are designed for men, company is out with a car especially suited for them. The Your Concept Car............ is a dream come true. It has a keyless entry, additional storage space, a lower hood and the back seat screen going all the way till the rear end so that you know exactly where the car ends. Add to this a parking aid for parallel parking and their most advanced technology, Ergo vision that scans the body at the dealership, stores the data and every time you hop into the car, automatically adjusts the height of the seat, the steering wheel, the distance between them and everything else to your specifications. Even though it is a concept car that will not hit the roads, its women-friendly features have been incorporated in some of the other cars.

(a) The first to be designed by experts

(b) The first to be launched by company

(c) The first to be the concept car

(d) The first to be designed by all women team

(e) The first to with so many features

20. The growing importance of Union excise amongst the shared taxes and the ascendancy of population as the principal basis of distribution are the two salient features of tax-sharing determined by the Finance Commissions. The finance Commission is called upon to determine the State that would be in need of grant-assistance of the quinqennium under reference and the amount of such assistance in each case. The first Finance Commission laid down some important principles governing the determination of grants -in-aid for States. ....

(a) These principles have been generally, endorsed by all the subsequent Commissions.

(b) These principles have been discarded by subsequent commissions

(c) These principles were taken from the Finance commissions of the other countries

(d) These principles were derivations from the elementary formulas of text books

(e) These principles cannot be changed and are fixed

21. The biggest attraction of the public sector is that, for women with the same qualifications and skills it almost always pays better than does private industry. For men the differences are much less pronounced...................... Figures are hard to come by, but in rich countries women typically hold 30-40% of senior managerial posts in central government. Hours and conditions too are usually more congenital and maternity arrangements more generous. So with better pay, conditions and promotion prospects, it is

no wonder that the public sector is the employer of the choice for so many women.

(a) The public sector is also more likely to promote women to senior jobs

(b) The public sector provide safe working environment for the women.

(c) Women are paid more than men in public sector

(d) Public sector is better pay master than private banks for women

(e) There is no issue in making a choice for women

22. The fiscal position of the Indian Governments - both Centre and States -has been under stress since the mid -1980s. The stress stems from the inadequacy of receipts in meeting the growing expenditure requirements. Reflecting the fiscal stress, the expenditure for development activities, which are directly related to growth, has suffered. On the other hand, expenditure on non-developmental purposes, largely committed, has witnessed a steady rise. ......in favour of developmental expenditure in order to enable higher growth. That the state of finances of States is in disarray is beyond dispute. The state finances have not been properly managed not only by the states but also by the planning commission and the central Government, which include economists who do not see states as autonomous responsible organizations.

(a) The crucial issue, therefore, is to bring about improvement in the finances with a view to restructuring expenditure

(b) The crucial issue, therefore, is to analyze the finances with a view to see what can be done to expenditure

(c) Hence, it can be said that management of finances is important vis-à-vis management of expenditures

(d) Therefore, Governments have to mend their way and balance the finances and the expenditures

(e) What is expected in this scenario is a policy shift

23. Under taxation is at the roots of the Indian fiscal problems. The available evidence shows that the tax -GDP ratio in India is lower than the level it should have for its per capita GDP by at least 2.5 percent. It is, therefore important to focus reform efforts to increase the tax ratio. Of course, this does not mean that strategy to increase the tax ratio lies in increasing the tax rates. The strategy is to reiterate that tax administration is tax policy. All exemptions will not go. Politically, it is not possible. The world over, there was a time when we thought that equity in tax policy meant reducing the incomes of the rich. But today's tax philosophy is that equity in tax policy is increasing the incomes of the poor. The incomes of the poor cannot be increased by reducing those of the rich..........

(a) As they are the central point of any economy their importance is peremptory

(b) As they have the real remote control in their hands and poor cannot see that

(c) As they have the capital for investment and give employment to the poor

(d) As they have lobbying power to decide the fate of the poor

(e) As they are capital rich and cannot be compared with poor

24. ....Enterprises worldwide are therefore, now putting in place an integrated framework for risk management, which is proactive, systematic and covers the entire organization. Banks in India are also moving from the individual silo system to an enterprise -wide risk management system. This is placing greater demands on the risk management skills in banks and has brought to the fore the need for capacity building. While the first mile-stone would be risk integration across the entity, banks would do well to aggregate risk across the group both in the specific risk areas as also across the risks.

(a) Banks are most risk prone of all the financial institutions.

(b) Banks were managing each risk independently, in isolation, which is no longer inadequate

(c) It is about risk level at which an enterprise is operating to have or not have risk management system

(d) Risk management in India is lagging for banks in comparison with other parts of world

(e) What if risk becomes unmanageable and looks right in your face?

25. One of the most stubborn fallacies about inflation is the assumption that it is caused, not by an increase in the quantity of money, but by a "shortage of goods." It is true that a rise in prices (which, as we have seen, should not be identified with inflation) can be caused either by an increase in the quantity of money or by a shortage of goods or partly by both. Wheat, for example, may rise in price either because there is an increase in the supply of money or a failure of the wheat crop. But we seldom find, even in conditions of total war, a general rise of prices caused by a general shortage of goods. ...." that even in the Germany of 1923, after prices had soared hundreds of billions of times, high officials and millions of Germans were blaming the whole thing on a general "shortage of goods"- at the very moment when foreigners were coming in and buying German goods with gold or their own currencies at prices lower than those of equivalent goods at home.

(a) Yet so stubborn is the fallacy that inflation is caused by a "shortage of goods"

(b) Yet people believe on such fallacy to unimagined level

(c) Yet so wide is acceptance

(d) Yet so timely and abrupt is response to fallacy

(e) Yet more and more people started to believe on 'shortage of goods' fallacy

26. The cure for inflation, like most cures, consists chiefly in removal of the cause. The cause of inflation is the increase of money and credit. The cure is to stop increasing money and credit..................... It is as simple as that. Although simple in principle; this cure often involves complex and disagreeable decisions on detail. Let us begin with the Federal budget. It is next to impossible to avoid inflation with a continuing heavy deficit. That deficit is almost certain to be financed by inflationary means-i.e., by directly or indirectly printing more money. Huge government expenditures are not in themselves inflationary-provided they are made wholly out of tax receipts, or out of borrowing paid for wholly out of real savings. But the difficulties in either of these methods of payment, once expenditures have

passed a certain point, are so great that there is almost inevitably a resort to the printing press.

(a) The cure for inflation, in brief, is to stop inflating
(b) The cure for inflation, in brief, is to think positively
(c) The cure for inflation is planning small things with little thoughts
(d) The cure of inflation lies in inflation itself
(e) The cure of inflation is hidden in understanding the cause of inflation.

27. The India Union has had more than 55 years of experience with fiscal federalism operating within the framework of the parliamentary democracy and planned economic development. A comprehensive review of fiscal federalism in independent India is, therefore, overdue. There have been feeble protests in form to time about the sprawling powers of the Central government eroding the foundations of fiscal federalism.................Now that single party has been dislodged from power in some of the States and parties of different hues and colours are holding office, a candid and comprehensive review of all the aspects of Centre- State relations and the working of fiscal federalism in particular is important and necessary.

(a) But these voices were curbed by all parties.
(b) But democracy does not allow a mechanism to redress this problem
(c) But fiscal federalism is all about ignoring and moving on with protests
(d) But these voices were drowned by the overwhelming influence of the same party at the centre and the States
(e) But these protests died in with time for their feebleness

28. Do firms need banks, or can they make do with stock markets? Do firms need stock markets, or can they make do with banks? Alexander Gerschenkron long ago argued that economically "backward" countries could not trust decentralized capital markets to provide their largest firms sufficient funds.................. More recently, finance theorists have reasoned from agency theory and the economics of information to much the same result. And the transition in Eastern Europe has given the issue a programmatic touch: what should scholars tell the new finance ministers to do about banks and stock markets?

(a) Instead, they needed banks
(b) Instead, they needed centralization mechanisms only
(c) Hence banks and Stock markets are not needed
(d) Therefore Banks score over Stock Markets for them
(e) Banks or Stock markets both are not needed simultaneously

29. The Japanese economy is one of the third largest in the world .... The Japanese currency is the Yen. Japan's main export goods are cars, electronic devices and computers. Most important trade partners are China and the USA, followed by South Korea, Taiwan, Hong Kong, Singapore, Thailand and Germany. Imports: Japan has a surplus in its export/import balance. The most important import goods are raw materials such as oil, foodstuffs and wood. Major supplier is China, followed by the USA, Australia, Saudi Arabia, South Korea, Indonesia and the United Arab Emirates. Industries: Manufacturing, construction, distribution, real estate, services, and communication are Japan's major industries today. Agriculture makes up only about two percent of the GNP. Most important agricultural product is rice. Resources of raw materials are very limited and the mining industry rather small.

(a) And it is going to achieve number one status sooner
(b) It is eying for number one spot in world economy riding on its recent technological developments
(c) Japanese Economy is going through recession and is bound to slip to lower stands in world economy
(d) Only USA and China have a higher GNP.
(e) It is only in terms of growth rate not in terms of GDP.

30. The prospect of renewed war between India and China is, for now, something that disturbs the sleep only of virulent nationalists in the Chinese press and retired colonels in Indian think-tanks. Optimists prefer to hail the $60 billion in trade the two are expected to do with each other this year. But the 20th century taught the world that blatantly foreseeable conflicts of interest can become increasingly foreseeable wars with unforeseeably dreadful consequences. Relying on prosperity and more democracy in China to sort things out thus seems unwise. Two things need to be done. First, the slow progress towards a border settlement needs to resume. The main onus here is on China. It has the territory it really wants and has maintained its claim to Arunachal Pradesh only as a bargaining chip. It has, after all, solved intractable boundary quarrels with Russia, Mongolia, Myanmar and Vietnam ....

(a) Surely it cannot be so difficult to treat with India?
(b) Surely it will be more difficult with India?
(c) Can it solve dispute with India with its non democratic values?
(d) With India intentions are not clear.
(e) In Indian markets, Chinese presence is increasing.

31. ....and the proponents of market reforms have no plans for those who do not have the resources and income to buy even two meals a day. The signals are clear that those who cannot pay for their food have no right to survive. These poorer sections of society are reduced to mere victims, beneficiaries, clients and recipients. In this dichotomous relationship, the state is seen as the 'dole giver' and the people the 'dole receiver'. It must be recognized that irrespective of market-governed politics, people remain bound to survival, livelihood and identity issues.

(a) The governments have ceased to govern.
(b) When the market is allowed to govern, the government becomes powerless to effect any radical social changes.
(c) Elections have failed to make democracy distributive and justice oriented.
(d) It is about market reforms and absence of plans for the poorest of the poor.
(e) A patron-client relationship defines modern governments and the masses.

32. To succeed in today's crowded marketplace where most of the products and advertising look exactly the same, a small business owner must stand out, shouting above the din with a message so clear and compelling that prospects stop and take notice. It's a matter of business survival. Unfortunately, most entrepreneurs quickly retreat to the supposed security of sameness, soon to be lost in a sea of

anonymity and a tidal wave of frustration. In effect, albeit at a subconscious level, they are saying, "I don't want to be different".

In back room offices and store fronts everywhere, salespeople are telling business owners they should do this or that kind of ad because it worked so great for their competitor. The owners nod and sign on. It's already proven to be a winner, right? WRONG..........

    (a)   To make your advertising work, follow the principle if your competition is doing it, don't.

    (b)   Following your competitor is a sure recipe for disaster.

    (c)   Win the battle without a fight.

    (d)   It will fill people with a sense of déjà vu.

    (e)   You will do it at your own peril.

33. Google, the internet powerhouse, seeks to organize the entire world's information. The company has told publishers it will delay until November its work on copyrighted texts and will not scan any items that the copyright owner does not want included. The Assn. of American Publishers was outraged by this offer, saying Google is trying to turn copyright law inside out. Google should have to ask permission to copy a book for its database, they say, it shouldn't be up to publishers to object. Google argues that it is making a fair use of the books. The dispute could easily wind up in the courts. Building a guide to the contents of books is hardly the same as making bootlegged copies or plagiarizing. It's a monumental and costly task, and publishers have given no reason to believe they can do it for themselves. Unless their works are as well integrated with the Net as other forms of information and entertainment, they may be left waiting on the shelves for an audience that no longer bothers to walk through the stacks...............

    (a)   This has put both the internet search engine and the publishers on an unwarranted collision course

    (b)   Since the case might drag on for years to the detriment of both the parties, an out of court settlement is well advised

    (c)   Isn't it rather difficult, or even in fructuous to protect copyright on published text in this internet age?

    (d)   Perhaps both the parties ought to try and appreciate the other's viewpoint, as well as legitimate apprehensions, but with the overall goal of the public good in mind.

    (e)   Meanwhile, Google should show more respect for publishers' rights - and publishers should not make the mistake of using the strictures of copyright law to tie their own hands

34. Relations between the factory and the dealer are distant and usually strained as the factory tries to force cars on the dealers to smooth out production. Relations between the dealer and the customer are equally strained because dealers continuously adjust prices - make deals - to adjust demand with supply while maximizing profits. This becomes a system marked by a lack of long-term commitment on either side, which maximize feelings of mistrust. In order to maximize their bargaining positions, everyone holds back information - the dealer about the product and the consumer about his true desires....................

    (a)   As a result, 'deal making' becomes rampant, without concern for customer satisfaction.

    (b)   As a result, inefficiencies creep into the supply chain.

    (c)   As a result, everyone treats the other as an adversary, rather than as an ally

    (d)   As a result, fundamental innovations are becoming scarce in the automobile industry.

    (e)   As a result, everyone loses in the long run.

35. The tax system of India encourages borrowing by granting its taxpayers tax relief for interest paid on loans. The system also discourages saving by taxing any interest earned on savings. Nevertheless, it is clear that India's tax system does not consistently favour borrowing over saving, for if it did, there would be no______

    (a)   tax relief in India for those portions of a taxpayer's income, if any, that are set aside to increase that taxpayer's total savings

    (b)   tax relief in India for the processing fees that taxpayers pay to lending institutions when obtaining certain kinds of loans

    (c)   tax relief in India for interest that taxpayers are charged on the unpaid balance in credit card accounts

    (d)   taxes due in India on the cash value of gifts received by taxpayers from banks trying to encourage people to open savings accounts

    (e)   taxes due in India on the amount that a taxpayer has invested in interest-bearing savings accounts

36. .... Unemployment typically continues to rise even after GDP starts to increase, so pain for workers is far from over. Already 9.5% of the workforce is unemployed, and all of country's metropolitan areas reported unemployment rates of at least 10% in June. More jobless will probably mean less shopping and a slower recovery. The latest consumer-confidence numbers show that people are jittery. The quarterly GDP report also makes it clear that consumer spending, which rose slightly in the first quarter, dropped again in the second, by 1.2%. The good news, therefore, was more a result of government stimulus than evidence of a real, sustainable recovery in private demand.

    (a)   A greater worry is the bleeding in country's labour market.

    (b)   The Finance Department has revised its estimates of just how bad 2008 really was.

    (c)   Figures released by Commerce Department confirmed what most had been expected

    (d)   New GDP figures suggest some hope for country's economy. But the pain is far from over.

    (e)   House prices still have a long way to go before they return to the level of a year ago

37. Everything in New Delhi is extreme. It is a city of the incredibly rich and the miserably poor. For the rich, there are expensive private schools and hospitals, concert halls and theatres - although fewer of those than formerly - and restaurants. The poor are on a hiding to nowhere: all public facilities, schools and hospitals and housing, are deteriorating. But then there are some world known social workers in it. There are thousands of heroin addicts, and an equal number of carriers of the Aids virus. ....This is Delhi for you.

    (a)   But then there are thousands of people who are social

workers

(b) But then some of rarest examples of humanity come from this city

(c) But then there is a faith in the City

(d) But then there are people addict to charity and altruism also.

(e) But then there are people who are totally against the drugs and faithful to their partners

38. Computers are used in banks for a variety of reasons. They help bank personnel operate more efficiently and effectively. Computers are used to track certain transactions and they help process other customer information as well. Without computers, it would be very hard for a bank to offer good customer service day in and day out. Computers help a bank save time and money, and can be used as an aid to generate profits. In nutshell they have become indispensible part of the banks. Bank personnel become so helpless in absence of their machine that nervousness is evident on their faces while technical glitch renders the computer systems dysfunctional for a small period of time. .... once again queues starts to move and crowd starts to thin with fingers starting to work on keyboards; nervousness has made way for confidence of knowing everything at just a click of mouse.

(a) Crowd starts to swell and nervousness starts to turn in fear of failure.

(b) A sense of relief spreads as the problem gets rectified.

(c) There is a condition of traffic jam in banks and everything comes to a halt.

(d) It is not their fault and they are excused for it.

(e) Technology comes with its own disadvantages.

39. Some of the world's most expensive land can be found in central Mumbai.......... However, housing costs are distinctly lower in Mumbai's suburbs, surrounding prefectures and in other regions and cities of India. Additional commuting costs are often more than compensated by the savings on the rent, especially as many companies pay part or all of their employees' commuting expenses. If you prefer to live close to city centers, rented houses are an inexpensive option to consider. Utilities such as gas, water and especially electricity are expensive, and phone rates are high. For international calls, consider internet phones, callback services and other offers for the expat community.

(a) Consequently; even tiny apartments in the city center are very expensive

(b) This land is unauthorized land usurped by Land Mafia in the city

(c) A new bubble - Reality bubble similar to housing bubble of West is waiting to burst

(d) City is breathing on its seams

(e) The prices will continue to rise till Government comes out with an effective policy for reality prices in coming months

40. Now digest the main historical event of this week: China has officially become the world's second-biggest economy, overtaking Japan. In the West this has prompted concerns about China overtaking the United States sooner than previously thought. But stand back a little farther, apply a more Asian perspective............ These two Asian giants, which until 1800 used to make up half the world economy, are not, like Japan and Germany, mere nation states. In terms of size and population, each is a continent-and for all the glittering growth rates, a poor one.

(a) China's longer-term contest is with that other recovering economic behemoth: India

(b) China's longer term contest with USA is going to end in near future

(c) China is now focusing on Asian Market space more than other markets

(d) China is going in tandem with other Asian economy - India

(e) China's long term border dispute with India affects Asian economy's growth rate

41. North India lies in the Indo-Gangetic plain. Towards the North is the Himalayas, which separates the country from Central Asia. The Vindhya ranges separate the North from the South. South India is situated in the Peninsular Deccan Plateau. This region has the Arabian Sea in the west, Bay of Bengal in the east and Indian Ocean in the south. When talking about the racial differences, the North Indians are termed as Aryans, and the South Indians as Dravidians. In physique as well, there are many differences between the people of the South and North. The North Indians are taller, and more strongly built than the South Indians. The South Indians are a bit darker than the North Indians.............. Salwar Kamiz is the widely used dress by North Indian women. On the other hand, women in the South wear saris. While men in the North wear Salwar, the men in South prefer dhotis. Another difference that can be seen between North and South India is their food. When compared to the North Indian food, the South Indian food is spicier. The South Indians use more tamarind and coconut when compared to North Indians. The North Indians use more milk products when compared to the people of South India. When talking about the culture, there is vast difference between North and South India. One can come across differences in their music (Northern Hindustani and Southern Carnatic), dance forms and folks.

(a) A big difference is in their style of living

(b) A big difference is in their fashion statements

(c) A big difference can be seen in their dressing styles

(d) A big difference arises in their taste for clothes based on their earnings

(e) A big difference can be seen in their climate that demands different dressing styles

42. An open economy is an economy in which there are economic activities between domestic community and outside, e.g. people, including businesses, can trade in goods and services with other people and businesses in the international community, and flow of funds as investment across the border. Trade can be in the form of managerial exchange, technology transfers, all kinds of goods and services. Although, there are certain exceptions that cannot be exchanged, like, railway services of a country cannot be traded with another. To avail this service, a country has to produce its own. This contrasts with a closed

economy in which international trade and finance cannot take place. The act of selling goods or services to a foreign country is called exporting. The act of buying goods or services from a foreign country is called importing.............. There are a number of advantages for citizens of a country with an open economy. One primary advantage is that the citizen consumers have a much larger variety of goods and services from which to choose. Additionally, consumers have an opportunity to invest their savings outside of the country. In an open economy, a country's spending in any given year need not to equal its output of goods and services. A country can spend more money than it produces by borrowing from abroad, or it can spend less than it produces and lend the difference to foreigners. There is no closed economy in today's world.

(a) Together exporting and importing are collectively called trade

(b) Exporting and Importing are exclusive classes of trade

(c) Both are independent of each other and do not constitute the term 'trade'.

(d) Together they make GDP of a country

(e) Together they are indicators of influence of a country on world map

43. A no budget film is a produced film made with very little, or no money. Young directors starting out in filmmaking commonly use this method because there are few other options available to them at that point. All the actors and technicians are employed without remuneration, and the films are largely non-profit,................. or uses a very minimum "crew" of volunteers to assist him/her on such projects where no money or financing is available, not including the cost of film. No-budget films are made every day with video tapes and consumer cameras.

(a) Usually the director works alone on such films

(b) These films are huge employers in entertainment industry

(c) A team of experts two or three in number starts without any significant infrastructure

(d) Director is the cameraman, lightman, scriptwriter, screen player and sometimes even act himself in the film

(e) It is difficult task to find suitable people with desired skills, hence director works alone on such films

44. In finance, the term 'yield' describes the amount in cash that returns to the owners of a security. Normally it does not include the price variations, at the difference of the total return. Yield applies to various stated rates of return on stocks (common and preferred, and convertible), fixed income instruments (bonds, notes, bills, strips, zero coupon), and some other investment type insurance products (e.g. annuities)......... It can be calculated as a ratio or as an internal rate of return (IRR). It may be used to state the owner's total return, or just a portion of income, or exceed the income. It may be used for production output in other industries. Because of these differences, the yields from different uses should never be compared as if they were equal.

(a) The term is a misnomer

(b) The term is understood differently by different people

(c) The term has no definite meaning

(d) The term is used in different situations to mean different things

(e) The term slightly differs in meaning from the textbook definitions

45. Market trends are fluctuated on the demographics and technology. In a macro economical view, the current state of consumer trust in spending will vary the circulation of currency. In a micro economical view, demographics within a market will change the advancement of businesses and companies. With the introduction of the internet, consumers have access to different vendors as well as substitute products and services changing the direction of which a market will go. Despite that, it is believed that market trends follow one direction over a matter of time, there are many different factors that can change this idea. Technology s-curves as is explained in the book The Innovator's Dilemma. It states that technology will start slow then increase in users once better understood, eventually levelling off once another technology replaces it......................

(a) This proves that change in the market is actually consistent

(b) Change is inevitable

(c) Fluctuations with these changes do not last long

(d) Be prepared for the change

(e) Changing changes the fortunes

46. Being one of the central banks which was involved in the exercise of drawing up the Core Principles, the Reserve Bank of India had assessed its own position with respect to these Principles in 1998. The assessment had shown that most of the Core Principles were already enshrined in our existing legislation or current regulations. Gaps had been identified between existing practice and principle mainly in the areas of risk management in banks, inter-agency cooperation with other domestic/international regulators and consolidated supervision. Internal working groups were set up to suggest measures to bridge these gaps and their recommendations have been accepted by the Board for Financial Supervision and are now in the process of being implemented. Given the spread and reach of the Indian banking system, with over 60,000 branches of more than 100 banks........ However, the Reserve Bank of India is committed to the full implementation of the Core Principles. The Bank also serves on the Core Principles Liaison Group of the BCBS, which has been formed "to promote the timely and complete implementation of these principles worldwide".

(a) implementation is a challenge for the supervisors

(b) implementation is impossible

(c) implementation should be done on trail basis

(d) implementation is a problem for supervisors

(e) implementation is a long process to take years

47. Indian banks having overseas operations are required to lay down internal guidelines on country risk management and fix limits based on risk rating of the country. Limits should also be fixed for a group of countries in a particular risk category subject to a maximum ceiling fixed by RBI. In the normal course, prudential exposure norms apply to all loans and investments overseas including loans to sovereign entities .... Adequacy of the bank's

policy on identification, measurement and control of country risk is assessed during onsite inspection by host country representatives. It is also monitored through a quarterly return on country-wise counter party exposure.

(a) The overseas branches are governed by the host country regulations also

(b) Host country is speculative for the success of these branches

(c) Banks and host countries conduct joint audits in branches in that country

(d) Host country regulations do not bind on these overseas branches

(e) Success of overseas branches depend on only the policies of host countries

48. The audiences for crosswords and Sudoku, understandably, overlap greatly, but there are differences, too. A crossword attracts a more literary person, while Sudoku appeals to a keenly logical mind. Some crossword enthusiasts turn up their noses at Sudoku because they feel it lacks depth. A good crossword requires vocabulary, knowledge, mental flexibility and sometimes even a sense of humor to complete. It touches numerous areas of life and provides an 'Aha!' or two along the way...

(a) Sudoku, on the other hand, is just a logical exercise, each one similar to the last.

(b) Sudoku, incidentally, is growing faster in popularity than crosswords, even among the literati.

(c) Sudoku, on the other hand, can be attempted and enjoyed even by children.

(d) Sudoku, however, is not exciting in any sense of the term.

(e) Sudoku, whereas, gives better enthusiasm

49. Mental illness is often stigmatized..................... It is not as obviously fatal as many physical illnesses. But it still takes a heavy human and economic toll. That is why it is important that politicians make good on their promises-and that ordinary people dig deep, too.

(a) Though the brain is extraordinarily complex, further scientific breakthroughs can be expected.

(b) Post-traumatic stress disorder was only defined in 1980; understanding of that condition has jumped forward in the past few years, as have the treatments for it.

(c) Past investigations into early interventions in psychosis have since repaid themselves many times over.

(d) Many illnesses afflict the old disproportionately, but mental illness tends to strike the young, undermining productivity.

(e) It lacks an effective lobby to match the groups that represent victims of cancer and heart disease.

DIRECTIONS (Qs. 50-54): *In each of the following questions a short passage is given with one of the lines in the passage missing and represented by a blank. Select the best out of the five answer choices given, to make the passage complete and coherent.*

(IBPS PO/MT 2011)

50. Women's rights around the world are an important indicator to understand global well-being. A major global women's rights treaty was ratified by the majority of the world's nations a few decades ago. ...... These ranges from the cultural, political to the economic. For example, women often work more than men, yet are paid less; gender discrimination affects girls and women throughout their lifetime; and women and girls are often the ones that suffer the most poverty. Many may think that women's rights are only an issue in countries where religion is law. Or even worse, some may think this is no longer an issue at all. But reading the report about the United Nation's Women's Treaty and how an increasing number of countries are lodging reservations will show otherwise. Gender equality furthers the cause of child survival and development for all of society, so the importance of women's rights and gender equality should not be underestimated.

(a) This treaty tackled and solved a number of issues related to women.

(b) Why is it then, that moment still face a number of problems on the domestic front?

(c) Thus, the woman today is ten times more empowered as compared to a woman say about a decade ago.

(d) Women's activists across nations have implored the respective governments to take this seriously.

(e) Yet, despite many successes in empowering women, numerous issues still exist in all areas of life.

51. Research has shown that air pollutants from fossil fuel use make clouds reflect more of the sun's rays back into space. This leads to an effect known as global dimming whereby less heat and energy reaches the earth. .... However, it is believed that global dimming caused the droughts in certain parts of the world where millions died, because the northern hemisphere oceans were not warm enough to allow rain formation. Global dimming is also hiding the true power of global warming. By cleaning up global dimming-causing pollutants without talking greenhouse gas emissions, rapid warming has been observed, and various human health and ecological disasters have resulted, as witnessed during the European heat wave in 2003, which saw thousands of people die.

(a) This though, does not bring any relief in the problems associated with climate change.

(b) This phenomenon thus is part of the climate change problem.

(c) Scientists thus believe that this phenomenon goes hand in hand with global warming

(d) At first, it sounds like an ironic savior to climate change problems

(e) The answer to all our problems with respect to climate change is definitely here

52. Poverty is the state for the majority of the world's people and nations. Why is this? .... Have they been lazy, made poor decisions, and been solely responsible for their own plight? What about their governments? Have they pursued policies that actually harm successful development? Such causes of poverty and inequality are no doubt real. But deeper and more global causes of poverty are often less discussed. Behind the increasing interconnectedness promised by globalization are global decisions, policies,

and practices. These are typically influenced, driven, or formulated by the rich and powerful. These can be leaders of rich countries or other global actors such as multinational corporations, institutions, and influential people. In the face of such enormous external influence, the governments of poor nations and their people are often powerless. As a result, in the global context, a few get wealthy while the majority struggles.

(a) Is it enough to blame poor people for their own predicament?

(b) What is the government doing about it?

(c) Are the wealthy ones in the nation even aware of this?

(d) The government has already taken measures to eradicate the same.

(e) The huge gap between the rich and the poor in the nation is now narrowing

53. Analysts and industry pundits forecast that notebook market, which has been growing faster than the desktop market for the past three years, is expected to overtake the desktop market by the year 2011-12. A fall in prices, large deals from governments and institutions, and demand from consumers and sectors such as education are expected to help the notebook numbers. According to research agencies, the year 2010-11 saw notebook volumes rise, and for the first time a million plus notebooks were sold in India in a single quarter. The market has grown nearly four times for notebooks. The demand is driven by all sectors and a very buoyant consumer market, which prefers mobile computers. Entry-level notebook prices have dropped below the ₹ 25,000 mark; this has helped break the ice with new customers. This drop in notebook prices has been helped by the drop in the prices of the building blocks that make a notebook. It's simple. With notebook volumes growing, the prices of the components are also bound to come down. ....

(a) All this has resulted in a noticeable change in a number of large government tenders for notebooks; which were traditionally for desktops.

(b) Because of this the government still prefers desktops to notebooks and has passed tenders for the same.

(c) Thereby making them more expensive.

(d) Thus the forecast for the coming year states that desktops will be the preferred technology choice only for consumers who cannot afford the exorbitantly priced notebook.

(e) Thus notebooks will become obsolete after a decade or so.

54. Next to China, India is the most populated country in the world. ...... Particularly, rush to technical and higher education has increased as the scope for arts and science has become lesser and lesser due to lack of reforms and up gradation in the course structure and materials according to the developments of the world. Also, qualification in higher education gives added advantage to face successfully competition in the job market.

(a) Keeping this in mind, the government has provided

concessions in the admission fees for the arts and science streams in the country.

(b) Naturally there is too much rush and competition in every field.

(c) Despite this the rush to higher education is lesser.

(d) This population increase, though, has not kept pace with the knowledge expansion around the world.

(e) In the next decade it will become the most populous.

DIRECTIONS (Qs. 55-59): *Which of the phrases (a), (b), (c) and (d) given below each statement should be placed in the blank space provided so as to make a meaningful and grammatically correct sentence? If none of the sentences is appropriate, mark (e) i.e., 'None of the above' as the answer.*

(IBPS PO/MT 2013)

55. Overlooking the fact that water scarcity intensifies during summer, ...

(a) the government issued guidelines to all builders to limit their consumption to acceptable limits

(b) provision for rainwater harvesting has been made to aid irrigation in drought prone area

(c) the water table did not improve even after receiving normal monsoon in the current year

(d) many residential areas continue to use swimming pools, wasting large quantities water

(e) None of the above

56. Refuting the rationale behind frequent agitations for formation of separate states, a recent report ....

(a) proved that such agitations result in loss of governmental property

(b) indicated that the formation of small states does not necessarily improve the economy

(c) suggested that only large scale agitations have been effective in bringing out desired change in the past

(d) recommended dividing large states into smaller ones to improve governance

(e) None of the above

57. Achieving equality for women is not only a laudable goal, ...

(a) political reforms are also neglected preventing women from entering legislatures and positions of power

(b) the problem is also deep rooted in the society and supported by it

(c) their empowerment is purposefully hampered by people with vested interests in all sections of the society

(d) it is also equally difficult to achieve and maintain for a long term

(e) None of the above

58. he has lost most of his life's earning in the stock market but ....

(a) he still seems to be leading his life luxuriously and extravagantly

(b) he could not save enough to repay his enormous debts

(c) stock market is not a safe option to invest money unless done with caution

    (d)   experts have been suggesting to avoid investments in stock market because of its unpredictable nature

    (e)   None of the above

59.   ....or else they would not keep electing him year after year.

    (a)   The party leader gave a strong message to the mayor for improving his political style

    (b)   Owing to numerous scandals against the mayor, he was told to resign from the post immediately

    (c)   The mayor threatened the residents against filing a complaint against him

    (d)   The residents must really be impressed with the political style of their mayor

    (e)   None of the above

DIRECTIONS (Qs. 60-69): *Which of the phrases (a), (b), (c) and (d) given below each statement should be placed in the blank space provided so as to make a meaningful and grammatically correct sentence? If none of the sentences is appropriate, mark (e) as the answer.*

60.   Although information technology has entered the homes offices and hearts of many citizens of India, __________ .

    (a)   India provides the highest number of IT experts to the world every year

    (b)   many people in rural areas still remain ignorant of its immense benefits

    (c)   government has done its best by funding research in this field appropriately

    (d)   the face of communication in the years to come would change completely from the by gone years

    (e)   None of these

61.   While the environment-friendly nuclear energy could make a large addition to the energy resources, __________ .

    (a)   experts have a lot of expectations from this cleaner method of producing energy

    (b)   the government is determined to extract maximum out of this technology in the near future

    (c)   international lobby has been pressurising the developing nations to shift their energy production from coal to nuclear power.

    (d)   the problem of locating adequate numbers of uranium reserves to run the reactors is yet to be sorted out

    (e)   None of these

62.   __________ experts proposed the idea of a common school system.

    (a)   Overlooking the fundamental right of quality education of every child in India

    (b)   Since the curricular requirements of a rural child is different from an urban child

    (c)   Based on the fact that difference in the quality of schools acts as a ground for discrimination

    (d)   Since a large percentage of Indian children are getting free education

    (e)   None of these

63.   ______ the soil today is nowhere as rich in native minerals as it used to be some centuries ago.

    (a)   As there is a growing consent among farmers regarding limiting the use of chemical fertilizers

    (b)   As the chemical inputs in agriculture improved the yield many folds

    (c)   Owing to the uninhibited use of chemical inputs in agriculture

    (d)   Awareness among farmers regarding the side-effects of chemical farming grew when

    (e)   None of these

64.   As allegations of crores of rupees changing hands to permit illegal mining began to fly thick and fast, __________ .

    (a)   government ordered an enquiry which exposed a nexus between mine operators and bureaucrats

    (b)   it caused great damage to the surrounding ecosystem and the environment in general

    (c)   the officials have been irresponsible in failing to bring it to the notice of the court in time

    (d)   the powerful mining lobby had bribed the officials to obtain permit for mining on ecologically sensitive land

    (e)   None of these

65.   In order to help the company attain its goal of enhancing profit, all the employees ________

    (a)   urged the management to grant paid leave

    (b)   appealed the management to implement new welfare schemes

    (c)   voluntarily offered to work overtime with lucrative compensation

    (d)   voluntarily offered to render additional services in lieu of nothing

    (e)   decided to enhance production at the cost of quality of the product

66.   His behaviour is so unpredictable that he ______

    (a)   never depends upon others for getting his work done

    (b)   is seldom trusted by others

    (c)   always finds it difficult to keep his word

    (d)   always insists on getting the work completed on time

    (e)   seldom trusts others as far as the work schedule is concerned

67.   Although initial investigations pointed towards him _____

    (a)   the preceding events corroborated his involvement in the crime

    (b)   the additional information confirmed his guilt

    (c)   the subsequent events established that he was guilt

    (d)   the subsequent events proved that he was innocent

    (e)   he gave an open confession of his crime

68.   The weather outside was extremely pleasant and hence we decided to ________

    (a)   utilise our time in watching the television

    (b)   refrain from going out for a morning walk

    (c)   enjoy a morning ride in the open

    (d)   employ this rare opportunity for writing letters

    (e)   remain seated in our rooms in the bungalow

69.   With great efforts his son succeeded in convincing him not to donate his entire wealth to an orphanage _____

(a) and lead the life of a wealthy merchant
(b) but to a home for the forsaken children
(c) and make an orphan of himself
(d) as the orphanage needed a lot of donations
(e) as the orphanage had been set up by him

DIRECTIONS (Qs. 70-74): *In each of the following questions a short passage is given with one of the lines in the passage missing and represented by a blank. Select the best out of the five answer choices given, to make the passage complete and coherent (coherent means logically complete and sound).*

(SBI PO Main 2016)

70. _______________Business is instead moving to digital-native insurers, many of which are offering low premiums to those willing to collect and share their data. Yet the biggest winners could be tech companies rather than the firms that now dominate the industry. Insurance is increasingly reliant on the use of technology to change behaviour; firms act as helicopter parents to policyholders, warning of impending harm-slow down; reduce your sugar intake; call the plumber-the better to reduce unnecessary payouts. Yet this sort of relationship relies on trust, and the Googles and Apples of the world, on which consumers rely day-by-day and hour-by-hour, may be best placed to win this business.

(a) The growing mountain of personal data available to individuals and, crucially, to firms is giving those with the necessary processing power the ability to distinguish between low-risk and high-risk individuals.

(b) Cheap sensors and the tsunami of data they generate can improve our lives; blackboxes in cars can tell us how to drive more carefully and wearable devices will nudge us toward healthier lifestyles.

(c) The better behaviour resulting from smart devices is just one threat to the insurance industry. Conventional risk pools (for home or car insurance, for example) are shrinking as preventable accidents decline, leaving the slow-footed giants of the industry at risk.

(d) The uncertainty that underpins the need for insurance is now shrinking thanks to better insights into individual risks.

(e) The data has enabled insurance companies to gauge the situation and plan accordingly.

71. By calling for exempting unionized businesses from the minimum wage, unions are creating more incentives for employers to favor unionized workers over the non-unionized sort. Such exemptions strengthen their power. _______________. Once employers are obliged to pay the same minimum wage to both unionized and non-unionized labor, workers often see less reason to pay the dues to join a union.

(a) High rates of unionization make minimum-wage rules unnecessary as collaborative wage setting achieves the flexibility goals of a low minimum wage and the fairness goals of a high one.

(b) Workers who have no real alternative to employment in the unregulated shadows of the labor market are even more vulnerable to exploitation and abuse than workers with the legal right to take low wages.

(c) The labor ethos of worker solidarity seems hollow if non-union workers are underpriced by union workers and left unemployed or scrambling for unauthorized work.

(d) This is useful because for all the effort unions throw at raising the minimum wage, laws for better pay have an awkward habit of undermining union clout.

(e) Unions have been demanding democratic vaues in the work cluture but on the contrary they have been practicing dictatorial ways.

72. The premise that the choice of major amounts to choosing a career path rests on the faulty notion that the major is important for its content, and that the acquisition of that content is valuable to employers. But information is fairly easy to acquire and what is acquired in 2015 will be obsolete by 2020. What employers want are basic but difficult-to-acquire skills. _______________.
They care about a potential employee's abilities: writing, researching, quantitative, and analytical skills. A vocational approach to education eviscerates precisely the qualities that are most valuable about it: intellectual curiosity, creativity and critical thinking.

(a) As students flock to the two or three majors they see as good investments, professors who teach in those majors are overburdened, and the majors themselves become more formulaic and less individualized.

(b) Often it is the art historians and anthropology majors, for example, who, having marshaled the abilities of perspective, breadth, creativity, and analysis, have moved a company or project or vision forward.

(c) Furthermore, the link between education and earnings is notoriously fraught, with cause and effect often difficult to disentangle.

(d) Ideas such as education is necessary to be successful in corporate life are unacceptable because education isn't that much relevant into day's society.

(e) When they ask students about their majors, it is usually not because they want to assess the applicants' mastery of the content, but rather because they want to know if the students can talk about what they learned.

73. What happens to our brains as we age is of crucial importance not just to science but to public policy. _______________However, this demographic time-bomb would be much less threatening if the elderly were looked upon as intelligent contributors to society rather than as dependants in long-term decline. It is time we rethink what we mean by the ageing mind before our false assumptions result in decisions and policies that marginalize the old or waste precious public resources to re-mediate problems that do not exist.

(a) The idea that we get dumber as we grow older is just a myth, according to brain research that will encourage anyone old enough to know better.

(b) By 2030, for example, 72 million people in the US will be over 65, double the figure in 2000 and their average life expectancy will likely have edged above 20 years

(c) Many of the assumptions scientists currently make about 'cognitive decline' are seriously flawed and, for the most part, formally invalid.

(d) Using computer models to simulate young and old brains, Ramscar and his colleagues found they could account for the decline in test scores simply by factoring in experience

(e) The reason it becomes harder to recall an acquaintance's name as you grow older is that there are so many more of them.

74. The expenditure of time, money and sparse judicial and prosecutorial resources is often justified by claims of a powerful deterrent message embodied in the ultimate punishment- the death penalty.__________
In 2010, the average time between sentencing and execution in the United States averaged nearly 15 years. A much more effective deterrent would be a sentence of life imprisonment imposed close in time to the crime.

(a) A single federal death penalty case in Philadelphia was found to cost upwards of $10 million - eight times higher than the cost of trying a death eligible case where prosecutors seek only life imprisonment.

(b) The ethics of the issue aside, it is questionable whether seeking the death penalty is ever worth the time and resources that it takes to sentence someone to death.

(c) Apart from delaying justice, the death penalty diverts resources that could be used to help the victims' families heal.

(d) But studies repeatedly suggest that there is no meaningful deterrent effect associated with the death penalty and further, any deterrent impact is no doubt greatly diluted by the amount of time that inevitably passes between the time of the conduct and the punishment.

(e) While some victims and their families supported and some opposed the decision, any expectation that Tsarnaev will be put to death might be misplaced.

DIRECTIONS (Qs. 75-79): *In each of the following questions a short passage is given with one of the lines in the passage missing and represented by a blank. Select the best out of the five answer choices given, to make the passage complete and coherent (coherent means logically complete and sound).*

[IBPS PO/MT Main 2016]

75. The Time Traveler (for so it will be convenient to speak of him) was expounding a recondite matter to us. His grey eyes shone and twinkled, and his usually pale face was flushed and animated. The fire burned brightly, and the soft radiance of the incandescent lights in the lilies of silver caught the bubbles that flashed and passed in our glasses. Our chairs, being his patents, embraced and caressed us rather than submitted to be sat upon, and there was that luxurious after-dinner atmosphere when thought roams gracefully free of the trammels of precision. (__________________).

(a) And slowly and steadily, the atmosphere grew stale and lost all the vibrancy it had

(b) And he put it to us in this way—marking the points with a lean forefinger—as we sat and lazily admired his earnestness over this new paradox (as we thought it) and his fecundity

(c) We sat like toddlers do in a nursery, eagerly anticipating the show the Time Traveler would put on for us

(d) We sat benumbed by the proceedings, for the radiance of the Time Traveler was unimaginable and unbearable

(e) I caught Filby's eye over the shoulder of the Medical Man, and he winked at me solemnly.

76. Let us understand the definition of metaphysics, a purely speculative science, which occupies a completely isolated position and is entirely independent of the teachings of experience. It deals with mere conceptions—not, like mathematics, with conceptions applied to intuition—and in it, reason is the pupil of itself alone. It is the oldest of the sciences. (________________)

(a) And it would struggle to survive without the architecture of mathematical support that it draws its strength from

(b) Yet it continued to baffle mankind because of its abstractions

(c) But it has never had and never will have the good fortune to attain to the sure scientific method

(d) And it would still survive, even if all the rest were swallowed up in the abyss of an all-destroying barbarism

(e) This critical science is not opposed to the dogmatic procedure of reason in pure cognition; for pure cognition must always be dogmatic

77. However, it is possible that the non -resident entity may have a business connection with the resident Indian entity. In such a case, the resident Indian entity could be treated as Permanent Establishment of the nonresident entity. ....During the last decade or so, India has seen a steady growth of outsourcing of business processes by non residents or foreign companies to IT -enabled entities in India. Such entities are either branches or associated enterprises of the foreign enterprise or an independent India enterprise. The nonresident entity or foreign company will be liable to tax in India only if the IT -enabled BPO unit in India constitutes its Permanent Establishment.

(a) The tax treatment of the Permanent Establishment in such a case is under consideration

(b) How would the profit would be shared is not decided yet?

(c) A lengthy and cumber some process requiring a lot of application of mind and revenue principles is ahead for the tax department of India

(d) A new trend is seen in last decade.

(e) Indian companies have a lot on stake as competition increases.

78. Aggregation of risks is somewhat quite new to banks in India. While some banks have started thinking in that line by trying to put integrated limits framework and integrated risk policies as well as using CBS solutions for technological integration, the effort required is beyond such requirement. Risk aggregation would mean aggregating the individual risk measures to decide most appropriate assets class that would contain the risk to the desired level dictated by the risk appetite .Capital allocation (about how much) would be based on such strategies............

   (a) Most banks are yet to conceptualize the same in their processes

   (b) Most banks have already integrated it in their functioning; it is working over the years satisfactorily.

   (c) Which would in long run prove to be the growth impeding

   (d) Of risk aggregation which is really a new concept to Indian banks

   (e) On expected lines of the regulation conditions laid down in the manual of the bank

79. After two years, high inflation moderated in the later part of 2011-12 in response to past monetary tightening and growth deceleration. High inflation had adverse consequences on welfare and on saving and investment, particularly household saving in financial assets. The most serious consequence of inflation is .... As growth slowed down, in part due to high inflation, it further reduced the welfare of the common man through adverse impact on employment and incomes.

   (a) its destructive allocation impact on the industries that were lately coming up.

   (b) its negative impact on the rich and high-profile people.

   (c) its adverse distributional impact on the poor, people without social security and pensioners.

   (d) its wayward consequences on the public distribution system meant for the poor.

   (e) its unfavourable bearing on day to day commodities that are used by the common man.

ANSWER KEY

1	(a)	9	(a)	17	(b)	25	(a)	33	(d)	41	(c)	49	(e)	57	(e)	65	(d)	73	(b)
2	(c)	10	(d)	18	(c)	26	(a)	34	(d)	42	(a)	50	(a)	58	(a)	66	(b)	74	(d)
3	(c)	11	(a)	19	(d)	27	(d)	35	(a)	43	(a)	51	(c)	59	(d)	67	(d)	75	(d)
4	(d)	12	(a)	20	(c)	28	(a)	36	(d)	44	(b)	52	(a)	60	(b)	68	(c)	76	(c)
5	(a)	13	(a)	21	(a)	29	(d)	37	(d)	45	(a)	53	(a)	61	(d)	69	(c)	77	(d)
6	(c)	14	(a)	22	(a)	30	(a)	38	(b)	46	(a)	54	(b)	62	(c)	70	(c)	78	(d)
7	(d)	15	(a)	23	(c)	31	(b)	39	(a)	47	(a)	55	(d)	63	(c)	71	(d)	79	(e)
8	(a)	16	(b)	24	(b)	32	(b)	40	(a)	48	(a)	56	(b)	64	(a)	72	(e)		

Hints & Explanations

1. (a) Passage is about the cheap labour and its advantage while competition from the other countries with even cheaper labour is there. Part before the blank space discusses the same thing like overtaking from these cheaper countries. Next part should have something (as sentence starts with 'therefore') that makes India vigilant about the fact and option (a) is having that part additionally it contains the information how India should build on the advantage it had of cheap labour as discussed in major part of the passage; hence, this is the best sentence to finish the passage.
From the other options, (b) is second best and can be an option in absence of (a). Option (c) ,(d),(e) are not logical.

2. (c) Option (a) is wrong as scrapping of the EIA is not discussed in any part of the passage. Rather improvement is discussed in subsequent part after the blank space. Option (b) and (e) are totally out of place as these do not go in with theme of passage. Only option which is brief and accurate for the blank space and connects two parts of passage is (c). As this is a general statement and can be inserted in without affecting the sense in which passage is flowing. Option (d) is also not right for its negative approach.

3. (c) It has been already given that all the institutes work in coordination; so, option (d) and (e) is redundant and repeating same thing in different manner. Sentence indicates that though these institutions work in coordination these are having different responsibilities to shoulder. But again there are two options which are nearly saying same thing -option (b) and Option (c). But in option (b) 'different direction' is not right. If they are working in different directions, then what is the need of coordinating? Option (a) is not correct for the context.

4. (d) Statement after the blank space contradicts what is said in the option (a). So it is not right. Membership is not being discussed here so option (b) is also not right. Reason of option (a) goes with option (c) also. Option (e) is totally wrong. Only option which comes appropriate with the passage content and position of blank space is option (d).

5. (a) Option (e) is too general and can be avoided. Option b) is not right as Issue is related to the India not the world, so role of World Bank looks irrelevant in this context. Discussion in parliament is too farfetched in option (c). Option (a) rightly indicates that Indian Government's policy for the matter discussed in passage would be instructive. Option (d) is out of context for its deviation from the topic.

6. (c) Market is being discussed here not the countries. Option (e) is fit for the context but not for the place of the blank space where immediately before it shielding the markets is being described and immediately after conflict between the Indian and foreign entrepreneur is given. Conflict of countries is not given. So this open is too wide in its scope for the blank space and hence cannot be appropriate. Other options are inappropriately distant from the context.

7. (d) Passage is a comparison of Centre and State Government's plans, finances and expenditures. In this particular portion of passage which has the blank part, it is mentioned that State finances are increasing at rapid rate and now they have more liberty for spending on expenditures; meanwhile, a comparison is also done with centre's expenditures in part following the blank space; so, option (d) which encompasses this sense of part of passage is correct filler. Option (a) is opposite of what is being said in the passage. Option (b) and (c) discusses revenues and borrowing of centre which is not mentioned or intended in the passage so these are incorrect. Option (e) is repetition of what is given in statement after the blank space.

8. (a) Option (e) is doubtful as it seems to be judgment than a closing sentence. Legality of budget cannot be ascertained through the passage. It is not a promise either. Only option (a) captures the theme of passage in single sentence. Hence it is the finishing sentence.

9. (a) Blank part should take some common perception of budget as the passage wants to indicate that the budget is not this…. but it is that…… and option (a) in best captures the essence of this logic.

10. (d) As a study report is not a legal document it is not binding on anyone. Sentence represents study in a lighter vein so it must not be taken seriously but as the study is done there must be some purpose of it and results at least is taken note of. This logic brings to the option (d) which is correct part to complete the incomplete sentence of passage.

11. (a) Only option (a) seems to be logical for the context. As subsequent part of passage shows how it was a problem to bail out one and to deny other the same resources. Option (d) and (e) are out of place.

12. (a) It is only logical option, other options do not follow any logic. If income is less than expenditure then there is definitely a loss.

13. (a) As the passage says that risk aggregation is new at the beginning of passage it can be inferred that most banks are yet to conceptualize it in their processes. Hence option (a) is correct. Option (c) is farfetched

conclusion. Option (d) is repetition of what is being stated in passage earlier. So it cannot be the answer.

14. (a) Passage is about non-resident Indian entity and its tax deduction. Other options are not in the context of passage as they talk about the things which are not given or can be inferred from the passage.

15. (a) Before the blank space, centre-state problems are discussed and after the blank, advantage of finance commission is given in this regard. So option (a) in right approach has shown finance commission in connection with both the problems and its own advantage. Option (c) is out of context. Option (d) is also mentioned in passage in later parts. Option (e) can be true but not the best answer.

16. (b) Option (b) is right as it has connection with what is said in the passage after the blank space. Mercy in this option connects well with not a trade, not a business etc.

17. (b) Last part of passage is about shortcomings given in the statement of option (b). New approach in option (d) can fit but leaves the passage stranded and two parts before the blank and after the blank cannot be joined through this option.

18. (c) The submarine is newly developed and introduced. It is like coming out from maternity ward to nursery.

19. (d) As this car is specially designed for the women it can be said that car is designed by all women team. This is the best option which emphasizes the point of passage.

20. (c) First finance commission laid down some of the principles which were followed by subsequent commissions is a positive statement which is the tone of passage. Passage presents the finance commission in positive light. Option (e) and (d) are doubtful and cannot be reached from the passage.

21. (a) In this part of passage a comparison of women with men in public or private sector is given with balance tilting to side of women. When preference is given to women in a particular sector then promotion to senior position is also imminent. Hence this option is best one to choose.

22. (a) Passage portion is not about the management of finances but the improvement in finances and restructuring of expenditures. Mending the ways of government is too strong a statement and does not apply here.

23. (c) Only option (c) is logical and sensible as rich cannot be centre point of any economy. They do not have the remote control either. Option (e) is just general statement and not in sync with passage. Fate of poor in the hands of rich seems irrational.

24. (b) Certain words in other options make them doubtful - 'most' in option (a); 'Risk level' in option (c). Comparison with other parts of world is not intended here as given in option (d).

25. (a) All options can fit. But the best one is (a) because It emphasizes the point said initially in the passage with word 'stubborn'.

It relates with German issue coherently.
It has detail definition of fallacy which is a requirement when one thing is being discussed again after a long gap in passage.

26. (a) Next sentence after the blank space suggests that blank should have something simple about the inflation. This simple thing should be logical and sensible. Option (a) is simple and goes well with the flow of passage. Option (d) is not right as cure cannot lie in inflation itself. Option (e) is repetition of what was said in the introduction of passage.

27. (d) Options like (e) and (b) are doubtful as passage does not mention such a thing in any of its part. Option (a) talks about all parties but the next statement after the blank space is contradicting it. Option (c) is negative and for fiscal federalism, passage discusses its plight not its shortcoming or of democracy as given in option (b). Only option that can fill the blank for matching with the content of passage is option (d). This sentence and next sentence both are a combination and coherent in flow.

28. (a) Other options cannot be inserted in the blank space as they are not logical and in sync with passage. Option (b) can be right if 'only' is removed from it. Use of 'only' makes it incorrect. Banks and Stock markets are decentralization agents and hence are needed as per passage in this way option (c) is against the passage. Then option (d) unnecessarily will introduce comparison between banks and stock markets while passage presents both in as a pair. Option (e) is also wrong on the basis of this logic.

29. (d) This question is to be solved by reading whole passage as no immediate connections can be derived with sentence preceding the blank space and one following it. If Japan is third then which one are two other - it is answered in option (d). USA and China are referred to in the entire passage. So they can be the other two. Option (a) is hypothetical in nature and needs some explanation to follow after it. Option (b) also needs some base. This is the case with option (c) and option (e).

30. (a) Last sentence shows that China has solved border dispute with a number of countries, while the passage is mainly about the relationship of India and China. This indicates that finishing statement should also be about improvement in relationships of India and China. This is given in all options. But option (a) poses a valid question as passage shows that relationships between two countries are improving.
From the other options (d) is not correct as positive improvements are illustrated in passage. Markets of option (e) are not discussed here in passage. Option (b) is opposite to the spirit of the passage.

31. (b) As per the passage in starting portion, it has been given that market oriented people do not have plans for poor people or in other words no social agenda which is definitely the priority of any government. But

if power of government is transferred to others (market forces in this case), then there would not be any radical social change. From the other options, (c) discusses elections but there is nothing related to elections in the passage. Option (d) is contradicting what is said in the statement following the blank space. Option (e) seems to be a finishing sentence rather than an opening sentence as it is related to last part of passage not with the starting part.

32. (b) Option (b) vehemently represents the sense of the passage; additionally it contains a message that author wants to convey. One more point that supports this option is it fits well with the capitalized word (which is of course used to emphasize) WRONG. Hence strong message should follow it.

33. (d) This option is right as it does not judge or present an opinion rather it comes up with a possibility with right approach i.e. positive and covers legal aspect of matter as well. Other options are more or less judgments or opinions that do not qualify as finishing /closing statement.

34. (d) All other options except (e) are rephrasing of already discussed facts of passage. But Option (e) is incomplete as it does not show what can be the loss specifically. But option (d) shows it. It can be inferred that holding back information would lead to lack of innovations in auto industry, these innovations can be in supply chain for dealers, new car models with improved performance at cheap pricing for customers/ end users and increased profit for company.

35. (a) Understand it this way - Although savings is discouraged, borrowings are not encouraged for a longer (persistent) period. This question is a difficult one. Best method to solve these types of questions is to use elimination method. Option (c) is out of context as talking about credit cards is rejected. Option (d) involves giving gifts by banks for opening saving account which seems to be giving triviality to the matter of paragraph. Option (e) is second best option. But contradicts what is said in passage.
Option (a) is best answer for the blank space as it supports only what is given in passage.

36. (d) Passage shall start with a hope in the GDP figures as in next sentence that hope fades away. See the use of word 'even after' this indicates that incident detailed here should have happened before it. Another thing that goes in favour of option (d) is that it shows the pain of unemployment and its sustenance which is a major issue highlighted in paragraph.

37. (d) 'Also' of this statement connects well with the preceding sentence. Passage presents Delhi in two different shades. And this statement complements the negative statement just before the blank space. The same example is given earlier in passage - on one hand, social amenities deteriorating while on the other hand world known social workers are also working in Delhi. In the same sense while there are people with addiction

for wrong things, there are also people with addiction to right things.

38. (b) Passage can be divided in two parts - one before the blank space and another after the blank space. First part says that bank people are nervous as computer systems are not working. Second part says that queues get thinner. It means problem mentioned in first part gets rectified and effect of it is seen in second part.

39. (a) This option connects well with the opening statement. Second option cannot be reached through passage. Third option also needs some mentioning in the passage. In absence of this linkage it does not qualify for the correct answer. Option (d) is irrelevant. Option (e) is again introducing governance issue that in absence of any elaboration in further reading of passage becomes inappropriate.

40. (a) 'These two Asian giants' hints reference of some Asian country in previous line. On this basis Option (b) is wrong. Option(c) is about only the China, Option (e) gives new dimension to passage by introducing border dispute which is unwarranted. Fight is between Option (d) and Option (a); latter scores over former as word 'behemoth' complements 'giants' of subsequent sentence.

41. (c) After the blank space two or three sentences are about the dressing styles of North and South Indians. It is not about the climate or earning based choice or fashion. Rather it is just the difference on general basis.

42. (a) This question is more of a checking of logic and sense than an understanding of the passage. Only export and import do not make GDP of a country. They are not the only indicators of influence of a country on world map. Option (c) is not logical and no sense prevails through it.

43. (a) Option (b) is not correct as it goes against the passage. Option (e) is illogical and does not fit as there is no reason why skilled people are not available. Option (d) seems frivolous on the basis of its impossibility. Experts are not discussed in passage. Only option which fits well in the context is director working alone on such films of low budget.

44. (b) See the part of passage after the blank space - this gives a number of meanings of term 'yield' taken in different fields. This is the same thing which is stated in the passage. From the other options, text definition angle is wrong in (e). Option (d) is linking the term with situations which is not correct. Option (a) and (c) are false.

45. (a) This is best option which expresses the fact illustrated in passage that the market is ever changing. Other options are generalized statements with no special linkage to passage.

46. (a) Implementation can be a challenge for such a wide banking system of India but it cannot be impossible or problem (supervisors are there to implement). It is foolish to implement on trail basis on a vast scale. Option (e) can be true or false as passage does not elaborate on it.

47. (a) A little reasoning is required to solve the question. If a foreign bank is operating in a country, then it shall be governed by the regulations of that country along with its original county. Then only that country will allow it to operate. On this logic option (d) can be rejected. Little extension of this logic discards the possibility of audit in country of origin. Hence rule out (c). Success does not depend on only policies of a country it demands a lot of other ingredients. Reject (e). Option (b) is inappropriate as passage does not support it.

48. (a) Option (a) is the answer. The paragraph, in the beginning, highlights the main points of difference between Sudoku and a crossword. Therefore, we are looking for a contrast, which is not present in options (b) and (d). Option (c) is too specific, which is why we pick Option (a).

49. (e) In the next statement after the blank, mental illness is compared with physical illness and is said that politicians and people should take this matter seriously. Now in option (e) also mental illness is compared with cancer and heart disease that are physical illness and it is said that it lacks effective lobby to match.. lobby-attempts.

50. (a) For attempting this type of questions it is important to correlate what is being stated before the blank space and what is stated after the blank.

    While it is also important to see in which direction the passage will go if a particular choice is selected.

    In this question, women's rights treaty being ratified by a number of countries is discussed so in the following sentence effects of these should be discussed. Option (b) can be rejected as for solving the problems treaty was ratified. (c) is a judgmental statement and should be avoided when no certain information is available. (d) can fit well before the ratification of the treaty but not after it. There should be a continuation in passage. Option (e) is incorrect for the logic that first basic rights will be achieved and then only empowering can be mentioned. This option is one step further and not about the women's right.

51. (c) Option (b) & (d) can be rejected as climate change is mentioned nowhere in the passage. After the blank global warming is mentioned and before it global dimming. So blank can work as a connector for both of these. Option (c) includes both. Hence this is the best option. (e) is like deciding in haste without understanding the intent of passage.

52. (a) Before blank space a question is posed. And after the blank space reasons which can be associated with poor people themselves is discussed so the blank space should have a special mention of poor people whether in form of question or a simple statement (b) & (d) won't fit well here so they can be ruled out.

    Rich is not even introduced in passage till this point, therefore option (e) can also be rejected. Additionally Option (a) gives a logical and sensible flow to the passage.

53. (a) Only option which is positive for notebooks and is in accordance with their prices coming down is (a). Option (b) is against what is being said in the last line of the passage. (c) is completely illogical and hard to come by as it talks about the prices of components coming down but prices note books soring high. (e) is also in different direction and is not related to spirit of passage. Option (d) is about desktops not note books.

54. (b) Sentence before the blank space is about the population and after it about the rush in for college education Option (b) is related to both the statements (before and after the blank) (e) is repetition of what is said in opening statement. (a) is like sudden intrusion of government's angle in passage with no relation to statements preceding and following the blank space.

75. (d) The description of the radiant lights and the last line logically invites option (d) we sat benumbed by the proceedings, for the radiance of the Time Traveler was unimaginable and unbearable.

76. (c) It is said that Metaphysics is a purely speculative science…. It deals with mere conceptions and the last sentence, It is the oldest of the science, logically concludes option (c), But it has never had and never will have the good fortune to attain to the sure scientific method.

77. (d) The second sentence--- In such a case…..Indian entity could be treated….. Again the sentence that runs after the blank….During the last decade or so, suggests option (d), A new trend is seen in last decade is the correct choice.

78. (d) Capital allocation (about how much) would be based on such strategies of risk aggregation which is really a new concept to Indian banks.

79. (e) The most serious consequence of inflation is its unfavourable bearing on day to day commodities that are used by the common man.

◇ ◇ ◇

DIRECTIONS (Qs. 1-15): *In the following questions, a part of the sentence is given in bold, it is then followed by three sentences which try to explain the meaning of the phrase given in bold. Choose the best set of alternatives from the five options given below each question which explains the meaning of the phrase correct.ly without altering the meaning of the sentence given as question.*

1. **The dichotomy is the striking feature.** An estimated 20 per cent of our population is economically advanced with access to the latest technology, while the rest wallows in inhuman conditions.
   - (I) The contrast can clearly be understood by the fact that an estimated one-fifth of our population is economically sound with access to the latest technology while the rest are still in critical condition.
   - (II) It is quite attractive that around 20 per cent of our population has access to the latest technology unlike the rest of the population thereby, contributing more in the economic development.
   - (III) It is shameful that the majority of our population is unaware of advanced technology and thus, they are not able to compete with the technologically advanced people of our country.
   - (a) Only (I) is correct.
   - (b) Only (III) is correct.
   - (c) Both (II) and (III) are correct.
   - (d) Both (I) and (III) are correct.
   - (e) None is correct.

2. It may have taken 20 years to develop the export market for UK garden furniture, but if there is to be a price war, **the industry could be back to square one within** 12 months.
   - (I) It took two decades to develop the export market for UK garden furniture, however, in case of high competition among its peers, it will always emerge victorious and that too within 1 year.
   - (II) The development of the export market of UK garden furniture took 20 years and it has reached to such a position that in case of price war, it can defeat all other industries within 12 months.
   - (III) Despite 20 years of hard work done to develop the export market of UK garden furniture, still the industry is sceptical about it success. It may fall down in case of a price war.
   - (a) Only (I) is correct.
   - (b) Only (II) is correct.
   - (c) Only (III) is correct.
   - (d) Both (I) and (II) are correct.
   - (e) None is correct.

3. As the situation got out of control during the match, **the captain of the team tried to put oil over troubled waters.**
   - (I) Seeing the situation going out of control, the captain of the team tried to calm down the players.
   - (II) As the situation was out of control, the captain of the team had no other option than to support his teammates and fight with the opposition.
   - (III) Taking advantage of the bad situation, the captain of the team too argued along with his teammates and tried to worsen the situation.
   - (a) Only (I) is correct.
   - (b) Only (II) is correct.
   - (c) Only (III) is correct.
   - (d) Both (II) and (III) are correct.
   - (e) None is correct.

4. **The manager had to eat a humble pie** after the workers decided to go on strike to protest against the biased salary hike and promotions.
   - (I) The manager politely refused to take his decision back despite knowing that the employees would go for a strike against the nepotism in salary hike and promotions.
   - (II) Seeing the urgency of the situation and the threat of strike given by the workers, the manager withdrew his decision of giving salary hike and promotions to his favourite employees.
   - (III) Knowing the fact that the employees would go for a strike against the biased salary hike and promotions, the manager gave up his pride and apologized for his mistake.
   - (a) Only (I) is correct.
   - (b) Only (II) is correct.
   - (c) Only (III) is correct.
   - (d) Both (II) and (III) are correct.
   - (e) None is correct.

5. The teacher tried his best to explain the importance of the chapter to the students but soon realized that he **was casting pearls before swine.**
   - (I) The teacher soon realized that whatever he was explaining to the students about the chapter was grasped by them the way he expected.
   - (II) Despite the hard work done by the teacher to explain the importance of the chapter, the students were busy making mockery of him.
   - (III) After trying his best to make the students understand the importance of the chapter, the teacher soon realized that they are not recognising its worth.
   - (a) Only (I) is correct.

(b) Only (II) is correct.

(c) Only (III) is correct.

(d) Both (II) and (III) are correct.

(e) None is correct.

6. Any curb on access to higher education, for instance, **would run counter to the prevailing mood** among the middle class, which wants further improvements to the overall standard of living.

(I) Any restriction on access to higher education would barely affect the mood of the middle class which expects further improvements to the overall standard of living.

(II) The present spirit of the middle class which wants further improvements to the overall standard of living will worsen if the access to higher education is paused for any reason.

(III) Any clampdown on the access to higher education is likely to alter the mood of the middle class which wants further improvements to the overall standard of living.

(a) Only (I) is correct.

(b) Only (II) is correct.

(c) Only (III) is correct.

(d) Both (II) and (III) are correct.

(e) None is correct.

7. We were all set for the picnic but the sudden change in the plan by my dad to go for the movie instead of picnic came **out of the blue.**

(I) The sudden change in the plan to go for the movie instead of picnic was a well- thought-out idea by my dad.

(II) The sudden change made in the plan by my father to go for the movie instead of picnic was unexpected for us.

(III) My dad had already made his mind to change the plan to go for the movie instead of picnic, however, we had intuitions about the change.

(a) Only (I) is correct.

(b) Only (II) is correct.

(c) Only (III) is correct.

(d) Both (I) and (III) are correct.

(e) None is correct.

8. The Supreme Court has **struck a blow for the rights of the disabled**, with a direction to the Central and State governments to provide full access to public facilities, such as buildings and transport, within stipulated deadlines.

(I) The Supreme Court has ordered all the states to provide full access to public facilities like building and transport to the disabled and they must not ignore the true spirit and purpose of the law made for these people.

(II) The Supreme Court has ordered the central government to provide the basic amenities to the disabled within the stipulated time period.

(III) The Supreme Court has warned the Central and State governments for the rights of the disabled which they are deprived of and has ordered them to provide full access to public facilities, such as buildings and transport, within stipulated deadlines.

(a) Only (I) is correct.

(b) Only (II) is correct.

(c) Only (III) is correct.

(d) All are correct.

(e) None is correct.

9. At the UN General Assembly, USA and India accused Pakistan of funding terrorism in South-East Asia but **Pakistan kept on beating around the bush.**

(I) USA and India accused Pakistan of funding terrorism in South-East Asia at the UN General Assembly however, Pakistan kept on refusing it.

(II) Pakistan was accused of funding terrorism in South-East Asia at the UN General Assembly by India and USA but Pakistan kept on avoiding this topic.

(III) The rising terror in the South-East Asia was the major concern at the UN General Assembly. USA and India accused Pakistan of funding terrorism in the area which was partially accepted by Pakistan.

(a) Only (I) is correct.

(b) Only (II) is correct.

(c) Only (III) is correct.

(d) All are correct.

(e) None is correct.

10. **Manish was in doldrums** after he was badly scolded by the teacher in front of all the students.

(I) Manish was in huge anger after being badly scolded by the teacher in front of all the students.

(II) Manish felt so insulted after being badly scolded by the teacher in front of all his colleagues that he started planning to take the revenge of the insult.

(III) Manish was depressed after he was badly scolded by the teacher in front of all the students.

(a) Only (I) is correct.

(b) Only (II) is correct.

(c) Only (III) is correct.

(d) Both (I) and (II) are correct.

(e) None is correct.

11. The Reservation system has long been a serious **bone of contention** for the government.

(I) The Reservation system has been one of the major issues for the government for a very long time.

(II) The government is yet undecided about the Reservation system despite various discussions done on it.

(III) For the government, the Reservation system has been an issue over which there have been continuing disagreements for a long a time.

(a) Only (I) is correct.

(b) Only (II) is correct.

(c) Only (III) is correct.

(d) All are correct.

(e) None is correct.

12. The government's new scheme was initially welcomed, but later **turned out to be a house of cards** when it was discovered how easy it was to perpetrate a scam.

(I) The new scheme of the government was initially welcomed, however, it proved to be a poor plan when it was discovered how easy it was to carry out a scam.

(II) The government's new scheme was initially welcomed, but later its importance got justified when it was discovered how easy it was to catch the people indulged in scams.

(III) With the motive to check the scams, the government came up with a new scheme which later proved to be successful.

(a) Only (I) is correct.
(b) Only (II) is correct.
(c) Only (III) is correct.
(d) Both (II) and (III) are correct.
(e) None is correct.

13. After taking the oath, **the minister hit the nail on the head** when he laid out a list of grievances which people had with the previous government.

(I) After taking the oath, the minister was shocked to see the list of grievances which people had with the previous government.

(II) Soon after taking the oath, the minister was given a list of grievances which people had with the previous government and he was astounded by it.

(III) As soon as he took the oath, the minister scratched his head with his nails when he saw the list of grievances which people had with the previous government.

(a) Both (I) and (III) are correct.
(b) Both (II) and (III) are correct.
(c) Both (I) and (II) are correct.
(d) All are correct.
(e) None is correct.

14. As powerful **men drop like flies** due to their inability to resist abusing their authority, it's clear that the problem is widespread.

(I) The problem remains widespread as powerful men succumb to their inability of abusing their authority.

(II) The problem is widespread as powerful men try hard to cater their authority but unfortunately, they fail.

(III) The problem can be solved only if powerful men use their authority in the right way rather than abusing it.

(a) Only (I) is correct.
(b) Only (II) is correct.
(c) Both (I) and (III) are correct.
(d) All are correct.
(e) None is correct.

15. Since he wasn't aware of the reason of dispute, he **decided to sit on the fence** during the argument between his neighbours.

(I) As he was not a part of the dispute between his neighbours, he decided to stay away from it.

(II) Since he was not aware of the reason of dispute between his neighbours, he decided to remain neutral.

(III) Since he was not aware of the reason of dispute between his neighbours, he didn't say anything in anyone's favour.

(a) Only (I) is correct.
(b) Only (II) is correct.
(c) Both (II) and (III) are correct.
(d) All are correct.
(e) None is correct.

DIRECTIONS (Qs. 16-30): *In each of the given questions, an inference is given in bold which is then followed by three paragraphs. You have to find the paragraph(s) from where it is inferred. Choose the option with the best possible outcome as your choice.*

16. **Triple talaq is banned now**

(I) The Supreme Court said triple talaq violates the fundamental rights of Muslim women as it irrevocably ends marriage without any chance of reconciliation. Triple talaq, or verbal divorce, is practised by some in the Muslim community to instantly divorce their wives by saying talaq three times.

(II) By ruling the discriminatory practice of instant triple talaq as unconstitutional and unlawful, the Supreme Court has sent out a clear message that personal law can no longer be privileged over fundamental rights. Three of the five judges on the Constitution Bench have not accepted the argument that instant talaq, or talaq-e-biddat, is essential to Islam and, therefore, deserves constitutional protection under Article 25.

(III) The Centre's proposal to make instant triple talaq an offence punishable with three-year imprisonment and a fine is an unnecessary attempt to convert a civil wrong into a criminal act. By a three-two majority, the Supreme Court has already declared, and correct.ly, that the practice of talaq-e-biddat, or instant divorce of a Muslim woman by uttering the word 'talaq' thrice, is illegal and unenforceable.

(a) Only (I) is correct.
(b) Only (II) is correct.
(c) Only (III) is correct.
(d) Both (II) and (III) are correct.
(e) All are correct.

17. **It is good to invest in Bitcoin**

(I) India's policy on Bitcoin regulation is still evolving and no legal framework exists. The RBI has cautioned against its use, informing users, holders, investors and traders dealing with virtual currencies that they are doing so at their own risk.

(II) One lakh rupees invested in bitcoin in 2010 would be worth a few hundred crore rupees today. That is the kind of extraordinary return the digital currency has given investors as its price has witnessed a meteoric rise, from just a few cents in 2010 to hit a lifetime high of over $11,000 last week.

(III) Even if you become a bitcoin miner, there is no guarantee that you would be able to mine a certain number of bitcoins. Any scheme related to bitcoins promising a fixed return is likely a tall promise best avoided.

(a) Only (I) is correct.
(b) Only (II) is correct.
(c) Only (III) is correct.
(d) Both (II) and (III) are correct.
(e) All are correct.

18. **Cyber security is a major concern for country like India**

(I) India is one of the key players in the digital and knowledge-based economy, holding more than a 50%

share of the world's outsourcing market. Pioneering and technology-inspired programmes such as Aadhaar, MyGov, Government e-Market, DigiLocker, Bharat Net, Startup India, Skill India and Smart Cities are propelling India towards technological competence and transformation. India is already the third largest hub for technology-driven startups in the world and its Information and Communications Technology sector is estimated to reach the \$225 billion landmark by 2020.

(II) To encourage development of new technologies in the field of cyber security, the Ministry of Electronics and Information Technology will offer challenge grants of up to Rs 5 crore to start-ups to spur research and development, Minister for Electronics and IT said on the previous day. "We are in the process of working with Data Security Council of India to conduct challenge grant for cyber security...," the Minister added.

(III) Two things set aside India's digital spaces from that of major powers such as the United States and China: design and density. India is a net information exporter. Its information highways point west, carrying with them the data of millions of Indians. This is not a design flaw, but simply reflects the popularity of social media platforms and the lack of any serious effort by the Indian government to restrict the flow of data.

(a) Only (I) is correct.
(b) Only (II) is correct.
(c) Only (III) is correct.
(d) Both (II) and (III) are correct.
(e) None is correct.

19. **Demonetisation has benefitted the Indian Economy**

(I) While the jury is still out on whether last year's demonetisation has harmed the Indian economy, the government's Chief Statistician maintains that the picture will become clear in the current fiscal only after data from the government and company accounts come in. He maintains he has reservations about "making quick" judgements about the note ban decision that had affected the economy at multiple levels, and that it should not be seen just from the perspective of cash replacement, but as one that produced many benefits too.

(II) Listing out the advantages of demonetisation, Union Finance Minister said that direct tax collections had risen 15.7% till September 18, adding that undisclosed income of ' ₹ 5,400 crore was also detected. "Net collections up to September 18 in the current financial year rose to ₹ 3.7 lakh crore, a growth of 15.7%. The revenue collections in case of direct taxes rose to ₹ 8,49,818 crore during 2016-17, a growth of 14.5%," he said.

(III) Indian Economy has witnessed close to 20% decline in currency in circulation, number of tax payers has considerably increased and a large number of shell companies have been identified.

(a) Only (I) is correct.
(b) Only (II) is correct.
(c) Only (III) is correct.
(d) Both (II) and (III) are correct.
(e) All are correct.

20. **The government is trying hard to lure FDI in India**

(I) In yet another significant move to attract Foreign Direct Investment (FDI), the government has opened the door wider in several major sectors of the Indian economy, through what it calls "path-breaking" amendments in the extant FDI policy.

(II) In less than a year, the Government of India has announced yet another set of "radical changes" in foreign direct investment (FDI) policies. The earlier announcement in November 2015 introduced changes in 15 major sectors, and the latest announcement covers nine sectors which seek to further simplify the regulations governing FDI in the country and make India an attractive destination for foreign investors.

(III) For India, the servicing burden of FDI in terms of repatriations, dividend payments and payments for use of intellectual property is now showing up prominently. About half of the inflows into India during the past six years were balanced by outflows.

(a) Only (I) is correct.
(b) Only (II) is correct.
(c) Only (III) is correct.
(d) Both (I) and (II) are correct.
(e) All are correct.

21. **Does India need Bullet Trains?**

(I) The proposed bullet train project is just a piece of stone that has been laid by our Prime Minister and Japanese premier, but it has already been written off as a white elephant by most analysts and commentators. They are probably right. The project, of course, is alarmingly expensive.

(II) The government had set an ambitious deadline to complete the bullet train project on August 15, 2022 when India marked 75 years of Independence. The project will be executed through a special purpose vehicle, the National High Speed Rail Corporation Ltd."The bullet train project will take care of high speed, high growth and high-end technology," Mr. Modi said, describing it as "a symbol of New India" that his government wants to build by 2022.

(III) Bullet train in India is a vanity project which has little or no justification on the grounds of economic viability or public service. Even the vanity angle - looking to position India among the ranks of developed countries - is a huge overreach. Only a handful of high-income countries with specific demographics have high-speed rail (HSR), while many have failed in their efforts, others have abandoned it after studying it. The main problem is viability, given the huge costs involved.

(a) Only (I) is correct.
(b) Only (II) is correct.
(c) Only (III) is correct.

    (d) Both (I) and (III) are correct.

    (e) All are correct.

22. **Indian art and culture is far ahead from Western art and culture**

    (I) Art in India is still very European centric. Why isn't Indian art given its due importance? "Indian art is spiritual, but it has nothing to do with any particular sect. A common misconception among society is that Indian art is religious. "The two should not be confused. It is more spiritual and less about rituals. For instance, the character Krishna means so many things. It is more of a symbol than just a god." Similarly, Arjuna is not just the character Arjuna, when depicted in a painting. He represents valour, action and mind.

    (II) Assertive cultural pride is understandable, even justified only when a group is breaking away from prolonged cultural subjugation and humiliation, as was the case in mid-19th century India, when profound distortions were introduced by cultural imperialism in our self-understandings. But already by early 20th century, in the expressions of Vivekananda, Tagore and Gandhi, we see an articulation of legitimate cultural pride that behoves a confident cultural community. What then is the need for such vociferous assertion now?

    (III) During the peak of the trade in mid-17th century, millions of yards of Indian cloth were being sold in markets as far as Japan, Africa, Middle-East and Europe. India's central location in the Indian Ocean basin was ideal for trading textiles to both East and West, with Gujarat, the Coromandel Coast and Bengal being the major trading centres.

    (a) Only (I) is correct.

    (b) Only (II) is correct.

    (c) Only (III) is correct.

    (d) Both (I) and (III) are correct.

    (e) None is correct.

23. **The Doklam issue between India and China no more exists**

    (I) The resolution of the Sino-Indian military stand-off at Doklam, that lasted close to two and a half months, is a much-awaited and welcome development where patient statecraft and deft diplomacy seem to have paid off. Even as several significant questions remain unanswered about the terms and conditions of the resolution, it provides New Delhi and Beijing an opportunity to reflect over what went wrong and rejig this important bilateral relationship.

    (II) Our Prime Minister at the BRICS summit was confident that the resolution of two-month old Doklam stand-off between the People's Liberation Army (PLA) and the Indian Army in Bhutan has gone into annals of military history. The resolution of the Doklam stand-off has now become a case study on how to deal with China, the rising global power, with our government employing deft, principled diplomacy and steely military resolve to checkmate hardline PLA generals in Beijing.

    (III) Our Union Home Minister said that India has become a powerful nation and that is why it was able to resolve the standoff at Doklam with China. "Had India remained weak, the Doklam standoff would not have been resolved till now. It was possible only because India has become a world power," he said. Troops from India and China had been locked in a face off in the Doklam region for over two months. "Everyone was expecting that relation between China and India will deteriorate due to the Doklam issue, but both the countries resolved the issue with comprehension," he added.

    (a) Only (I) is correct.

    (b) Only (II) is correct.

    (c) Only (III) is correct.

    (d) Both (I) and (III) are correct.

    (e) All are correct.

24. **There is no provision for banning a film in the certification rule**

    (I) Constitutional guarantees of freedom of expression are under threat in India. How can some people threaten to kill or maim persons associated with films they don't like and haven't even seen? Censorship is nothing but a dictatorial weapon used by people who do not want the public to know what is really happening in the country. Banning a movie is clearly not only illegal but shockingly naive and unwise.

    (II) Some of the burning issues that confront us are: How does the Constitution of India define freedom of speech and expression? What are the limits on the said freedom? Why are films banned? Are these bans constitutionally valid? What views have been expressed by the final interpreter of the Constitution, the Supreme Court of India, about these bans on the films? Are we on the right constitutional path when we ban films? What consequences would these bans have on our freedom of speech and expression and on the rule of law?

    (III) To ban a film in India, reacting to demands from some, is grave constitutional impropriety. We tolerate such foolish and sometimes dangerous appeals not because they may prove true but because freedom of speech is indivisible. That liberty cannot be denied to some ideas and saved for others. The endeavour here is to highlight that banning a film is not only unconstitutional and illegal but also imprudent.

    (a) Only (I) is correct.

    (b) Only (II) is correct.

    (c) Only (III) is correct.

    (d) Both (I) and (III) are correct.

    (e) All are correct.

25. **Pollution is adversely affecting the health of children**

    (I) A study conducted on Delhi children and released recently in the Journal of Indian Paediatrics provides powerful evidence that shows children growing up in polluted environments like the Capital have reduced lung growth compared to children in developed countries like the United States.

(II) Bad food habits is taking a toll on our children, warn doctors. A group of doctors have published a multi-centric study to drive home the ill effects of moving away from healthy eating habits and opting for easy-to-use and widely accessible processed food.

(III) Children living in big cities such as Delhi, are likely to grow susceptible to allergic ailments, more than adults, due to urban pollution, especially air, health experts said. Infants and children living in metro cities are inhaling polluted air and therefore their resistance to allergic ailments is lowered at a very young age, making them more susceptible to contract various allergies when they grow up, compared to adults.

(a) Only (I) is correct.

(b) Only (II) is correct.

(c) Only (III) is correct.

(d) Both (I) and (III) are correct.

(e) All are correct.

26. **Salary hike of teachers will motivate them to impart knowledge with utmost diligence**

(I) About eight to nine lakh teachers in higher educational institutions are set to get a salary hike, with the Centre ready to take the proposal to the Cabinet. The hike would range from 20-25%, said an official of the Ministry of Human Resource Development. "It is already done and it is ready to go to the Cabinet for approval. Once Cabinet approval comes, teachers in colleges and universities will get their revised salaries," he said.

(II) Since salaries have not been hiked in accordance with the University Grant Commission's (UGC) Seventh Pay Commission recommendations long after the panel submitted its report, teachers in many colleges and State universities across the country may go on strike. The All-India Federation of University and College Teachers' Organisations (AIFUCTO), which has a presence in about 400 State universities across India, will hold its national executive to discuss the future course of action.

(III) The citizenry does not see higher education as an intellectual resource. Nor do political leaders. The only commonly understood purpose that the system of higher education serves is to alleviate - and keep under tolerable levels of discomfort.

(a) Only (I) is correct.

(b) Only (II) is correct.

(c) Only (III) is correct.

(d) All are correct.

(e) None is correct.

27. **All is not well in the Indian Army**

(I) After years of wait, the Indian Army will finally get an advanced medium-range surface to air missile (MRSAM) system by 2020 which will be able to shoot down ballistic missiles, fighter jets and attack helicopters from a range of around 70 km.

(II) The 'controversial' appointment of the new Indian Army chief who assumed office on January 1, 2017 is perhaps the appropriate occasion to discuss the rising uneasiness within the Indian Army on a number of significant issues.

(III) Almost contrasting statements by the Army and Air Force Chiefs in recent days about military preparedness has kicked up much discussion about India's real military preparedness.

(a) Only (I) is correct.

(b) Only (II) is correct.

(c) Only (III) is correct.

(d) Both (II) and (III) are correct.

(e) None is correct.

28. **Farmers are distressed all across India**

(I) The year 2017 was marked by several farmers' protests nationwide, with a few turning violent. Last month, in New Delhi, 184 farmer groups came together from Tamil Nadu, Maharashtra, Madhya Pradesh, Uttar Pradesh, Punjab and Telangana to take part in a 'protest walk.' The protest once again highlighted the plight of farmers and the extent of agrarian agony. The agriculture sector is characterised by instability in incomes because of various types of risks involved in production, market and prices.

(II) Indian agriculture today is structurally different and more robust compared to even the Green Revolution era. Between the early-1970s and the late-nineties, India's annual farm gross domestic product (GDP) expanded from about $25 billion to over $100 billion. Not only was growth sluggish over three decades from a low base, it was also largely cereals-centric, limited to wheat and rice..

(III) The Prime Minister has asked the private sector to invest more in contract farming, raw material-sourcing and creating agri-linkages, and said there are huge opportunities for global super-market chains considering India as a major outsourcing hub.

(a) Only (I) is correct.

(b) Only (II) is correct.

(c) Only (III) is correct.

(d) Both (I) and (II) are correct.

(e) None is correct.

29. **Indian youth are becoming modern in both looks and thinking**

(I) Unlike advanced industrial societies, where age is a significant social factor and there are sharp differences of opinion across generations, there is a strong continuity of belief in India. While this guards against disruption of social and family life, it means that there are limits to perceiving the youth as harbingers of change.

(II) Youth are seen as the country's future, as the carriers of new values and attitudes, and as the agents of social, economic and political change. The findings show that Indian youth are not a homogenous category. The usual social factors the urban/rural divide, class, gender, caste and community play a role in shaping their attitudinal profile.

(III) Indian youth are certainly becoming more modern in their appearance and consumption habits, "but their

thoughts and views reflect a troubling inclination towards intolerance and conservatism", says a national survey of their attitudes, anxieties and aspirations, released in New Delhi this weekend.
- (a) Only (I) is correct.
- (b) Only (II) is correct.
- (c) Only (III) is correct.
- (d) All are correct.
- (e) None is correct.

30. **Robots are better workers than humans**
- (I) Currently, various automation technologies are in the process of overhauling the mass employment-generating but low-skilled blue-collar labour markets. They could also threaten skilled white-collar workers.
- (II) As we ask ourselves how employment is threatened by technology, we should look at how labour has changed in recent decades. Before we get so attached to the current job market, and feel we must defend it from an eventual robot takeover, we should examine how unfair the labour system has become and how robotics could contribute to change that.
- (III) According to Microsoft chairman Bill Gates, the robot industry is "developing in much the same way that the computer business did 30 years ago." Just as that industry has overcome many obstacles to become utterly central to our lives so, says Mr. Gates, robot-makers are meeting the challenges of building truly useful androids.
- (a) Only (I) is correct.
- (b) Only (II) is correct.
- (c) Only (III) is correct.
- (d) Both (I) and (II) are correct.
- (e) None is correct.

DIRECTIONS (Qs. 31-40): *In the question given below few sentences are given which grammatically correct and meaningful. Connect them by the word given above the statements in the best possible way without changing the intended meaning. Choose your answer accordingly from the options to form a correct, coherent sentence.*

---

31. Yet
- (A) The tragic death of Bajirao, one of India's breeding tigers from the Bor reserve in Maharashtra, on a highway is a reminder that building unsuitable roads through wildlife habitats has a terrible cost.
- (B) An assessment by the Wildlife Institute of India states that tigers in at least 26 reserves face the destructive impact of roads and traffic.
- (C) The fate of the big cat, and that of so many other animals such as leopards, bears, deer, snakes, amphibians, butterflies and birds that end up as roadkill, highlights the contradictions in development policy.
- (D) Losing a charismatic tiger in its prime to a hit-and-run accident is an irony, given that it is one of the most protected species. Successive Prime Ministers have personally monitored its status.
- (a) Only D-C　　　　　　(b) Only B-A
- (c) Both C-D & D-B　　　(d) Both B-A & D-C
- (e) None of these

32. But also
- (A) A reconsideration of the flawed verdict in Suresh Kumar Koushal is now in prospect.
- (B) In contrast, the latest petition has paved the way for a comprehensive hearing on all dimensions of the right of individuals to affirm their sexual orientation. In this, the court must not confine itself to the issue of privacy.
- (C) The formulation in Koushal that constitutional protection is not available to a tiny fraction of the population can be overturned only on the touchstone of Article 14, which protects the right to equality.
- (D) Address the discrimination inherent in Section 377 on the basis of sexual orientation.
- (a) Only D-C　　　　　　(b) Only B-D
- (c) Both C-D & D-B　　　(d) Both B-A & D-C
- (e) None of these

33. Yet
- (A) It is not, according to many who cover the White House, a work of journalistic merit, or a rigorous factual account backed by catalogued evidence.
- (B) Consequently, the debate has circled back to the question of his mental health and his ability to discharge the duties of his office.
- (C) Even if one discounts many of the claims made in Fire and Fury, it paints an unmistakable picture of profound instability in Mr. Trump's office.
- (D) Twenty-seven psychiatrists, including those from top universities, have described Mr. Trump's mental state as "dangerous"; some have called for an emergency evaluation of his mental capacity.
- (a) Only A-C　　　　　　(b) Only B-D
- (c) Both A-C & B-D　　　(d) Both B-A & D-C
- (e) None of these

34. However
- (A) The winter session of Parliament saw more political positioning than appraisal of a legislation to make instant triple talaq a criminal offence.
- (B) The dilemma before the Congress is that it cannot be seen as reprising the role it had played over 30 years ago in the Shah Bano episode, when it brought in legislation to scupper a Supreme Court verdict in favour of a Muslim woman's claim for maintenance.
- (C) Hasty legislation passed in the commotion of a divided House may not help the cause. A sound legal framework to deal with all issues arising from instant talaq ought to be crafted after deeper consideration.
- (D) On the one hand, it says instant triple talaq in any form is void, thereby declaring that the marriage continues to subsist; but it also talks of issues such as the custody of children and maintenance.
- (a) Only A-D　　　　　　(b) Only B-C
- (c) Both A-D & C-D　　　(d) Both B-C & A-D
- (e) None of these

35. Above all
- (A) Therefore, action against the groups that threaten India is unlikely to be an immediate priority. New Delhi must also be mindful of the impact of a more fractured U.S.-Pakistan relationship on regional security.

(B) While welcoming all moves to address India's core concerns on terror, New Delhi must ensure it doesn't get ensnared or triangulated in the equation between Washington and Islamabad.

(C) From India's point of view, any attempt to hold Pakistan's feet to the fire on its support to terror groups is a positive development.

(D) The U.S.-Pakistan relationship, like that between India and the U.S. and India and Pakistan, is a long-standing bilateral one.

(a) Only A-D   (b) Only B-C
(c) Both A-D & C-D   (d) Both B-C & A-D
(e) None of these

36. But

(A) To innovate with health-care delivery models to tackle the challenges it faces.

(B) India has no choice

(C) First proposed in 2016, the Bill aims to overhaul the corrupt and inefficient Medical Council of India, which regulates medical education and practice.

(D) Despite its plus points, the NMC isn't the game-changing legislation it could have been. One of its goals is to rein in corruption in the MCI through greater distribution of powers.

(a) Only A-B   (b) Only C-D
(c) Both B-A & C-D   (d) Both A-C & B-D
(e) None of these

37. With

(A) Both developed and emerging markets benefiting from it.

(B) The return of higher economic growth in the U.S.

(C) Inflation is bound to spike up and force the next Fed chair to raise rates at a faster pace.

(D) The strong start suggests that stocks may be all set to carry on their momentum from 2017, which saw major indices offering solid double-digit returns to investors. A significant feature of the present bull market in stocks has been its broad-based participation

(a) Only D-A   (b) Only B-C
(c) Both D-A & B-C   (d) Both B-C & A-D
(e) None of these

38. Since

(A) That the list of aliens will only increase is daunting given the absence of a deportation treaty with Bangladesh.

(B) There are important humanitarian concerns at play, concerns that go beyond identification and numbers. Nearly five decades have elapsed

(C) The cut-off date of March 25, 1971, and individuals who have sneaked in illegally have children and grandchildren by now.

(D) The situation has been muddied with the Centre's intent to pass the Citizenship (Amendment) Bill and make Hindu illegal migrants and those from certain other minority communities in Afghanistan, Bangladesh and Pakistan eligible for Indian citizenship.

(a) Only A-D   (b) Only B-C
(c) Both A-D & C-D   (d) Both B-C & A-D
(e) None of these

39. Based on

(A) The commitment made in Copenhagen in 2009, has been positive.

(B) The climate question presents a leapfrog era for India's development paradigm.

(C) They are moving ahead with specific instruments for loss and damage they suffer due to destructive climate-linked events. India's progress in reducing the intensity of its greenhouse gas emissions per unit of GDP by 20-25% from 2005 levels by 2020.

(D) This has to be resolutely pursued, breaking down the barriers to wider adoption of rooftop solar energy at every level.

(a) Only C-A   (b) Only B-D
(c) Both A-D & C-D   (d) Both B-C & A-D
(e) None of these

40. Including

(A) So, it is impossible to dispute the legal reasoning behind Chief Justice Dipak Misra's ruling that no one but he can decide the composition of Benches and allocation of judicial work in the Supreme Court.

(B) It is a fact that in the Prasad Education Trust case, the petitions alleging that some individuals.

(C) There is absolutely no doubt that the Chief Justice of India is the master of the roster.

(D) A retired Orissa High Court judge, were plotting to influence the Supreme Court, had been heard by a Bench headed by Chief Justice Misra.

(a) Only C-A   (b) Only B-D
(c) Both A-D & C-D   (d) Both B-C & A-D
(e) None of these

41. Nevertheless

a. The Securities and Exchange Board of India (Sebi) on Thursday approved norms to improve governance in mutual funds and credit rating agencies and deepen the securities markets

b. War between the two countries had never happened before

c. the decision will help participants in various markets to be part of a highly regulated, safer, more transparent trading, clearing and settlement framework when implemented fully.

d. they were headed straight down that path.

(a) a-c   (b) b-c
(c) c-a   (d) b-d & a-c
(e) b-d

42. However

a. The Union government has given about Rs133 crore so far and Prime Minister Narendra Modi on 20 December said he will consider the requests for more funds, pending an ongoing assessment of the damages.

b. Last week the Union government moved an amendment to Union finance minister Arun Jaitley's supplementary demand for grants, without including a major central compensation package for Ockhi victims, a move sharply criticised last week in Parliament by Kerala MPs such as Shashi Tharoor.

c.   The next mention of Qatna after the Story of Sinuhe comes from Mari in the 18th century BC, during the reign of Iš?i-Addu of Qatna.

d.   A tablet found in Tuttul, dating to the early reign of the Mariote king Yahdun-Lim in the late 19th century BC, mentions a king named Amut-pi?el, who is most probably the father of Iš?i-Addu; this would make him the first known king of Qatna.

(a) a-b   (b) c-d
(c) b-c & d-a   (d) c-b
(e) a-b & c-d

43. Besides

a.   handing out compensation for loss of equipment for affected fishermen, such as boats and nets, apart from promises to address re-employment, education and rehabilitation of the affected families, the package includes awarding Rs20 lakh to the kin of 74 killed so far by the cyclone.

b.   The state's coffers are severely short of money, as the shock from goods and services tax (GST) continues, according to Kerala finance minister Thomas Issac

c.   When Cyclone Ockhi slammed Kerala's coast on 30 November, chief minister Pinarayi Vijayan asked the state's inmates to generously donate to his disaster relief fund to help the victims.

d.   In the face of shortage of money, the Kerala government devised a rehabilitation package that goes far ahead in terms of scope and extent of coverage in the state's history.

(a) a-b   (b) c-b
(c) b-c& a-b   (d) d-a
(e) a-d & b-c

44. Moreover

a.   The Supreme Court had outlawed instant triple talaq in August and asked the government to frame a law within six months. Ending the controversial divorce practice was also the BJP's electoral promise.

b.   Trading in non-agri commodity contracts will be launched first on the BSE platform. SEBI's move is welcome.

c.   BSE is all geared up for action and will provide commodity trading facility to more than 3.71 crore registered investors

d.   E T Mohammed Basheer of the Indian Union Muslim League (IUML) and Asaduddin Owaisi of the AIMIM alleged that through the bill the government was trying to bring in a Uniform Civil Code.

(a) a-d   (b) b-c
(c) c-b   (d) a-c
(e) a-b

45. Although

a.   it often(and in its better moments)has that quality. Major "literary" historians include Herodotus, Thucydides and Procopius, all of whom count as canonical literary figures

b.   there are many historical prototypes, so-called "novels before the novel"

c.   the writing in these fields often lacks a literary quality

d.   the modern novel form emerges late in cultural history-roughly during the eighteenth century

(a) a-c   (b) d-b
(c) c-d (d)   a-b & c-d
(e) a-c & d-b

DIRECTIONS (Qs. 46-50) : *In each question below, there are two or three sentences. Those are to be synthesised into one sentence. Such synthesised sentences are denoted by (A), (B) & (C). You have to find out which one or more of these three are most similar in meaning of the original two or three sentences.*

46. Petroleum industry is going to face certain challenges. These challenges would be imminent in the next two decades. For success, it must predict these challenges now.

A   In the next two decades, petroleum industry must face the challenges which it has now predicted.

B   If petroleum industry determines to succeed in facing the challenges which are likely to be posed in the next two decades, it must be able to predict them now.

C   If petroleum industry wants to predict the challenges it is likely to face in the next two decades, it must successfully face them.

(a) Only A or B   (b) Only B or C
(c) Only A or C   (d) Only A
(e) Only B

47. Two men can now do this job. Previously it required sixteen men.

A   Two men can now do a job formerly requiring sixteen.

B   Two men, instead of the previously sixteen, can now do this job.

C   In place of two men who can do this job now, there is a requirement of sixteen men in the past.

(a) Only A   (b) Only B
(c) Only C   (d) Only A or C
(e) Only B or C

48. They were curious. They asked us a question. They wanted to know why we had left the comfortable hotel and gone to the desert.

A   Out of curiosity they inquired why we had gone to the desert leaving the comfortable hotel.

B   They asked us why we were curious to leave the comfortable hotel and go to the desert.

C   They were curious to know the reason for our leaving the comfortable hotel and going to the desert.

(a) Only A or B   (b) Only B or C
(c) Only A or C   (d) All the three
(e) None of these

49. They could play exceedingly well. They were defeated in the last round. The captain motivated them to overcome the defeat.

A   The captain's motivation helped them to overcome the earlier defeat and play exceedingly well.

B   Despite earlier defeat they played exceedingly well due to the captain's efforts to motivate them.

C   Despite the captain's motivation, they were defeated earlier but could play exceedingly well now.

(a) Only A   (b) Only B
(c) Only C   (d) Only A or B
(e) None of these

50. His marriage is at a far-off place. I do not want to undertake such a long journey to attend it. In fact, there is no earthly reason to justify such a long journey.

   A   There is no reason to justify such a distant place for his marriage as it would take me a long time to reach it.

   B   There is no earthly reason for me to undertake a long journey to attend his marriage.

   C   Because his marriage is at a far-off place, I would not be able to undertake such a long journey as it is not justifiable.

   (a) Only A or B   (b) Only B or C
   (c) Only A or C   (d) Only C
   (e) Only B

DIRECTIONS (Qs. 51-65): *In each question below, two sentences are given. These two sentences are to be combined into a single sentence without changing their meaning. Three probable starters of the so combined sentence are given which are denoted by (A), (B) and (C). Any one or more or none of them may be correct. Find out the correct starter(s), if any, and accordingly select your answer from among the given five answer choices.*

51. He has lost his immunity. Therefore, he is vulnerable to any disease.

   (A) His loss of immunity....
   (B) Because of his vulnerability to his...
   (C) His vulnerability to any disease...
   (a) Only (A)   (b) Only (B)
   (c) Only (C)   (d) Only (A) and (C)
   (e) Only (A) and (B)

52. You must sign your railway ticket, write your name and age on it. It becomes valid only after that.

   (A) To make your railway ticket valid, the railway authorities should sign...
   (B) Without validating your railway ticket, you cannot...
   (C) To validate your railway ticket, you must...
   (a) Only (A)   (b) Only (B)
   (c) Only (C)   (d) (A) and (B) only
   (e) (B) and (C) only

53. Are you satisfied with this information? Please contact me for any further clarification.

   (A) If you need...   (B) In case you need…
   (C) Should you need...
   (a) None   (b) All the three
   (c) (A) and (C) only   (d) (A) and (B) only
   (e) (B) and (C) only

54. How much you earn is less important. What is more important is how you earn, i.e., your methods of earning?

   (A) How you earn is as important
   (B) How much you earn is as important
   (C) How you earn is not as important
   (a) Only (A)   (b) Only (B)
   (c) Only (C)   (d) All the three
   (e) None of these

55. You must submit the proof of your being a US citizen. Only then your NRI account will be made operative.

   (A) Unless you prove...
   (B) Unless your NRI account is made operative...
   (C) Without your NRI account, you must...
   (a) Only (A)   (b) Only (B)
   (c) Only (C)   (d) All the three
   (e) None of these

56. The hijackers' real identity will always remain a secret.

   (A) No one will ever know the hijackers'...
   (B) The secret identity of the really...
   (C) The real identity of the hijackers would have remained...
   (a) Only (A)   (b) Only (B)
   (c) Only (C)   (d) Either (A) or (C)
   (e) Any one of the three

57. "I'm extremely sorry: I'm late," said Sushma.

   (A) Sushma apologized for my being…
   (B) Sushma tendered apology for her…
   (C) Sushma apologized for her being…
   (a) Only (A)   (b) Only (B)
   (c) Only (C)   (d) Either (A) or (C)
   (e) Either (B) or (C)

58. They have displayed arrogant behaviour; they will therefore be punished.

   (A) As a result of their arrogance, they...
   (B) They will be punished because...
   (C) They will punish because they have...
   (a) Only (A)   (b) Only (B)
   (c) Only (C)   (d) Either (A) or (B)
   (e) Any one of the three

59. Not everyone among them was able to perform the act flawlessly.

   (A) None among them could...
   (B) Few of them could not perform...
   (C) Some of them could perform...
   (a) Only (A)   (b) Only (B)
   (c) Only (C)   (d) Either (A) or (B)
   (e) Either (B) or (C)

60. Most US citizens have made generous donations for rehabilitation of the victims of war.

   (A) These generous donations...
   (B) The generous donations made by the victims of...
   (C) The rehabilitation of victims of war was generous...
   (a) Only (A)   (b) Only (B)
   (c) Only (C)   (d) Either (A) or (B)
   (e) None of these

61. This judgement has been given by the highest court in the land. It therefore assumes finality from legal point of view.

   (A) Being the judgement of ...
   (B) In spite of the judgement...
   (C) As it is the judgement of ...
   (a) Only A   (b) Only B
   (c) Only C   (d) Only A and B
   (e) Only A and C

62. On this special occasion the Chief Minister of the state would be welcomed first. After that the Prime Minister would be extended a warm welcome.
    (A) Although the Prime Minister would ...
    (B) As per the prevalent practice the Prime Minister...
    (C) In spite of the Chief Minister...
    (a) Only A   (b) Only B
    (c) Only C   (d) Only A and B
    (e) Only A and C

63. India is rich in bio-resources. It has no clear legislative framework to regulate access to and use of these resources.
    (A) As India is rich...
    (B) But India is rich...
    (C) Although India is rich...
    (a) Only A   (b) Only B
    (c) Only C   (d) Only A and B
    (e) Only A and C

64. I did not receive any packet from Dipti. I also did not receive any phone call from her.
    (A) Neither did I receive...
    (B) Clearly I did not...
    (C) Because I did not ...
    (a) Only A   (b) Only B
    (c) Only C   (d) Only A and B
    (e) Only A and C

65. I was to reach home a little early but I got delayed. On reaching home I found that guests had left a little while ago.
    (A) Hardly had I reached...
    (B) As long as I reached...
    (C) Besides few minutes...
    (a) Only A   (b) Only B
    (c) Only C   (d) Only A and B
    (e) Only A and C

DIRECTIONS (66-75): *Select the phrase/connector from the given three options which can be used in the beginning (to start the sentenc(e) to form a single sentence from the two sentences given below, implying the same meaning as expressed in the statement sentences.*

66. He was unwilling to go any further. He returned home.
    (i) Returning home....
    (ii) Unwilling to go.....
    (iii) To go any further.....
    (a) Only (i)   (b) Only (ii)
    (c) Only (iii)   (d) Both (i) and (ii)
    (e) None of these

67. They saw the uselessness of violence. They changed their policy.
    (i) Seeing the uselessness....
    (ii) Changing their policy....
    (iii) See the uselessness.....
    (a) Only (i)   (b) Only (ii)
    (c) Only (iii)   (d) Both (i) and (ii)
    (e) None of these

68. He lost a large sum of money. He gave up speculation.
    (i) Giving up speculation.....
    (ii) Large sum of....
    (iii) Loosing a large....
    (a) Only (i)   (b) Only (ii)
    (c) Only (iii)   (d) Both (i) and (iii)
    (e) None of these

69. The hunter took up his gun. He went out to shoot the lion.
    (i) Taking up his.....
    (ii) Took his gun....
    (iii) Shooting the lion.....
    (a) Only (i)   (b) Only (ii)
    (c) Only (iii)   (d) Both (i) and (iii)
    (e) None of these

70. A crow stole a piece of cheese. She flew to her nest to enjoy the tasty meal.
    (i) Flying to steal.....
    (ii) Stealing a piece.....
    (iii) Enjoying the tasty......
    (a) Only (i)   (b) Only (ii)
    (c) Only (iii)   (d) All
    (e) None of these

71. My sister was charmed with the silk. She bought ten yards.
    (i) Buying ten yards....
    (ii) After charming....
    (iii) Charmed with the......
    (a) Only (i)   (b) Only (ii)
    (c) Only (iii)   (d) All
    (e) None of these

72. The letter was badly written. I had great difficulty in making out its content.
    (i) The letter having.....
    (ii) Having great difficulty.....
    (iii) Making out the content.....
    (a) Only (i)   (b) Only (ii)
    (c) Only (iii)   (d) Both (i) and (iii)
    (e) None of these

73. I was walking along the street one day. I saw a dead snake.
    (i) Walking along.....
    (ii) Walking with.....
    (iii) Seeing a dead.....
    (a) Only (i)   (b) Only (ii)
    (c) Only (iii)   (d) Both (i) and (iii)
    (e) None of these

74. Neeraj lost the favour of his master. He was dismissed from his high offices.
    (i) Lost the....
    (ii) Having lost....
    (iii) Dismissed from his.....
    (a) Only (i)   (b) Only (ii)
    (c) Only (iii)   (d) Both (i) and (iii)
    (e) None of these

75. He was occupied with important matters. He had no leisure to see visitors.
    (i) No leisure to see.....
    (ii) Being occupied.....
    (iii) Occupying important matters....
    (a) Only (i)   (b) Only (ii)
    (c) Only (iii)   (d) Both (i) and (ii)
    (e) None of these

ANSWER KEYS

1	(a)	11	(c)	21	(d)	31	(a)	41	(e)	51	(d)	61	(e)	71	(c)
2	(e)	12	(a)	22	(e)	32	(b)	42	(e)	52	(c)	62	(e)	71	(b)
3	(a)	13	(e)	23	(e)	33	(a)	43	(d)	53	(b)	63	(c)	72	(d)
4	(c)	14	(e)	24	(d)	34	(b)	44	(c)	54	(e)	64	(a)	73	(a)
5	(c)	15	(c)	25	(d)	35	(a)	45	(b)	55	(a)	65	(a)	75	(b)
6	(c)	16	(d)	26	(e)	36	(c)	46	(c)	56	(a)	66	(b)		
7	(b)	17	(b)	27	(d)	37	(a)	47	(a)	57	(e)	67	(a)		
8	(e)	18	(e)	28	(a)	38	(b)	48	(c)	58	(d)	68	(c)		
9	(b)	19	(d)	29	(e)	39	(a)	49	(d)	59	(c)	69	(a)		
10	(c)	20	(d)	30	(b)	40	(b)	50	(b)	60	(e)	70	(b)		

Hints & Explanations

31. (a) 'Yet' is correctly makes a link between (D) & (C); the last part of sentence D explains though the successive Prime Ministers have personally monitored its status, yet the fate of them highlights the contradiction.

32. (b) The last part of the statement (B) ends with 'the court must not confine itself to the issue of privacy' which makes a link to the phrase 'but also' and then add up to the sentence (D) i.e. address the discrimination inherent in Section 377....

33. (a) The tone of the sentence (A) demonstrates 'despite the fact that', then it adds up to the statement 'even if one discounts...' linking with 'yet'.

34. (b) The statement (B) correctly links the statement (C) with the conjunction 'however'. However is an adverb, and it's used to introduce a new sentence in circumstances where you would use to join the sentences.

35. (a) If we study the statements (A) & (D), we are directed at (D) from (A) with the linking phrase 'above all' i.e. more so than anything else.

36. (c) Both (C) & (D) appear to be co-related with the linking conjunction 'but'. Similarly, the phrase 'India has no choice' (B) may be followed by 'but' linking to statement (A).

37. (a) The ending of statement (D) takes us to the statement (A) with linking to 'with'. Similarly, statement (B) may be preceded by 'with'.

38. (b) Statements (B) & (C) may be linked with conjunction 'since'.

39. (a) The ending part of the (C) appears to have something missing which if linked with 'based on' takes us to the statement (A) making it a complete statement.

40. (b) Statements (B) & (D) appear to be closely related with conjunction 'including'.

41. (e) nevertheless is used "to contrasts a second point with the first point. It has a similar meaning to despite this" a-c combination is not contradictory because the decisioin of sebi is helping the participants.

42. (e) You use however when you are adding a comment which is surprising or which contrasts with what has just been said.

43. (d) Besides= besides means in addition to / moreover. It tells about additional information.

45. (b) Although = used to show a contrast. After although we use a subject and a verb.

66. (b) From (ii) Unwilling to go any further, he returned home.

67. (a) From (i) Seeing the uselessness of violence they changed their policy

68. (c) From (iii) Loosing a large sum of money, he gave up speculation

69. (a) From (i) Taking up his gun, the hunter went out to shoot the lion

70. (b) From (ii) Stealing a piece of cheese, a crow flew to her nest to enjoy the tasty meal.

71. (c) From (iii) Charmed with the silk my sister bought ten yards.

72. (d) From (i) The letter having been badly written, I had great difficult in making out its content.
From (iii) Making out the content of the letter was difficult for me as it was badly written.

73. (a) From (i) Walking along the street one day, I saw a dead snake.

71. (b) From (ii) Having lost the favour of his master, Neeraj was dismissed from his high offices.

75. (b) From (ii) Being occupied with important matters he had no leisure to see visitors.